The Management
of Service Operations

The Management of Service Operations

Second Edition

J. Nevan Wright and Peter Race

THOMSON

Australia • Canada • Mexico • Singapore • Spain • United Kingdom • United States

THOMSON
ᵀᴹ

The Management of Service Operations, 2nd edition

Copyright © 2004 J. Nevan Wright and Peter Race

The Thomson logo is a registered trademark used herein under licence.

For more information, contact Thomson Learning, High Holborn House, 50–51 Bedford Row, London, WC1R 4LR or visit us on the World Wide Web at: http://www.thomsonlearning.co.uk

British Library Cataloguing-in-Publication Data
A catalogue record for this book is available from the British Library

ISBN 1-84480-051-2

First edition published 1999 by Cassell
Reprinted 2001 by Continuum
Second edition published 2004 by Thomson Learning

Typeset by Photoprint, 9-11 Alexandra Lane, Torquay

Printed in Croatia by Zrinski d.d.

I dedicate this book to Joy, my wife and best friend.
I also dedicate this book to my grandchildren,
Daniel, Brad, Georgia and Sam.   *JNW*

To Gay and Jevon.   *PR*

Contents

Part Two 43

List of figures

List of tables

Preface

T his book is specifically about the management of service operations. It will be of practical use for:

- managers;
- students of management at undergraduate and postgraduate level (especially MBA students);
- anyone engaged in a service industry (private or public sector).

Although the focus is on service the importance of the extended supply and value chain cannot be ignored. To this end in this edition chapters have been added to:

- give a more complete appreciation of the extended supply chain, from suppliers' supplier, through the manufacturing process and out to the direct customer and finally to the end-user;
- consider the influence and impact of e-business and B2B alliances.

The book is based on the theory of operations management but links theory to practical everyday management of performance; its purpose is to provide an understanding of the management of service industries and to show how to turn policy and objectives into reality.

The book's central philosophy is that people make the difference in providing an efficient and 'quality' service. It might seem trite to say that people are any organization's greatest resource, but nonetheless it is true – and especially true – for service industries. It is also true to say that people in service industries will generally be the most expensive resource. However, this book is not designed as a human resource manager's handbook: it is designed for the general manager, and in particular the operations manager, so that they can make the most effective use of resources – primarily by the involvement and motivation of the people with whom they work, including suppliers of goods and services through to the end-user of the service.

The text contains tools and techniques for developing and implementing strategies, and draws on everyday examples to provide basic day-to-day 'tips' in making the most efficient use of resources to gain a competitive edge through a focus on customer satisfaction. The book concludes with chapters on how to develop measures that will make a difference, and how to change the culture of an organization in order to self-motivate the people of the organization.

Case studies

In addition to the everyday examples given in the book, additional case study material (including questions and answers) is included. The cases were selected to illustrate and reinforce theory provided in the book and to provide an additional basis for study. Questions are included with the cases that are designed for you to check your understanding and to relate theory to practical management situations.

J. Nevan Wright and Peter Race, 2003

Acknowledgements

T his second edition of *The Management of Service Operations* was written in collaboration with Peter Race. I wish to acknowledge the hard work that Peter has put into this 'project' to bring the book up to date and in particular for writing Chapter 12 and for identifying and editing the case study sections of the book. I am also grateful to Ross Milne for writing Chapter 11, supply chain management. Special thanks also to Ron Basu (my co-author for *Total Manufacturing Solutions*, and for *Quality Beyond Six Sigma*) for contributing the General Electric and Fresh Food case studies.

In the first edition I acknowledged Professor Ray Wild's involvement and support. The original intention was to write a service industry companion book for Ray Wild's definitive work *Production and Operations Management* (5th edition, 1995) republished as *Operations Management* (6th edition, 2002). While it is true that much of the material in *The Management of Service Operations* is derived from Ray Wild's *Operations Management*, much has been re-ordered and new material introduced which will not be found in his book. So, although *Management of Service Operations* does not differ in basic philosophy, it cannot be considered as just the 'service' version of *Operations Management*. However, once again I wish to sincerely acknowledge Ray's generosity in allowing me to quote so freely from his book and for the use of four of his case studies.

Readers of *Total Manufacturing Solutions* (1998), and *Quality Beyond Six Sigma* (2003), both written by Ron Basu and myself, will recognize the continuation of the theme of a whole systems approach in *The Management of Service Operations*. *The Management of Service Operations* draws on sections of both these books.

Finally, I accept full responsibility for any errors and omissions. To a large extent this book is drawn from my own experiences, the experiences of others and from a wide reading of contemporary management issues. It would not be possible to acknowledge the sources of all the concepts that have been used: in some cases the source has been lost in the mists of time, on other occasions I have read ideas and suggestions which I am almost sure I first propounded in past lectures, journal articles or conference papers! Suffice to say I have made every endeavour to credit materials and ideas of others (see References at the end of the book). I offer apologies to the authors of any works that I have failed to mention.

My thanks also go to Anna Herbert and Jennifer Pegg at Thomson. It is obvious that they know the meaning of good service.

Nevan Wright
Auckland, New Zealand
February 2003

Introduction

Growth of service industries

Around 78 per cent of the workforce in the United Kingdom are engaged in service industries (www.statistics.gov.uk 2003). This high percentage is not unique to the United Kingdom: it is representative of employment statistics for developed nations throughout the world. Indeed the US Bureau of the Census (www.census/gov/ 2003) show that 80 per cent of the workforce in the United States is employed in service industries or with the government. Although a shift back to manufacturing industries has been identified (Basu and Wright, 1998), it is obvious that the greater percentage of the workforce of developed nations will continue to be employed in service-type activities. There are two reasons for this:

1. Continual advances in technology mean that manufacturing is considerably less labour intensive than in previous times. Automation, robotics, advanced information technology, new materials and improved work methods have all led to the decimation of manual labour.

2. For larger organizations, manufacturing has become internationalized. For example a company such as Xerox, once an American-based manufacturer of photocopiers, now regards itself primarily as a marketing and service company, with its manufacturing being supplied by contractors or allied companies situated all round the world.

Additionally, organizations can no longer regard themselves as being purely in manufacturing and hope to survive. The market first and foremost now demands quality of product and service. Market expectations of the level of quality are driven by perceptions of what technology is promising and by perceptions of what the competition is offering.

Organizations now operate in a global market where national barriers, tariffs and customs duties no longer provide protection for a home market. Any manufacturer, even if it has concentrated its efforts on supplying a local market, is in reality competing on the world stage. Competition is no longer limited to other local organizations, and the fiercest competition in the home market will be from goods produced overseas. This fact alone has meant that manufacturers can no longer make products to suit their engineering strengths, but must now be aware of what the market wants and what global competition is offering. And what the competition is offering is service, in the form of delivery on time, marketing advice, training, installation, project management or whatever else is required to provide a total service as well as a reliable product.

Finally, it has to be recognized that never has the customer been better travelled, more informed and had higher expectations. Many of these expectations for continuously improved product and service have arisen from global competition, the well-publicized total quality management (TQM) drive of the 1980s and the success of quality crusaders such as the charismatic Tom Peters. Customers expect and take for granted a reliable, high-quality product for their money, and most organizations realize that their products actually differ very little from those of their competitors, and any technological improvement is soon copied; thus the difference – the 'competitive edge' – comes from service.

Service separated from production operations

If no serious operation can ignore market demands for service and world-class quality, why bother to try and separate manufacturing from service in the study of operations management? Indeed, for a manufacturing organization aspiring to world-class status I would agree, most emphatically, that the operations managers of such organizations must concern themselves with service and quality if they are to compete on the world stage.

However, operations managers in service industries such as health, retail, distribution, education, travel, real estate, consultation, brokering, law, accounting, administration of central and local government, transportation of goods or people – where no direct manufacturing is involved, or where the manufacturing is light and simple (such as in a restaurant) – do not have to know much about manufacturing. Although all the above industries are reliant on manufacturers to varying degrees for the equipment they use, or in the case of a retailer for the goods they sell, the actual physical heavy work of making the goods is not their concern. The analogy is that of a driver of a car: one can be a very good driver without knowing very much about what happens under the bonnet. Some knowledge of when to change gear and the danger of overheating due to lack of oil or water will be of advantage, but not much more is really necessary. Likewise with the operations manager in the service industry: a detailed knowledge of line balancing for a high-tech mass production line of washing machines is not necessary for a retailer of white wear. Some knowledge of lead times for deliveries, operating instructions and the capacity of the washing machine will be sufficient for the salesperson as a basis for good service to the customer.

Thus there can be a separation of operations management into two distinct streams: the management of operations management in production including service; and the management of operations in service industries (for whom this book is written) where only some rudimentary knowledge of manufacturing is required.

The operations manager that is involved directly in production and manufacturing needs to be well versed in strategies, tactics and methodologies of production operations management and also has to be very aware of what constitutes service and quality from the customer's point of view. Books such as *Operations Management* (Wild, 2002) or *Total Manufacturing Solutions* (Basu and Wright, 1998) are recommended for operations managers who need to take a total operations approach to providing a quality product coupled with the service required to better the competition.

However, operations managers who are primarily engaged in service industries do need some knowledge of production systems and methodologies.

Over recent years more and more members and associates at Henley Management College and at the Auckland University of Technology have asked me to recommend an operations management book that is specifically designed for the service industry practitioner. I was not able to recommend one book alone that met this requirement, and as a result, at my students' request, the first edition of this book was written.

At Henley Management College and at the Auckland University of Technology we believe it is important that members of programmes are able to apply course material to their own working environment. Therefore *The Management of Service Operations* was designed so that those employed in service industries will find this book practical and user-friendly. The 'theory' is brought to life by the use of carefully researched case studies from a wide spectrum of service industries. In the first edition the case studies were provided on a CD Rom, but in practice it was found that students saw this as an unnecessary refinement. In this edition the cases are therefore included in the text.

Theme of the book

The underlying theme of this book is the elimination of non-value-adding activities and the provision of customer satisfaction in service industries. The book takes a whole systems 'supply chain' approach, from supplier through service provider to customer, and back again. Above all, it is stressed that particularly in a service industry, people are an organization's greatest resource. People include management and staff at all levels. It is concluded that if the organizational culture is 'right' there is little that an organization cannot achieve. The final chapter therefore deals with how to attain the 'right' culture: this has been reached when any member of staff, faced with an unusual or difficult problem, reacts instinctively in the manner in which management would have hoped they would act.

1 Part One

Part One is the foundation for the rest of the book. This Part consists of two chapters.

- **Chapter 1** begins with some basic definitions, establishes the framework in which the operations managers work, looks at the constraints of policy, and shows how what can be achieved is limited by resources and systems structure.

  It is acknowledged that operations management theory draws heavily on manufacturing practice. The distinction between manufacturing and service industries is explored. In particular, the intangible nature of service is considered.
- **Chapter 2** discusses the dimensions of customer service, competition and resource utilization.

  The inherent conflict between achievement of customer satisfaction and efficient resource utilization is identified.

1 Making it happen

Objectives

Issues covered in this chapter are:

- the mission of organizations;

- the theme of a whole systems approach;

- definitions;

- the importance of systems structure.

Introduction

The title of this book is *The Management of Service Operations*. Although written as a companion to Wild's *Operations Management*, *The Management of Service Operations* is a stand alone book. To understand the function of the operation manager some understanding of manufacturing operations is required. Often the service operations manager will be working for a division of a larger organization which has a manufacturing arm, or the service operation will have manufacturing organizations as clients. Thus, to give a complete understanding of operations management, some explanation of manufacturing operations is included. If a manager is working purely in manufacturing, it is strongly recommended that they acquire a copy of Wild's definitive work *Operations Management* (2002). In this chapter we consider the role of the operations function and the operations manager in organizations. We look at the important role the customer plays as an input into the operation. A framework for analyzing the structure of the operating system for both service and manufacturing is introduced.

The mission

Customer service is the mission – the reason for existence – of organizations. Operations management is the function within an organization which interacts with and delivers products/services to customers, and therefore efficient operations management is crucial to the success of the organization. The role of a manager of operations is to provide customer satisfaction within the framework of the organization's policy, and to use resources as efficiently as possible. Simply put: the operations manager 'makes it (the mission) happen'.

Techniques and strategies

This book tells you how operations managers make the mission happen and introduces techniques to make the operations manager's life easier. Some of these techniques are new, but most of them are tried and proven. All of the techniques covered have a particular relevance to service organizations. Operations managers do not work in a vacuum; their options are influenced by factors over which they may have little control. These influencing factors and how to recognize their operational significance are considered, and strategies that can be adopted to make the most of operational situations are given.

Theme

The overall theme of this book is the elimination of non-value-adding activities within an organization and the provision of excellent customer service. A whole systems approach, from supplier through to the successful delivery of service to the customer out to the end-user is taken.

Definitions

The terms 'operating system' and 'operations management' will be referred to throughout the book. 'Service organizations' – the focus of the book – is also referred to. We need to begin by defining these terms.

Definition 1: Service organization

> A service organization is when two or more people are engaged in a systematic effort to provide services to a customer, the objective being to serve a customer.

A service organization exists to interact with customers and to satisfy customers' service requirements. For any service to be provided, there has to be a customer. Without a customer, and interaction between customer and the service organization, the objective of providing service cannot exist.

The degree of intensity of interaction between the customer and personnel within a service organization varies and depends on the type of service offered. For example, a specialist medical consultant will have a high degree of 'face-to-face' interaction with the customer, and so will a hairdresser. Further down the scale of face-to-face interaction is a restaurant, where the customer will judge the quality of service by the level of interaction (wine waiter's knowledge, waiting staff's attentiveness) as well as by the standard of the goods provided (wine and food). The restaurant in turn will, however, have a higher degree of personal interaction than will a fast-food takeaway. A scale of personal interaction is shown in

Figure 1.1. The bottom of the scale on Figure 1.1 is automatic 'cashpoint' banking where customer interaction is purely with a machine.

Irrespective of the level of 'face-to-face' interaction, without some customer interaction service cannot be provided. However, this does not mean that the customer always has to be present when the service is being provided. For example, when a car is being serviced by a mechanic, the owner of the car need not be present; but without the owner providing the car and giving instructions ('Grease and oil-change, ready at five?') no service can be provided.

Manufacturing operations

In manufacturing operations customer interaction is not essential. For example, cars can be assembled, hamburgers can be made and houses can be built, all without customer input. In these three examples although it might be desirable that the customer has input into the design and the specifications of the product (be it a car or a hamburger), customer input is not essential.

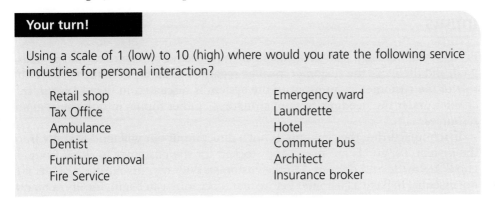

Your turn!

Using a scale of 1 (low) to 10 (high) where would you rate the following service industries for personal interaction?

Retail shop	Emergency ward
Tax Office	Laundrette
Ambulance	Hotel
Dentist	Commuter bus
Furniture removal	Architect
Fire Service	Insurance broker

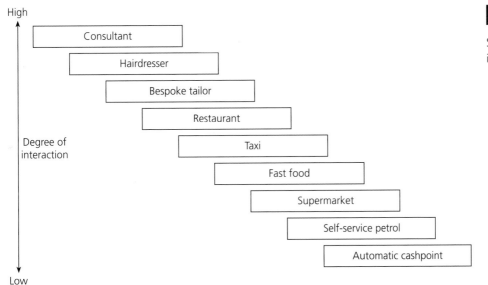

Figure 1.1

Scale of personal interaction

▶
Where does your own organization lie on the scale?

For manufacturing organizations often the end-user will not be specifically known, and the distance between the factory and the actual customer will be considerable. An example is the processing and freezing of vegetables for a supermarket. The interaction between customer and the factory will often rate as zero on the above scale.

Definition 2: Manufacturing organization

A service operating system describes the manner in which customers and resources combine to give service outputs.

A manufacturing operation system is the manner in which resources (people and machines) are used to transform input materials into outputs (goods).

Inputs

For a service industry without a customer the objective of service cannot be delivered, and therefore the customer must be regarded as an input to the system. The role of the customer as an input to the system is discussed in detail later in this chapter under the heading 'System structures'. Other inputs into the system are resources.

In manufacturing the customer is not a direct input but will tend to draw from the system, i.e. goods are made and stocked for the customer to draw from, or goods are made and delivered to the customer. With manufacturing systems it is not essential to have a customer before manufacturing can begin. Inputs in manufacturing will generally be materials to be transformed, and consumed utilities.

Resources include:

- *Materials*. Materials used by the operating system include utilities such as energy, water and gas. Materials also include goods that are consumed by the system, goods that are transformed by the system, and goods held for sale. Transformation refers to changing the shape or form of inputs to produce an output. For example, by placing lettuce leaves, a beef burger and a slice of tomato between two halves of a bun, we have combined and transformed several goods to produce a new good, commonly known as a hamburger.
- *Machines/equipment*. These include plant, fittings, vehicles, display racks, etc., available to the operating system.
- *Information systems*. This includes information technology and the flow of information within the organization, and to and from external sources (in particular suppliers and customers).
- *People*. People not only means the number of people employed in the operating system, but includes knowledge and skill levels, and also includes the intangibles of dependability and attitude.
- *Real estate* (offices, warehouses, factories, display areas, i.e. available space).

All of the above represent either a capital investment or an ongoing expense to the organization. Tangible inputs are physical and can be seen and touched, and the amount or rate of use can be measured in quantifiable terms. Intangible inputs, which cannot be seen or touched, include knowledge (intellectual capital) and information.

Money is not regarded as an input resource. Money is used to buy resources (people, machines, buildings etc. are the resources). Likewise time itself is not an input but is used to measure efficient use of resource or performance (for example, on time delivery).

Measurement of effective use of time and information is less obvious than for the tangible resources. Nevertheless, the amount of time and information available will be important issues for the operations manager

With today's technology, information would seem to be readily available. The concern of the operations manager, however, will be knowing what information is required and then being able to interpret and use information so as to achieve the organization's operational objectives.

The flow of resources through the operating system is shown in Figure 1.2. In a service organization, customer and resources are brought together to provide a service output. For manufacturing, input resources are transformed to provide an output, and the customer draws from the system, i.e. the product is made and the customer buys the finished good. With a service operation, output cannot be stocked and the service cannot begin without customer input.

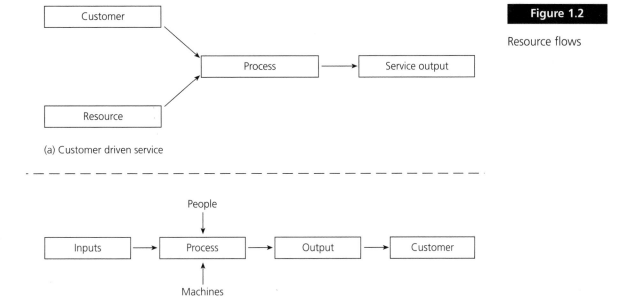

Figure 1.2

Resource flows

Examples

- *Bus service*. A bus can travel on its advertised route, but until a passenger is carried the function of the bus service is not achieved. Without a passenger the mission of the bus service – to carry passengers – cannot be fulfilled. An empty bus travelling on the bus route is nothing more than an unutilized or 'stored' resource. Apart from the bus itself, other resources such as fuel and the time (wages) of the driver are being used.

- *Hotel room*. Until a guest checks in, the service function of the hotel cannot be performed. The room can be 'serviced' and prepared in advance, but until a guest arrives there is no service output.

- *Restaurant*. With a restaurant it is possible for the chef to make up salads, and even to prepare and cook meals in advance, before any customer is seated. This may not be the policy (strategy) of a topline restaurant but nonetheless the decision (strategy) can be changed, i.e. it is not essential to have a customer before a meal is prepared. However, the mission of the restaurant is not to prepare meals, it is to serve meals, and the delivery of service cannot take place without the customer – it is not possible for the meal to be served unless there is a customer who has placed an order.

All three examples – the bus travelling on its route, the prepared hotel room, and the partly prepared meal in the restaurant – involve stored resources waiting for the input of a customer. Without customer input no service output will be delivered. With manufacturing operations, outputs can be stored and the customer served from stocked outputs. With a service operation it is not possible to stock outputs.

Definition 3: Operations management

Operations management is the ongoing activities of designing, reviewing and using the operating system, or systems, to achieve outputs as determined by the organization.

The operations manager is a decision-maker. Decisions range from long-term strategy to short-term day-to-day operational concerns. As the operations manager is at the hub of, and responsible for 'making it happen', it follows that the most pressing decisions are of a day-to-day nature.

The operations manager will be limited in the decisions that can be made. The limitations are set, on the one hand, by the objectives of the organization, and on the other by what is feasible with the resources available and by the structure of the system.

In short, decision-making is limited by what is:

- *Desired* by the organization (mission and policy of the organization).
- *Feasible* with the amount and quality of resources (tangible and intangible) available, and given the nature – in particular the structure – of the operating system being used.

Figure 1.3 shows the constraints of an operations manager. The mission and policy of the organization set the scope of the operations manager. How business policy

Figure 1.3

Making it happen

is determined is covered in Part Two (Chapter 3). Once the policy has been decided, then what is desirable is expressed as the objectives of the organization, and what is feasible is limited by the resources and structure of the organization.

The more demanding the objectives, the fewer the resources and the more limiting the structure, the less choice the operations manager will have in making decisions, and vice versa. The aim of the operations manager will be to use resources as efficiently as possible to achieve the highest level of customer satisfaction within the constraints of policy objectives, available resources and the system structure.

Service system structures

In considering system structures we find it convenient to use the following symbols:

O =   the process of combining resources to add value.

V =   'store' of resources, or queue of customers waiting to enter the system.

⇨ =   the flow of resources through the system.

C =   the customer. Note, the customer does not have to be external to the organization, but may be an internal customer.

The 'internal customer' can be defined as the next person, or department, in the process.

Overall there are three basic service structures (Figures 1.4, 1.5 and 1.6), but often organizations will consist of a combination of systems.

Figure 1.4 shows service being provided direct to the customer from a stock of resource. The stock of resource could be the bus moving from stop to stop,

Figure 1.4

Service direct from resource to customer

an accident ward waiting for patients, a fire brigade waiting for a call-out, a restaurant waiting for diners, an accountant waiting for customers or a betting shop waiting for punters. In this structure the customer does not normally wait: the resources do.

Figure 1.5 shows how most service providers would like to operate. Customers form a queue for services. An example is the dentist. Customers phone in for service and are given an appointment. The dentist then draws patients from a stock of customers, with no waiting (by the dentist) between jobs. Evidence of this type of system can be seen at banks, post offices and supermarkets. Refuse collection is another example; the customer puts the wheelie bin out and the bin 'waits' to be emptied.

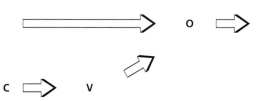

Figure 1.5

Customers form a queue for services

Figure 1.6 shows a structure where there is spare resource waiting for customers, and customer queues also form.

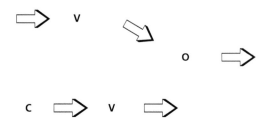

Figure 1.6

Spare resource waiting for customers; queues also form

In reality, the dentist, the accountant, the lawyer, the real-estate agent, the taxi driver, the travel agent and the social service worker operate in this manner. In effect all inputs are stocked and customers accumulate in queues. Although the dentist would prefer not to wait for customers, but to draw customers from the accumulated stock in the appointment book, in practice the dentist will be obliged to set aside some time each day for emergency treatment. If no patient arrives during the time set aside for emergency patients then the dentist will become an unused resource.

Another example of this structure is where customers are waiting at the airport, but all the taxis are in the city at hotels. In this scenario neither the customer nor the taxi operator will be happy.

Some readers will ask why a service system could not be 'just-in-time', i.e. no spare resource and no customer queues. The answer is that if customers are never kept waiting there has to be spare resources; or alternatively, if resources are going to be fully utilized with no idle time, there has to be a stock of customers to be drawn from. From time to time a perfectly balanced system might appear to exist but this will only be a temporary phenomenon.

Combined structures

Although three basic service system structures are shown above, in reality most service organizations will employ a combination of structures.

The structures we have looked at so far are customer 'push' systems. Another type of structure is a customer 'pull' system, which occurs where activities take place in anticipation that eventually a customer will arrive. Sometimes the projected demand is known with a fair amount of certainty in advance, and activities can therefore be safely scheduled in advance. In this scenario the expected demand 'pulls' the system, rather than waiting for direct customer input to 'push' the system.

Example   *Motel*

A small motel consists of twenty rooms. Occupancy varies but is on average 80 per cent. Some guests book in advance but mainly the motel relies on passing traffic. Each day, previously occupied rooms are cleaned and linen changed in anticipation of guests arriving. The system structure can be depicted as in Figure 1.7.

In Figure 1.7, 'O_i' is the preparation of a room, 'V' represents that cost has been incurred and resources transformed and held – 'stored' – in anticipation of a customer. The service operation doesn't actually occur until 'O_{ii}', i.e. a guest, arrives ('C') and a room is allotted.

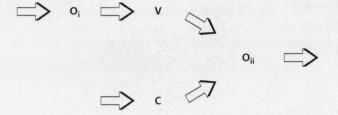

Figure 1.7

A customer 'pull' structure

Retail/wholesale operations

The system structure for an operation that stocks goods for sale or for delivery is as shown at Figure 1.8. In this structure goods are stocked and the function is to make a sale, or to deliver to a customer, and ownership of the goods changes hands.

Figure 1.8

Retail/wholesale structure

Manufacturing system structures

As discussed above with manufacturing operations no direct input from the customer is essential for the function of the operation to be carried out. Figure 1.9 shows that input materials are stocked, that materials are drawn from stock and transformed and that finished goods are stocked. Customers draw from the system.

Figure 1.9

Input and output stocks

Figure 1.10 shows that no input materials are stocked, but materials when received go straight into production. An example is food processing; once the crop is harvested it must be processed or it will deteriorate. Processed stock is held for eventual delivery to customers. The customer draws from a stock of finished goods.

Figure 1.10

No input stock

Figure 1.11 shows that input materials are stocked and once manufactured are delivered direct to the customer. For this to happen the demand must be known otherwise the structure will not be valid. An example is McDonald's where input materials are stocked, hamburgers are made in anticipation of demand, but if the demand does not eventuate, after four minutes the hamburgers are thrown away. A further more extreme example is ship building. In theory it is possible to build to stock, but as a ship is capital intensive it is generally built to order, and once completed ownership passes direct to the customer. Nonetheless a shipyard can build ships without a customer order. Note Figure 1.11 is the same as for retail operations.

Figure 1.11

Manufacture from stock direct to customer

The structure in Figure 1.12 shows no input stocks of materials and no output stock of materials. This is known as a just-in-time or 'lean' structure. An example is a small house builder who acquires a block of land and builds a house. Materials are ordered when required (pre-mixed concrete arrives and is poured when required, etc.) and hopefully the house is sold before it is completed. A small speculative builder can generally not afford to have a 'stock' of finished houses for sale. The same structure applies when the builder is building to a customer specification. In this case the structure could well be a combined structure. Just-in-time is the structure that also applies to some manufacturing operations where materials are ordered to arrive to go straight into production just as required, and finished

Figure 1.12

Just-in-time

goods are not stocked but delivered direct to the customer. This type of operation is discussed in further detail in Chapters 8 and 9.

Example

The owner of a block of land asks advice from a builder as to what type of house can be built. The builder has a book of standard plans but the client can change the specification to some extent. Eventually both parties agree but as the builder is currently working on another house, the client might have to wait six weeks before the builder can begin. Once the house is completed, and final payment made, ownership of the house passes to the client. This combined structure is shown in Figure 1.13.

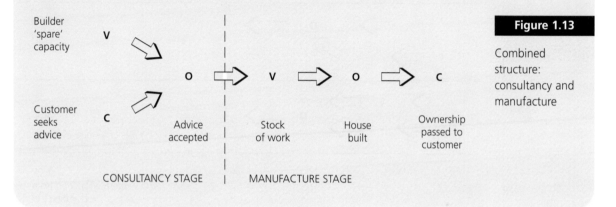

Figure 1.13

Combined structure: consultancy and manufacture

Importance of structures

It is important to realize which structure(s) applies to your organization. The structure employed will determine what is feasible, and an understanding of the structures which are in force will enable consideration to be given to changing structures so as to best meet the aims and objectives of the organization. For example it will be a policy decision that decides that:

1. resources will be stored in advance of customer requirements: such a structure implies some surplus capacity in the system;
2. no surplus resource will be held and it is accepted that customers will queue for service.

System structures are derived from Wild (2002; p.17). Wild's seven basic structures are shown in Figure 1.14.

Your turn!

Consider your organization and identify the structures that apply to it.

Figure 1.14

Structure of
operating systems

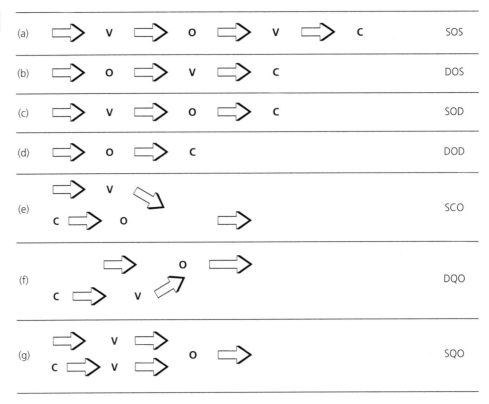

S = stock
O = operate/function from
D = direct to
C = customer
Q = customer queue

Chapter summary

In this chapter we have defined operations management as the function within a service organization which interacts with customers and delivers service to customers. The role of the operations manager was shown to be to use resources as efficiently as possible to achieve the highest level of customer satisfaction within the constraints of policy objectives, available resources and systems structures. The chapter concluded with an explanation of the seven basic systems structures that can exist in an organization, and it was shown how system structure will determine what is feasible.

Case Study *'When NICE isn't good enough'*

The case study that adds value to this chapter is 'When NICE isn't good enough'.

Questions

1. Describe the nature of operations at 'Nice Framing'. Discuss the constraints and challenges of Nicola's existing business.
2. Acting as Nicola's father, advise her of the implications for operations if she changes the business to include the 'smart-artgallery' system

When NICE isn't good enough

Nicola Evershed sat at her office desk reviewing her 3rd quarter, 2000 accounts. She wasn't skilled in accounts but intuitively knew that her business was going downhill. She only had to look around her picture-framing workshop to know why. Every available wall space had been fitted with storage racks, and they were bulging with 3-metre lengths of frame moulding. Framed and partly-framed pictures cluttered the floorspace, and her staff were finding it increasingly difficult to access their workbenches to get the work done.

The figures didn't lie; since 1996 turnover had stagnated, gross margins were 20 per cent lower than at their peak, stock was accounting for 15 per cent of sales and her agreed overdraft was at its maximum of £35 000.

Nicola knew she had lost focus, and decided it was time to act.

Thirteen years earlier, her problems were of a differing nature. It was a time of entrepreneurship and taking the initiative. Nicola had decided to take up the challenge of starting her own business. She had an unusual background of having studied sculpture at art college but had then changed course and took up engineering with a small private manufacturing company, based in West Yorkshire. Whilst manufacturing was a tremendous challenge, as she approached the age of 30 she felt it was

time to take the gamble of self-employment with its lure of personal wealth and control over her own destiny. But, what should she do, and where should she start?

For some time she had yearned to get more involved with her main interest . . . the world of art. A friend of hers who worked as an interior designer had suggested she speak to an acquaintance working in the estates department at a local brewery.

Dave Hutchings was Senior Designer for Lancashire Breweries, and responsible for the internal maintenance and fabric of their portfolio of Managed Public Houses. What he told Nicola was the catalyst she needed.

The Mergers and Monopolies Commission had recently made a ruling, known as the 'Beer Orders' which declared that breweries could no longer act as monopoly suppliers of their own products to their own 'tied' public houses. From now on, each brewery was required to reduce their 'managed' portfolio to a maximum of 2000 premises and allow independent beer producers access to their estates, all within the next 2 years.

The implications were that the introduction of competition would force the breweries to upgrade their 'managed' portfolio in order to attract and retain customers. One of the key areas would be the development of branded interior schemes, incorporating framed pictures.

Nicola knew that her interest in art, in combination with her manufacturing know-how, was ideal for this situation. All she needed to do was learn how to become a picture framer.

After several months of investigation, and a week long training course, Nicola had mastered the framing equipment, borrowed some capital, and 'NICE Framing' (**NICE**vershed) was up and running with a small 'test' contract from Dave Hutchings.

It was the start of a profitable relationship. Nicola had quickly realized that Lancashire

▶

Brewery demanded excellent and reliable service. They had embarked upon a programme of projects to rapidly upgrade their 'managed-house' premises, of which pictures constituted an average contract price of £3000. The 'City' was extremely supportive of this investment and share prices rose in relation to the market.

What this meant for Nicola was that it was imperative for her to be able to satisfy demand very quickly and schedule contracts onto site in accordance with the project's required delivery slots. This usually meant 'round the clock' availability, as picture delivery and installation often took place at unusual hours, in order to reduce the congestion that was characteristic of such internal refurbishment projects.

As well as overseeing manufacture, and managing delivery schedules, Nicola was also warned by her father, a successful business-man, to carefully manage both inventory and working capital. To Nicola this seemed to be a completely contradictory statement.

Nicola decided that she needed to have good levels of raw material and 'finished picture' stock, if she was going to be able to satisfy the needs of her main client. After all, if she didn't have the stock, she wouldn't get the order. At the margins she was achieving, this was an opportunity not to miss. 'Stock' would rule and she would worry about the 'working capital' issue later. In any case, her local bank was extremely supportive of her business plan, and aware of the fact that she had already invested her own capital and a bank loan in her business premises and facilities. A working overdraft facility of £20 000 was quickly agreed.

Nicola soon became aware that the framing of pictures was actually quite a complex operation, requiring different tasks to be performed by different staff members.

First of all there were many suppliers of wood mouldings, that formed the actual frame, and each of these suppliers offered a huge range. Mouldings had different widths, depths and profiles, necessitating frequent changes to the cutting (mitre) machine, and to

the 'underpinning' machine that joined the four sides into a complete frame.

Similarly the machines used for cutting the mounts (the overlay that creates a border around the picture), and the glass cutting machine (for the glass that sits between the mount and the inside of the frame), also needed to be changed for each different size.

However, one of the key factors that gave 'NICE' an edge over their competitors was the ability to supply a wide variety of framed pictures, rather than a more standard offering. Whilst it added to manufacturing complexity, especially with regard to the frequent changes to the machine settings, it also enabled 'NICE' to charge a higher price.

To overcome the problems of frequent machine-setting changes, Nicola decided to make small batches of same-sized framed pictures instead of one at a time, and put the unused pictures into stock for future use. As demand was continuing to grow, she knew that it would only be a short time before she could supply them on a particular contract. In fact this was to become a useful strategy as several projects were of a 'last minute' nature, where a designer had forgotten to order the pictures. Nicola's ready stock became extremely valuable and helped build her reputation for reliability and responsiveness.

Nicola felt quite proud of her management expertise: she had positioned 'NICE' in a 'virtuous circle' where immediate availability of finished stock enabled the completion of more contracts, at higher than average margins, enabling further investment in finished stock for servicing future requirements. Nicola's staff were driven by her mantra, 'stock wins orders'. Any periods where demand was slacker than usual enabled the re-building of stock levels. The thought of 'idle' time was too much for Nicola to accept.

For the next few years, NICE Framing successfully completed projects for Lancashire Breweries, and extended their service into several other breweries across the UK. 'NICE' also became an approved supplier for the international hotel chain 'Holiday Inn' in 1994, and began supplying pictures on their 2 and 3 star hotel upgrades.

By 1996 NICE had relocated to larger premises and employed 6 framing staff, with Nicola continuing to do the sales visits and contract negotiation. Turnover had risen to £210 000 with a gross margin of 70 per cent, and Nicola's profits were in excess of £35 000 pa.

After 9 years in business, she felt confident that the systems she had put in place would enable her to grow the business even more, and achieve her own personal goals. But times were changing, and there were new challenges around the corner.

First, the contracts for Holiday Inn were of a different nature to the 'pub' contracts. Instead of being able to take a large stock to site, and arrange the layout and design 'in situ', the designers for Holiday Inn specified the schemes with Nicola at design meetings, held in advance of the order placement. Holiday Inn would then place the order, to the agreed specification, four weeks in advance of the installation date.

This meant that Nicola could no longer select from finished stock, but had to make the order to a particular specification. This situation created problems in deciding when to make the order, as early completion would tie up capital and require 'double-handling' of the finished pictures.

Second, the nature of competition in the 'pub' sector was beginning to change. This new industry was now 8 years old. Breweries were no longer gaining the high returns on their investments that had characterized the early 1990s, and as the industry had matured, more suppliers were attracted into the market, drawn by the large levels of investment.

The brewery buyers were also more sophisticated, and had started to introduce competitive tendering, based against defined specifications, rather than their previous practice of allocating a budget, and judging 'value' at the completion of the contract.

Of course, the newer suppliers were keen to make an impact, and with their willing compliance, the price level in the whole industry plummeted.

Whilst Nicola's reputation for design expertise, reliability and availability continued to win her orders with some of the designers, finance departments were demanding price cuts.

Further problems appeared in October 2000, when Nicola called to make an appointment with Nancy Lopez, one of her key customers at Holiday Inn's design department.

Nancy had recently met with a salesman from a new picture framing company called EasyArt who had persuaded her to try their new 'online' design service. EasyArt believed that designers would prefer to design and specify jobs by selecting from an 'online' website catalogue and viewing the picture within a range of mounts and frames, rather than the time-consuming process of selecting from catalogues. And the designer would be able to 'see' the finished framed picture before placing an order. Nancy had been so impressed by the amount of time she had saved, that she had decided to place a trial order with them.

As Nicola sat in her office that late November evening, she wondered what to do. Whilst sipping her coffee, she flicked through the catalogue from the last trade show in February, and recalled a particular meeting.

Amongst all the usual trade stands promoting images, frames, materials and machinery, there was also a company demonstrating some new 'framing software'. As she searched for the contact details she recalled how dismissive she had been of this innovation, claiming that 'online' design would never take the place of face-to-face meetings.

Here she was 9 months later, with evidence to the contrary.

The next morning she phoned Grenville Ridley and asked him to tell her about 'smart-artgallery.com'.

Grenville reminded her that 'smart-artgallery.com' was similar to the EasyArt system, except for one important difference. Where EasyArt was a direct retailer, competing

▶

against other picture framers, 'smart-art-gallery' was a business system that individual framers could incorporate into their existing website. It was a B2B service which offered framers a 'safe' technological leap, and provided a simple and time-efficient design service for their customers.

Grenville assured Nicola that customers would also benefit from the knowledge that their Internet orders were being sent to their local framer and not to a company with whom they had no business relationship. After all, a local framer was much better placed to deal with 'face-to-face' issues such as deliveries, payment and 'returns'.

Nicola's meeting with Nancy and the increasingly intensive competition for the 'pub' business had provoked an internal dilemma. Should she carry on as she had traditionally done, and accept declining returns, or should she embrace the new technology, and with it a different way of working?

In times of crisis, Nicola did what she always did, and phoned her father.

	1996	2000
Profit and Loss – extract		
Turnover	210 000	212 000
Cost of sales	63 000	95 000
Staff and overheads	106 000	97 000
Capital expenditure	4 000	0
Owner's Profit	37 000	20 000
Balance Sheet – extract		
Inventory	26 000	32 000
Raw materials	6 000	12 000
Finished stock	20 000	20 000

Written by Keith Heron, 2002

2 Operations objectives

Objectives

Issues covered in this chapter are:

- Basic service requirements.

- The importance of stakeholders and their needs.

- Dimensions of resource utilization and efficiency.

Introduction

Managers of operations have two key objectives. The first is to satisfy customers' wants. Without customers the organization will cease to exist. The second key objective is the efficient use of resources. If an organization cannot afford the level of service it is providing, it will soon go out of business. The twin objectives of an operations manager must therefore be the provision of customer satisfaction combined with efficient use of resources. This chapter considers the dimensions of customer satisfaction and resource utilization.

Customers are sophisticated

Never have customers been more travelled, better informed and had higher expectations. Customers now take it as a matter of right that they will get a reliable, high-quality product and courteous, well-informed service. World-class organizations know that new products, services and technological improvements are quickly copied and improved upon and thus offer only a short-term advantage in the marketplace. They also know that the 'competitive edge' comes from providing a higher level of customer satisfaction than does the competition.

The role of competition

The quality of product and the level of service provided in a competitive market must at least equate to what the competition is providing or is perceived to be providing. Customers' expectations are influenced by what they have previously experienced, by what the competition is claiming to provide in advertisements, by what the media is saying and by the promises of technological improvements.

Basic service requirements

When introducing the concept of customer satisfaction it has to be understood that the first requirement for the customer is that the product or service must meet his/her specification and second that it will meet time and cost requirements.

Specification – providing the customer with what he/she expects to receive or is prepared to accept – is the essential requirement.

Time and cost are the next requirements. The product or service has to be available at a time that is acceptable to the customer, and the price must be reasonable.

What is acceptable or reasonable will always be open to question, and will depend on the circumstances of how important the product or service is to the customer and the alternatives available.

Example

Consider a commuter bus service – if a bus is not going from near where we live ('A') to near where we work ('B') then we will not catch it; and if the service does not get us to work on time and quickly, we will not use it. Also, if the cost is too high we will seek alternatives. Thus the essential dimension of customer satisfaction is specification (the bus must be going from 'A' to 'B'). In this example, if the specification is not right, time and cost are irrelevant.

Usually customers will accept, or tolerate, a service that does not perfectly meet their requirements. The amount of tolerance will be dependent on what the competition is offering or, if there is no immediate competition, what the alternatives are. Customers might be prepared to trade some specification for cost or timing; for instance, the passenger may be prepared to walk an extra block to catch a train, rather than take the bus, if the train fare is considerably cheaper.

Provider's perspective

From the perspective of the provider, what is provided has to be what can be afforded, and must be at least up to the same standard as the competition. The determination of what to provide is based on economic considerations rather than altruism. Customers are needed for income, but in the long term the organization cannot afford to run at a loss. Many an organization has failed to survive although customers have received excellent service. (Efficient use of resources is covered later in this chapter.)

Competitive advantage

As described in the opening sentences of this chapter, in today's environment of world-class standards and sophisticated customers, and where new products are quickly copied and improved upon by the competition, often the only competitive advantage will be from the level of service provided. Thus customer satisfaction goes past the basics of specification, time and cost to include *quality*. Quality has two dimensions: customer satisfaction and efficient use of resources. What constitutes quality, how it is judged and controlled, and the culture of quality is detailed in Chapter 13. However, because of the importance of the quality of service in gaining a competitive edge, our discussion on customer satisfaction would be incomplete if we were to ignore the rudiments of what can be done to enhance the basic attributes of specification, cost and time.

In our example of the bus service, having offered a service that attracts customers – specification, cost and time are acceptable – it will be possible to look at ways of adding a perception of increased service without adding to the cost.

Adding value

Generally some perception of added service can be provided at very little cost. Using our bus service as an example; assuming that specification, cost and timing meet the customer's basic needs (the bus is going to the right place, at the right time and the price is right) additional quality service attributes which probably would be appreciated by the passengers might include punctuality, cleanliness, a friendly and well-presented driver and consistency of service. A punctual service will be achieved by good planning and should not cost the company any extra to achieve; keeping the bus clean might add marginally to the cost (cleaning materials and wages). Issuing the driver with a smart uniform will obviously be a cost, and training a driver to be courteous and well-groomed might also incur some cost. Although all such costs are minimal when compared to the total operating cost of a bus company, the overall perception will be an improved service, although the basics of specification, timing and costs have not changed.

It is important to recognize that, above all, customers expect a reliable and consistent service. A service that is sometimes excellent and sometimes indifferent will only confuse the customer. Once a service level has been established, then the standard must be maintained.

For any organization, increased service at little or no cost will require a special culture. The workforce has to be enthusiastic and has to have some authority to make limited operational decisions. Creating a quality culture resulting in staff motivated to reduce inefficiencies and to give friendly and consistent service is covered in Chapter 13.

Reverting to our bus service, if having achieved the basics – right route, right time, right price, clean bus, friendly well-presented driver – the customers were now surveyed, it might be found that they would also like a more frequent service, sheltered waiting areas and more comfortable buses. Additional service at this level, such as a bus every ten minutes rather than one bus every half-hour, the provision of bus shelters, and an upgrade of the fleet will add an appreciable amount of cost, and the economics of doing so, rather than what the customer wants, will determine if such additional services are provided.

In Chapter 9 we examine scheduling strategies and techniques, but suffice to say that for this example it might be possible (if we have sufficient buses and drivers) to provide a ten-minute service at peak periods and to reduce the service to once an hour at other times without adding to the overall operating cost and at the same time providing a better service for peak-hour passengers.

To recap, customer satisfaction has three levels:

- The basics of specification, cost and timing have to be acceptable to the customer.
- The perception of an improved quality service can be achieved at very little cost, i.e. cleanliness, consistency, reliability, friendly and helpful front-line staff, etc.
- Added tangible value will cost money.

What is offered has to be affordable and sustainable.

We will now concentrate on determining who the customer really is, who are stakeholders, and how to rank the relative importance of the various requirements of customers and influential stakeholders.

Who is the customer?

In Chapter 1 we established that the customer is an input into a service process. Quite simply, without a customer no service can be performed (see Figure 2.1a), whereas in a manufacturing operation the customer is not a direct input but draws from the system, see Figure 2.1b.

Internal customers

In Chapter 13 we discuss the philosophy of total quality management (TQM). Some of the proponents of TQM consider the customer to be the next step in the operating process. For example, with TQM a writer when passing a manuscript to a word-processing person would consider the word processor to be the customer. The TQM approach would appear to conflict with our stance which is that in a

Figure 2.1

Push and pull

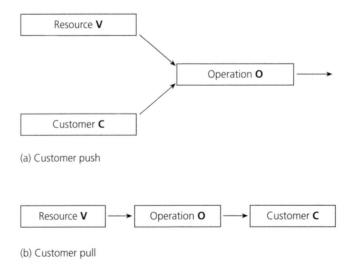

(a) Customer push

(b) Customer pull

service industry the customer is an input into the process, rather than the next step in the process; thus we would show the writer as the customer.

The TQM concept of the internal customer was always a contrivance, initially aimed to get factory workers on an assembly line to reduce waste and to pass on a good job to the next operator in the process. It was easy to say that without customers we will not sell our goods, and without sales the factory will close, but for the operator wielding the screwdriver, faced with a seemingly never-ending assembly line, the customer was remote and faceless. Making the next person on the line the customer gave the customer a face. We do not criticize this approach: anything that serves to make work more meaningful, gives people more esteem and reduces costs has to be applauded. However, in reality it has to be accepted that the factory worker has very little control over the quality of the product – the worker does not decide on the quality of the material used or decide on how many coats of paint will be applied, and even if a worker tried to take a craft worker's approach to the job, the time available to add the finishing touches to his or her small step in the overall process will be restricted by the speed of the line. Suffice to say that the suggestion that the next step in the process is an internal customer will not help to determine what the end-user (the true customer) of the product or service really wants, nor will it help when trying to analyze the structure of a service system.

There can, of course, be customers drawn from within an organization.

Example

A large organization with its own research department has moved to establish cost/profit centres. Previously the research department relied on other departments of the organization for research projects. The research department was not proactive in seeking work. The operating structure is shown in Figure 2.2.

Using our systems structure approach it is apparent that without input from the customer no research would begin, and it is also likely that the product manager and his or her staff will be consulted at various stages as the research proceeds; therefore the customer, although internal to the organization, is more (in TQM terms) than just the next step in the process. To limit the department to being the next step in the process does not encourage pro-action, but encourages the department to think of themselves as the 'customer'. As a 'customer', the culture would not be to go out looking for work but to wait for work to come to them.

Once it is realized that the customer is an input, rather than the next stage in the process, it will be appreciated that the department cannot afford to passively wait for briefs from other departments. To survive, the research department will have to be proactive. They will need to promote themselves within the organization, and if sufficient customers are not available from within there should be no reason why they should not promote themselves outside the organization, i.e. look for work external to the organization.

▶

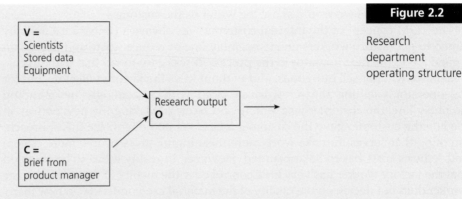

Resource of the department is the knowledge of the team, the data that has been collected and stored, test equipment, computers and so on. The customer's input is the brief for the project.

Example

A pension fund department of a water board is now seeking to manage funds for outside companies. Even five years ago this would not have been contemplated by the department, and even if such a suggestion had been put forward – 'to go outside the organization for pension customers' – it is likely that the board would not have sanctioned such a move. This is just another example of how the move towards deregulation and privatization around the world has changed the environment for government-type organizations to allow them to become commercially orientated.

Satisfying the stakeholders or who pays the ferryman?

A stakeholder is anyone who has an interest in what an organization does. This might seem a very broad definition, and indeed it is. Knowing who stakeholders are and how their concerns might affect the operation of an organization is becoming more and more critical.

With some organizations, usually public sector-type operations such as education, health and social welfare, the person with the direct input into the system – the student, the patient, the welfare beneficiary – has to be satisfied. Without these people (the direct customers) the need for the service will disappear. However, in many cases the direct customers do not personally pay for the service they receive. Funds for the operation come from the government, or in some cases charitable trusts. The body that provides the funds (government or charitable organization) obviously has a stake in the efficiency of the operation. These stakeholders, the fund providers, should, and increasingly do, seek value for money. In their eyes value for money will not only include providing a level of service to the customer but will also include efficient use of resources. There are also other stakeholders who do not directly provide money, such as the general public in the guise of tax-payers; they also are concerned that their money is being spent wisely.

Example

For a government-funded university the customer is the student (the direct input into the teaching process). A major stakeholder is the government (major source of funds) and their concern will be that they are getting value for money. Other providers of funds include fee-paying students and their sponsors (parents or work organizations) and business houses who make grants or sponsor a chair. All these stakeholders have a stake in the quality of the outputs. There are still other stakeholders who do not directly provide funds for the university, but who will have a very real interest in the quality and relevance of the teaching provided. If the university offers law and/or accountancy degrees then relevant professional bodies and societies will have a special interest, and perhaps even some direct say, in what is taught. Likewise others who may not directly contribute funds, such as some parents, employers and prospective employers of graduates, and the staff of the university are all stakeholders. Each group of stakeholders is likely to have different priorities in judging the service provided. Some fund providers and taxpayers will be anxious that resources are being efficiently utilized (money is not being wasted); others will be more concerned with what is being taught, and the value of qualifications (perceived standard or status of the university).

Determining stakeholders

For commercial businesses a stakeholder is anyone with a pecuniary interest in the organization (such as shareholders, banks, financiers, investors, suppliers of goods and services, and the people who work in the organization and their families). Other more general stakeholders include investors in the share market, local bodies in the district of the operation, people who live and work in the operation's general neighbourhood, and the green movement. For government and quasi-government organizations, charitable trusts and other like bodies, stakeholders are fund providers, bankers, suppliers, people who work in the organization and their families, and the community at large.

Your turn!

Identify the stakeholders for your organization and their concerns.
(Identifying stakeholders and determining their concerns should prove to be an interesting exercise.)
Now rank their importance.

Customer/stakeholder priorities

Customer satisfaction therefore has two elements:

1. We have to know exactly what the customers want in terms of specification, price and timing.
2. We have to ensure that what is being offered and the manner in which we operate, to satisfy the customer, is not conflicting with the interests of stakeholders.

The matrix in Figure 2.3 is designed to allow an industry to analyze customers' and stakeholders' needs.

Figure 2.3		Specification	Timing	Price
	Direct customers			
A service industry matrix	Stakeholders a			
	b			
	c			
	d			
	Total			

Example

The direct customers for the Refuse Collection Department of the Highvale Borough Council are considered to be householders. The service provided is a weekly collection of refuse. The Borough Council has recently decided to add a surcharge to the rates to partly offset the cost of refuse collection; until now there has not been a separate charge. The commercial (or business) district of the town also has refuse collected by the department, but commercial organizations are charged separately for this, and some organizations use alternative means of rubbish disposal. No competition yet exists for household refuse collection, but two private refuse collectors operate in a neighbouring town. The fee that will be charged by the Highvale Borough Council does not cover the full cost of the service and is much cheaper than neighbouring independent operators. Local body elections are due in eighteen months' time.

The operations manager (the manager of the Refuse Department) is worried that the charging of a fee by the Council suggests they are concerned with the cost of running the department. His other worry is that if householders are to pay for the service, they might become more critical and demand a higher service. In other words the Council has indicated that they are concerned with the cost of running the department, and customers are now likely to expect a higher level of service. The other worry for the operations manager is that the Council might consider outsourcing (buying in) the service.

To determine what is wanted by the direct customers and by the Council, and to see if there are any other stakeholders, the operations manager commissioned a survey. The survey was designed to determine, first, what the customers and stakeholders (if any) wanted; and second, their perceptions of what they are currently getting. Results of the survey are tabulated in Figure 2.4.

Desired service (rating: 3 = very important; 2 = important; 1 = not important)

Figure 2.4

Desired service

	Bins emptied	Timing	Price	Keep to budget
Direct customers	2	2	3	1
Stakeholders:				
Council	2	1	1	2
Commercial ratepayers	1	1	1	3

Perceptions of present service (rating 3 = excellent; 2 = acceptable; 1 = not good

	Bins emptied	Timing	Price	Keep to budget
Direct customers	3	3	2	2
Stakeholders:				
Council	3	3	2	1
Commercial ratepayers	3	3	1	1

Requirements

The results of the survey by the customer/stakeholder group showed that:

1. Householders' requirements are as follows:

Specification
Householders require a good service (ideally bins always fully emptied and left in a tidy manner with no rubbish scattered on the road).

Timing
Timing is important – householders want a regular service (same day each week).

Price
The price is most important to the customers. They rate price (cost) above service, and they do not see a need for the Council to make a profit on refuse collection (being close to budget is sufficient).

2. Council requirements are:

Specification
To maintain a reasonable service (they are not concerned if the occasional bin is missed).

Timing
Timing is not vital.

Price
Keeping to budget is regarded as essential.

3. Requirements of important stakeholders:

Commercial ratepayers see that keeping to budget is essential. Some even suggested that the Refuse Department should actually run at a profit, and others suggested that the service should be outsourced. Commercial ratepayers provide 70 per cent of the Council's income, and have a strong lobby group. They believe that they are subsidising the householders.

4. Other stakeholders' requirements:

The concern of the people who work in the department, and their immediate families, is with job security. They are confident that they can improve the efficiency of the service, and already some useful suggestions have been made.

Perceptions of existing service

Customers and all the stakeholders see the service as excellent. If the operations manager was only concerned with what the customers want then he would have been very pleased with the outcome of the survey. But as the other stakeholders do not rate service as being the critical area of measurement, this suggests a rethink of the priorities of the department.

From this analysis, the operations manager can see that the Council cannot afford to run the service at a loss. Prior to this analysis, as the Council was not suggesting an increase in fees for the commercial sector, the operations manager had not realized that the commercial ratepayers had an interest in the service for householders, and he had certainly not considered that the commercial sector could actually threaten the future of the department.

The results of the survey indicate that if the department cannot keep to budget, the Council will put the price up or perhaps consider subcontracting to private providers. Likewise householders are very price conscious and if the Council does contemplate a price increase the householders could themselves lobby for private subcontractors. Now that the operations manager realizes the importance for the department of not only keeping to budget but actually reducing costs, he is looking to see if some efficiencies are possible. Until now regular and high-level service rather than cost had been his main objective; keeping to budget had been of secondary importance.

Adaptation of matrix

This type of matrix analysis can be adapted to any industry. Even if there are no stakeholders, and there are only customers to be satisfied, then the analysis can be extended to include different groups or segments of customers. Pareto analysis will be a useful tool (see Chapter 3) where it may be found that a vital few will account for up to 80 per cent of the business.

Stakeholders such as banks and creditors (suppliers of goods and services) will generally only be interested in the financial security of the business. Other stakeholders such as people living in the neighbourhood of the operation will have other concerns such as pollution, noise and perhaps even heavy traffic flows. If local concerns are known in advance then action can be taken to prevent offence. Actions that have to be taken as a result of protests or legal initiatives not only taint an organization's reputation but will prove more costly than if the operation had been set up correctly and stakeholders' concerns addressed in the first place.

Composite customer service rating

Christopher (1992) gives another method of rating customer service, as illustrated in Table 2.1.

Table 2.1	Service index	Weighting %	Performance %	Weighted score
Rating customer service		(a)	(b)	(a × b)
	Order fill	45	70	0.315
	On time	35	80	0.28
	Invoice accuracy	10	90	0.09
	Returns	10	95	0.095
		100		0.78
	Composite customer service rating			78%

In this example the key criterion has been established as filling orders (specification): this is the most important criterion and has been given a rating of 45/100. On-time delivery is the next most important, and other important criteria (but of lesser rating) are invoice accuracy and the number of returns (return represents faulty goods).

Column 'b' shows that 70 per cent of orders are filled, 80 per cent of orders are sent on time, the accounts department are 90 per cent accurate, and 5 per cent of goods are faulty. Christopher's composite customer service rating is calculated against internally set standards of service, and is also calculated on internally gathered data, rather than on feedback from customers.

However, no matter how good or how relevant we think our own internal measures are, such as Christopher's composite service rating, there is no better method than to ask the customer. Ideally, internal measures should be set against targets established by the customer.

What might seem trivial to the business could, in the customer's eyes, be seen as a major problem. For example, we might find that an important customer claims that they can never get through on the phone. Once this is appreciated we could set the target that the phone must be answered within three rings. We might also do away with automatic recorded telephone answering: leaving a message on voice-mail is a very poor option. To stress the point that we are easy to communicate with, we could also set a target that all faxes and e-mails are replied to on the day received. No internal measures of such targets are needed if the culture of the organization is such that the staff are all driven by a desire to satisfy the customer (see Chapter 13).

Gap analysis

The level of service offered stems from the business policy which, in turn, to a large extent is driven by what the competition is doing or is threatening to do. When deciding upon and specifying a level of service, management tends to rely on the advice of the marketing function. If the marketing function does not correctly interpret the requirements of the customer then there will be a gap between the level of satisfaction the organization believes it is providing and what the customer believes he or she is getting. The concept of service gaps arose from the research of Berry et al. (1988) and his colleagues (Parasuraman et al., 1985, 1991; Zeithaml et al., 1990). As Lewis (1994: 237) says: 'They defined service quality to be a function of the gap between consumers' expectations of a service and their perceptions of the actual service delivery by an organization, and suggested that this gap is influenced by a number of other gaps which may occur in an organization.'

The magnitude of the gap will be compounded by the number of steps in the service process and by the distance of the operational function from the customer.

► **Example**

Suppose that the marketing department's interpretation of what the customer wants is only 90 per cent correct, then the actual performance can never be better than 90 per cent of what the customer really wants. If, however, business policy is such that it is deemed sufficient to provide resources to meet 90 per cent of customers' requirements (this 90 per cent will be set on the understanding that marketing is 100 per cent correct) then at best the customer will now only get 81 per cent of what they want. Let us assume that the operation consists of a back office and a front office. Supposing the back office slightly misinterpret what management want and also set themselves an internal target of 90 per cent, and then further suppose that the front office is so resourced that to the best of their ability they can only achieve 95 per cent of the standard set, this means the final result will be that the cus-

tomer satisfaction is at best only 70 per cent. The calculation is shown in Table 2.2.

Unless gap analysis is attempted, management will firmly believe that the overall result is somewhere near 90 per cent of what the customer wants. And each department when queried will fervently believe that they are reaching between 90 and 95 per cent of required performance levels.

If an organization is close to its customers and aware of what the competition is doing, then a gap of this magnitude should not happen. The larger the organization and the greater the delineation of responsibilities between departmental functions, and the further the operations function is removed from the customer and from consultation in business policy decisions, the greater the likelihood of gaps occurring between what is provided and what the customer really wants.

Table 2.2	Customer requirement	100
	Marketing misinterpret (they get it 90% right)	90
Gap analysis	Business policy sets target at 90% of 100 (but this actually equates to 90% of 90)	81
	Under-resourced back office set internal standard of better than 90% of target. Due to slight ambiguity and misunderstanding of management target, even when 92% of internal target is reached, it is only 90% of what was set by management (90% of 81 = 73)	73
	Front office, also under-resourced, are 95% on target (95% of 73 = 69)	69

Summary: customer satisfaction

To summarize, generally an organization will aim to consistently achieve certain standards or levels of quality as determined by business policy. The decision about the level of service to provide will be an economic one, and will be driven by what the competition is doing or is likely to do. The intention should be to define accurately what the customer wants, in terms of the basic requirements of specification, time and cost. Normally an organization will not be able completely to meet all the requirements of the customer and some trade-off will be possible. It is also wise to understand who the stakeholders are and what their concerns might be.

Where a strong organizational culture exists, with enthusiastic and helpful staff, the perception of service can be enhanced at very little extra cost to the organization.

Dimensions of resource utilization

Given infinite resources any system, however badly managed, might provide adequate customer service. (Wild 2002: 11)

Many an organization has failed to survive despite the customers having been more than satisfied with what they have received. Thus customer satisfaction is not the only criterion by which an operations manager will be judged. Customer satisfaction must be provided simultaneously with an effective and efficient operation. The level of customer satisfaction offered must not only be affordable to the organization but it must also be consistent and sustainable.

Efficient use of resources

A prime concern of any operations manager is the efficient use of resources and the elimination of non-effective (non-value-adding) activities.

The resources available will consist of a mix of the following:

- People.
- Information technology.
- Equipment and machines (including display racks, checkout facilities, etc.).
- Vehicles.
- Space (buildings, offices, warehouses, display areas, etc.).
- Materials (including 'intermediate' materials such as wrapping and packing materials, etc.).
- Inventory (raw materials, work in progress and stock for sale).
- Time and information.

Obviously not all organizations will have, or need, all of these resources.

There will never be an unlimited amount of resource and often resources will be limited in quantity and quality. An increase of resources will be dependent on funds available. When funds are not an inhibitor there can be other constraints; for example, we may need specialized packing materials which we order but it might be some weeks before delivery is made.

Prioritizing resources

The above list of resources may appear formidable, but generally it will be found that the list can be reduced or modified to show the three most important resources for the particular organization with which we are concerned. The important resources are those which are most necessary to satisfy the customers' essential requirements of specification, time and cost.

Example

For a travel agent the three most important resources could well be people, information technology and space. Certainly stationery and other office supplies and equipment will be needed, but these will be of only minor significance. Likewise the branch manager might see his car as an important resource, but it might have minor impact on the achievement of customer satisfaction.

Suppose that the travel agency has determined that they are valued by the customers for friendly service and useful advice on means of travel and accommodation, accurate bookings and ticketing, speedy service, and competitive prices and 'special' deals. This would enable the agency to say that 'our customers judge satisfaction by specification, time and cost'. *Specification* is advice and accurate ticketing, *time* equates to speedy service, and *cost* is competitive prices and special deals. To achieve customer satisfaction as defined in this manner the agency will need a reliable integrated computer system which gives on-line information, communication with airlines, hotels and so on, and confirmation of bookings, tickets and vouchers. The agency will need sufficient office space to accommodate several staff members and customers at any one time. Finally, the agency will need reliable, systems-trained, well-presented and courteous staff.

Using the travel agency example we can now extend our matrix approach for customer satisfaction to include resource utilization:

Assume for this example it has been established that customers rate advice and accurate ticketing as most important and that they are prepared to wait for information and for tickets, but they do not expect to wait more than five minutes before a consultant is available. Cost, although important, is of a lesser consideration to accuracy and to receiving speedy service. Having established this rating the next step is to determine the most vital resources needed to give the customers satisfaction.

In this example it is found that a reliable integrated computerized information and ticketing system is essential. When the system is 'down' little can be achieved, information on prices, schedules and availability of seats cannot be provided, nor can bookings be made and tickets and vouchers issued.

A back-up 'manual' system consisting of the telephone, bound books of pamphlets and handwritten tickets has proved in the past to be not only unwieldy and slow, but expensive due to mistakes being made through information not being up-to-date and bookings being incorrectly recorded.

Trained staff are important but of lesser importance than the system, for without the system the staff can do little. Space is an issue, but in our example generally has not proved too much of a problem. With a good system and well-trained staff, customers can be turned around quickly; when the system is slow or staff are inexperienced then the time taken to serve a customer is extended and space can become a problem.

Customer satisfaction			Resource utilization		
Spec	Time	Cost	People	Information technology	Space
3	2	1	2	3	1

Example

Another example concerns a computer service bureau. The bureau writes specialized software to order. The customer satisfaction matrix showed that customers rated specification as important, time as not so important (they were prepared to wait to get exactly what they wanted), and were prepared to pay a reasonable amount. Thus:

	Specification	Timing	Price
Required	3	2	2

But the perception of the service actually received by customers showed a gap between expectations and performance.

Perception of service	2	1	1

It can be seen that customers were not satisfied. The software was not always to specification, time delays were unacceptable, and cost was too high (in comparison to what the competition were offering).

A self-analysis by the bureau found that the key resources were skilled people, own hardware and software used for developing new programs. Other resources such as office space, materials, stationery, etc. were of comparatively minor importance.

Resource analysis

Actual performance:

Hardware	Software	People
3	1	3

The analysis revealed that the hardware was adequate, the staff were well skilled, but there were problems with the in-house software. It had always been realized that there were problems with the software, but it was also thought that the time delays had been caused by not having enough trained people; indeed, consideration was being given to increasing staff numbers. However, as pointed out by the accountants, an increase of staff would add to the costs. When the staff were asked for their opinion they advised that delays and costly rewrites were due to software problems.

The efficiency factor

The discussion above concerning resource utilization has been from the stance of customer satisfaction.

Traditional production and operation management texts tend to suggest that the role of the operations manager is primarily efficient use of resources in transforming inputs into outputs and that customer satisfaction is almost a subservient objective. While this might be so for certain types of capital-intensive operations where the customer is not an input into the system, such as a factory where goods can be produced irrespective of whether a customer order is held or not, we have concluded for service industries that resource utilization is subservient to customer satisfaction. This is not to say that efficient use of resources is unimportant; indeed efficiency is vitally important. However, total efficiency would mean making the optimum use of resources, i.e. elimination of all waste, no spare space, no idle time and minimum of time spent with clients, customer queues so that service staff are fully employed, and so on.

Example

An example of where resource utilization takes precedence over customer satisfaction can be found with some airlines where the policy is to accept bookings for 440 passengers when the aircraft only has 400 seats. This strategy has evolved from past experience which shows that not all passengers arrive for flights, and consequently rather than having aircraft fly with empty seats, the policy is for some passengers to be offloaded and to be offered seats on a later flight.

Precedence of objectives

Some organizations will concentrate on customer satisfaction at an affordable and sustainable level as being the over-riding objective, and others will focus on efficient use of resource utilization ahead of customer satisfaction. This is not to suggest that the organization which is resource focused ignores customer satisfaction, and often resource utilization will be in harmony with customer satisfaction.

Example

Aircraft passengers will value getting to their destination (specification) on time and will be prepared to pay a certain price. If the airline meets these criteria (specification, time and cost) customers will be basically satisfied, and if at the same time the airline has a full aircraft (no empty seats) and keeps its operating costs to a minimum then simultaneously efficient resource utilization and customer satisfaction will have been achieved.

In our first airline example it is only when pre-booked passengers are turned away that the objectives will conflict. Suffice to say that passengers travelling first class, those who have been prepared to pay for extra service, will not be the ones to be off-loaded. First-class passengers could well rate the service and all the personal attention that they get as being truly first class. Thus although some passengers will be less than happy (those who have been off-loaded) the airline company could still claim in its mission statement, and in its advertising, to provide world-class service, although the over-riding objective is clearly resource utilization.

Your turn!

For your organization what limits the level of customer service provided? Also, is resource utilization the over-riding objective, or does customer satisfaction have first priority?

Balance of objectives: potential conflict

The two basic objectives for an operations manager are customer satisfaction and resource utilization. The examples given above show that having understood the key requirements of the customer it is then important to attempt a match with the resources available. It will not always be possible to totally gain a balance between what the customer wants and what the organization is able to do. For the operations manager the further restraint will be the objectives of the organization. If the objectives are driven primarily by the need for efficient use of resources, then customer satisfaction will be more difficult to achieve. As stated in our opening sentence to this section, given infinite resources any system, no matter how badly managed, might provide adequate service. The truth will be that there are not infinite resources, and often existing resources will not completely mesh with the achievement of total customer satisfaction. Nonetheless, the operations manager will be expected to achieve adequate use of resources and a reasonable level of customer satisfaction.

Customer satisfaction
matched with resource utilization

If the over-riding aim is to make the most efficient use of existing resources, it might mean that the product has to be rethought and repromoted. Thus the product and service will be altered to meet the competences of the organization, rather than extra resources being added to enhance a product or service. Before any change to the specified product is contemplated it would be expected that the operations manager would seek improved methods of operating and better ways of doing things using existing resources. Rather than saying 'It cannot be done' the positive approach is to look for ways to make the impossible possible with existing resources.

Chapter summary

In this chapter we have determined that the prime objective of an organization is customer satisfaction through the provision of a consistent and sustainable product and level of service. The determinant of the level of service to be provided will be driven by the competition and demands of customers and stakeholders. The operations manager is vitally concerned with efficient and effective use of resources. We also noted that resources will generally be limited in quantity and quality. Therefore the operations manager must balance the two, potentially conflicting, objectives of customer satisfaction and efficient resource utilization.

Case Study *Qormi Post Office*

The Case Study and study notes for Qormi Post Office (Malta) illustrates how the Qormi Post Office was able to improve customer satisfaction by better use of existing resources.

Questions

1. What are the current operating system structures at Qormi?

2. What are the present operations objectives for the subsystems in Qormi Post Office?

Introduction

The branch Post Office at Qormi, on the Mediterranean island of Malta, provides a postal service to a community of about 10 000 persons. It operates from a building which is located in a central position on the main road in the town.

It comprises three main sections: a big sorting room where mail is stamped, sorted by locality and arranged for local delivery; a transport storage room where bicycles are kept; and a receipt and despatch depot.

This local branch Post Office undertakes to collect letters and similar postal items (e.g. postcards, printed matter, etc.) in the town and deliver them to addressees in the minimum time possible, and to deliver in the town items from elsewhere. Items collected locally meant for local addresses are 'processed' wholly within the branch, while other items addressed for outside the local area are date-stamped, bundled and later collected by Head Office, Valetta for onward transmission.

The Qormi Post Office operates only as a mustering room. It does not operate a counter service, so there are no facilities for accepting parcels and heavier items which need weighing, rating and certification prior to being accepted for posting, or for the registration of letters which demand treatment (i.e. listing) upon acceptance. Nor does it have the facilities to sell stamps and advise people on postal tariffs and rates, nor to offer any philatelic services like the special first day of issue date-stamp. Local customers needing such services have to travel to the nearest town – Valetta (the capital of the island).

The operation

Collection of letters from post boxes at strategic points around the town is made twice daily, at 7 am and again at 9 am, by postmen using bicycles as a means of transport. The mail is brought to the Post Office where it is date-stamped and sorted according to the locality postcode. Letters for the local area are immediately passed to the sorting room for sorting by postmen ready for delivery the same day. Postal items for outside areas are packed in bags for collection by Head Office.

Mail from outside areas for local addressees arrives by van from Head Office. This van then carries away local mail for 'foreign' destinations. Incoming mail is sorted according to postal beats, then passed to the sorting room for re-sorting into the postmen's rounds. The postmen then start delivering the mail. The inner town routes (or 'beats') are usually made on foot, while mail for outlying areas is delivered by bicycle.

Figure 2.5 shows the normal process of operation. It should be noted that although there are various levels of postal tariffs relating to the quality (i.e. speed) of service required (e.g. first class mail for closed letters, second class mail for postcards and newspapers), all mail is afforded first class treatment in what is called an 'all up' service. Thus all mail is processed and delivered in one batch.

The staff employed consist of an officer in charge of the whole operation, plus seven postmen. There are five beats so five of the postmen are totally dedicated to sorting and delivery. Another postman acts as a 'reliever'

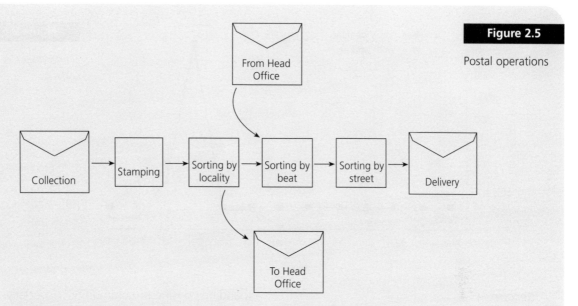

Figure 2.5

Postal operations

who stands in whenever another postman is absent, which is frequently, as each postman is entitled to five weeks vacation leave (there are no scheduled shutdowns) plus other absences due to illness, etc. The seventh postman takes care of the collection of letters from letter boxes, date-stamping of letters and despatch and receipt of mail from Head Office.

The customer

Post Offices in Malta deal with three sets of customers. The first is the domestic consumer market where the Post Office offers a service primarily aimed at collecting and delivering household mail (mainly letters).

The second is the business and industrial community and offers such services as fast transmission of documents and packages, bulk postings and a reliable and fast commercial parcel service.

The third is a 'niche' market that only the Post Office could satisfy, and concerns the needs of the philatelic enthusiasts.

Qormi branch Post Office deals mainly with the first market although lately pressure has been mounting to extend operations so as to be able to accommodate demand from industry and philatelists.

Demand

Demand for the postal service is uniform and stable with a peak during the Christmas festivities period when mail posting tends to double (see Figure 2.6). Demand forecasting is therefore straightforward, the more so since the Post Office, having a monopoly on the postal business, is not subject to real competitive pressures (although some competition exists in alternative ways of communication; for example, telephone, telefaxes and electronic mail).

Objectives

The aim of the Malta Post Office is to serve the community by offering a fast, reliable and cheap postal service. It commits itself to collect and deliver within the island of Malta, all items posted up to a certain time (7 am) on the very same day. Items posted between 7 am and 9 am and addressed within the local area will also be delivered on the same day. Mail posted after 9 am will get a next day delivery.

The Post Office also commits itself to deliver the articles intact and at the lowest possible prices. The very low level of complaints testifies to a high degree of customer satisfaction.

▶

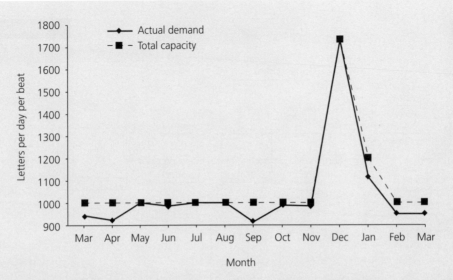

Figure 2.6

Demand versus capacity

Resources

The most important resource employed is labour. Few materials are consumed in the process and the machinery/tools employed are minimal and comprise, beside the building, some bicycles, date-stamps, racks, chairs, mail-bags, tables and uniforms.

To solve the Christmas demand problem, the Post Office withholds all staff leave during December. A double shift working arrangement is introduced at the peak demand period, where postmen are required to collect, process and deliver mail a second time. (Temporary labour is not used because using inexperienced workers might lead to errors and a subsequent drop in quality, with the risk of complaints from customers. Moreover, inexperienced workers will be slow and thus costs will be higher). Transfer of labour from other Post Office branches is not feasible because they also have the same seasonal demand.

The development of the Qormi Post Office

Although this branch Post Office has been operating very effectively, pressures have been mounting on the central Post Office management to extend the Qormi operations to accommodate the growing demand from the expanding business community, especially since the setting up of an industrial area in the vicinity of the town.

In addition to this, local philatelists have also been complaining about having to travel to another office in order to satisfy their needs. They argue that a local branch with a customized 'first day of issue' date-stamp would be a further service to philately and might increase demand.

These public demands have been echoed in the press and by local politicians, and Post Office management has felt obliged to have the situation investigated, prior to considering whether to reformulate their business policy in relation to the Qormi branch.

To do this they set out to:

- Identify and forecast the level of expected extra demand that would be generated following the proposed change.

- Identify any possible threats and risks (e.g. expected demand not materializing), whilst also

- Acknowledging the needs of the public as major stakeholders, and

- Accepting the Post Office's responsibility as a public utility to cater for the requirements of society.

After some preliminary market research and an analysis of the Qormi branch operations, it was found that the level of expected demand was enough to warrant expanding the service. Moreover, it was noted that this presented an excellent possibility to use available spare space on the premises and also of improving significantly resource utilization (which for most of the time was operating at less than maximum capacity).

The decision was therefore taken to set up a counter section in the Qormi branch with the following objectives:

- To provide services to satisfy the needs of a variety of markets, in search both of greater market penetration (domestic market) and market development (business and philatelic communities).
- To make far greater use of available resources, thereby minimizing costs.

Branch resources

The determination of the level of resources to be used for the new counter service depended on forecast demand for counter services. It was anticipated that demand would take some time to pick up, so initially only one counter

assistant was allowed by Head Office. Other resource requirements were considered to be minimal and amounted to some counter furniture, weighing scales and a limited stock of stamps (stocks of stamps were replenished from Head Office whenever they fell below a minimum amount).

Whilst in practice this set-up gave rise to some customer queuing, it was nonetheless thought to be minimal and considered by Head Office to be quite normal and acceptable in such situations.

Branch economics

Previously, resource utilization levels had enabled the Qormi Post Office to achieve its most economic level of operation at around one thousand letters processed per day, per beat (see Figure 2.7). Any increase in output or demand will involve an increase in costs (overtime) and will change the unit cost/output relationship.

In fact the new services increased demand significantly and generated a substantial rise of 45 per cent in revenue (from Lm19 000 to Lm27 500). This was achieved at an increase in fixed costs of Lm4000 and a smaller increase in variable costs (from Lm2000 to Lm4500 pa)

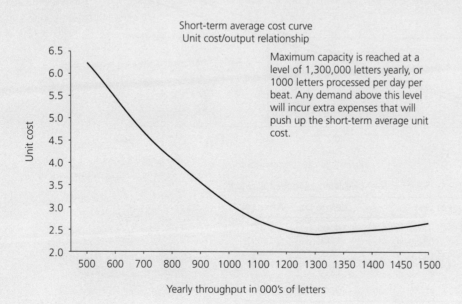

Short-term average cost curve
Unit cost/output relationship

Maximum capacity is reached at a level of 1,300,000 letters yearly, or 1000 letters processed per day per beat. Any demand above this level will incur extra expenses that will push up the short-term average unit cost.

Figure 2.7

Output/cost relationship

Yearly throughput in 000's of letters

mainly due to increased expenditure on over-time and the employment of a counter clerk.

This new situation lowered slightly the break-even percentage capacity which has been lowered from an estimated level of approximately 60 per cent to 53 per cent as illustrated in the figure and table (see Figure 2.8).

Impact on customers

Given the new methods of operating, it was recognized that customer service could suffer. However, since the increased demand was not initially expected to exceed the available capacity, it was reasoned that any problems could easily be dealt with through the careful adjustment of capacity, as and when required, by overtime work. Certainly this seemed to be the only possibility as central management was not prepared to consider employing additional labour which might be under-utilized at periods of normal demand.

The manager, however, did consider other options available to deal with the problem:

1. *Mechanization*, that is, some form of mechanization to increase capacity, e.g. an automated stamp cancelling machine to release labour time to devote to other activities, or motorcycles instead of bicycles, to save time on collection and delivery rounds.

2. *A 'Two Level' Service.* Normally the 'all up' service has applied. However, now that available capacity may not always be enough to meet demand, the second class type of mail could be left to 'queue'.

3. *Revised Scheduling.* Operating at near to full capacity means that the timing of activities becomes much more crucial. Demand for the new counter service is expected to be fairly stable and regular, but the main effect of the new decision was to increase demand so as to utilize available capacity effectively all of the time. This however, had implications for the quality of service through:

- an occasional inadequacy of the system to process all demand and therefore to ensure prompt delivery;

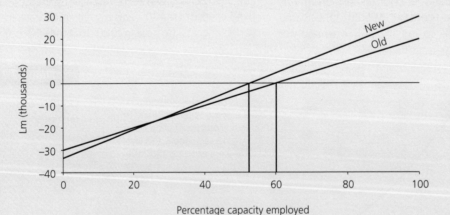

Figure 2.8

Break-even capacity calculation

The graph above has been calculated using the following:

Nature of cost	Before Lm	After Lm
Fixed costs (overheads)	4500	5000
(wages)	24500	28000
Variable costs (overtime)	2000	4500
TOTAL COSTS	31000	37500
SALES	50000	65000
PROFIT	19000	27500

- a tendency to introduce mishandling and delivery errors in the various phases of the process through sheer pressure of work.

Thus quality became a major concern for the Branch Manager who took the view that the provision of good quality service is above all a result of a good operating system and a quality culture. Procedures and individual functions should be clearly defined so that responsibilities can be easily identified; commitment should be clearly visible from the operations manager downwards. Work standards and specifications need to be emphasized; supervision and internal communication, coupled with continuous on-the-job training would also facilitate the quality process.

The human aspect of ensuring quality through a satisfied workforce should also be highlighted by providing work variety and in allowing employees a degree of autonomy in determining methods of work and problem-solving. Job rotation and job enrichment methods should also be studied.

In this context it was noted that the nature of the service has two particular advantages:

1. The postman comes in direct daily contact with his customers, developing a friendly relationship that not only helps to build a good image for the organization but effectively motivates the postman to produce a quality service. Any errors on the postman's part have to be explained directly to the customer.

2. The postal operation is a continuous and cascading mail-sorting process, which immediately detects any errors made in a previous stage. For example, if a letter has been incorrectly sorted by locality, it cannot be re-sorted by beat, let alone by household order, and will be re-directed to the previous sorting stage straightaway. The chances of misdelivery are therefore much reduced.

© Anthony Vella, Ray Wild 1995

▐▌ Part Two

In Part Two we consider the context of operations management. As no one is an island unto themselves, likewise no organization can isolate itself from the external environment, and within the organization no one department or function can stand alone. Every business is now competing on the world stage, and to survive must strive to reach world-class standards. National and geographic boundaries no longer afford a protective barrier for competitors. Customers today are well travelled and well informed and are quick to make value judgements on performance.

- In **Chapter 3** the link between the business policy and operations objectives are explained, and the importance of understanding the true mission is discussed. Factors which influence business policy, including external and internal influencers, are identified and explained. This chapter also establishes the importance of a good rapport between the operations and marketing functions.
- **Chapter 4** focuses on the efficient use of resources and takes a total value-chain approach, from supplier through to the ultimate customer. This chapter also expands on the need for co-operation between departmental functions within the organization if the overall corporate mission is to be achieved. Operational planning, implementation and the control process necessary to make the business policy happen are also discussed in this chapter; and the importance of communication and transfer of information in the control process is recognized.
- **Chapter 5** links back to the structure of organizations, and shows ways of establishing value-adding activities with a view to minimizing non-value-adding activities. It is seen that activities which are deemed to add value are those that are required to achieve customer satisfaction. It is accepted that some activities are essential to the overall operation but in themselves do not directly add value to the service, and thus these activities should be critically examined with a view to reducing the effort and cost incurred.

3 Business policy

Objectives

This chapter examines:

- How business policy is determined.

- Who the customer is, and how satisfaction is judged.

- Internal capability and feasibility (the competence of the organization).

- The external factors which influence policy.

In Chapter 1 we said that the role of the operations manager is to arrange and use resources efficiently and effectively to achieve the goals or mission of the organization. We also said that although operations managers may not always be involved in determining goals and objectives, nevertheless they are the people responsible for turning the goals and objectives into realities.

Ideally the operations manager will be involved in shaping the corporate policy and objectives of the organization, establishing and acquiring resources, and setting specific operational targets. But organizations seldom operate in an ideal fashion. The reality is that in many cases the operations manager will inherit an existing structure, and less than adequate or unsuitable resources will already be in place. More importantly, the principal objective (be it customer satisfaction or efficient resource utilization) will not be clearly defined in the business policy. Indeed, most organizations will have both customer satisfaction and resource utilization as twin and equal objectives without realizing that inherently there is a conflict between these objectives. The operations manager will then have the task of making the seemingly impossible possible. Operations managers need to be optimists and adept at employing structured thinking, as well as unstructured or lateral thinking, to problems to achieve the goals imposed on them. Various techniques and models to aid operational decision-making are given in subsequent chapters.

Business policy

The business policy sets for the organization:

- The objectives.
- The product/service to be provided.
- The market to be served.
- The way in which the service will be provided.
- Level of quality to be aimed for.
- The resources which will be employed.

The vision

Business policy does not happen by accident. It is a conscious attempt by organizations to provide long-term goals and to plan resources to achieve those goals. Business policy will start with the purpose of the organization – the very reason it exists. This is often referred to as the vision of the organization. As explained by Dulewicz, MacMillan and Herbert (1995):

> A vision depicts the aspirations of the company, a desired and attainable picture of how the company will appear in a few years' time, which can capture the imagination and motivate employees and others. The mission is to achieve the vision, expressing the commitment and will to do so. On the way, decisions will have to be made according to the values of the company, as indicated in the decision-making behaviour of the board – according to what the board believes is good or bad, right or wrong from the company's point of view.

Mission statement

The purpose of the business is often articulated in a mission statement. Frequently what the mission statement says may be at variance to the true mission of the organization. For example, I know of no organization with a mission statement that says 'Our aim is survival and to survive we will reduce our workforce by 25 per cent', or 'We will aggressively advertise our service levels, but we will not spend any money on training our staff'. Such organizations are more likely to publish missions that proclaim 'We value and respect the importance of our highly trained and dedicated staff', and 'Our aim is to provide outstanding world-class service'. It is important for the operations manager to understand what the true mission is, irrespective of what might be stated in the published mission. For instance, if survival is the mission, and this could well be a legitimate mission, this has to be understood and thus will shape the strategies to be employed.

Making the vision happen

The next stage in business policy is to determine what has to be done, and what can be done, to make the vision happen. If the vision cannot happen then it is no more than a dream. Determinants of whether the vision can happen, and of the consequent business policy decisions, are shown in Figure 3.1. The inter-relationships to policy are shown in Figure 3.2. Figure 3.1 provides a framework for analyzing the strengths and weaknesses of an organization and of opportunities and threats.

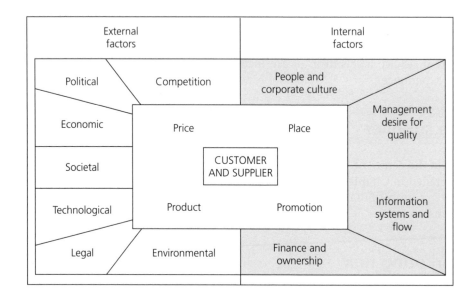

Figure 3.1

Determinants of business policy

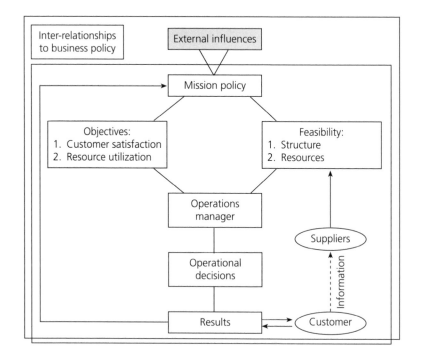

Figure 3.2

External influences

The customer

At the centre of Figure 3.1 is the customer. Without a customer the organization will cease to exist. But although the importance of satisfying the customer cannot be denied, it is important to appreciate that customer satisfaction is only one determinant of business policy. As Wild (2002: 11) points out 'many organizations have gone bankrupt despite having loyal and satisfied customers'. In short the level of customer satisfaction provided has to be affordable and sustainable. Most organizations can provide a high level of customer satisfaction for a short period, but the level offered has to be sustainable. In service industries customers will be very aware if service levels drop or are inconsistent with what they expect based on past experience.

The supplier

Also at the centre of Figure 3.1 is the supplier. With the supply chain philosophy, as detailed in Chapter 11, the supplier is as important as the customer. Without a reliable supply of materials and services the organization will not be able to satisfy the customer.

Marketing mix

Before an organization can attempt to satisfy the customer it must first be known what the customer wants. Generally the marketing function has to establish:

- what the customer wants in terms of the service being offered (product);
- the price customers will be prepared to pay;
- where the service should be provided (place).

To complete the 'marketing mix' the marketing function will have the responsibility of promoting (advertising) the service. The marketing mix influence on policy is shown in Figure 3.1 in traditional marketing terms of product, price, place and promotion. Unless operations can perform there is little point in promotion!

We accept that in marketing textbooks there are more than 4 'P's shown in the marketing mix (process, people, performance, profit, and perhaps pleasure and passion could be added. Pleasure in the sense of pleasing the customer by providing more than expected – surprising the customer – and passion in the sense of our people having a passion for excellence). However, our contention is that marketing does not determine people, process, profit, performance or pleasure and passion, whereas it has a very direct influence on product, price, place and promotion.

Product/service to be provided

Definition of the service to be provided is at several levels. The first and crucial level is the *specification*. Unless the product/service is what the customer wants then it will not be used. In Chapter 1, with reference to a commuter bus service we said if the bus is not going from 'A' to 'B' then we will not catch it. The service offered might include other 'nice to have' attributes, but unless the basic service is right, the extras, the 'nice to have' features, become irrelevant. In the case of a bus service, no matter how clean, how comfortable, and how polite the driver, unless the essential service is right (the bus stops somewhere close to our home and gets us somewhere close to where we work) we will not be interested in all these 'nice' extras.

The second important issue is *consistency*. Customers expect the service to be at the same level, or better, each time it is experienced. With the bus service we would expect the bus to follow the same route each day and to keep to the published timetable.

Timing is also an important issue; unless the service is available when the customer wants it the bus company will more than likely lose the customer. With the bus service, not only is it important that it is going from 'A' to 'B', but when is also important. If the bus does not get the potential customer to work on time, or if it does not connect with another service such as a train, then the service will not be used. Time will be of lesser importance in some circumstances and for some services. For example, we are conditioned to make appointments in advance for services such as consultancy services and often we are prepared to wait to get the person we consider will give us the best service (be it advice, the dentist, or the beauty salon).

Once the bus meets the basic requirements then all the other 'extras' such as cleanliness, comfort, plenty of seats, polite driver, waiting shelter, and perhaps even music interspersed with announcements from the driver, will add to the perception of quality and could provide the edge in a competitive environment.

Some specification issues are taken for granted by customers. Examples of this in the bus service are that the bus is roadworthy and the driver is licensed. Often, what the customer takes for granted will be crucial to the whole operation and will take a good deal of effort on behalf of the operations manager to achieve (such as keeping the fleet maintained and roadworthy).

Other 'requirements' of customers can be traced back to the marketing team 'selling' features that the customer had not previously considered important but which once 'sold' will come to be expected by the customer. Carlzon (1989) calls this the olive in the martini. In some service industries, for many customers, appearance and status will be every bit as important as the actual service received. Overall once a level of quality of service has been promoted or actually provided, customers will be quick to notice if it is not achieved or sustained. There is no point in setting a high standard of service if the operation cannot consistently meet the standard.

Price (profit)

Once the marketing team is satisfied that they know what the customer wants – the specification – then they will determine the price that can be charged. What can be charged depends, of course, on what the customer is prepared to pay. The issue for the operations manager will be 'Can the service be provided to the given specification (including all those fussy extras added by marketing) within the price set (marketing again) and still provide a profit?' Thus the operations manager in achieving a defined level of customer satisfaction will simultaneously be required to minimize the use of resources (cost) to an affordable level. It will be noted that price has a direct impact for the profit 'p'.

Where (place)

The location of the service is a marketing issue and the decision will be affected by where the customers are. Location issues are discussed in detail in Chapter 6. Location of services will have a great impact on operational decisions concerning supply and choice of suppliers, and distribution and logistic issues.

Promotion

Marketing will advise on promotional strategies, but the overall thrust and philosophy of the promotional drive is very much a business policy decision. The purpose of promotion being to increase demand, no promotion activity should ever take place without the full involvement of the operations manager.

Examples

1. Recently a major TV campaign announced a special offer in aluminium ladders. Being a keen do-it-yourself person (and the offer really was too good to miss), I hurried down next morning to the store only to be advised that the factory was behind schedule and the ladders would not be available for another month! I went to the competition and bought a ladder although the price was higher. Marketing had created a demand but lost a sale (I only needed one ladder and my needs had now been satisfied elsewhere).

2. A golf club advertised a free open day for prospective new members; the day chosen was a non-competition day when the course would be relatively free of club players. Noting that no play was scheduled for that day and unaware of the open day, the green-keepers had made an early start on coring and re-sowing the greens, and temporary rough greens were cut. The overall impression gained by the prospective new members was not good and the time and money spent on the promotion was to a large extent wasted.

Marketing mix and operational feasibility

It can be seen that the marketing team have a great influence on business policy. They determine who the customer is, what the product offered will be (specification, time, place and price) and they promote the product. The operations manager has to determine the overall feasibility; in other words, does the organization have the capacity to consistently provide the desired service and meet the expected demand and quality attributes within the price set, and return a profit? If not, what extra resources are required and what else could be done to make the impossible possible? In short: can the product/service, with all the desired features, actually be provided? A key resource is of course the people of the organization. The People issue is covered in Chapter 7.

Feasibility and structure

Although we can accept from the outset that with less than adequate resources and overly ambitious targets, the operations manager is expected to, and frequently does, make the impossible happen, nonetheless it is helpful to know what is feasible – *what is the capability of the operation?*

Feasibility is limited by the structure, as discussed in Chapter 1, and understanding the limitations of the existing structure is essential for the operations manager.

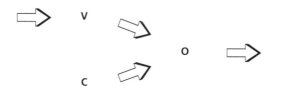

Figure 3.3

Customer satisfaction as the prime objective

Example

If the structure is as shown in Figure 3.3, then it can be deduced that customer satisfaction (timing) is the prime objective and the organization operates with some spare capacity or a 'buffer' stock of resources. This structure also indicates that if customers cannot be served as they arrive, the customer is likely to be lost to the system. The challenge for the operations manager, with this structure, will be to gauge the extent and timing of the demand and to have adequate resources on hand so as to meet the primary objective of customer satisfaction. The secondary objective will be to minimize the amount of time that capacity is not used, or to minimize the amount of buffer stock held. Thus the first concern will be to establish feasibility – that is, how much capacity is available and the limits at which the organization can operate. The operations manager will be required to satisfy expected customer demand by making the best use of capacity so as to prevent customer queues and lost business. 'Best use' means that although the structure includes surplus, or stored (buffer) stocks of resources (spare capacity), it is incumbent on the operations manager to minimize idle capacity.

Your turn!

At the end of Chapter 1 you were invited to consider the structure(s) that exist for your organization. Now analyze the structure(s) of your organization to determine challenges the operations manager faces as a result of the existing structure. Perhaps your structure implies that the primary objective is customer satisfaction, or is resource utilization the primary focus?

Feasibility and resources

As shown in Chapter 1, without input from the customer the function of providing service will not happen. Logically the operations manager plans ahead and has certain resources in place in anticipation of customer needs. In a service industry the major resource is likely to be people, and we need to know what their competences are, i.e. how skilled they are, their attitudes and dedication, and whether they are resourceful and capable of taking initiatives. Other resources include premises, information systems, time, plant and equipment, materials and vehicles. The location of premises, the reliability of the information system and other necessary equipment, the reliability of suppliers, and most importantly the quality of the people of the organization will determine the overall capability or competence of the organization. Establishing a quality of culture, how to motivate people and continuous improvement are covered in Chapters 7, 13 and 15.

Feasibility is one side of the equation. The other side of the equation is knowing what is required (demand), and anticipating what might be required. Demand issues and forecasting techniques are covered in Chapter 8.

To summarize: feasibility is the determination of how able or competent the organization is to achieve the business policy. Limitations of specific structures and what has to be done to change structures are discussed as we progress through the book and are further illustrated in the case studies.

Policy influencers

Figure 3.1 has an outer band which includes on the left-hand side the traditional PESTLE of strategic management (Political, Economy, Societal, Technology, Legal and Environmental issues) and to these we have added Competition. PESTLE and Competition are external to the operation and can be considered as a Threat or an Opportunity.

These factors are all external to the organization. They affect customer expectations and also limit what the organization is able to do.

On the right-hand side of the outer band are internal factors which can be Strengths or Weaknesses:

- People and corporate culture.
- Management's desire for quality.
- Information systems and information flow.
- Finance and ownership.

These are certainly influenced by external factors but they can be managed by actions of the organization. In a traditional SWOT analysis (strengths, weaknesses, opportunities and threats) the opportunities and threats are 'external' to the organization, and the strengths and weaknesses are 'internal' issues. Opportunities and threats are on the left side and strengths and weaknesses are shown on the right side of the model.

Knowing the organization's own strengths and weaknesses will help determine feasibility and will also indicate areas where corrective action should be taken. For the external factors, using the SWOT approach, the aim is to determine opportunities and threats, and to determine how the organization is, or might be, affected by these external factors.

Competition

In the determination of the service and the level of quality to be offered, at the very least the organization has to meet the service provided by the competition. Today the competition is worldwide. No matter that we believe we are providing a service to a local market, people today are well travelled and very well informed, and our customers judge us by their perceptions of world-class standards. For any organization, competition, although not yet present, might soon present a challenge. Technology and innovation is no protection: technology can soon be copied and new methods and systems are readily available to anyone. Often customers are influenced by what the immediate competition says it can do, or will do (which may not be quite the same as what actually happens). Nonetheless it is the perception of what the competition is offering that sets the market standards.

Knowing what the competition is offering is only possible if it is known who the competition is, and who the likely new (world-class) competition might be. For example, ten years ago insurance companies would not have appreciated that the banking profession would soon be their competitors for life insurance, and who would have expected that French companies could own or compete with British utilities? On the other side of the world many Australians still can't believe that one of their major breweries is owned by a New Zealand company, and New Zealanders in turn have recently been shocked to find that one of their major breweries is now owned by a Japanese company.

Economic

The economy, exchange rates, interest rates, population growth, house sales, building permits, the consumer price index, the average wage, unemployment and other statistics relevant to your service industry are all areas of vital information when considering business policy. The problem is to identify what is relevant to your industry, and to know where to find information.

Political, legal and societal factors

Laws and regulations might be seen as limitations, but laws and regulations also serve to protect an organization. Whatever the laws are, it is important that an organization is aware of how they will affect its operations. Laws could limit the number of hours drivers work, the amount of maternity leave people are entitled to, and so on. For our own home market we will have a reasonable idea as to what is legally possible, and what our legal responsibilities (for example, taxation, and health and safety issues) are. But when operating in other countries it is essential that the organization makes the effort to find out what legal restraints exist and what is socially acceptable before commitment is made to any action.

Generally, laws are for the benefit of the people as a whole, and are enacted as the result of pressure from the people to add a safeguard. Thus it is useful to be aware of popular issues and to make adjustments to operations so as to be seen to be a responsible organization (safeguarding the environment) within the pervading culture, rather than wait for legislators to take action as a result of public pressure. When a safeguard is made the subject of rules and regulations, it is likely to have more stringent conditions than when organizations or industries abide by their own self-imposed safeguards.

Technology

Customers will often be beguiled by technological promises as exaggerated in the popular press. On the other hand, an organization will be limited by the technology that it has at its disposal. Keeping up-to-date with technology for the sake of keeping up is expensive. Often it is best to be aware of changes, be aware of what the competition is doing, and try to delay decisions to change until the new technology is tried and proven (and cheaper).

Environmental

Many organizations are now aware that sustainability and minimizing pollution (green issues) can lead to improved performance. For example, the Japanese company Canon reports savings through recycling of materials, reduced costs through more efficient use of energy, and more efficient ways of packing and thus reduction in transportation/distribution costs. In 2002 Canon, under the leadership of Fujio Mitari was one of the few Japanese companies to improve profits.

Your turn!

What external economic or societal influences affect your organization and how do you keep abreast of what is happening?

People and corporate culture

Corporate culture is the amalgam of beliefs, norms and values of individuals making up an organization ('the way we do things around here'). For a business policy to be successful it has to be accepted by the members of the organization and it has to mirror their goals and aspirations. The Chief Executive might be the one who articulates the vision, but unless there is a cultural fit and the people of the organization buy into it, it won't happen. Culture and values are deep seated and may not always be obvious to members and to newcomers to the group. Chapter 7 is our People chapter. Culture and change of culture are discussed in greater detail in Chapters 13 and 15. Suffice to say that if the organization has a strong culture then each individual will instinctively know how things are done and what is expected. Conversely, if the culture is weak, then the individual may not react in the manner that management would hope.

Management's desire for quality

The level of quality offered is very much a business policy decision. It has been said that quality is free. Certainly doing things right the first time and every time should cost us nothing apart from training our people to know what is right and what corrective actions they can take. But if we refer back to our earlier example of a bus service we will see that higher-level service and quality will cost. With the bus the aim was to run a regular service, keeping to a defined route, and to a set timetable. In addition the driver had to be licensed and the vehicle maintained to a roadworthy level. We could add the perception of extra quality at little if any additional cost by simply getting things right first time, and every time. For example, if the bus kept to the timetable, the drivers took a pride in their appearance, were polite to customers, and the bus was kept clean, the perception of a quality service is enhanced at no appreciable extra cost to the organization. There might be a minor cost in providing uniforms, and in the cost of cleaning, and perhaps in training the driver in customer relations. If, however, we wished to increase the service by running a bus every ten minutes rather than one bus every half-hour, this would mean extra buses, more fuel, and extra drivers; thus to increase the service would now become very expensive. And yet this might be what the customers have asked for – a more frequent service. What determines our policy: the customer or economic considerations? No doubt we would consider how many extra passengers we would get and whether their extra fares would offset the extra costs. Then too, any change in policy would depend very much on whether we had competition on the route.

Quality, therefore, is an economic consideration. At one level it is cheaper to do things right, and to do them only once, and it is also helpful to have happy and eager staff who will give customers friendly, helpful service. This shouldn't add to our costs, but extra service above these levels will cost. Thus the level of quality we can afford and sustain is very much a business policy decision, and to a large extent it will be driven not by what the customer wants but by what the competition is doing or threatening to do.

Any quality initiative has to have strong and overt support from management. Our contention in Chapter 13 is that in an organization quality is everybody's business, but unless management provide the vision and the drive any quality initiative will fail.

Information systems and information flow

With the information technology available today there is no reason why every member of an organization cannot be kept up-to-date and understand what the policy of the organization is. Few of us do not have a personal computer on our desk with access to electronic mail systems. Two-way communication is now commonplace and many organizations go to great lengths with staff magazines, bulletin boards and so on to keep staff informed about company policy as well as social events.

The old method of management was for the bosses to do the thinking, set the goals and to give directions. The workers were not paid to think; their job was to obey orders. With such an approach there is little wonder that many people were reluctant to show initiative and thus few really had the interests of the organization at heart. This is often referred to as 'Taylorism',[1] and is as relevant to service industries as it is to manufacturing organizations. Today, most of us work where we do because we understand the policies of the organization, believe in the product or service we are offering, and we enjoy being involved even in a small way in helping to shape the policy.

Financial ownership

Most organizations are limited by money. The necessary funding comes from the owners and from profits (equity or shareholders' funds) and from borrowing. Unless owners are getting a reasonable return on their investment they are going to ask questions.

Owners, investors, the share market and bankers will judge the organization on the bottom line in the accounts. If you work for a government department, or are funded by the government or the public, the return will be seen in terms of value for money, and the persistent question will be 'Can we get better value for our money by using private enterprise (out-sourcing)?'

Financial strength, being profitable, or getting value for money is a major shaper of business policy. More than anything else lack of funds will determine policy.

Chapter summary

The business policy is long term, takes an organization-wide perspective and is concerned with the setting of goals and targets for the whole enterprise and the best use of the available resources. Business policy must take into account several factors as shown in Figures 3.1 and 3.2. The effective operations manager will maintain a keen interest in all facets of the organization and be aware of, and study, external trends and factors that could influence the organization. We do not condone politics in organizations but the operations manager, to be effective, must be politically aware to the extent that policy changes should not come as a surprise; and ideally the operations manager should be sufficiently well informed of external pressures to make policy suggestions. In Chapter 4 we discuss ways in which all the functions of an organization can work together for the common good of the organization and to achieve the overall corporate mission.

Key points

- Business policy is not made in isolation. There are external and internal factors which influence the shaping of policy.
- The marketing function is the interface with the market and has the responsibility of advising on product (specification), price, place (distribution), and for promoting the product. The market is influenced by the external factors of competition, technology, politics and the economy.
- In setting the business policy it is important to determine the capability of an organization so as to know what is feasible. Feasibility depends on structure and the availability and quality of resources. Internal factors are: culture, information, desire for quality and financial strength. Recognizing the

competences of the organization is an important consideration when determining the business policy. The operational structure of the organization is a key element in determining what can or cannot happen.

Note

1. The American F. W. Taylor was known as the father of scientific management at the turn of the twentieth century. His philosophy was that management, by scientific means, should find the best way of doing a job (method and equipment), train the workers in the best way, and offer incentives to increase productivity. Supervisors were employed to maintain the best method. Workers were not expected to make suggestions; their job was to do what they were told while management did the thinking.

Case Study *Hua Hin Golf Tours Ltd*

The Hua Hin Golf Tours Ltd case study is set in Thailand, and illustrates how policy decisions are driven by outside influences.

Question

Frank has gained a full licence for the company to operate as a holiday tour organization. Advise him on how best to make use of the licence and how your recommendations will affect the objectives and strategies of the future operation.

Setting the scene

The town of Hua Hin is on the south-eastern (Gulf of Siam) coast of Thailand. It is traditionally a fishing harbour – and still accommodates around 40 fishing boats. However, it has now become a small tourist centre – being famous as the place where the Thai royal family has often taken their holidays. The beach is sandy and provides safe swimming and snorkelling and other water sports. The town has a population of approximately 40 000. Hua Hin is a 3-hour road journey south of Bangkok. Cha-Am is a slightly smaller coastal fishing town about 20 minutes drive north of Hua Hin.

Golfing came to Thailand during the property boom of the 1980s. At that time, property developers bought agricultural land cheaply in the region and succeeded in putting together sufficient acreage to construct golf courses as well as sell off surrounding plots for residential development.

Now both Hua Hin – with 10 international standard hotels – and Cha-Am – with 5 hotels – are surrounded by around 12 golf courses which attract serious golfers from many parts of the world.

The company

The company, Hua Hin Golf Tours Ltd., was set up by Frank Gilbride, an English golf professional, who first came to Thailand in the 1980s in order to help design golf courses. Later he decided to create the company (now based in Hua Hin) to promote golf in the area and to provide a service for the many visitors. In addition to acting this way – as a specialist tour organizer – Hua Hin Golf Tours founded and organized the annual Thailand World Pro-Am contest.

Hua Hin Golf Tours are licensed by the Ministry of Tourism to conduct their present

▶

types of activity – promoters rather than operators. They describe their services as follows:

Hua Hin Golf Tours Ltd offers golfers and their family exclusive holidays. As well as offering exclusive hotel accommodation rates and green fees, the company provides transfers to and from the courses, tee reservations and a personal service which overcomes language barriers and cultural problems. Where to eat? What to eat? What to buy? Hua Hin Golf Tours will be pleased to help. The company also arranges golf tournaments which can be tailor-made to an organizer's wishes. Each tournament can be complemented by a series of cocktail parties and dinners which provide a unique and memorable experience.

The company is not licensed as a holiday tour operator and relies upon the sub-contract services of other local organizations to provide activities such as sightseeing visits to its golfing clients.

The company employs 15 people, has a fleet of 5 vehicles and has agents in Australia, South Africa and the UK. Their advertising is mostly by word-of-mouth, but increasingly a major portion of their enquiries come through their website, www.frangipani.com.

Hua Hin Golf Tours Ltd provide the following services:

- Transport service from Bangkok city hotels and airport to Hua Hin and Cha-Am – using mini-buses or hired coaches where appropriate.
- Meet and greet arrangements at Bangkok airport.
- Hotel reservation in Hua Hin and Cha-Am.
- Green fee reservations and booking for clients at any local golf course.
- Transport for clients from hotels to and from golf courses.
- Equipment sales and rentals.

- Group dinners, parties and presentation events.
- Tournaments and competitions.
- Local tours of attractions, literature and advice.
- Sightseeing tours for clients using local tour companies.

The season

The busy season for the company – as indeed for the area – is from November through to March, the dry season. Eighty-five per cent of the company's customers arrive during this popular season.

The management of the company

Frank and two partners run the company. They share the managerial responsibilities between them, but Frank is the Chief Executive. In the following interview, Frank identifies some of the problems he now faces.

When we first began, we got only golfers coming here. Few golfers came with non-playing partners. Over the years that situation has changed, partly because of the increased popularity of Thailand as a holiday destination. Now we get far more people – accompanying golf players – who do not play golf, and also golf players who do not necessarily want to play all the time. More of our time now goes into advising them about other things to do and other places to go, but of course we can ask other local organization to arrange these things for them.

Furthermore, being readily accessible by e-mail and via our website we are now being contacted by non-golf players looking for local hotel bookings, airport transfers etc. On some occasions recently we have been contacted by tour and holiday companies in the UK and South Africa asking if we would be their local agent, looking after their clients when they are here. This would take us into what is known in the trade as the 'Destination Management Business'.

   As things are going at present, we need to respond to these developments for, if we do not, our competitors will, or others may combine golf with traditional holiday packages. For this reason we have decided to apply for a holiday tour organization's license from the Ministry. We expect to get this in time for next November and we are beginning to ask ourselves now what impact this will have on our operations and what changes we will need to make.

Written by Ray Wild

4 Operations management and inter-relationships

Introduction

The concern of the operations manager is to provide the goods and services, defined by the business policy, as efficiently as possible. A principal operations objective, although sometimes subservient to customer satisfaction, is the efficient use of resources.

Internally, efficiency means making the best use of resources and the elimination of any activity that is not adding value. It is not possible for an organization to rely on operations alone to be efficient; operations is only one part of the whole organization. World-class organizations are totally efficient, and each department or function meshes with the others to support the drive to achieve the common mission.

Value-chain approach

The value-chain approach transcends the traditional manner of departmentalizing stages of the business process. The value chain highlights the importance of the operations manager being involved in all aspects of the process, from suppliers right through to the customer. The 'old' approach was that one department or function would be responsible for purchasing goods and services, another for planning. Scheduling of activities was often a separate function, as was warehousing and distribution, and operations were just one step in the whole process of providing services. With the value-chain approach functional boundaries are ignored and in many organizations it is now accepted that the operations manager has to control the whole process from buying in goods and services to the final stage of satisfying the customer. Marketing, accounting, human resources and other support functions do not show up on the value chain as such but, as discussed below, operations managers must be vitally interested and involved in these internal functions of the organization. The value chain, shown in Figure 4.1, is derived from Porter (1990) and from Basu and Wright (1998).

External efficiency

External efficiency is measured by customer satisfaction and by market share. To achieve customer satisfaction the organization requires, and is dependent on, the timely receipt of goods and services to specification by external suppliers. The efficiency of suppliers to the organization is of as much concern to the operations manager as is the ultimate satisfaction of the customer. In this chapter we consider the importance of communication and teamwork within the organization between the various functions, and externally with suppliers at one end of the value chain and customers at the other. As can be seen from Figure 4.1, the key to the whole process is information flow.

Suppliers

In some organizations suppliers are treated with distrust, and the business strategy adopted is to shop around and to get the best deal on each occasion. With this approach little loyalty is shown to any supplier, and the supplier is almost treated as an adversary. The value-chain approach is to treat the suppliers of those goods and services important to the smooth operation of the service system as part of the team. In some cases the supplier can become involved in the day-to-day operations of the organization and might be expected to advise and assist. Cost no longer becomes the key issue. Instead, suppliers will be judged on their loyalty and ability to deliver goods and services to the required standard and on time. Suppliers can also become part of the information-gathering arm of the organiza-

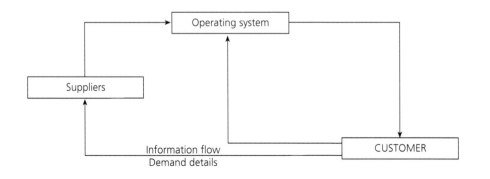

Figure 4.1

Flow of information for the value chain

tion; often suppliers have a different perspective as to what the competition are up to (changes in buying patterns, timetables, new packages, use of new materials and so on). Suppliers are also in a good position to offer technical advice regarding new technology and alternative materials.

The prudent operations manager, however, will always have a fall-back position. No matter how well-intentioned your supplier, it is foolish to be in a position where you are so reliant on one supplier that you are seriously embarrassed if the supplier is unable to perform for some reason (a fire or an unfriendly takeover).

Operations and other functions

Generally organizations are divided into functional departments; and even if the organization has re-engineered, and no matter how flat the structure, some people's tasks will be primarily marketing, others will be primarily concerned with accounting, others will be purely administration, human resource management and so on. We have already shown in our value-chain approach the importance of the operations manager having the responsibility for purchasing goods and services right through to delivery of service to the customer.

The customer and operations

As was shown in Chapter 3, Figure 3.1, the customer is the central focus for any organization, and the marketing department is responsible for knowing what the customer wants and what the competition is doing.

The total quality management (TQM) approach of the 1980s propounded the philosophy of delivering a quality service in excess of customer expectations. 'Surprise the customer' was the catch-phrase. As we have discussed in preceding chapters, what is provided has to be within an organization's capability, sustainable and affordable. Shareholders, fund providers and financiers will measure performance in terms of return on investment and value for money. On the other hand, customers are becoming more and more sophisticated and expect continuous improvements in quality of services, but always at no extra or even less cost. Another of the many conflicts faced by an operations manager is how to provide more for less!

Polarization of marketing and operations

Chapter 3 described the essential job of marketing as being the definition (specification) of the service. Attributes may range from the essential down to the desirable and perhaps include extras that the customer does not even want.[1] As well as defining the service to be offered, marketing has to establish the price, forecast demand and finally promote the service. Marketing also has to sell the product/service internally within the organization to the operations and other functions of the organization.

The responsibility of operations, using the value-chain approach, is to determine feasibility; do we have:

- the know-how;
- the skills;
- the specialized equipment;
- reliable sources of supplies and services?

Finally, taking into account existing priorities and workloads, can the product and/or service be provided for the customer to specification, within the time frame required and at the price set by marketing?

Thus arises the traditional polarization of marketing and operations. Marketing see themselves as the entrepreneurs, the go-getters, the trigger for making things happen. For them the bottle is always half full, whereas they believe that their colleagues in operations will see the same bottle as half empty! Operations see themselves as the realists, they are the ones who have to make things happen, and meet impossible demands with make-shift and insufficient resources. Marketing see the realistic, sometimes cautious approach of operations as negativity. They are apt to believe that operations are always looking for reasons why things can't happen instead of looking for ways that make things happen. Operations in their turn see marketing as going ahead with doing their own thing, making extravagant promises without bothering to determine the operational situation. They see marketing as having no appreciation of capacity or scheduling constraints and the time and effort required for the development and testing of new services.

Marketing is likely to ask questions such as 'Why are we always late?' or 'Why do we always keep customers waiting?'; 'Why do we always seem to have insufficient capacity?'; 'Why are our costs so high?', and then add that 'the xyz group (competitor) always out-performs us'. (Of course xyz has exactly the same problems but marketing listen avidly to what xyz are saying rather than noting what xyz are actually achieving.) In this scenario operations is on the back-foot and is likely to reply: 'Forecasting was not accurate'; 'Rush orders were taken'; 'We were not consulted'; 'Fancy extras, extra service, all cost time and money'. In other words 'It wasn't our fault'. The above examples, which at first might be seen as one department 'communicating' with another, are in fact no more useful than the pointless exchanges of two children along the lines 'You did so!' – 'No! I didn't', 'Yes you did' – 'Did not', 'Did' – 'Didn't'.

Bunker mentalities

Communication has to be two-way and has to be aimed to help rather than just to apportion blame or to criticize. With traditional hierarchical organizations a bunker mentality can develop whereby each function is walled off from the other, and any suggestion, no matter how helpful, is taken as a threat or a challenge. World-class organizations are noted by the manner in which the figurative fences that separated functions have been broken down, and by the teamwork that exists between all functions to achieve the common goal as determined by the business policy. This requires that everyone in the organization knows what the goals and objectives are and that the culture is conducive to the enthusiastic pursuit of the goals for the common good of the whole, rather than for the specific interests of one department. Information is open to all, and there are no secrets.

Benefits of being an open organization

With an open organization marketing will welcome any approach by operations to get closer to the customers. Operations managers will not be able to meet with all the customers, but a derivation of the Pareto principle[2] can be adopted whereby the operations manager asks to meet with the top ten customers, with a view to gaining first-hand information as to how operations can improve the service, and to gaining some appreciation of what the customer really values. This should not be seen by marketing as an attempt by operations to usurp 'their' authority but as a genuine effort by operations to serve the customer better. Most customers will be surprised and delighted to meet someone from the back room; they will find this far more meaningful then being asked to fill out a questionnaire that invariably doesn't give the customer the scope to say what they really want, or to express what really annoys them. Once the operations manager fully understands first-hand from the customer what is really needed – and often this can only happen through visiting the customer's place of business and by first-hand observation as to how the customer is operating – it is more than likely that changes can be made which will benefit the customer and at the same time be more economical to provide.

From time to time, usually due to pressure from the competition, it will be necessary to offer new products (in this context product and service are synonymous), or to upgrade existing products. Before any new product is finalized, operations should be invited to meet and to discuss with the main customers so as to understand what they really want. However, for some new products, customers will not know what they want. For example, it took many years before instant coffee became popular.

Life cycle of products

Products have definite life cycles (see Figure 4.2).

- *Development* of a new idea. This stage requires research, market testing, no income is received and costs (often substantial) are incurred.
- *Launch* of the new product. This stage can include heavy marketing costs and small initial returns.

Figure 4.2

Product life cycle

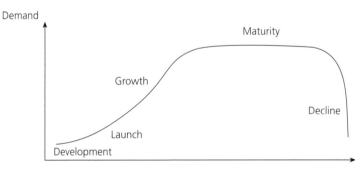

- *Growth* marked by rapid market acceptance and increasing profits.
- *Maturity*: income stabilizes as growth levels off.
- *Decline*: sales fall and eventually the product is phased out or updated and the cycle begins again.

For some industries, the maturity stage for the essential product can last for many years; however, products are always changing and businesses find themselves constantly in new areas of endeavour.

Example

Once accounting firms kept the books and filled in the tax returns, but today accountants specialize in all sorts of areas and offer additional consulting services such as recruitment (head hunting), benchmarking, business brokering, and so on. Still other service providers have entered the 'boutique' market where they deal only in specialized niche areas, such as a law firm that only handles property title searches.

Different stages – different actions

Each stage of the life cycle will require different actions and decisions. The development stage will require operations to be involved in determining feasibility, acquiring necessary resources, training people and establishing a standard procedure. The introduction or launch stage will need the ability of operations to service fast-growing demand, and to be able to handle novel and unexpected problems. Procedures might have to be modified and people retrained to act in a standard fashion. With the growth phase, operations are likely to be challenged by fluctuating and uncertain demands. By the time the maturity stage is reached, standard procedures should be in place, people will know instinctively how to react when problems arise; in short stability should have been achieved. This is the stage when there should be time to look for improvements to the service and to improve efficiency. Unfortunately, when the pressure is off, sales are good and objectives are being comfortably achieved, the temptation will be to not look for changes (complacency sets in). Nonetheless there will always be room for improvements and ideally the culture of the organization will be to seek to make incremental improvements. The decline stage will bring another set of problems, either changes of a decisive nature will have to be made to the product to arrest the decline, or an entirely new product will have to be developed.

New initiatives

Changes to the product might include 'repackaging' – this would mean essentially the same product but promoted in a different manner and to a different target market.

Outdoor adventure tours (white water rafting, etc.), once for young backpackers, might now be tuned down (safer water) and repackaged as 'grey power adventure experiences' for the older market.

Other initiatives might mean the same basic service but with extra benefits, a reduced price, or at a different time. Whenever changes are being contemplated, the operations manager needs to be in a position to make suggestions and to be involved in the final decision.

In the public service, with the move to privatization of public sector management since the late 1980s, health services and utilities, such as water and sewage, power generation and distribution, now find that they are operating in a totally different way and are surprising themselves with what they can offer commercially.

Water Boards, now privatized in the UK, have moved to establish and promote consultancy services for their customers and for new customers, and are finding themselves competing against organizations that once they would not have thought of as being in the same market.

Development process

The design process for a new product, or for the development of a variation to an existing product, has six distinct phases. They are:

- Concept – determination of a need.
- Systematic and rapid screening of various alternatives.
- Research, including market analysis and cost analysis.
- Development of the product.
- Testing the offerings developed.
- Launching on a commercial scale.

Speed is important

In today's fast-moving market, operations have to be able to react quickly to marketplace changes. Speed is important in gaining the initiative over the competition with a new product, or in catching up and reacting to a new service or product offered by a competitor. Customers are fickle and once lost are hard to regain.

Innovation and product development

There are several strategies available to the development of new services:

- Some organizations will position themselves as market leaders; this can be a high-risk strategy as time and money will be required to develop and set up the infrastructure needed. On the other hand, being first in the market can reap large benefits.
- Others will seek to imitate the innovations of other organizations and will attempt to join in the initial growth phase of a new product.
- Others will join in with adaptations before the market becomes saturated with suppliers or will endeavour to find a specialized niche market.
- Others will add nothing new except to rely on size and efficiency to enter the market at lower prices.

Whichever strategy is adopted, certain conditions have to be met:

1. Close links between operations, marketing, research and suppliers are essential.
2. Lead time, from concept to market, has to be minimized.

Overall it is essential to be continually monitoring the product life cycle and to be aware of what the competition are doing.

Simultaneous development

Simultaneous development uses multi-functional project teams to design and develop the new product, and relies on strong two-way communication. In manufacturing, a prototype can be developed or tested. Because service industries are reliant on customers as input for the service to happen, the design of the new service will mainly involve the process by which it will be delivered. It is difficult in service industries to produce a prototype 'product', although a new service can be tested in a small localized market. As customers must be involved, a flow process chart will be a useful tool for development and comparison of alternatives. The flow process chart will show, in detail, all the processes through which the customer will pass. In many services the customer will never come in contact with the back-office activities, such as exist for a post office, an insurance office or a restaurant. However, such activities are essential to the provision of the service and it is crucial that these areas, and the suppliers to the system, are not ignored in the consideration of the feasibility of providing the new service. Therefore the flow process chart will need to cover the value chain from supplier to customer, and should consider the time taken for each activity. The technique of flow process charting, with examples, is given in Chapter 6.

Sequential versus simultaneous product development

Figure 4.3 illustrates a sequential approach to product development for a manufactured product. The figure shows one-way communication, and that each

Figure 4.3

Sequential product
development

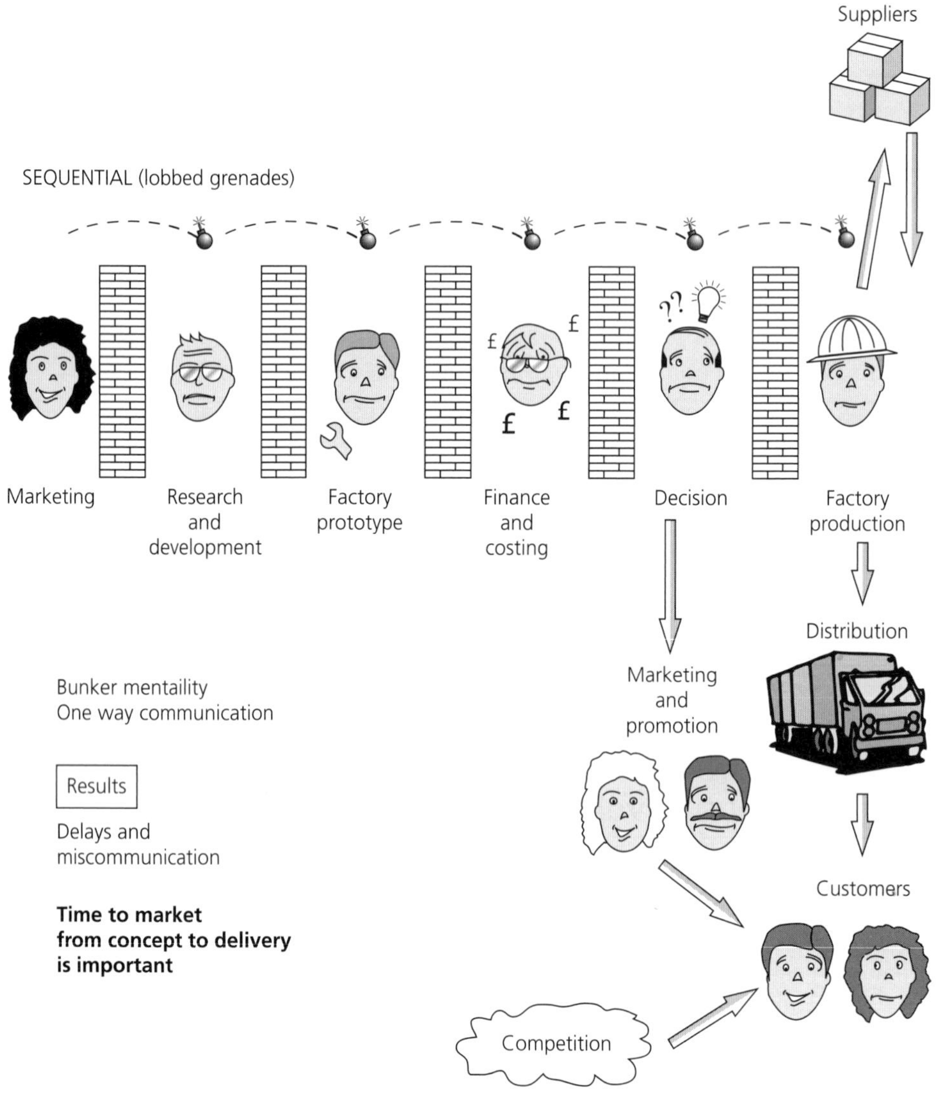

SEQUENTIAL (lobbed grenades)

Suppliers

Marketing   Research   Factory   Finance   Decision   Factory
             and   prototype   and   production
             development   costing

Bunker mentaility
One way communication

Results

Delays and
miscommunication

**Time to market
from concept to delivery
is important**

Marketing
and
promotion

Distribution

Customers

Competition

department is separated by a 'brick wall'. Communication is here shown as a series
of lobbed grenades. The result is miscommunication and mistrust and unnecessary delays. In today's market the time taken from concept to launch of a new
product can be crucial in gaining market share.

Figure 4.4 shows the advantage to be gained by a cross-functional project team
approach in developing a new product; the same approach applies when developing a new service. It will be noted that in Figure 4.4 suppliers and customers are
shown as part of the project team. Simultaneous development will enable each
department, including key suppliers, to understand and explain each other's competencies. Overall the time taken for development will be considerably reduced.
What is more customers will get substantially what they want.

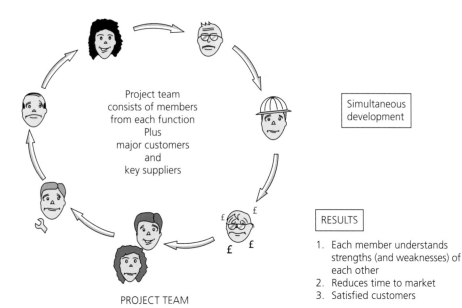

Figure 4.4

Simultaneous development

Project team
consists of members
from each function
Plus
major customers
and
key suppliers

Simultaneous
development

RESULTS

1. Each member understands
   strengths (and weaknesses) of
   each other
2. Reduces time to market
3. Satisfied customers

PROJECT TEAM

Your turn!

What advantages might be gained by including the key suppliers in the design team for a new product or service? Does your organization involve customers when developing a new product, or an upgrade to an existing product?

Finance and accounting issues

Many new businesses have a very short life span (over 70 per cent of small businesses fail within five years of beginning operations), and every month there are reports of medium and large businesses in financial difficulties. Like it or not, the continued success of any organization relies on financial stability. Often operations managers see the accountants as soulless people devoid of imagination, interested only in short-term returns on assets. However, unless there is a positive cash flow and a strong balance sheet, long-term business plans for the future are meaningless. It is vital that any organization has a reliable accounting system in place to provide fast and accurate information.

The minimum requirement is a budget and reliable feedback of actual results for comparison to the budget, in time for corrective action to be taken where required. In Chapter 14 we discuss key financial figures, and how the operations manager can make best use of financial information. Rather than the accountants pressing operations for returns and figures, it should be remembered that the accountants are a support function, and it should be the operations manager who is pressing the accountants to provide essential information! Budgetary control is discussed in Chapter 5.

Chapter summary

In this chapter we considered the direct inter-relationships of an operations manager with internal functions and with the external elements (suppliers and customers as part of the extended team) of the value chain. The need for understanding where a product is on its life cycle was discussed and the importance of speed in developing new products was stressed. It was concluded that accountants are not the enemy, but rather provide an important support service to the overall operation. It was recommended that operations should be pressing accountants to provide more information.

Notes

1. Why are some brands of golf balls wrapped in tissue paper? The paper is a nuisance when you are out on the course and decide to use a new ball (your last one having just disappeared into the river), and serves no useful purpose; after all, a golf ball is not fragile, indeed it is designed to be hit with some force by a lump of steel. The answer is that at some stage a marketing person decided that individually wrapped golf balls added to the prestige of the product. Another example is the way new shirts are presented. Why do they have so many pins stuck in them, and does the customer really want the pins? Both these examples illustrate the adding of cost, rather than value, to a product.

2. Wilfredo Pareto was a nineteenth-century Italian economist who concluded that 80 per cent of the wealth was held by 20 per cent of the population. The same phenomenon has often been found in businesses, where for example 80 per cent of the sales come from 20 per cent of the customers, or 20 per cent of the stock held accounts for 80 per cent of the inventory value. In other areas 80 per cent of road accidents occur in localized areas (20 per cent of the roads have 80 per cent of the total accidents). Lorenz, early in the twentieth century, produced a graph for demonstrating the cumulative dominance of the 20 per cent. Juran (1988) refers to the 80/20 phenomenon as the 'vital few and trivial many'.

The case study that adds value to this chapter is Burton Fashions.

Case Study *Burton Fashions or what the butler heard*

Question

Analyze what went wrong and why. Suggest a better method of operating.

Burton is sitting in the club house deep in conversation with long time friend and confidant Jenny Sonata. Jenny is a management consultant, Burton is the principal of Burton Fashions. Jeeves the butler notices that Burton seems to be doing all the talking. Let us join Jeeves as he listens in . . .

Our marketing team, against stiff opposition, gained from the Excess chain a *very large order for fashion sports wear. To get the sale they had to reduce our normal price. Because my marketing manager had not fully understood our production capabilities the factory was always going to have some difficulties in making exactly what the marketing team specified. However, we overcame these problems, although it meant some new gear had to be installed. Later we found out, purely by chance, that the extras that marketing had added, such as zip up pockets, were not seen as being important by Excess. But what gave us real problems were the* delivery dates: we realized right from the start that we had little chance of delivering the full order on time.

Because of the fine margin, in placing our order for raw materials, I decided that price would be a key factor in choosing a supplier. However we were careful to specify the standard, quantity and delivery dates. Materials were ordered to be delivered well in advance of when we needed them (that is our standard practice). In any case we were not certain how reliable Acme, our new supplier would be.

In our order quantity, based on past experience, we also built in a factor for wastage during manufacture. When the materials arrived from Acme, somewhat late but not drastically so, we checked them for quantity and quality. We found that we had been short supplied, and a large proportion was below our specified quality; also, on further checking, some material was found to be totally the wrong colour! We reluctantly kept and used the below standard material. Of course we had to return the wrong coloured materials and we requested urgent replacement. At the same time we also pointed out that we had been short supplied.

Acme was slow to reply, and they were very vague as to what they could do to remedy the situation.

So in desperation I went to our usual supplier, Zachary and Co. Naturally Zachary was not sympathetic (did I tell you they had missed out on our initial order because their price was slightly higher than Acme's?). Actually Sam Zachary was rather churlish with me and refused to give the discount we normally expect. However, Zachary and Co. did deliver within a few days and the material was up to standard and the right colour, although far more expensive than I would have liked.

Unfortunately, much to our surprise, the same day that the Zachary's stuff arrived,

Acme made good their shortfall. We now had more material than we really needed, and neither supplier was prepared to accept a return of goods. The factory, as per our normal allowance, wasted 10 per cent, and at the end of the run our quality inspector rejected 10 per cent of the finished goods as she considered the stitching was not up to standard. However, as we had fallen behind our delivery date and the customer was threatening to cancel the order, I overruled her and we delivered what we could including the below standard product.

Fifteen per cent of what we despatched was subsequently returned as being below standard, but by the time this happened we had been able to make and store sufficient replacements from our 'surplus' materials. We were therefore able to make good the order, although we were now several weeks behind the original delivery date. The customer, Excess, took 50 days to pay although our agreed terms were 30 days. Naturally, Acme and Zachary invoiced us promptly. However, there are errors on both sets of invoices (wrong prices, wrong quantities, no credit for returns, and wrong discount calculations). I have tried holding off paying, but will be obliged to pay most of the amount owing as we require further materials for a new order from Sunshine Fashions. Sam Zachary said that there was no way that he will deliver until we pay our outstanding accounts and that if his accounts department has made a mistake they will send us a credit note next month.

Our first calculation shows that on the Excess deal we broke even. But if we calculate the interest charge on the materials, and the time it took for us to be paid, and the overhead costs of ordering, checking and paying, plus all the problems associated with each stage of these activities, then our large order has cost us money. The unknown cost is the loss of our

▶

reputation with Excess who will probably be reluctant to buy from us again, and the loss of goodwill with both Acme and Zachary who now see us as difficult people to deal with.

Jenny I need you, I need to know how we can work better in future to prevent another disaster.

Hear Hear! said Jeeves sotto voce as he exited stage left.

Written by J. Nevan Wright 2003

5 Planning, implementing and controlling

Objectives

In this chapter we examine:

- The need to provide an operating surplus – the financial imperative.

- The need for long-range planning.

- The planning process.

- Implementation of plans.

- Control systems, including budgetary control.

- The importance of an effective information technology system.

Introduction

In Chapter 3 we considered external influences on business policy and in Chapter 4 we considered the importance of open communication between the various functions of an organization and externally with suppliers and customers. We used our derivative of the value chain to show the total process. In this chapter we begin by noting the financial imperative, and then consider the three stages of operations. These stages are planning, implementation and controlling. We also consider the benefits of information technology and the necessary steps to consider in introducing an effective information technology system.

The financial imperative

As stated in Chapter 1 the operations manager is the person who is responsible for using the resources of the organization as efficiently as possible to make goals and objectives happen. Central to the goals and objectives will be the need to make a profit, for without a profit a business will not survive. Apart from mere survival there will also be a need to satisfy fund providers (owners, shareholders, financiers) that their investment is secure and that they are receiving, or will receive, a satisfactory return on their investment. If an organization is a non-profit institution (such as government-funded) the central objective will be to show fund providers that they are getting value for money. The requirement to satisfy fund providers (value for money invested) can be considered as the financial imperative. In accountants' parlance this is known as 'the bottom line'.

Customer satisfaction

At the end of the value chain, as shown in Chapter 4 (Figure 4.1) is the customer and, as demonstrated in our study of structures in Chapter 1, without a customer no service industry is able to carry out its function. Thus to satisfy the financial imperative (value for money invested) a necessary requirement will be to satisfy the customer, for without customers there will be no income. To achieve these two complementary objectives – the financial imperative and the satisfaction of the customer – the operations manager is limited by the structure of the organization, the policies of the organization and the resources available (including the reliability of external suppliers).

Planning and control cycle

The overall planning and control cycle is depicted in Figure 5.1. It will be seen that the cycle is continuous and includes subsidiary cycles. It is recommended that you refer to Figure 5.1 as you progress through this chapter.

The need for long-range planning

Planning takes place at several levels and can cover several different time frames. Thus an organization might have a ten-year plan, a five-year plan and will

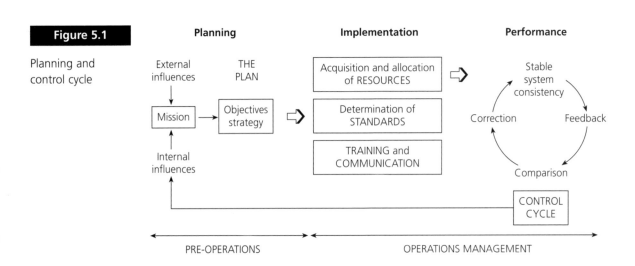

Figure 5.1

Planning and control cycle

certainly have a twelve-month plan (e.g. 'the budget'). There will be a corporate-wide plan, business unit plans, department plans, and at the operations level the operations manager will have medium, short-term and daily plans.

Here we are concerned with the *corporate plan*. The corporate plan establishes the objectives of the organization which, as we said in Chapter 3, is made after consideration of external environmental factors balanced against the internal competences of the organization (see Figure 3.1). The overall thrust of the corporate plan is often articulated in a mission statement. The corporate or business plan, however, requires more than just the few well-chosen words of a mission statement. Generally the plan will need to be supported by sales figures which will include past trends, broken down into product group and market segments, and forecasts of future demand. The plan is also likely to include capital equipment budgets, cash flow forecasts, profit-and-loss forecasts, human resource and training requirements, property requirements and so on, and a budget will be produced every twelve months at least. Then, some time after the end of a twelve-month accounting period (often months after balance date), an annual report with financial statements showing actual results will become available. The success of the plan and budgets could be compared and judged against these actual results, but seldom are.[1]

For the operations manager, annual reports are likely to be of historical interest only (unless there is a bonus payable which is tied to past results). Operations managers naturally will be more concerned with meeting immediate and short-term future demands rather than looking back to what happened last year; likewise with higher-level long-term planning which will often take on an unreal dimension as far as the operations manager is concerned. The cynic would say that each year much time and effort will go into the business plan, and each year before the plan is issued it will be out of date, and due to the dynamic nature of business there is a measure of truth in this. However, unless an organization has a long-range plan it will not be possible to develop appropriate capabilities as conditions change. Changes (or additions) to location, computer systems, recruitment and training of people, etc. cannot happen overnight. But once such decisions have been taken, and carried out, they cannot be undone in a hurry.

The operations manager, pressed with 'real', day-to-day operational problems, could be tempted to avoid involvement in what might be seen as esoteric long-term planning. If the operations manager is only marginally involved in long-term planning, business policies with important long-term operational ramifications will be made by strategic planners, accountants and marketing directors, and ratified by the board. Generally these people will not fully appreciate the time and effort needed to develop a distinctive operational competence. Indeed, they might consider that the real work has been done in gathering the information and in making the plan, and that implementing the plan is by comparison a straightforward matter. Rather than trying to avoid involvement in long-term planning, the astute operations manager will press for inclusion in the planning process. Only by involvement in the long-range planning process can the operations manager hope to influence future operations.

The planning process

Establish goals and objectives

The first step in the planning process is to define the organization's goals and objectives, and to set priorities. This step will be built on the vision (the reason for being of the operation) and is likely to be presented as a mission statement.

Competence of organization

The second step is to determine competences in relationship to the organization's market. As discussed in Chapter 3 this is done by reviewing external influences under the headings of political, economic, technology and competition, and by carrying out a SWOT analysis. Opportunities and threats are external to the business, and strengths and weakness are internal aspects. Examples of strengths might be financial stability and a particular operational competence; a weakness might be lack of skilled staff. An opportunity might be an emerging new market, and a threat will surely be new and emerging competition.

It is not sufficient merely to list strengths, weaknesses, opportunities and threats. The real purpose is to determine what actions have to be taken to capitalize on the strengths, eliminate weaknesses, counter threats and exploit opportunities. Often a threat, if considered in a positive manner, can be turned into an opportunity.

Example

Consider a new ambulance service. The objective as articulated in the mission statement might read:

To provide a quick response, first aid and transport service for the sick and injured in the Hillvale District.

The necessary strategies would include:

- purchase of a reliable vehicle and necessary first aid equipment;
- recruitment of trained staff;
- premises in a central location of Hillvale township;
- 24-hour on-call service/staffing;
- communication links with police and local

hospital, and other ambulance services in nearby districts;

- maintenance of vehicle and equipment;
- ongoing training of staff.

Note the simplicity of the mission statement: no grand statements such as to be the best, to provide excellent service, or that people are our greatest resource, and so on.

Note also the brevity of the strategies, and how each is limited to supporting the mission. It could be said that ideally strategy is specific in the abstract, but not specific on detail. By not attempting to provide the specific details, plenty of scope is left for operational contingencies within the broad framework of the general strategy.

Strategy

The third step is to develop strategies to enable the business objectives to happen. In simple terms objectives/goals are what we want to do, and strategies are how we will do it, i.e. the necessary actions required to make the objectives happen.

In Figure 5.1 mission, objectives and strategy are shown as pre-operations planning.

Implementation of plans

Action plans

Once the strategy is finalized then action plans can be made. In our ambulance example one action plan would be to locate suitable premises central to the area of operations (Hillvale District) large enough to house a vehicle and with room for offices, sleeping quarters and a communication centre. Once specific details are built into a plan it will be found that one strategic step will overlap with another. For example, before we can determine the amount of space required we first have to determine how many people have to be accommodated, and so on.

The ambulance example is a start-up scenario, but in day-to-day operations the resources, premises, people and equipment will already exist.

Implementation of the plan is an operational function. Operational plans will be based on forecasts of demand and the plan will consider systems, processes and resources to meet that demand. Invariably there will be several operational plans, at different stages of fulfilment, running at any one time.

For new projects, such as the development of a new service as discussed in Chapter 4, in order to cut across functional boundaries and to streamline the process, a project team approach will be desirable.

For other projects, such as a move to new operational premises, then the operations manager will act as a co-ordinator and might take a project approach to the problem without actually setting up a team as such.

Network and/or critical path analysis is one technique commonly used by project managers to monitor the timely progress of projects. Chapter 9 includes a section on how to manage using a network analysis approach.

Performance control/control systems

Planning, it is said, creates standards of action, and controlling keeps the plans and actions in line.

The traditional approach to management is to control subordinates by supervision and measurement of performance to make sure that what is being done is what was intended. However, because the supervisory method of control relies on feedback of results, control tends to be in the past tense rather than in the present. That is, the manager checks after the event to see what has been done against what was intended. In this method of control the manager cannot control without a plan consisting of goals and targets. The more detailed the plan, the more control can be achieved.

The alternative method of control is to empower the worker, or a team of workers, so that control is exercised directly by the subordinates. The management responsibility in this model is to provide the workers with resources and support. Control, when exercised by the worker, can under certain circumstances be concurrent with carrying out the operation rather than retrospective.

It would seem logical that the earlier a variance to a standard is detected and corrected, the less cost will be incurred in subsequently correcting deviations.

Control elements

For any activity, no matter who exercises control, whether control is top-down (the manager's aim is to control the activities of subordinates) or a culture where control is exercised directly by the workers, the same four control elements apply. These elements are:

1. setting standards of performance;
2. feedback of actual performance;
3. measuring performance against the standards;
4. correcting deviation from the standards.

This is shown on the right-hand side of Figure 5.1, and is expanded upon in Figure 5.2.

Stable system

An appropriate stable system exists when standards are known and are consistently being met. The difficulty is in setting the standards and then ensuring that deviations do not occur.

1. Setting standards of performance

Standards are usually expressed in terms of specification, time, quantity and cost, and include 'quality' elements. They can be imposed from above, or set by the

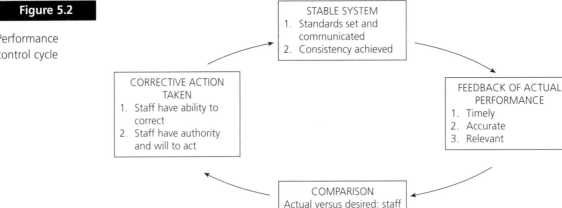

Figure 5.2

Performance control cycle

STABLE SYSTEM
1. Standards set and communicated
2. Consistency achieved

FEEDBACK OF ACTUAL PERFORMANCE
1. Timely
2. Accurate
3. Relevant

COMPARISON
Actual versus desired: staff know what to compare

CORRECTIVE ACTION TAKEN
1. Staff have ability to correct
2. Staff have authority and will to act

workers themselves, either as individuals or as a team. If the workers are setting the standard, they have to know the overall limits (goals such as minimum outputs and quality levels). It is hoped that when the culture is right 'empowered' workers will voluntarily aim to exceed the minimum levels.

In a service industry it is often considered difficult to set quantifiable standards. How, for example, do you measure 'courteous service'? (Nevertheless, if customers perceive that there is a lack of courtesy then corrective action must be taken.) In other areas of service, standards can be set quite readily. For example, how long do customers wait before being served? Did the customer get what was ordered? Was the service effective? and so on. Measurements that matter are covered in Chapter 13.

The only true way of knowing if a standard is being achieved is by 'hard' measurement criteria. Hard criteria are measurements such as quantity, size, number of failures, wrong deliveries, time taken to attend to a customer, down to the length of time taken to reply to a letter or an e-mail. Such measurements are quantifiable, are easily understood and cannot be disputed. However, even when the hard criteria are met it is often the soft or intangible criteria that influence a customer to come back (or not), or encourage a customer to recommend your service to others. Word of mouth in service industries can be very telling for or against a service provider!

Aesthetics is an example of a soft criterion. Depending on the service provided, aesthetics can include the atmosphere of the office or showroom (cleanliness, fresh air, well-groomed people, situation in an appropriate part of town and so on), and of course will include the attitude of the people (are the people friendly and is the advice given helpful?), is there empathy, is the smile genuine and do the people really mean what they are saying? If the service offered is a product or the installation of a product, then other intangibles will become important such as evenness of colour, texture, finish, rough edges, flush fittings, etc. If the service includes a food product then smell, colour, taste, temperature of food when served and clean utensils all become important. When the culture of the organization is right and all the staff genuinely believe in the value of what they are doing, then a genuine enthusiasm and a desire to help will overcome the adverse effect of a late delivery, or some other shortcoming. No manner of control imposed from above can substitute for people who want to get things right and who want to help the customer, provided that they are empowered to do so.

2. Feedback of actual performance

The operating control system shown in Figure 5.2 includes a means of feedback of actual performance. Feedback needs to be reasonably precise, recognizable and

Your turn!

Standards of performance

1. List hard measurements for your department.

2. Consider what soft measurements might be important to the 'customers' of your department.

3. Can service from your department be improved without extra cost?

timely. For example, budgetary control is virtually useless if actual results are achieved three months after the event. The importance of key measures cannot be emphasized enough. What should be measured is what really matters. Too often the desire for total accuracy and the detail of information provided takes too long to prepare and is so detailed as to be of little use to the recipient. Effective control requires a few key measurements that are sufficiently accurate to enable corrective action to be taken.

3. Comparison: actual to standard

As shown in Figure 5.2, the crucial issue at this stage of the control cycle is knowing what the feedback means and knowing how to compare results so as to be able to recognize deviations. This might seem obvious, but in reality how many people truly understand financial reports and know exactly what they should be looking for – or more importantly, why? In other areas, how many of us really understand what the computer is telling us when we get an error message, or for that matter what the red light means on the dashboard of the car? It is up to the operations manager to determine what information is required and to train staff in what to look for, and then what action they should take. Appropriate action might mean merely asking for help; staff who try to do too much when not sure can lead to interesting results. A willing and enthusiastic amateur can do irreparable damage!

4. Correcting deviations from standard

Once steps 1, 2 and 3 of the control cycle are in place, then whether in an office, a retail shop, a restaurant, a hospital, or a factory, the output of the system can continually be compared with the plan or standard, and where necessary, corrections made to eliminate divergences. Ideally the level at which this is done is as low as possible. If a corrective action has to be reported up through five levels of management and down again before action can be taken, time is lost and often errors can be compounded; and if a customer is waiting for a decision to be made, customer satisfaction will diminish at a rapid rate. If a member of staff is facing a customer, that staff member needs to know the limits within which decisions can be made. The ability and knowledge of the staff member has to be taken into account when limits of authority are given. Some staff will welcome flexibility of action whereas others are afraid to make decisions.

Not everyone is comfortable with being empowered, and this also will need to be taken into account when limits of authority are being set. Members of the organization have to have mutual trust and confidence in each other. Management needs to be confident that staff are well trained and competent and that every person understands the goals. Staff have to be confident that they are empowered to take action and will be supported by management in difficult situations.

Budgetary control

Budgetary control is one example of a control system. With budgetary control the standard is the budget. Feedback of actual results after the event is provided by weekly or monthly reports. Often the report will show the actual, the budget, and the variance between budget and actual. Deviations from the budget will be investigated. Part of the investigation will be to determine if the report is correct – has there been a misposting? – and to correct the entry. If the deviation is not a result of a misposting then the question is: why has the deviation occurred? With budgetary control, the corrective action will be either passive or reactive; seldom will it be proactive. An example of passive action would be the correction of a misposting of an expense to a wrong account. As far as the end result (the bottom line) is concerned this might not make any difference if it merely transfers an expense from one category to another. Other actions are likely to be reactive.

Example

If an expense category is above budget, the reactive corrective action could be to issue an edict that no more overtime will be worked without the direct permission of a senior manager. Rarely is action proactive. A proactive decision would be to note that sales are below budget, and rather than reducing expenses (reactive) to actually increase the advertising expense in an effort to attract more sales in the future. Generally with budgetary control the thrust will be to control expenses.

Accuracy and timeliness are important. It is not much use learning three months after the event that expenses are above budget, when there are only four months of the year left. The result will usually be panic measures to reduce expenses and much writing of reports justifying why expenses are above budget. With budgetary control the danger is that managers will be judged on their ability to meet budget, and their expertise in shifting expenses from one category to another. All this frenetic action is counterproductive, does not add value but does add to overhead costs.

Changes to standards

Where it is found that deviation from the required standard is consistently above or below the set level of performance, then the original conditions must be checked. If the level being achieved is above the set standard it could be that conditions have changed, such as new suppliers, improved technology, an improved process, or the workers themselves have found better ways to provide the service. Once the cause of the improved performance has been checked, and it is found to be legitimate and not a dangerous short cut, then it should be incorporated into the standard. If the level of performance has however fallen below the standard then it is important that action is taken to determine why this should be and what needs to be done to restore the system to stability.

Information technology

From the above we can see that control is exercised by comparison of actual results with intended results and with corrective actions taken when deviations occur. We have also noted that effective control relies on timely, accurate and relevant feedback of information.

A properly designed and integrated information system will provide prompt and accurate feedback of results and highlight deviations from plans. A further major advantage of a well designed system is that it will facilitate communication and the sharing of information between functional departments of an organization. In this section we consider the necessary actions to be taken, and areas that should be considered when installing a worthwhile information technology system.

Information technology (IT) is rapidly changing and becoming cheaper, more user-friendly and more powerful. Today, for most of us the personal computer on our desk has more computing power than most top organizations had ten years ago. International information networks (e-mail, Internet, high-speed data and video links, video conferencing and so on) have simplified global communication and operations. Electronic Data Interchange (EDI) technology has made possible extended supply chains between organizations and their suppliers. For example, cash register transactions will not only update accounting information, stock records and marketing statistics, but may also trigger automatic reordering from a supplier without the need to print and post an order to the supplier.

Problems

The rapid growth of information technology has not been without problems for the users. Most senior managers of organizations lack any detailed understanding of the complexity of information technology. They either don't want to know or try to believe that knowledge of the technology is not important. This attitude is fostered by computer salespeople who are adept at selling the idea of 'user-friendly' systems (i.e. 'You don't have to be an automotive engineer to drive a car, so why do you have to be a systems specialist to use a computer?'). After being told for over a decade about the amazing things that apparently low-cost computer technology can do, we can be pardoned for feeling let down when a systems specialist says 'It will take three years to develop and to install'. We will be even more upset when the installation project bogs down and there are overruns in cost and time budgets.

Another problem is that not all computers can easily communicate with each other, and in some cases not at all. Incompatible information systems usually result from looking at bits and pieces of systems to solve an immediate problem. For example, one distance-learning polytechnic in Australasia standardized on Apple Mac word processors for their production department (some twenty word-processing staff) and then provided the tutors and writers with incompatible PCs. Another Australasian organization, with 32 wholesale stores, found that when the head office mainframe was updated (by the installation of an expensive 'new generation' machine) the printers in the branches were no longer compatible, and thus 100 new printers (not allowed for in the budget) had to be purchased.

Need for planning

Properly planned information technology provides tremendous benefits, but an unplanned piecemeal approach costs time and money, and is demoralizing. Technology is brilliant when it works, but at least frustrating and at worst disastrous when it fails. For example, the $60 million accounting system for a major bank in America had to be scrapped because it could not keep accurate accounts.

We are all aware that computer technology is constantly changing and genuinely becoming more user-friendly and that versions of specific software and systems technology will continue to change. Therefore it is vital that any organization formulates a software strategy by careful planning.

The first step is to identify the areas of application. The software policy should be to include standard 'off-the-shelf' packages for the organization in specific areas of application. In the selection of software, consideration should be given to:

- user requirements;
- reputation of the supplier;
- availability of software support.

The earlier examples of application software were relatively inflexible and the approach was for the user to conform to the system rather than to customize the system to fit the user. Many disillusioned users attempted to build their own software, which usually proved to be expensive and resulted in cumbersome systems. Today off-the-shelf software should be adequate for most organizations. We all believe that our organization is different and has different requirements from any other organization, but in essence, in areas that really matter, the differences are minor rather than radical. Bitter experience shows it is not prudent to let an enthusiastic IT manager attempt to develop or customize software. My earlier statement about the dangers of enthusiastic amateurs certainly applies in the area of information technology!

IT support

The supplier of hardware and software should be reputable and it is important that support should be available locally and on call. Every organization should also have its own IT support staff who are primarily responsible for:

- first-level users' 'Help' desk service;
- user training;
- back-up and maintenance of the system;
- disaster recovery planning,

but not for developing new software and new systems.

IT systems: senior management support and project team

As for any company-wide programme, the implementation of a new IT system must have top management commitment. This should be reflected in setting up a project team comprising members from users (operations, marketing, sales, accounts, warehouse, human resources and, where appropriate, suppliers) and from the systems providers of hardware and software. Logically the project manager should be chosen from the main user group. For example, if the application software is for supply-chain management then the project manager should ideally be selected from the operations function.

The project team should receive both basic technical training and operational training (functionality of the software). The project manager will then prepare a clearly stated action plan with target dates, and resources for key activities. The project will also have a budget. The plan must include review points, and senior management should be kept informed of progress in writing on a regular basis (maybe weekly but certainly not less than monthly).

Opportunity to increase operational effectiveness

It is essential that the existing procedures and processes are thoroughly and systematically reviewed before an IT system is changed. Various tools for analyzing the flow and requirements of existing systems are included in Chapter 6.

The introduction of an IT system is an ideal opportunity to eliminate non-value-adding reports and activities and to break down barriers between departments. If this opportunity is not taken the new technology will only serve to speed up data collection, which in itself will not mean that information will be disseminated. It is important that all departments work together to achieve a common goal if the benefits of an investment in information technology are to be realized, otherwise the 'investment' could end up as an expensive addition to overheads with little benefit to operations.

User training

After the training of the project team the training programmes should be extended to all potential users of the system. The training features should contain both cultural education to establish acceptance by everyone concerned, and operational training to understand the functionality and operations of the new system.

Dry run

The next stage is the data input and 'dry run' of the new system in parallel with the existing system before the new system goes live. There are benefits in forming a users' group for exchanging experience with users drawn from both within and outside the company.

System maintenance

We have not discussed uninterrupted power supply, disaster recovery, the need to back-up files, system security (log in, fire walls, etc.) and so on. All these issues are nuts and bolts and should be second nature to your IT manager. This section was not written for the professional IT manager, but to give the average manager an understanding of the strategy of IT implementation. However, don't be afraid to ask the systems manager if there is a disaster recovery plan!

Chapter summary

In this chapter we discussed the planning and control cycle. We began with the mission (the reason for being for an organization), and we showed how the business plan is formulated to convert the mission into reality. Plans identify objectives, and strategy determines the steps that are needed to make the objectives happen. The operations manager is the person responsible for making the plan happen and for establishing a stable system that gives a consistent and reliable service in line with the standards set by the plan. The operations manager will control the situation by ensuring that staff at all levels:

- know what the standards are;
- get accurate and timely feedback of results;
- are capable of comparing results to standards;
- are empowered to take corrective action.

The lower the level of decision-making for corrective action, the quicker will be the response. An organizational culture that inspires staff at all levels requires mutual goodwill and trust by management and workers. However, not everyone wants to be empowered; some people prefer to be told what to do and not to take responsibility.

Communication and prompt and accurate feedback of information are essential if control is to be exercised. An information technology system that has been properly designed and installed is essential for any organization. The pitfalls of not properly planning an information system are legion. In this chapter we have detailed areas that should be considered when planning a new information technology system.

Note

1. Sharemarket analysts generally make investment recommendations after consideration of published results, the 'strength' of the balance sheet and the use of 'common size' benchmarks in the form of ratios (gearing, return on equity, stock-turn and so on). Share prices are generally not calculated on how well the business performed against budget (usually the past budget will not be shown in the published result); rather, share prices change daily on the basis of interim announcements, rumours, speculation and sentiment. Calculations such as Profit/Earning Ratios and Dividend Covered, etc. as shown on financial pages of newspapers are by necessity based on the last published annual or interim accounts, which are by nature historical and often many months out of date.

Case Study *Paua Bay (New Zealand)*

Questions

You have been hired as a consultant to analyze the situation for Hinemoa and John. In particular:

1. Comment on past shortfalls in planning and operational control.
2. Identify key system areas for control and suggest relevant measurements.
3. Show diagrammatically the principal control loops that will be used for the control of flows through the systems you have identified.

November 2001

John has just been made redundant from the Acme Bank. He and his partner Hinemoa are having a few days holiday at Paua Bay, a well-known holiday area some 100 kms from Auckland. They are staying at Kapai, a low budget accommodation complex which is located close to the beach and 500 metres from the famous Paua Bay hot springs, but a good 12 kms from the town centre of Pauapaua. Kapai consists of:

- 20 cabins each sleeping up to three people. For each set of five cabins there is one shared kitchen, and a block of showers and toilets.

- A main two storey 'lodge'. Upstairs there are 25 double bedrooms each of which has its own facilities (stove, small refrigerator and a bathroom with shower and toilet).

  Downstairs there is a large 'games' room with one table tennis table and one small pool table and plenty of room to add extra tables. The games room is seldom used. Adjoining the games room is a comfortable bar complete with a large screen TV which seems to be permanently set to the sports channel. The bar is well patronized by locals, visitors to the hot springs and

people staying at Kapai. Although there is a large kitchen, complete with modern equipment, no food is made or served on the premises. The owner of Kapai Enterprises Ltd, Erik Hermsdorf, lives in a smallish house at the rear of the main building. A map showing the location of Kapai is at Appendix A (p. 89).

While staying at Kapai John and Hinemoa have become friendly with Erik. They find he is keen to sell Kapai Enterprises Ltd and to return to Holland (Mrs Hermsdorf has recently died after a long illness and Erik is feeling lonely for his extended family in Holland. He adds that there is too much work for one person in running Kapai).

John and Hinemoa ask to see the accounts for the last two years. These are shown at Appendix B (pp. 90–1). Being an 'ex'-banker, although with no formal qualifications, John feels able to analyze the accounts. He convinces Hinemoa that the accounts are showing an excellent return on the capital invested. John and Hinemoa do their sums and decide that if they sell their apartment in Auckland, with the redundancy cheque plus the proceeds of a small legacy from Hinemoa's aunt they could meet Erik's asking price of $450 000. Hinemoa feels a bit mean, she wonders if they are not taking advantage of Erik's situation. John points out that Erik has set the price, not them, and that really they are doing him a favour. Secretly John can't believe the bargain they are getting.

Hinemoa thinks that probably due to his wife's illness Erik has let the place run down, in her opinion it needs sprucing up. She can also see potential for opening a coffee bar or a restaurant – after all there is plenty of room. John also suggests that a small convenience store is needed. They both realize that to make any improvements at all they will need to borrow from the bank. At John's exit interview his manager had made a promise to 'see John right' if he needed any financial help.

June 2004

'I can't believe it', says John to Hinemoa in the privacy of their house. He is looking at the annual accounts just back from the auditors. These accounts (for the last two years) are shown at Appendix C (pp. 92–3). 'Two years hard labour and we are more in debt than ever'.

'Hard labour – you make it sound like a prison sentence', replies Hinemoa.

'Well it's the same as a prison sentence, two real estate agents have now told us we won't get more than $350 000, and it owes us at least $600 000. Let's face it, we can't afford to leave', grumbles John.

'Correct. So what can we do now to turn the place around?'

During the time that John and Hinemoa have owned Kapai (from 1 January 2002) they have learnt the following:

1. The business is seasonal. From December to the end of February they are booked out. At Easter there is about 90 per cent occupancy, and at various other times, such as long weekends and school holidays, occupancy is about 75 per cent, but for the rest of the year there are few guests. Most guests are repeat family groups rather than backpackers as such, although Kapai is listed in tourist information centres as a backpackers resort.

2. When they applied for a loan of $100 000 to convert the games room to a dining room and to add a convenience store, the bank only valued the whole complex at $350 000. This was mainly because the land is leased and only has twenty years to run with no automatic right of renewal. Erik had 'forgotten' to mention this to them when they had negotiated the purchase of Kapai! At first they weren't too worried as they thought this was just the

bank being ultra conservative and anyway as Hinemoa said 'twenty years is a long time'.

3. Although Hinemoa did go ahead and open the restaurant, (Erik had assured her that this would be a goldmine), few guests used it as they preferred to do their own cooking. However, some locals were beginning to appreciate her excellent cooking. The restaurant was now only open Saturdays and Sundays, and was catering for locals rather than holiday-makers.

   It was still however going to be a long time before the restaurant repaid the amount spent on tables, chairs, crockery and cutlery purchased by Hinemoa.

4. On the other hand, the small convenience store started by John has been a marked success. (On hot summer days he frequently runs out of ice cream.)

5. The bar is popular, and is making a profit, but John believes the profits should be higher. John wonders if the bar staff (Bill and Mavis – a husband and wife team) are helping themselves. Whenever John does a stock take he can never make the figures tally. John has to admit that Bill and Mavis are very popular with the patrons.

6. Hinemoa is popular with guests and 'her' staff. Hinemoa looks after house-keeping staff, the restaurant and the accommodation desk (bookings, reception and checking out). Hinemoa's staff are all capable of doing several basic jobs. For example, the housemaids as well as 'making up' the bedrooms double as waitresses. Julie the head waitress has also indicated that she would like to learn how the accommodation side works. Julie has also recently enrolled in a tourism course with The Open Polytechnic. Perhaps Hinemoa's only weakness is that she is too 'soft'. Her staff know that if they arrive at work late Hinemoa is willing to believe any excuse that they give. Nonetheless, generally jobs get done, although

▶

pre-booked guests often have to wait until their rooms are 'made up'. Most guests accept the relaxed atmosphere and there have only been a few complaints.

Hinemoa's team consists of three full-timers and four part-timers who all work well together. None of Hinemoa's staff have job descriptions or formal contracts.

John looks after maintenance, gardening, the bar and the convenience store. He is also the 'purchasing' manager for the bar, the store and the kitchen. John also pays the wages, files tax returns and does the 'paper' work. He uses a manual cash book system and records cash when received (bankings are done daily); payments are recorded when they are made. The cash book is the basis for preparing the annual accounts. Stocks for the bar and for the store are recorded manually. Unfortunately, due to all the other work pressures, John often gets behind in keeping records, thus stock is frequently sold before it is 'entered' into the system. Often profits look quite good until a belated invoice for goods (such as a crate of wine) arrives a month after the sales have been made. No one else knows how to do the

paperwork but John. Hinemoa has no idea of how to complete the monthly tax return or how to make up the wages, and John has always been too busy to show her. Julie, the head waitress, has a Diploma in Business which she gained at the Auckland University of Technology. As a result of this study she believes she has an understanding of how an integrated computor system could help with the accounts, wages and stock records. John believes she has a point but has been too busy to explore the situation further.

John has problems with staff, he does not cope well under pressure. The bar staff (husband and wife team – Bill and Mavis), have threatened to walk out more than once. John has then had to grovel to get them to stay. Other staff often become confused when John gives instructions. For example, recently the maintenance man repainted the tennis court, when all John wanted was the seats by the tennis court repainted. When things go wrong John is quick to blame everyone else. He believes that he is a good delegator, but that people simply don't listen. None of John's staff have formal employment contracts.

Appendix A Location of Kapai

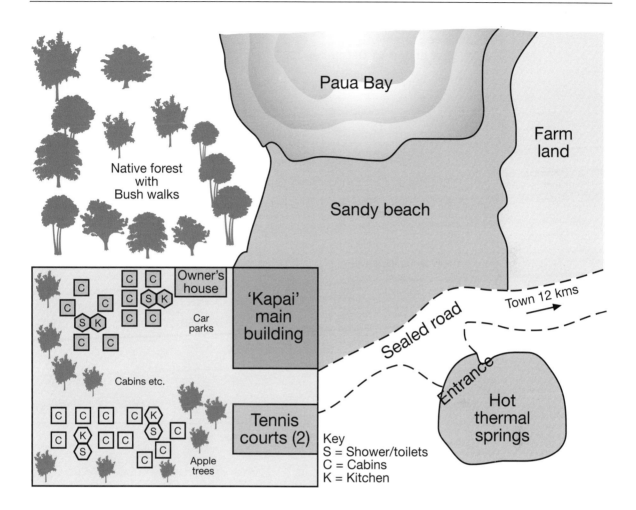

▶

Appendix Bi

KAPAI ENTERPRISES (1996) LIMITED
Performance Statement
For the year ended 31 December 2001

$'000

Revenue	*2000*	*2001*
Bar trading		
Sales	101	110
Less cost of stock sold	41	44
Bar wages	40	42
Profit from bar	20	24
Revenue from accommodation	90	93
Total income	110	117
Less Expenses	63	71
Interest	2	1
Profit before tax	45	45
Taxation	15	15
Profit after tax	**30**	**30**

Note to accounts:

Two shareholders as at 31 December 2000 – E. Hermsdorf and J. Hermsdorf.
Not audited (unanimously agreed by shareholders).
Depreciation at taxation rates.
Company is exempt as per the Companies Act 1993 and Financial Reporting Act 1993.

Appendix Bii

KAPAI ENTERPRISES LIMITED
Position Statement
As at 31 December 2001

		$'000		
Revenue	2000		2001	
Capital 250 000 $1 shares (fully paid)	250		250	
Revaluation reserve	150		150	
Retained earnings	100		100	
Profit current year	30		30	
Dividend	(30)		(30)	
		500		500
Current assets				
Bank	1		1	
Debtors	3		2	
Tax refund due	5		4	
Stock bar	23		18	
Stock line/cleaning materials	5		6	
		37		31
Less current liabilities				
Creditors	20		15	
Prepaid deposits	2	22	4	19
Working capital	15		12	12
Fixed assets (net of depreciation)				
Property: buildings and improvement	290		287	
Machinery	50		45	
Furniture & equipment	65		61	
Goodwill	100		100	493
Liability				
Mortgage	20		5	(5)
	500		500	500

▶

▶

Appendix Ci

KAPAI ENTERPRISES (2002) LIMITED
Performance Statement
For the year ended 31 December 2003

	$'000	
Revenue	*2002*	*2003*
Bar sales	120	135
Cost of stock sold	72	85
Bar wages	50	55
Loss on bar operations	(2)	(5)
Store sales	85	115
Cost of stock sold	42	55
Wages	18	20
Profit on store operations	25	40
Restaurant sales	36	40
Cost of materials	12	12
Wages	20	22
Profit restaurant operations	4	6
Accommodation revenue	105	115
Total revenue	132	156
Expenses	80	89
Interest	15	17
Profit before tax	37	50
Taxation	12	16
Profit after tax	**25**	**34**

Appendix Cii

KAPAI ENTERPRISES (2002) LIMITED
Position Statement
As at 31 December 2003

	$'000			
Revenue	2002		2003	
Capital 450 000 $1 shares (fully paid)	450		450	
Profit prior period carried forward	–		25	
Profit for year	25		34	
Equity		475		509
Current Assets				
Cash	1		1	
Debtors	2		2	
Stock: Bar	30		35	
Store	10		15	
Restaurant	1		1	
Accommodation	5		2	
Goods and Service Tax	1		(2)	
		50		54
Current Liabilities				
Overdraft	5		10	
Creditors	30		45	
Current portion term loan	10		10	
Taxation	4	49	6	71
Working capital		1		(17)
Fixed Assets				
Property, buildings and improvements	350		385	
Furniture and equipment	110		135	
Machinery	50		46	
Goodwill	50		50	
Term loan	(86)	474	(90)	526
		475		509

Written by J. Nevan Wright 2003

III Part Three

Parts One and Two have tended to take a broad-brush or macro approach to management of service operations. In Part Three a micro approach is adopted and specific operational problems are considered. Issues discussed are location of operations, layout of premises, workplace layout, method study and ergonomics in **Chapter 6**. In **Chapter 7**, job enrichment, empowerment of workers and other motivational factors are considered.

- This Part begins (in **Chapter 6**) with location and then moves on to layout. It is maintained that it is generally necessary to understand the flow of work and the work relationships of people, before the layout of the premises is finalized. This is important when new premises are being contemplated, but these considerations are equally important when considering existing premises, as a changed layout can markedly improve efficiency. Chapter 6 also shows how the structured approach of method study will improve efficiency, including layout of premises, work flow and design of workplaces.
- From the worker's perspective, convenient and comfortable workplace location and layout, coupled with work flow and work methods designed to reduce unnecessary or complicated work are likely to have motivational aspects. Thus it is considered logical to include in this Part a chapter (**Chapter 7**) covering job enrichment and empowerment of workers.

6 Facilities and work

Objectives

In this chapter we consider:

- Location problems and decisions in relationship to customer service and to efficiency of operations.

- Layout of premises to gain the best use of space and efficient work flows.

- Layout of individual workplaces.

- Safety, health and ergonomics.

- Method study to improve the efficiency of staff.

Introduction

As discussed in Part Two, the operations function and day-to-day operational issues (problems and decisions) exist within the broader framework of the total organization and its external environment. It has been shown that business policy determines the services offered and the level (quality) of service that will be provided. It has also been seen that business policy will limit the resources available to operations and, to a large extent, establish the operating structure. We have seen that operations objectives include customer satisfaction and at the same time efficient use of resources. These, often conflicting, objectives have to be balanced by the operations manager within constraints of price, quality and overall feasibility as limited in the short- to medium-term by existing resources. The challenge for operations managers therefore is to make the best use of existing resources. A major resource, and a major constraint, will be the premises from which the business of the organization is carried out. In the long term new premises can be acquired but, in the short term, operations have to make do with what already exists.

Location of premises

The location problem applies to two basic situations, i.e. new premises and existing premises.

There are several factors to be considered when deciding on location:

1. Any business policy that requires speed of service to customers, or ease of access by customers, will lead to a choice of location near where the customers are. Example: the location of a corner shop.

2. Any policy that stresses efficient use of resources will lead to the question 'Can we make do with less?' Example: with the increasing popularity of automatic teller machines, telephone banking and the introduction of Internet banking, banks are tending to reduce the number of branches and opting for smaller premises.

3. Any business policy which takes the value-chain approach, wherein the suppliers are dedicated and regarded as an extension of the whole organization, might well take into consideration proximity to suppliers as a criterion when determining location. Example: an advertising agency and a print shop.

For an existing location, operations managers will be accustomed to handling input and output relationships, and will have views on what can be achieved with the existing location. The operations manager will therefore wish to be closely involved in any business policy decision concerning a new location. Operational concerns will be either material related (access to suppliers) or market related (proximity and ease of access for customers).

Location – new operations

Wild (2002: 111) says 'The choice of location is vital for any new business; indeed there are numerous examples of new businesses which have had brief and troubled lives solely because of their disadvantageous location.' Poor location decisions are expensive and have long-lasting effects. A wrong initial location decision will lead to further expense and disruption if a subsequent move to a new location has to be made. If it is decided to stay with the existing unsuitable location, ongoing costs will continue and frustration is likely to escalate. Often the ongoing effects of a poor location decision are hidden as the costs will be in the form of lost opportunities.

Opportunity costs of a wrong location, such as lost sales and extra operating expense, cannot be separately accounted for (often they will not be known) and thus they are not shown in annual financial reports. This lack of exposure for scrutiny and comment generally means that perhaps only the operations manager will be truly aware of the extra effort required, the extra costs of transport, the cost of double handling and so on due to poor location. However, the marketing department may also have some ideas on lost opportunities (sales) due to a poor location.

Location decisions – new and existing operations

Basic location questions are:

- Why?
- Where?
- How much space (demand issue)?
- Lease or buy?
- Cost/benefits?
- Evaluation of alternatives.
- And 'Why?' again!

Why?

A new operation will require premises For a new operation the reason for acquiring premises is self-evident; premises and facilities will be needed to achieve the objectives of the organization. The decision to acquire premises will therefore be part of the overall consideration of the resources needed by the new organization.

Existing operation – why move? When it is suggested that an existing operation should move to new premises, the obvious question would seem to be 'Why move?' The answer, however, is not always obvious. Perhaps the question should be rephrased to ask 'How will the move to new premises improve the business operation, or improve customer service?' If a satisfactory answer can't be given, then why move?

Prestige versus operational efficiency Many decisions to move to new premises (such as to build a new head office) are made for prestige purposes rather than to improve the efficiency of the operation or to give a better service to the customer. If the reason given for a planned move is nebulous (it cannot clearly be demonstrated that the move to new premises will improve operations or add to customer satisfaction) but the decision to move is still made, then the operations manager must clearly state what is required to safeguard existing levels of operating effectiveness.

To meet increased demand If the reason for new premises for an existing business is to satisfy an increase in demand then the question must be 'Is it possible to expand the existing premises, (rather than relocate)?' It might even be found to be possible to rearrange the layout of the existing premises so as to make better use of what already exists. On the other hand, if a move is really necessary, then piecemeal additions or *ad hoc* solutions can result in facilities that will always be inefficient. Money thrown at an inadequate facility will be money wasted.

Long-term demand? Many organizations, with enthusiasm fuelled by rapid initial growth or in periods of national economic growth, have committed themselves to costly new premises only to find that growth has not continued at the same initial meteoric rate. It has to be recognized that the economy is cyclical, and when there is an economic downturn expensive premises are hard to unload. Before committing to expensive premises it must be reasonably certain that the increase in demand is ongoing and not short term (i.e. based on a fashionable trend in the marketplace – yesterday's must-haves are tomorrow's junk).

Where?

Having determined that new premises are genuinely needed and demand will continue, then the next question is: 'Where?'

Service and transport industries have different criteria from each other. Service industries will generally evaluate location alternatives in terms of accessibility by customers (distance to be travelled by customers), and transportation (delivery system) industries will consider accessibility to customers (time to reach customers). In both cases, customer numbers and market density will be important, and in the case of supply services proximity of suppliers might also be important.

If the focus is on maximizing revenue the considerations will be market density and volume of business.

If the focus is on cost minimization, the considerations will be cheap premises, cheap labour, cheap energy, etc.

Manufacturing industries have a totally different set of criteria such as access to transport, deep sea ports, suppliers, cost of energy, reliable energy supplies, cheap/skilled labour supply, government and legal requirements, tax incentives, waste disposal and so on.

Your turn!

What are the criteria that you would use in determining the optimum location for your department?

Fixed or delivered operations

Service industries can operate as a 'fixed' operation. With a fixed operation the customer comes to the location for the service. With a 'delivered' operation the service is taken to the customer. This applies to supply, service and transport industries. For example, a pizza shop might operate both ways: some customers come to the shop for service, and some customers phone in and the pizza is delivered to their homes.

For fixed operations high visibility is necessary and accessibility to customers is essential. This can include adequate car parking, or a situation in a busy part of a town for foot traffic. Distance from customers and market density is obviously important in deciding on the location.

For delivered operations accessibility to the market, i.e. time taken to reach the customer, becomes important. Thus rather than being in the centre of town (if that is where the market is) the operation can be on the outskirts of town, which is likely to be cheaper in property costs, provided there is ready access into town to serve the customers. An example would be an insurance consultant/financial adviser working from a home office and visiting clients at their place of business.

How much space?

The amount of space is dependent on two issues, the first being demand and potential growth, and the second being how efficiently space is used. It is a truism that the more space is available, the more wasteful of space we will be, i.e. space requirements expand to use up the space available. It is also true that in a growing organization there never seems to be enough space. It could be argued that an organization can never have too much space, but on the other hand space costs money, and too much space, distance to travel between departments etc. will add to time taken/wasted in getting a job done. Use of space and space requirements is further covered in the sections on layout and method study.

Lease or buy?

Once land has been purchased and buildings erected, large amounts of money will have been spent. If subsequently it transpires that the location or the buildings themselves are not suitable, it is often found that a substantial loss will be made if a decision is made to sell. Accountants have a term 'borrowing short, lending long'. Large capital expenditure in land and buildings equates to large amounts of funds (own or borrowed funds) tied up in real estate (lending long), which reduces the amount of funds available for working capital for the business. Reduced working capital results in the business being forced to raise a series of short-term loans. If short-term borrowing cannot be serviced out of cash flow, or short-term loans cannot be repaid on the due date, then although the business has large amounts of fixed assets on the balance sheet, it will face insolvency. Generally in a forced sale situation buildings will not realize their balance sheet value.

In the late 1980s, after a period of rapid growth in property values, and following the stock market debacle of October 1987, there were sudden and dramatic falls in property values and many organizations found themselves with 'negative equity'[1] for their property holdings. It is no wonder that even now, many years on, some organizations prefer to lease properties rather than to purchase. Leasing of property has two advantages: first it does not tie up working capital, and second if a poor decision has been made, leases are not for ever. Even with a long-term lease it is usually possible to negotiate out of the lease or to sub-let.

Although leasing is less final than building or buying, nonetheless the location decision must be made just as carefully. If it later transpires that a leased property is in the wrong location, the disruption (internally to the smooth running of the operation, and externally to the customer), and the effort and money expended in finding new premises and moving, could have been avoided if the correct decision had been made initially.

Cost/benefits?

Break-even analysis can be a useful tool to determine location. Break-even analysis is a technique that shows the amount of sales revenue required in a given situation to cover the costs of the operation. For break-even purposes costs are divided into fixed costs, i.e. those costs which don't change no matter how many sales are made, and variable costs which are those costs which increase or decrease in proportion to sales activity.

Example

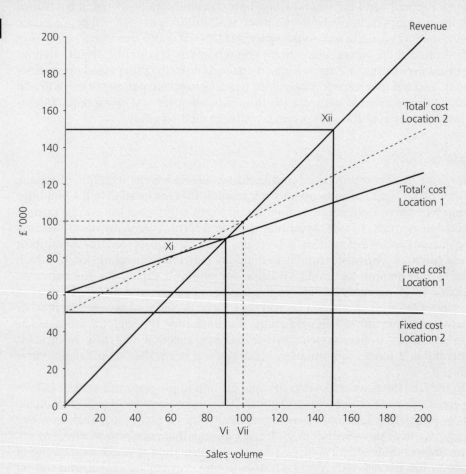

Figure 6.1

A location break-
even chart

Figure 6.1 shows a break-even chart which compares two possible retail locations. Location 1 is the centre of the town with a high pedestrian count and with a corresponding high cost for premises. Location 2 is one block away from the centre where premises are cheaper, but the pedestrian count is much lower. This particular business relies to some extent on attracting people off the street.

Explanation of Figure 6.1

Fixed costs do not change no matter how much is sold. In this example, fixed costs for both locations consist of any combination of:

mortgage interest, interest forgone on money invested in the purchase of property, rent or lease of property, local government taxes/rates, insurance, any other property costs.

Variable costs for both locations include all costs which are directly attributable to making a sale. In this example variable costs would include purchase cost of goods sold, packing costs, advertising and delivery costs. As sales increase so will variable costs.

Other costs not included in our break-even calculations are any costs that are the same irrespective of location. Such costs would include wages, electricity, etc.

In our example, Location 1 has the more

expensive fixed costs, but less variable costs (less advertising and delivery costs). Location 2 is in a cheaper part of town, but with a lighter market density. By comparison more advertising will be necessary and more delivery costs will be required per sale made.

Sales price per unit will remain the same irrespective of the location, therefore only one revenue line is shown.

Vi (Location 1) and Vii (Location 2) show respective break-even points (where revenue equals respective total costs).

Xi shows the point where, with the same amount of sales, both locations make the same level of loss, i.e. at £60 000 of sales, Location 1 will give a loss of £20 000, likewise Location 2 with £60 000 of sales will also have a loss of £20 000. From this point on, the profit gap, that is the gap between the revenue line and 'total'

costs, increases at a greater rate for Location 1 than it does for Location 2.

Clearly in this example Location 1 is the better choice: break-even is reached with fewer sales. A further factor, not shown in the break-even analysis, is that with the higher pedestrian count at Location 1 the potential for sales is greater than for Location 2, thus the shop at Location 1 is more likely to reach the £150 000 sales sooner than will Location 2.

Break-even can also be demonstrated in the form of a simple profit and loss statement as shown in Table 6.1.

In Figure 6.1, Xii shows the difference in profit for Location 1 and Location 2 when a certain level of sales revenue has been reached. This can also be demonstrated with profit and loss statements as shown in Table 6.2.

Table 6.1		Location 1	Location 2
Profit and loss statement (a)	Sales	90 000	100 000
	Variable cost	30 000 33.3%	50 000 50%
	Gross profit	60 000 66.6%	50 000 50%
	Fixed costs	60 000	50 000
	Profit	Nil	Nil

Table 6.2		Location 1	Location 2
Profit and loss statement (b)	Sales	150 000	150 000
	Variable cost	50 000 33.3%	75 000 50%
	Gross profit	100 000 66.6%	75 000 50%
	Fixed costs	60 000	50 000
	Profit	40 000	25 000

Evaluation of alternatives

Checklists   Given a choice of locations, perhaps the easiest method of evaluation is by a checklist of relevant requirements. In the checklist shown in Table 6.3 a point rating system has been incorporated. The importance of each criterion is given a weighting and then in the second column a further rating is given as to how well the criterion is met.

For example, the criteria might consist of:

	Weighting	×	Criteria met	=	Total
Customer access	9		7		63
Car parking	7		8		56

Table 6.3

Point rating system checklist

	Importance weighting (1 to 10) ×	Meets criteria (1 to 10) = TOTAL
Access for customers		
Access to customers		
Parking space		
Proximity to suppliers		
Availability of transport		
Fixed costs of location		
Variable costs of location		
Labour supply		
Cost of labour		
Industrial relations		
Government: (local/national as appropriate)		
Zoning restrictions		
Capital restrictions		
Funds transfers		
Taxation rates		
Tax/other incentives		
Stability of government		
Reliability of sources: of energy of other utilities		
Cost of utilities		
Other factors		
TOTAL		

Overseas ventures   If overseas locations are being investigated, it is most important that the broader issues, such as political and economic stability, local customs and culture, tax structures and incentives, reliable communications, energy supplies and so on are considered. Obviously an overseas venture for an organization will require very detailed considerations. Often local problems do not emerge until the project is well under way. It is most sensible to solicit local assistance and knowledge from the outset when contemplating an overseas venture.

Transportation models

Transportation models are an iterative, mathematical approach to determining location and for solving transportation and distribution problems. However, transportation models are not only used for distribution problems; for example, they can be adapted to determine whether to have few or many retail branches and where branches should be located so as to best serve (attract) customers. The transportation model approach can also be used to solve location problems in other service areas where cost or time of providing a service can be related to location. For example, a transportation model could be used to determine the location of appliances for a fire brigade service, or to determine where satellite (local) outpatient departments should be set up for a health service, and so on. Here we will provide a general method, based on the location of warehouses to supply known customer markets. As this is an iterative approach, a computer spreadsheet approach would help. There are 'off-the-shelf' transportation computer programs available. The example given is a simplified problem designed to give an understanding of the overall approach.

Example

A distributor has three warehouses:

Location	Capacity
Able	5 000
Baker	6 000
Charlie	2 500
TOTAL	13 500

Forecasts show that demand for four different regions will be:

North	6 000
South	4 000
East	2 000
West	1 500
TOTAL	13 500

Each region can be served by any one of the three warehouses.

We therefore have three warehouses to supply four markets, thus in total there are twelve possible routes. Each route will have a different cost of transport (if we were considering a fire brigade or ambulance service, then the 'cost' would be the 'time' taken to get to an incident). The aim of transportation problems is to minimize cost (or time).

For example, transport costs are:

From: Supplier	To: North	South	East	West
Able	3	2	7	6
Baker	7	5	2	3
Charlie	2	5	4	5

Solution one: North–West Rule

A simple transportation allocation approach is known as the North–West Rule. With the

North–West Rule a table is used to get an initial feasible solution. We begin by allocating as much as possible from the first supplier to the customer shown in the top left-hand (north-west) corner of the table. The cost of transportation is also shown on the table, in the right-hand corner of the cell for each of the twelve routes (see Table 6.4).

After the initial allocation (see Table 6.5), which totally depletes Able, North still requires 1000 units which are allocated from Baker. The remainder of Baker's stock will go to South and East. North and South are now satisfied but East and West are still to be fully served. Charlie can be used to complete East's requirements and also

to satisfy West's requirements. This allocation is shown in Table 6.6.

We will call this **Solution one**. This approach gives a feasible solution, but ignores the costs, or time elements. If we apply the 'costs' to our solution we obtain the results shown in Table 6.7.

This is not likely to be the optimum solution! Actually the optimum is less than 40 000!

Solution two

An alternative approach begins with the largest supplier making the initial allocation, in this case Baker 2000 to East, then stopping to re-evaluate

Table 6.4	From	North	South	East	West	Supply
Table before any allocations	Able	3	2	7	6	5000
	Baker	7	5	2	3	6000
	Charlie	2	5	4	5	2500
	Required	6000	4000	2000	1500	13 500

Table 6.5	From	North	South	East	West	Supply
Table after initial allocation of 5000 units from Able to North	Able	5000				–
	Baker					6000
	Charlie					2500
	Required	1000	4000	2000	1500	

Table 6.6	From	North	South	East	West	Supply
Allocation of remainder	Able	5000 ^{3}	2	7	6	5000
	Baker	1000 ^{7}	4000 ^{5}	1000 ^{2}	3	6000
	Charlie	2	5	1000 ^{4}	1500 ^{5}	2500
	Required	6000	4000	2000	1500	13 500

to determine who is now the largest supplier. In this example Able still has 5000 to dispose of and Baker has been left with 4000. As Able is now the largest supplier, Able will allocate the maximum possible to the cheapest route – 4000 to South. After this allocation Baker again becomes the largest supplier and would allocate 1500 to West and so on. Carrying this method to its conclusion we have the allocation and costs shown in Table 6.8. Again not the optimum solution!

Another method is to begin with the cheapest route for the biggest supplier. In this case the biggest supplier is Baker with 6000, and the cheapest route for Baker is to supply East. As East

can only accept 2000, Baker will still have 4000 to dispose of, and using the cheapest routes Baker will give West 1500 and South 2500. Able is the second biggest supplier, and the best allocation still available for Able is 1500 to South and 3500 to North. Charlie will then deliver the balance required for North of 2500. The result, **Solution three**, is shown in Table 6.9. But is Solution three the best possible result?

Stepping-stone method

Another approach is to use any of the Tables as shown above and from any cell subtract one unit and follow through the resulting flow-on effects.

Table 6.7	From	To	Volume	Unit 'cost'	Total 'cost'
Solution one	Able	North	5000	3	15 000
	Baker	North	1000	7	7000
	Baker	South	4000	5	20 000
	Charlie	East	1000	4	4000
	Charlie	West	1500	5	7500
	TOTAL				53 000

Table 6.8				
Solution two	Able	1000 × 3	=	3000
	Able	4000 × 2	=	8000
	Baker	2500 × 7	=	17 500
	Baker	2000 × 2	=	4000
	Baker	1500 × 3	=	4500
	Charlie	2500 × 2	=	5000
	TOTAL			42 000

From	North	South	East	West	Supply
Able	1000 3	4000 2	7	6	5000
Baker	2500 7	5	2000 2	1500 3	6000
Charlie	2500 2	5	4	5	2500
Required	6000	4000	2000	1500	13 500

Assume for our example using Table 6.9 that for the cell Baker–South one unit is added. The flow will be as shown in Table 6.10. The cost of making the adjustments is also shown. The net effect of this first set of steps is to reduce costs by 1. This shows that for every unit shipped from Baker to South there will be a cost benefit of 1. The process is then repeated cell by cell throughout the table. This approach is known as the stepping-stone method. Following through the stepping-stone method we find that the optimum solution is the same as Solution three, i.e. $39 500.

As we said, this is a simple example. All assignment or transportation models are based on an iterative approach which is suitable for a computer package approach. For a more detailed study of algorithmic transportation and assignment models see Wild (2002: Appendix 1, Linear Programming).

Table 6.9					
Solution three	Able	3500 × 3	=	10 500
	Able	1500 × 2	=	3000
	Baker	2500 × 5	=	12 500
	Baker	2000 × 2	=	4000
	Baker	1500 × 3	=	4500
	Charlie	2500 × 2	=	5000
	TOTAL			39 500

From	North	South	East	West	Supply
Able	3500 ^{3}	1500 ^{2}	^{7}	^{6}	5000
Baker	^{7}	2500 ^{5}	2000 ^{2}	1500 ^{3}	6000
Charlie	2500 ^{2}	^{5}	^{4}	^{5}	2500
Required	6000	4000	2000	1500	13 500

Table 6.10	From	North	South	East	West	Change
Stepping-stone method	Able	1000+1 ^{3}	4000–1 ^{2}			+3 −2
	Baker	2500–1 ^{7}	+1 ^{5}			−7 +5
	Charlie					
	Total					−1

Layout of premises

Having determined where our organization will be located, the next issue is to consider the layout with the overall objectives of facilitating efficient operations and first-class customer service. As in most areas of operations the first criterion is to establish the relative importance of customer satisfaction *vis-à-vis* efficient use of resources.

In most systems there will be a physical flow of people or materials. Layout planning aims to:

- optimize movement;
- reduce congestion;
- maximize use of space.

Optimize movement

In an office, or a backroom area, the aim will be to reduce movement. However, in a retail store situation such as a supermarket, the aim might be to have a layout that will increase the distance to be travelled by the customer. For example, customers are channelled up and down aisles, and the actual distance travelled is maximized rather than minimized so that the customers are obliged to pass by brightly coloured and attractively presented goods and, hopefully, be tempted to buy up 'big time'.

Reduce congestion

The objective of operations management is to add value, and to eliminate non-value-adding activities. Seldom is value added by having customers waiting in queues. Time spent waiting does not add to sales, and merely adds to congestion. There is a limit to how long people will queue, no matter how good the service or product at the end of the queue. What can't be quantified is the number of sales lost by people who are put off by a queue. Recently in Australia there have been reported cases of 'supermarket rage' where shoppers have become extremely agitated by waiting in queues.

Maximize use of space

As we have seen in the section on location, space costs money; thus it is important to make the best use of space. For example, if there is spare space it can always be used for display purposes. Likewise, with the customers' interests at heart it follows that where possible more space per person should be allocated to customer areas (front office) and less space to backroom facilities. One large insurance company allocated the top floor of its new building as the staff cafeteria. Thus the floor with the best views was given to the staff who used it for about two hours a day (tea breaks and lunch). Two years later a new Chief Executive found space in the basement for the cafeteria, and leased out the top floor at a premium rate. We are not condoning relegating the staff to the dungeons, but on the other hand to be over-generous with premium space is not good economic sense. Sensible initial planning would have prevented staff subsequently becoming upset at losing 'their' cafeteria (what they hadn't had they wouldn't miss).

Types of layout

The basic types of layout are:

- Process
- Product
- Fixed position
- Hybrid

Process layout

With process layout all operations of a similar nature will be grouped together. Examples of process layout will be found in hotels, libraries, supermarkets and warehouses.

Example

In a library the reference section with computer terminals and indexes may be grouped together, the books will be grouped according to subject, journals and periodicals will be in another section, CD Roms in another area, and the librarians' check-out department will be behind a counter near the exit. The customer goes to the section required and will bypass some sections.

Product layout

Here facilities are arranged according to the needs of the service.

Example

Self-service fast-food outlet (without seating) (see Figure 6.2).

Another example is the diagnostic department in a hospital where patients are given sequential tests, i.e. different types of specialized equipment are located adjacent to each other, and a mixture of specialized skills and tasks is required.

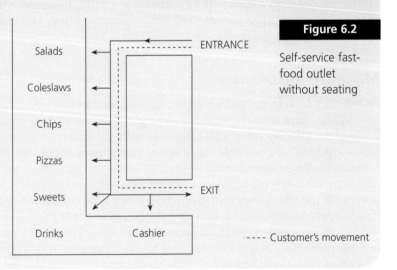

Figure 6.2

Self-service fast-food outlet without seating

---- Customer's movement

With product layout floor space is minimized, and ideally the process should be continuous with the person who is being 'served' moving from facility to facility.

Fixed-position layout

For process layout and product layout the customer moves past stationary service sections. In a fixed-position layout neither the customer nor the service provider moves, an example being the hairdresser or the dentist.

Hybrid layout

As the name suggests, this is a mixed form of layout. A restaurant is an example of a mixed product/process layout, where a buffet for self-service (product layout) and table service is also offered (process layout).

With some service operations the choice of layout will be limited by the service offered; in other cases it is often worth considering if a change from, say, a process-type layout to a product-type layout might improve flow of customers or save space. There can be no hard and fast rules, but being aware of the different types of layout and daring to question, i.e. 'Can the customer become more involved in self service?' might well trigger a better use of space. Consider the old-style grocery store (before the advent of the supermarket) where customers stood still and the grocer and his staff 'picked' at the request of the customer. In today's supermarket customers do their own picking. Most supermarkets allow customers to travel up and down aisles, and customers can choose to bypass aisles; however, other supermarkets are laid out in such a way that the customer can only travel one way and once the journey has started there are no short cuts – no aisle can be avoided as in essence there is only one long meandering route to follow (see Figure 6.3).

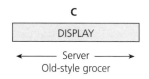

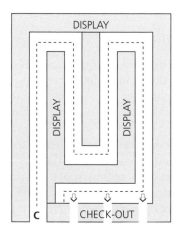

Figure 6.3

Possible grocery store layouts

Layout planning

Here we consider the layout of a new department. The approach will be the same irrespective of whether the decision is to remodel an existing area or to obtain new premises.

The two key issues for layout planning are *demand* and *capacity*. Demand will determine the capacity required, and the system structure will determine if storage space for goods is required where goods are being supplied so as to meet demand fluctuations. Thus detailed demand forecasting and capacity planning are required before layout planning can begin. Method study and the determination of a standard system (see the next section) coupled with capacity planning will lead us to establish the amount of resources that will need to be housed. Resources include people, equipment, furniture, fittings, display stands etc. Other factors include customer waiting areas, rest rooms/toilets for staff and customers, additional services such as lunch-room facilities and so on. Health and safety regulations will also have to be considered. Once all the above has been agreed then layout planning can begin. It follows that every stakeholder should be invited to indicate requirements; no one person can hope to know it all!

Project approach

It is recommended that the layout of a new department should be treated as a project. Projects are defined as 'one-off' novel endeavours, and certainly a new layout meets this criterion. The intricacies of project management are discussed in Chapter 12.

Layout planning methods

The tendency today is to use computer simulation for layout planning, but in reality the same result can be achieved through the use of more mundane traditional methods. The methods we show here have stood the test of time and are simple to apply. The strong point with each method is that the planner must get personally involved and collect factual evidence.

Visual aids

Visual aids are an important element of layout planning. These include scale representations, including drawings, templates, three-dimensional models and movement patterns. One simple way to illustrate movement is to use coloured cottons on a scale plan to show the movement of materials, people, documents, or information. The power of this method lies in vividly highlighting inefficiency.

In a service industry the criterion may not always be to reduce the distance travelled. As discussed earlier, for a supermarket the criterion might be to make the most use of selling space by increasing the distance travelled by customers. Alternatively, if space is at a premium, then the criterion might be to reduce the amount of space needed. Before planning can begin the criteria for the layout have to be clearly established and agreed. It really comes back to the old conflict of operations: is the objective primarily customer satisfaction or resource utilization? For

Example

Figure 6.4 shows a 'before-and-after' string diagram. Imagine how much more graphic this would be with the use of different coloured cottons to indicate each person/department visited.

Note: With the string diagram the floor plan must be drawn to scale. Once the recording has been completed the string can be measured to determine the exact distance covered.

Figure 6.4

A 'before-and-after' string diagram

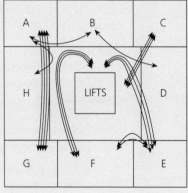

Before

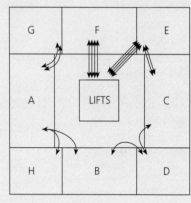

After

backroom operations resource utilization will generally be the objective, i.e. minimal movement and minimum space; for the front office the reverse could well be the objective.

Relationship diagrams

A relationship chart looks at movement and the need for one department to be near another; relationship diagrams also consider the underlying reasons for the relationships.

In all but the simplest of layouts, planning by hand can be a long and tedious process, and generally a computer-based approach can be used. The two basic methodologies in computer-based layout planning are proximity of departments or processes, and movement minimization of workers, customers or flow of work.

Proximity maximization

The approach is to begin by placing the departments with the highest proximity rating together and working in descending order-of-closeness rating until all departments have been included. There will be other constraints such as space required and access and egress considerations. The programs work by assigning a value to closeness ratings and the aim is to maximize the score. At first glance you could be pardoned for thinking that if proximity can be maximized then movement will automatically be minimized. However, the closeness rating will often

Example

The following simplified example for a hospital shows the space requirements for each department.

Visitors' lounge*	1500 square metres
Gift shop	1500
Pharmacy	1200
Autopsy	2000
Morgue*	2000
Accident and emergency department*	1500
X-ray department	1500
Toilets	1000
Stairs and lifts	1000
Routine admissions and enquiries*	1000
TOTAL	13 200

* Denotes external access to street required.

The first step in constructing a relationship diagram is to consider the importance of why one department should be close to another, or conversely why one department should not be next to another. A code is generally used, or a numeric scale, to determine the importance of adjacent locations. The code used in our example is:

Adjacency:
A = Absolutely essential
E = Extremely important
I = Important
O = Ordinary
U = Unimportant
N = Not at all desirable

Figures 6.5, 6.6 and 6.7 demonstrate how the codes are used, and are translated into a rough diagram from which a more precise layout can be determined.

Figure 6.5

Relationship diagram

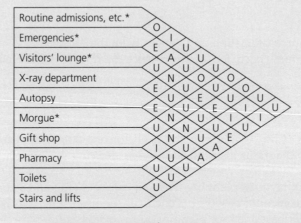

*Outside exit/entrance required

Importance
A = Absolutely
E = Extremely
I = Important
O = Ordinary
U = Unimportant
N = No way!

Figure 6.6

Rough diagram

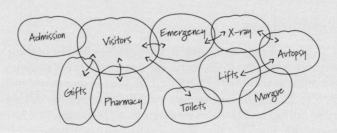

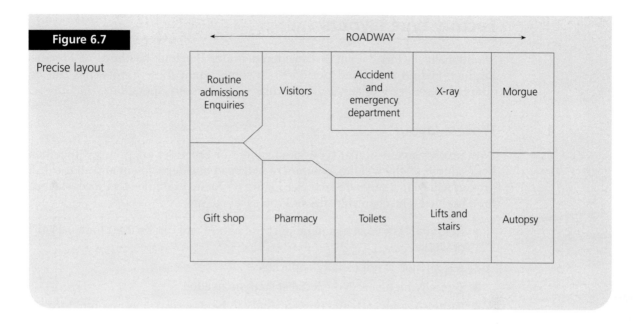

Figure 6.7

Precise layout

include other factors such as customer convenience or safety issues, and movement will be only one of the factors considered.

Movement minimization

Movement minimization concentrates on reducing movement. Movement may be measured in the number of journeys, distance and cost, and may be related to movement of customer, worker, or materials.

Movement minimization uses factual information that can be quantified, i.e. metres travelled, cost of travel, number of journeys, volume moved and so on.

Proximity maximization is more general and some of the measures will be qualitative rather than quantitative.

A combination procedure allows an initial layout to be developed using one criterion, and then by adding other criteria changes will be made until the best 'mix' is achieved. The advantage of computer systems is the interactivity which enables the layout designer to change criteria and to try 'What if' scenarios.

Flexibility

Ideally layouts should be flexible and easily changed. To this extent movable and preferably free-standing partitions are recommended. Open-planned offices do make the most of floor space but generally staff, given the choice, prefer their own offices. Workstations which combine desk, filing cabinet, bookshelf and computer terminal, all ergonomically designed for the comfort and convenience of staff, can overcome the resistance to open planning to a large measure. Additionally a properly designed workstation will afford a measure of privacy and will have some acoustical properties to deaden extraneous office noise.

Factory type layouts

Traditionally factory layout is considered under the four headings of Process, Product, Hybrid and Fixed positions. To some extent these approaches can be adapted to service industries, in particular to 'back room' operations.

Process layout

With process layout similar types of machines or processes are grouped together. For example, all the welding equipment will be in one department and all the drill presses will be in a separate area. See Figure 6.7 for an example of a Process layout for a hospital. The characteristics of Process layout are;

1. Resources can be of a general purpose nature and can be used for a variety of work.
2. Automation is not usually applicable.
3. Typically highly skilled/specialist staff are needed.
4. For the overall cycle the process time can be slow as delays and build-up of work can occur at each process.
5. Material handling costs are higher than with Product layout. Jobs move from department to department in the overall process, and in some cases the production of one product might have to revisit a department several times in the overall process (e.g. welding might take place at several different times in the production of one item).
6. Material can accumulate (stock pile) at each stage.
7. Scheduling activities to balance the workload is difficult.

Product layout

Resources are arranged to enable production to move sequentially through each step of the total process. Examples are the assembly line in car manufacturing, a staff cafeteria and going through the various check points for international air travel (baggage check in, customs, security, final ticket check at departure lounge, etc.). Product layouts have the following characteristics, some are positive others are not.

1. The layout uses specialized (capital intensive) equipment to increase throughput. Automation is a feature of product layouts.
2. Speed of each process rate is important, resources are arranged sequentially, and in the factory the line has to be balanced
3. Material handling costs in the factory are minimized, work flows continuously from one work station to the next and workstations are in close proximity to each other (*note*: this is not so in the international airport, but very much so in the car assembly line).
4. Inventory storage between each stage is kept to a minimum and overall stocks of materials can be minimized.
5. There is a lack of flexibility (try going back to the beginning of the line in a cafeteria – see Figure 6.2).

In the factory situation, mass production work was broken down to small specialized tasks and the process relied on standardization to push through high volumes. Flexibility was non-existent and production was in large batches. Using this approach, in 1913, Henry Ford was able to make 250 000 Model T cars per year. Ford turned the car into a consumer item affordable by most families. Prior to this cars were made one at a time and were so expensive that only wealthy people could afford them. The production line was characterized by large batches and no flexibility. It would sometimes take days to change a production line over to produce another model. Today, with the Toyota approach, a production line can be flexible and one-off products can be made with single minute exchange of dies etc.; for more detail on flexibility in production lines see Chapter 9 (scheduling).

Hybrid layout

Most organizations use a mixture of Product and Process layouts. For example, in car manufacturing there will be an assembly line, with a high degree of automation for various steps of the process; and feeding the assembly line there will be cells, such as a department assembling components where automation is not possible.

Fixed positions

With fixed position the assembly of the complete product is done at one work station, and each workstation is equipped with all the necessary resources, or resources have to be brought as required to the workstation. Generally yachts, aircraft, and high-voltage transformers, are built in this fashion.

Safety, health and ergonomics

Occupational safety, health and ergonomics might be considered a moral issue, but even the Romans realized that well-maintained slaves were more efficient and more valuable. The average fully-employed adult will spend 25 per cent or more of his or her life at the workplace, and additional time in travelling to and from work. It could well be argued that employers have a moral obligation in addition to various legal obligations to provide a safe working environment, and that the worker who 'sells' his or her time has a right to a safe and healthy workplace. Sadly history shows that voluntary safety arrangements do not provide adequate standards, and thus legislation has been necessary. The fault has not always been with employers, as it is the employees who are often found to take short cuts. Statistics show that the home is still the most dangerous place for most people!

It is a fact that most health and safety requirements are only common sense. It is common sense to have adequate light, correct temperatures, proper ventilation, noise controls and so on.

Ergonomics

Ergonomics is the science which seeks to improve the physical and mental well-being of workers by optimizing the function of human–machine environments. In today's office, workers are surrounded by machines, most of them electronic, and long hours are spent hunched over keyboards and in front of VDU screens. In particular ergonomics concentrates on:

- Fitting the work demands to the efficiency of people, to reduce physical and mental stress.
- Providing information for the design of machines, keyboards, etc. so that they can be operated efficiently.
- The development of adjustable workstations and chairs etc. so that individuals can self-adjust the workstation to meet their needs.
- Providing information on correct body posture to reduce fatigue and to minimize OOS (occupational overuse syndrome – formerly known as RSI or repetitive stress injury).
- Giving guidelines for lighting, air conditioning, noise limits and so on.

The following web site provided by the US Department of Labour Occupational Safety and Health Administration is recommended, http:/www.osha.gov/SLTC/computerworkstation

Method study

In service industries – no matter how automated the process, how clever the information technology – there will always be the need for people to interface with the customers, or by backroom endeavours to provide support for front-line staff. Method study aims to make the life of the workers easier and more rewarding by:

- providing an efficient layout (be it office, showroom, or warehouse);
- providing a well-designed workstation with adequate lighting, ventilation/heating/air conditioning;
- implementing standard work procedures;
- providing personal satisfaction – modern method study encourages workers to become involved in looking for improvements at the workplace.

Method study also considers the health and safety requirements for the workplace. The study of work, to streamline and to make work easier and more efficient (productive), will always be of importance.

The standard method study approach is through a systematic investigation of all factors that affect the efficiency of a particular work situation. Generally, method study is applied to existing work situations and problem areas. The seven-step approach of method study is not limited to the workplace: it can be applied with equal effectiveness in the home, in the sports club and indeed any situation where a problem is encountered.

Seven steps of method study

The systematic method study approach consists of the following seven steps (some steps can be combined depending on circumstances).

1. Select
2. Record
3. Examine
4. Develop
5. Define
6. Install
7. Maintain

1. Select

The select stage of method study includes recognizing that there is a problem and then defining the problem. Before the study proper is commenced it is advisable to determine the aim (e.g. to increase the number of customers served per staff member), the standards by which the results of the study can be judged (such as savings in cost or time) and the boundaries or scope of the study.

2. Record

This stage requires the recording of all the facts relating to the existing way the work is carried out. Much of the success of the whole method study procedure relies on the accuracy with which the facts are recorded. How the recording will be done depends on the nature of the study, e.g. a localized process or a functional procedure which accounts for the activities of an entire section, department or branch.

Information recorded will include existing data, such as outputs, specifications, job descriptions, methods, hours worked, time sheets and so on. However, it is important that all information used is tested to see if it is current and accurate.

The best information is that which is gathered from direct observation. Flow charts can be used to chart the job process for people, machines or combined person/machine. For example, a person/machine process chart might show: worker accesses computer (worker and machine involved), worker leaves machine to answer phone – computer idle. Alternatively the computer system prints a report while the worker has a cup of coffee (worker idle). Flow charts can be used to show the flow of work, materials, people or information.

The symbols used are:

Operation (value added)	O
Transportation (movement of people or material)	⇨
Inspection (checking of work)	□
Storage (e.g. filing of paper records, goods on display, items in warehouse)	∇
Delay (idle time)	D

In all the above activities the only time where value is added is when an operation takes place. All other activities add time and cost to the overall process. A simple example of a flow process chart is given below.

Person		Inwards goods	
To inwards goods	⇨	Goods held in arrival dock	D
Locates paperwork	O		D
Matches paperwork to parcel	O		D
Carries parcel to desk	⇨		⇨
Unwraps parcel	O		O
Checks against specification	☐		D
Records receipt of goods	O		D
Goods taken to store	⇨		⇨
Goods placed on storage rack	O		▽
Returns to desk	⇦		

To the above could be added distance travelled and time taken.

The amount of detail recorded depends on the nature of the study. For some studies an overview is sufficient to gain an appreciation of what is causing a problem, or where a bottleneck is, and only two symbols are used: O and ☐.

3. Examine

The traditional method study approach is a step-by-step critical examination of each element of the job or process. The main question is 'Why?' The first question being 'Why is this job or element of a job done at all, and what would the ramifications be if this job or element was not done?' If the answer is 'If it wasn't done it would make no difference', then the study is over, i.e. eliminate that job or element. This means of course being absolutely sure that the job can be eliminated; on the other hand, if the only answer is along the lines 'We have always done it this way', this is in itself a very good reason for not doing it that way again!

There are six sets of questions and they are used in the sequence shown below.

1. What is being done, why, what else could be done, and what should be done?
2. Where does it happen, why there, where else, and where should it be done?
3. When is it done, why then, when else, and when should it be done?
4. Who does it, why that person, who else, and who should do it?
5. Who checks it, why that person, who else could, and who should?
6. How is it done, why that way, how else could it be done, and how should it be done?

Asking the above questions requires tact, otherwise resentment or defensive reactions are possible. It is also important to distinguish between facts and opinions. Opinions can be argued, facts can only lead to valid conclusions. The analyst must have an open mind and not have preconceived ideas. In considering what else, where else, when else, who else, and how else, lateral thinking will be needed. Although the method might appear to be a pedestrian step-by-step approach, the aim is to find a creative solution which will ease work and increase efficiency. It is also important to determine the cause of a given condition rather than its effect.

The Japanese approach is to ask 'Why?' five times.

Example

An invoice for an important customer is wrong, and the customer complains and in doing so claims that 'your invoices are always wrong'.

Using the five-'Why?' approach the questions will be:

- Why was the invoice wrong? Answer: The discount amount allowed by Accounts differed from that quoted by Sales.
- Why was a different rate quoted? Answer: Sales had been sent a memo from Marketing with a new rate. Accounts did not use this rate.
- Why did Accounts not use the new rate? Answer: Because they did not receive advice of the new rate.
- Why was Accounts not advised of the new rate? Answer: Because Marketing thought it was Sales' responsibility to advise rates to Accounts, and Sales thought that the responsibility was Marketing's.
- Why did this confusion exist? Answer: The procedure had changed but the administration manual had not been updated.

Solution: Update the manual, and in future Marketing will send a copy of rate changes to both Accounts and Sales (previously rates had been set by Sales and not by Marketing, the policy had changed so that Marketing and not Sales set rates).

In the above example if the effect alone had been addressed, Accounts would have checked with Sales, as per the standard procedure in the manual, and asked what the rate was. Sales would have given Accounts the new rate, and Accounts could have been excused in thinking that the problem was a one-off oversight by Sales. In this scenario Marketing would not have been aware of their responsibility. As rates only change every six months or so, the same problem would therefore re-occur, and the customer would get several wrong invoices before a further correction was made.

4. Develop

Answers to the questions in the Examine stage furnish clues to improvement. If it is found that a particular task or an element of a task is unnecessary it should be eliminated or modified. Wherever possible, related tasks should be combined to reduce movement of people or paper, i.e. if a clerk is properly trained and given responsibility, then a check of work by a supervisor may not be necessary. Likewise delays can be cut to reduce time and expense. Changing the sequence of activities is another possibility for developing a better work pattern.

Once a new method has been developed then it should be subject to the same questioning technique before final installation. Quite often an initial solution can be adopted with existing resources and layouts as an interim measure until more radical improvements can be made. Sometimes a radical improvement will take time to develop and to implement, but there is no reason why a lesser improvement could not be adopted as an interim measure, if only to get people used to working with the proposed overall changes.

The input of all stakeholders to any proposed changes should be sought throughout the method study. The biggest problem with method study is resistance to change; this can be overcome if people are won over through being involved in developing the new method. If they take 'ownership' the chances of successful implementation will be enhanced. Unless people wholeheartedly support a new method it is suggested that sometimes it might be wise to settle for a less than optimum solution, if it is more acceptable to the workers.

5. Define

Once the new method has been developed, it is important that it is defined in writing. It should be described in sufficient detail for others to be able to install it and for it to be used in training and instruction.

6. Install

This is the ultimate goal of the preceding stages – the effective application of the improvement. If this stage fails the earlier stages will be wasted effort. Installation needs careful planning, communication and training. Often modifications might be needed; however, a careful watch should be made to ensure that modifications are really necessary and are not just the result of people slipping back to old systems or misunderstanding new systems. When computer terminals were introduced it was not unusual for mistrusting people to secretly keep the old manual system running in parallel, and then blame the computer for creating extra work and bottlenecks.

7. Maintain

Although an improved process has been installed it does not follow that the benefits will automatically be maintained. Reasons for variations need to be examined and corrective action taken to return to the standard system.

Example

A building society was taking over three weeks to approve home mortgage applications. This delay was causing problems for clients and often a client would 'miss out' on a house. The reason given was that time was needed to arrange a qualified survey for any house before a mortgage could be approved. On examination, using flow process charting with times shown for each activity, it was found that on average surveyors took less than half an hour to inspect a property and the entering of a survey report on a standard format in the computer system took no more than fifteen minutes. All the rest of the three weeks' delay in giving approval to the client was in the 'processing' of paper from desk to desk, and to the regional office for approval of recommendations. It was quite possible that, if the building society had streamlined its paperwork and communication lines, and given branch offices some authority with clear guidelines, mortgage approvals could be given within 24 hours of application, and certainly within 48 hours. Although a report was made and accepted, the same building society two years later is still taking ten days to approve mortgages, and clients are going elsewhere for their mortgages!

Chapter summary

This chapter has covered the practical aspects of location, layout and method study. All of these areas are intertwined. It is obvious that a method study could also recommend changes to a layout, and in itself layout will be limited by the size and shape of the space available.

Location, layout and method study are very much operational issues, and exist in the broader strategic context of the organization.

Location decisions are essentially to do with where a service operation is best placed to serve the market. The alternatives are speed to customer, or ease of access by customer. Although a location decision will not ignore the extended supply chain, nonetheless the supplier will generally be of lesser importance in the determination of service locations.

Business policy will to a large extent determine location; it will not be so evident on layout decisions, but will not be entirely absent. The nature of the product or service can also affect the system structure which in turn will influence the layout.

Method study deals with increasing efficiency down to the smallest element of the operation, and it can be carried out irrespective of the business policy. Method study can be done with the express aim of making the most efficient use of existing resources with no need for increased capital expenditure. Method study, however, is not limited to just increasing efficiency, but also includes making work more enjoyable for staff by involving them in improvements, and considering and improving aspects of the working environment such as noise, ventilation, lighting, ergonomically-designed workstations and so on.

Note

1. Following a serious share market downturn in October 1987 many home-owners in the UK and other parts of the world found themselves in a position of negative equity. That is, the price they could sell their home for did not cover the amount still owing on their mortgages. The same applied to commercial properties. With the Asian economic crisis of the late 1990s the same problems re-emerged in Asia, Australia and New Zealand (ten years after the property 'crash' of the Eighties). In 2004 property markets are now again buoyant, or maybe even overheated! Our forecast is beware in 2007!

Case Study *Cyclone Furniture*

This is a large chapter and many important issues have been covered. The case study which adds value to the chapter is Cyclone Furniture.

Questions

1. What are the overall immediate concerns for the business?
2. Give an overview of factory situation.
3. Identify the current factory operation and strategies.
4. Recommended actions for the factory manager.
5 Should they outsource to Indonesia?

Cyclone Furniture Company

The Cyclone Furniture Company is a well established family business. It consists of an 'exclusive' furniture retail show room in the downtown business centre of a large New Zealand city, and a manufacturing plant in a neighbouring satellite town. The plant manufactures furniture for their own retail showroom (25 per cent of the output) and for export to Australia. The plant also makes top quality office furniture, all of which is exported to Australia. Overall 75 per cent of all output is exported to Australia.

Three weeks ago you were recruited as General Manager for the company. Until you were appointed, Winston Prebble had managed the business. Winston was the son of the founder of the business. Winston, although only forty, has decided to retire from running the business to pursue other interests. Yesterday, 31 May, he left with his new wife for an extended world trip. His parting words to you were 'You have full authority, treat the business as your own, keep in touch, phone or email me once a month'.

You have a tangible incentive for the business to perform well as your remuneration package includes a bonus calculated at 2.5 per cent of the pretax profit of the company (if the budget is achieved your bonus will be $16 500). Today, 1 June, is the first day Winston has not been breathing down your neck and you get to the office early, keen to get started. (The 'Head Office' is on the mezzanine floor of the retail showrooms.) You are particularly anxious to visit the factory, for although you have met Rangi MacDonald, the factory manager, you have not as yet visited the factory. Winston had shown little enthusiasm for the manufacturing side of the business. In fact he had said to you 'I sometimes wonder if we would be better to close the factory, outsource to Indonesia where the timber is sourced and just concentrate on the show room and export side of the business'. You have to admit that Winston certainly seems to know the retail side of the business. The decor and presentation of the store, for which Winston takes personal credit, exudes just the right atmosphere of sophisticated elegance which has given Cyclone their reputation as 'the' place for finely crafted furniture.

On arriving at the office you are pleased to see that Rachel Huntress the accountant is already at work. Your sense of pleasure however does not last long! Rachel shows you the trading results for the first three months (up to 31 March), which she has just finalized. You are shocked to see that the results show profit to be below budget by over $100 000! On being pressed Rachel says that she won't be able to produce the detailed May/June results for at least another 3 weeks.

Extracts from Rachel's financial statements are shown at Appendix A (p. 128). You do some quick calculations and come to the conclusion that the debts are far too high and that the organization as a whole is carrying too much stock. The sales figures also look low for the first six months when compared to budget. Rachel blames the recession brought on by the economic downturn in Australia. She says 'If sales don't improve, and I don't see why they will, the loss for the year will be about $200 000. I suggest that we cut back heavily on staff numbers'. You ask Rachel what she knows about the factory. She replies she has only been with the company nine months and hasn't had time to visit the factory. You suggest that Rachel visit the factory that afternoon with you.

While you and Rachel are talking, Ransom the Bank Manager, phones. Her concern is the high level of the overdraft. She asks you to visit her office in two days' time. Ms. Ransom says that one of the terms of the overdraft is that a balance sheet and key trading figures be supplied to the bank at the end of each quarter, she says she has yet to see the results for the March quarter. Ms. Ransom adds that in view of the high level of overdraft a cash flow and profit forecast up to 31 December is required. Once Ransom hangs up (you had turned the speaker on so that Rachel could hear), Rachel says 'Well I can't visit the factory now, I'm going to have to put all my efforts into getting the forecasts together'. You reply that without information from the factory you don't believe a forecast can be made.

You call for Silver Fern the Marketing Manager and ask her for sales figures for the last few years, and also for an updated forecast of sales through to December.

Silver returns in five minutes with the following information

Silver says 'By the way, don't worry about being behind budget, in the ten years I have been here Winston has always set an impossible budget, he seemed to think this would make us try harder'.

Before you can consider the figures in detail you realize that you are due at the factory and that Rangi will be waiting for you. You invite Silver to come with you. Silver agrees, she says she hasn't seen the factory since the new extension. You don't comment, but you know that the extension is at least two years old!

When you get to the factory (90-minute drive), you explain to Rangi and Silver that 'we' have a temporary cash flow problem and that we are going to have to cut back on expenses. Rangi looks concerned and says that in his opinion Head Office is over-staffed and that the factory is very efficient, 'so there is no point expecting me to cut back'.

On a tour through the factory Silver comments on how clean and tidy it is. You also note how cheerful the workers are and that there is an overall sense of people taking pride in their work. You then inspect some of the finished products in the large warehouse and there is no doubt that the quality is first-rate. You and Silver congratulate Rangi on the high standard of workmanship. Somewhat mollified Rangi begins to relax.

You are surprised to find that Rangi has an office staff of five people including an accountant. You have also noted that a large number

Actual sales by quarter $'000

	2000	2001	2002	2003	2004
Jan–Mar	800	660	945	930	940
Apr–Jun	1050	900	1080	1055	1080*
Jly–Sept	975	865	1040	1005	–?–
Oct–Dec	1085	1075	1135	1115	–?–
Full year	3900	3500	4200	4105	–?–
Budget	4200	4000	4200	4400	4600
Net profit (actual)/ before tax	390	315	360	310	?

*April–June figures are based on sales invoiced, and goods on order for delivery in June. Silver is comfortable with the figure of $1 080 000.

▶

of machines are idle, you know that most of the plant is leased and you wonder if some can be returned to the lessors. You are also surprised to see just how large the stock of raw material and finished stock is and how much space it takes up (you think 'no wonder they had to build an extension').

While Silver has a cup of coffee with the factory accountant you ask Rangi how work is scheduled. Rangi explains he has 22 factory workers and that they are all kept fully employed. He schedules work up to 12 months in advance and has standard times for each element of every job. For simplification he aggregates the standard times up to 20 hours, and each 20 hours of standard time equals a unit of work. For example, a Queen Anne bed takes 1.2 units of work (24 hours of labour).

His schedule for the next six months shows:

(Using June as an example for calculations; June has 22 work days × 8 hour per day × 22 people = 3872 hours. Divided by 20 gives 193.6 available units of work.)

	Total available units in month	Units of work scheduled	Demand (required for delivery at end of month)
June	193.6	192	140
July	184.8	184	165
Aug	193.6	192	165
Sep	184.6	184	160
Oct	184.6	184	150
Nov	193.6	192	200
Dec	150	150	160
Jan	125	125	70
Feb	176.0	175	200
		1578	**1410**

June, July and August are definite orders, the balance is based on past experience. February (and March) are always big months for exports.

Your quick calculation is that for the next six months Rangi is planning to make enough stock to cater for about seven months demand. This suggests to you that the factory staff could be reduced and that there would still be adequate capacity. You also recall that Rachel's figures show that the factory has four months' finished goods on hand at the end of March. Rangi partly explains this by saying a big order was sent to Australia in April, but he does admit that as demand has been a little slower than expected he does have about three months' of uncommitted stock of finished goods on hand at present. He adds that most of this is office furniture which traditionally sells well in February and March. He says part of their good reputation is that they always deliver on time and that this is company policy. He agrees that customers usually order some weeks in advance, and he agrees that perhaps it could be possible to make to order.

You then ask Rangi how he calculates the amount of raw materials to order. Referring to Rachel's figures he says that at the end of March there appeared to be at least three months' of raw materials on hand. Rangi explains that 25 per cent of the timber used comes from South America and there are three shipments a year. Shipments arrive December/January, April/May and August/September. Orders are placed in October (for December/January), February and June. Thus an order placed in October has to cover requirements up to the end of May, and therefore Rangi has to make generous estimates to avoid stock outs. Rangi advises that 12 months ago a computer package was installed which has made ordering easier. Rangi says that the computer specialists had explained that by using an economic order quantity (EOQ) and a reorder point for each item of stock holding calculated on lead times that a reduction in stock holding of about 30 per cent could be expected. However, Rangi thinks that actually more stock is being held than before.

He explains that the formula used by the system is:

EOQ which equals the square root of (2 DA/IC) where:
A = $ cost of placing an order
D = Annual demand in units

I * = Carrying cost for holding inventory for a year

C = Unit cost of the item.

*(the carrying cost interest rate is 30 per cent pa, being 20 per cent cost of funds, 5 per cent for obsolescence, 5 per cent for storage and an ordering cost of $10 per order).

Rangi is not sure of how the EOQ works. 'It is based on the last four years' usage. The computer people said it would work very smoothly because the system would self adjust'. Before the new system was installed Rangi said he didn't rely on past usage but calculated orders on known future demand. He believes that all stock should turn over at least three times a year 'but now I think about 25 per cent of the stock is just taking up space and gathering dust and apart from the imported stuff (about 25 per cent of the materials needed) you can usually get the rest locally more or less when needed.'

You note that the factory is arranged into three sections, each with its own dedicated plant.

The first section (Domestic) makes furniture *only* for the retail shop;

The second section (Exports) makes export orders, and the

Third Section (Commercial) makes office furniture.

Work from each of the three sections then moves to a single finishing department (staining and french polishing), and where appropriate to an upholstery department.

Rangi explains workers for the three manufacturing furniture sections are interchangeable, but that the finishers and upholsterers are specialists.

Silver, who has rejoined you, asks 'Why are three sets of machines required, and wouldn't it be more efficient to have just one manufacturing section?'

Rangi says rather brusquely that office furniture is different from domestic furniture. 'For example, this month Domestic is making beds, Export is making coffee tables and Commercial is making desks. We prefer to work in small batches and to keep each type of work separate. We have always done it this way, and no one has queried our quality.'

You and Silver have much to discuss as you drive back to Head Office.

/— Domestic Furniture **O** ⇨ \

V — Export Furniture **O** ⇨- —- Finishing **O** ⇨ Upholstery ⇨ **O** ⇨ **V** ⇨ **C**

/— Office Furniture   **O** ⇨ /

V = stock; **O** = operation; / = direct to next operation/customer

Appendix A

Performance Statement
For the three months ended 31 March 2004

	Actual	Budget	Full Year Budget
Sales $'000	940	1200	4600
Cost of sales			
Labour	235	300	1200
Materials used	235	300	1200
Gross profit	470	600	2400
Selling expenses	140	180	720
Head office expense	250	250	1000
Interest	25	5	20
Profit before tax	55	165	660

Relevant information from Position Statement as at 31 March 2004

	$'000
Accounts receivable	1050
Inventory raw materials	400
Inventory of finished goods (cost of materials plus labour)	600
Fixed assets: Factory buildings and plant	2000
(The retail store and head office are in leased premises)	
TOTAL ASSETS	4050
LIABILITIES (bank and creditors)	550
EQUITY (Shareholders funds)	3500
TOTAL	4050

Written by J. Nevan Wright, 2004

7 People power: the most valuable resource?

Objectives

Although much has been written about motivation, and many theories have been developed, the reality is that few organizations have a staff of high-performing, self-motivated people.

In this chapter we consider the importance of the human resource to any industry, but in particular to a service industry, and how the operations manager can make the best use of this resource. In particular we look at:

- The importance of motivated people.

- Motivation theories.

- How to create a culture for self-motivation.

- The need for continuous learning.

Introduction

As most of us will have read, or heard in the chairperson's annual address, an organization's most 'valuable' resource is its people. The chairperson could also probably have added 'the most expensive'.

In any operation, but particularly in service industries, the level of service provided to customers and the internal efficiency of the organization, depend heavily on people – the human resource – and their consistent performance. The operations manager has to manage this valuable and expensive resource just as carefully as any other resource. But the difference between managing non-human and human resources is that actions taken with inventory, equipment and machines will lead to predictable results (if the input into a computer is correct the output is predictable), whereas people are not predictable. In a given set of circumstances people will react one way and in similar circumstances, for no apparent reason, they may react in a different way.

Motivated people will provide high levels of service for the customer at no extra cost to the organization and at the same time they will constantly be looking for the most efficient way of using the other resources. Although much has been written about motivation, and many theories have been developed, the reality is that few organizations have a staff of high-performing, self-motivated people.

Basic requirements leading to self-motivation

Getting the best out of the human resource will be achieved partly by:

- making sure that the people of the organization have all the necessary materials and equipment to do the job;
- making sure that staff know what to do and how to do it;
- encouraging self-motivation and development.

In Chapter 6 we looked at the physical aspects of working conditions with a view to increasing efficiency. These physical aspects included location and layout, safety and health, ergonomic issues and methods of simplifying work. If the physical aspects are not right – that is, if the layout does not make it easy to be efficient – if conditions are uncomfortable, and if the work includes unnecessary steps, then it is not likely that staff will be motivated to extend themselves. Indeed, much of their energy will be used up in combating, or adapting to, the difficult conditions in which they are expected to work. In this chapter it is assumed that the physical aspects are right, and the non-physical or intangible aspects which will encourage self-motivation are considered.

The importance of motivated people

The importance of motivated staff can perhaps best be shown by example.

Example

In Chapter 2 we discussed what customers expect from a commuter bus service. We said that achieving specification, cost and timing would meet a customer's basic needs (safe journey from 'A' to 'B' at the right time and at a reasonable price). We also said that meeting basic expectations would not in itself be considered to be a 'quality' service. We said that on top of basic requirements customers would appreciate punctuality, a clean bus, a friendly, well-presented driver, and consistency of service. We agreed that cleaning the bus, issuing the driver with a smart uniform, and training the driver to be courteous and well groomed would incur some minimal costs, but that the overall perception to the customer would be an improved, or perhaps even a 'quality' service.

If drivers can be sufficiently motivated to think of the bus as being 'their' bus, then it is possible that much of what management would like – bus kept clean, timetable adhered to, friendly helpful service to customers and so on – can be gained at no extra ongoing cost to the organization. The only cost will be the investment in the time to change the culture of the organization. Once the culture is right no longer will the drivers think of their job as just a means to get a weekly pay packet; they will be proud of what they are doing, believe that their actions can make a difference and will constantly surprise management with their helpful suggestions.

An organization with motivated staff does not need service questionnaires filled out by customers. Unsolicited feedback from customers will all be positive.

Sounds too good to be true, doesn't it!

'Front-line' staff motivated by desire to serve

Many front-line staff in service industries enjoy customer contact, and generally prefer to be cheerful and helpful. They do their best to give good service. This attitude will often exist despite poor pay, indifferent working conditions and bad management. Social workers, teachers and nurses are obvious examples of people who have a desire to serve (even when their pay and conditions may be less than satisfactory). People who have a desire to serve are able, in their minds, to separate the employing organization from the customer. Thus good service is provided in some cases despite lack of resources, poor organization, or poor pay and working conditions, not for the benefit of the employer nor to please management, but purely from the personal satisfaction gained from meeting the needs of the customer.

Other front-line workers, such as restaurant waiting staff, might provide good service irrespective of poor pay and conditions, in the expectation that the customer will leave a reward (a tip) – the suggestion being that it is the expectation of a reward that encourages the serving staff to provide higher-level service. However, in some countries, such as Australia and New Zealand, tipping is not common and it is noticeable that restaurant service is every bit as good, if slightly less formal ('there yer go mate') than in countries where tipping is expected. This suggests that people who are drawn to front-line service genuinely like working with people and given the opportunity or encouragement prefer to give good friendly service, and that an extra reward is not necessary to motivate these people to give better service. But where a tip or other reward has become the custom it is not likely that people would remain motivated for long if tips suddenly stopped coming, and indeed the tip is regarded as part of their remuneration.

'Back-office' workers

Back-office service workers, such as clerical and administration support people, seldom come face-to-face with external customers and thus to a large extent lack the incentive of seeing or interacting with satisfied 'end-user' customers, or conversely of having to field the complaints of dissatisfied customers. Back-office staff therefore are less likely to be motivated by management pleas that customer satisfaction is important. Of course all workers, front and back office, will pay lip service to a credo of customer satisfaction; after all no one is going to say that customer satisfaction is anything but important. To a large extent it is on the efforts of back-office people that the overall efficiency and eventual customer satisfaction will rest. For example, in a restaurant, no matter how friendly the waiting staff, if the food is badly cooked the customer will rate the service as poor.

Thus front-line staff might provide reasonable service to customers, despite poor conditions and poor management, simply because they are people-oriented and like positive relations with the people whom they are serving; these types of people do not need management to tell them that the customer is important. On the other hand, back-office staff lacking direct customer contact are less likely to be motivated by a plea to provide customer satisfaction, even when management tries to promote the concept of internal customers. The internal customer theory is that within the organization the next person in the process is the customer. For example, a writer giving a manuscript to a word processor would, in theory, consider the word processor as the customer. Human nature being what it is, although the writer might even buy into this concept, the writer is still going to be irritated when work is not completed on time. Therefore, in reality, the writer will never truly consider the word processor to be the customer.

Motivation theories

As indicated in our introduction to this chapter an operations manager needs to have at least an understanding of the various motivational theories. However, it has to be remembered that theories are just that – and what will work for one person will not necessarily work for another.

Sometimes management does not understand that motivation is up to the individual. People motivate themselves; all management can do is to provide the environment to encourage self-motivation.

Economic man and scientific management

Scottish economist Adam Smith in 1776 (*The Wealth of Nations*) and F. W. Taylor, the late nineteenth-century American industrialist, both said that people are primarily motivated by money. This is known as the economic man principle. Both Smith and Taylor also studied the conditions necessary to allow workers to be efficient.

Adam Smith in a famous study on pin-making showed how division of labour (standard procedures and specialized work in a team situation) would dramatically increase productivity. His study showed that one man working on his own could scarcely make 20 pins a day whereas ten people working together, each with specialist tasks (division of labour) would make up to 48 000 pins a day! Of course the team would not make any pins at all unless it was worth their while (economic man principle).

Taylor is known as the father of scientific management. Taylor's approach to motivating people was to find by 'scientific' means the best way of doing a job. The best way included finding the right tools and the most efficient process. Once the best way was established it became the standard method. People were trained in the standard method and supervised to see that the method was kept to. Bonus payments were offered to encourage above-average performance (economic man approach). In one celebrated case, 'the Bethlehem Steel Works', Taylor reported that he was able to reduce the number of men in a gang shovelling coal and iron ore from 600 to 220 (increase productivity by 270 per cent), increase profit by 140 per cent and also increase the wages for each man (on average) by 65 per cent. This was achieved by experimenting with the length of the shovel handles and the size of the shovel. He found that a different shape and size of shovel was needed for coal from that required for shovelling iron ore. He therefore issued the men with a standard shovel for coal and a separate standard shovel for iron ore and had them trained in the easiest way to shovel. He also paid them an incentive to increase productivity. Prior to the study each man brought his own shovel to work and used the same shovel for coal and iron ore. Taylor also reported that each worker earned far more and that 'they were almost all saving money, living better, happier, they are the most contented set of [workers] seen anywhere'. Taylor's approach was for management to develop the best method with little, if any, input from the workers. (Management did the thinking and workers did what they were told, and were rewarded if they performed above a set standard.)

Today, over 225 years after Adam Smith, it is evident that productivity will increase if work processes are simplified and if people are trained to follow a standard process. To this extent the approaches of Smith and Taylor cannot be disputed, and neither can it be argued that people work for money. What can be questioned is that if people are encouraged to make suggestions and given a measure of autonomy will they take 'ownership' of a job and become more productive? It can also be questioned whether people can be motivated to be more efficient and customer-focused without being paid extra to do so.

Before these questions are answered it is necessary to discuss the importance of money.

Money: a necessity and a means of keeping the score

Our belief is that, depending on their circumstances, some people are motivated by money more than by anything else (people with children and mortgages need money – lots of it). Money is also a method of keeping the score – it is the one sure way of knowing if our efforts are appreciated. A pat on the back is nice, and so are kind words, but money is tangible – it is a certain measure of the value given to our efforts. There is also the question of equity. If we are being paid a certain amount for doing a job, even if initially we thought the pay was good, we would be less than human if we didn't get upset if we found a colleague was being paid substantially more. Our belief is that money is important, and it is more important for some people than it is for others.

Money is only one factor

We believe that if people are being paid a reasonable amount then it is possible to increase motivation without paying extra amounts, but, conversely, simply by paying more money increased productivity cannot be taken for granted. Money is important, but money alone is not the answer. All we can be certain of is that the amount paid must be reasonable, and must be equitable.

Need theories

Motivational theorists fall into two broad schools: those that state people are motivated by the desire to satisfy internal needs, and those that state people react to external stimuli.

Hierarchy of needs

Abraham Maslow (1943), a clinical psychologist, claimed that people have five levels of needs and that each level has to be covered before the next level can be addressed.

- Level 1 (the lowest) is physiological and includes food, water, shelter and so on.
- Level 2 is safety needs which include a desire to feel secure and free from threats to existence.
- Level 3 is the need to belong, which includes being accepted in a group of people.
- Level 4 is self-esteem – this includes feeling positive about yourself and being recognized by others for our achievements.
- Level 5 (the highest) is self-actualization, which roughly translated means development of our capabilities so that we reach our full potential.

Maslow accepted that each level did not have to be completely fulfilled before people moved on to the next level, but that until a level had been substantially covered it was unlikely that people would address a higher level in the hierarchy of needs. In prosaic terms, if you are grubbing around in the gutter for fag-ends, wondering when the soup kitchen will open, you are not interested that the ballet company is offering free tickets to the first twenty people who arrive.

It should be noted that Maslow's hierarchy-of-needs model was developed from a very small sample. (He observed fourteen close friends and studied the lives of nine famous people – including Lincoln, Jefferson, Eleanor Roosevelt, Einstein and Sweitzer.) His theory has often been questioned because of this lack of depth in his research.

Two-factor theory

Following Maslow's line of reasoning, Herzberg (1966, 1968) developed a two-factor theory based on satisfiers and dissatisfiers (or motivation and hygiene factors). Herzberg's theory (like Maslow's) is that until the lower-level needs – the hygiene factors – are covered then the higher-level satisfier factors will not motivate. Roughly translated hygiene factors include:

- adequate wages;
- safe working conditions;
- job security;
- non-threatening supervision and control.

Motivators are the higher-level needs and include:

- recognition;
- responsibility;
- the importance of the work;
- prospects for growth and advancement.

Herzberg's initial study was based on questioning 200 accountants and engineers in the United States. The study was therefore not based on the typical worker (accountants and engineers would of course have been well above the national average for wages and working conditions).

Nonetheless the theory does merit consideration. For example, using Herzberg's approach it might be considered that spending money on improving the staff cafeteria in itself will not motivate people to work harder if they have little responsibility. (The cafeteria would be considered a hygiene factor, and increased responsibility would be seen as a motivational factor.) On the other hand, responsibility and recognition of achievements might not motivate if people feel that their pay is inadequate or if there are threats of redundancies. Thus being asked to accept extra responsibility without extra benefits might only be seen as an attempt by management to give the recipient extra work (job enlargement rather than job enrichment).

Expectancy theory

Victor Vroom (Vroom *et al.*, 1973, 1988) argued that people are motivated by expectations, and performance is linked to the assessment of the probability that increased performance will lead to increased rewards: rewards may be extrinsic, that is, money and promotion; or intrinsic, that is, sense of achievement. Bateman and Zeithaml (1993) added that the assessment of whether the rewards will be sufficient to induce increased performance depends on self-evaluation of own abilities and the availability of necessary resources.

In other words, unless the chances of success, and consequent rewards, are reasonable, people will not be motivated to make an extra effort. (It won't be worth their while.)

All the above theories are cognitive theories, that is they are concerned with people's thought processes an as an explanation of behaviour.

Reinforcement theory

The other broad school of thought is that people's behaviour can be conditioned by external stimulus and there is no need to seek cognitive explanations. B. F. Skinner (1971) claimed that if good behaviour is rewarded and poor behaviour punished, people will be conditioned to act in a positive rather than a negative manner. An example would be if a worker stayed until midnight to complete some urgent work and was subsequently given favourable recognition. It is likely that that person would be encouraged to act in this way again. If, however, the worker was criticized for some minor error then the worker might feel that the effect of staying on late resulted in a negative outcome and consequently would be less willing to put in extra effort on a future occasion.

Skinner's theories were based on tests with rats and pigeons. One experiment included rats in a maze; if the rat took the right option it received a reward in the form of food, if it took the wrong action it received an electric shock. It was found that it did not take long for the rats to learn the correct route, and rewards and shocks were no longer necessary. This approach, reward and punishment, is also known as reinforcement theory.

The one common thread that all these theories have is that people's behaviour is goal-directed.

Combined approach

It is probable that most people have many needs:

- To have a job that pays enough to meet personal commitments (family, mortgage, social activities).
- To be in a job they like.
- To feel they belong.
- To have the opportunity of increasing self-esteem (important job, status and responsibility).
- To feel comfortable that they can do the job.
- To have job security.
- To have sufficient leisure time to enjoy/follow personal interests.

Work a necessity?

For most people work is not the be-all and end-all but a necessity. To achieve personal needs people need adequate wages and job security, and it seems obvious that ideally if they have to work, people would prefer to do something they enjoy, and to be given some authority (sense of belonging) and recognition for skill and above-average effort (esteem factor). It would be reasonable to suppose that people will not be motivated to make an extra effort if they think the job is beyond their scope or if the chances of success are limited. It would also seem that people can be conditioned to act in certain ways by reward or punishment. I would suggest however that people, rather than acting as robots as a result of conditioning, are aware (cognizant) of likely outcomes (rewards/punishments) and consider likely consequences before they act. I know that I do, and I am sure that you do!

The above would seem to cover the reasons why people work and what they would like in a job, but it does not necessarily follow, given the individuality of people, that even if all the above factors are taken into consideration, people will necessarily be motivated to be more efficient, to make suggestions or to go out of their way to provide extra service for customers. I could give plenty of examples of well-rewarded middle managers with autonomy to make decisions who do not appear to be overly motivated. To achieve a situation where every worker in the organization is excited about what the organization is doing and willingly puts in extra effort, requires a special type of organizational culture.

Culture

Organizational culture is the amalgam of beliefs, norms and values of the individuals making up the organization ('the way we do things around here'). Organizations are made up of many individuals, each with their own set of values. The culture of the organization is how people react or do things confronted with the need to make a decision. If the organization has a strong culture then each individual will know instinctively how things are done and what is expected. Conversely, if the culture is weak, people may not react in the manner in which management would hope.

The value to an organization of a dedicated, enthusiastic workforce cannot be underestimated. Such a culture begins with everyone in the organization, from the chief to the cleaner, believing in what the organization is trying to achieve. This means that not only is every person customer-focused, but each person is determined to eliminate any cost that is not adding value. For this culture to exist there are several prerequisites, and these prerequisites apply to everyone in the organization. As already discussed in this chapter:

- Working conditions have to be right (location, layout and process).
- Wages and rewards have to be equitable.
- There has to be job security.
- Staff must have a chance for self-development (self-esteem).
- Staff must feel 'good' about the job: it has to be meaningful.

And as discussed in earlier chapters:

- Everyone in the organization has to know who the customer is and ideally know what the customer values.
- The level of service which the organization is aiming to provide must be known by all.
- Service has to be affordable and sustainable.
- Service has to be consistent, and standards need to be set and communicated to maintain a consistent level.
- Controls have to be in place to ensure that the standards are being met.

- People must know how to make corrections.
- People must know their individual level (limit) of authority for taking action.

Finally, but importantly, everyone must feel free to make suggestions, and management must listen and treat suggestions with respect. Management must give more than lip-service to the above; they must passionately believe in the capabilities of their staff, and show this by their actions. This does not mean that management abdicates responsibility. Far from it! Management still has to make the important decisions and set the policy. Staff will be expected and encouraged to contribute to policy, but once a policy decision has been made, workers have to conform to the policy. Policy cannot be changed at the whim of individual people! Such actions would lead to chaos. In summary:

- Objectives must be clearly communicated.
- Management sets policy and guidelines.
- Staff have freedom to act within the guidelines.
- People are encouraged to make suggestions to change policy.

Bureaucratic culture

In a bureaucratic culture, some people (management) do the thinking, and workers do what they are told. In this type of culture the bigger the organization, the more rules and procedures will be required and control will be achieved by supervision and reports. In this type of culture, communication is one-way, top-down. Such a culture is sterile, and fosters a nine-to-five attitude (sign on at nine in the morning and leave promptly at five in the afternoon). Staff will pay lip-service to service and customer satisfaction, but will not have the authority, let alone the motivation, to actually provide above-average service, for to do so will result in breaking rules and the possibility of a reprimand.

Open culture

An open culture is where management is highly visible and approachable, there are few rules and procedures and the staff know instinctively what is right and what has to be done to correct a situation. The 'way we do things around here' is second nature, not just a slogan or a mission statement. People have authority to act and are self-motivated. Chapter 12 discusses how to engineer a quality culture.

Mission statements

Where the culture has been bureaucratic, and staff have a nine-to-five mentality, then to change the culture will require a major effort. Research (Wright, 1996) has found that major change can begin with the issuing of a mission statement. The mission statement, however, must be more than mere words or clichés such as 'People are our most valuable resource, we will provide excellent world-class service'. The sentiments cannot be argued, but like any platitude they are only words – 'full of sound and fury signifying nothing'.

The fad over recent years has been for new chief executives to feel it is mandatory to issue a new mission statement with the ostensible reason of communicating a change of direction. In this sense, the mission is given as a statement of *where* we are going (the vision) and *how* (the strategy) we are going to get there. But often the real reason for the new statement is for the new chief executive to establish authority, (the 'I'm the new boss, and things are going to change around here' syndrome). Sadly, from a study of over 1000 mission statements, I have come to the conclusion that most mission statements are mere rhetoric, full of sound and fury, and signify nothing.

To be meaningful a mission statement has to give the 'vision' – where we are going; and the strategy – how we are going to get there. To be successful the mission statement has to be in tune with what the staff believe and want to do. The mission has to reflect 'the way we do things around here'.

Your turn!

Write a mission statement for an ambulance service.

A mission statement for an ambulance service might read 'To provide a quick response, first aid and transport service for the sick and injured' – this is the central vision of the mission. The statement might continue to include a strategic element along the lines of 'To operate from a central location, to be on call 24 hours a day, to have well-maintained vehicles and equipment, to have well-trained staff, to network with hospitals, police and the fire service'.

Thus, as shown in this example, the mission statement shows what is going to be done and who it is being done for (the central vision) and outlines how it will be done (the strategy). There is no need for statements such as 'To be the world's best', or 'We value our staff'. These will be embodied in the culture of the organization and do not need to be put into words.

Mission – only the beginning

A well-written mission statement gives a clear statement of vision and strategy which will give the people of the organization a focus, and provide the reason-for-being for the organization. The mission statement is, however, only the beginning – albeit an important beginning.

Having established the mission the chief executive must show a real desire to involve all levels of staff in the decision-making of the organization. As previously stated, this does not mean an abdication of responsibility; the chief executive will always be the person who is accountable for the success or otherwise of the organization.

Leadership

Getting effective decision-making down to the lower levels of the organization requires the creation of the right structure so that people can get involved, can become committed and are able to make things happen. This can never happen with a centralized bureaucratic structure. The flatter the structure, the closer the leader will be to the real workers; that is, the people who are actually involved in adding value in the process, rather than those who are administering and regulating. A true leader creates leaders, whereas a manager tries to retain control and in doing so creates or perpetuates a culture of compliance and conformance. To become a leader, rather than a manager, requires a major paradigm change. 'Real leaders communicate face-to-face not by memos.' Organization structure and change management are further developed in Chapter 15.

Accepting responsibility

For an organization to change from a top-down bureaucratic culture to an open culture requires managers to trust the workers. For some managers the giving up of 'power' will be extremely difficult to handle. But it is just as difficult for those who have been used to receiving orders and being told what to do to accept responsibility. It has to be accepted that some people prefer to be told what to do and are not comfortable with making decisions and accepting responsibility. Empowerment is a two-way street; managers have to be prepared to let go and trust, and workers have to be prepared to accept responsibility. As Schein (1988, 1991) points out, any change process involves not only learning something new, but unlearning something that is already present. Chapter 15 is our 'change' chapter and discusses the management of change.

Learning programmes

Human resource management can create real strategic advantage by proper planning for people with the right skills and calibre to suit the corporate strategy. If it is recognized that 'people make things happen', then there will be a continuous need for recruitment, training and development of the workforce at all levels. Schonberger (1986) describes training as the catalyst for change programmes such as total quality management – TQM (the TQM philosophy is explained in Chapter 13). Related to this, education and training are critical components of an empowered work environment.

Basu and Wright (1998) discuss a status distinction between the terms 'training' and 'education'. For example, training is associated with imparting skills (how to do) and education with imparting knowledge (why it should be done). Training is thought of as being needed by people at a lower level to yourself, and education is for your level and above (see also Tompkins, 1989). To overcome this implied snobbishness, many prefer to use the term 'learning' to cover both training and education. Learning includes the development of people in their career progression.

Learning programmes of a leading-edge organization should comprise five elements:

1. Continuous recruitment and development.
2. Annual appraisals.

3. Learning for a company-wide change programme.
4. Learning resources.
5. Learning performance.

1. Continuous recruitment and development

The development of people starts at the recruitment stage. Organizations, in the drive for efficiency and capitalizing on the benefits of technology today, require fewer people than previously but the people required do need greater knowledge and flexibility. The ability to attract high-calibre people is an indication of the future of an organization. A recognized world-class organization will attract high-calibre people. The recruitment policy of a leading organization will seek high qualifications at the entry level. For example, as a minimum requirement a management trainee should have a degree, with above-average grades, from a reputable university. All other staff should have a polytechnic or equivalent diploma in a suitable discipline.

2. Annual appraisals

World-class organizations take time to consider development plans each year in order to respond to changing needs.

The learning programmes for staff should include appraisal procedures. Key people should be given the opportunity to move to higher levels, provided that they have the skills, experience and performance requirements. A well-administered and fair appraisal system which includes a personal development plan will help an organization to gain a competitive edge. An ineffective appraisal scheme will lead to dissatisfaction and cynicism, and will do more harm than good. On the other hand, when the scheme contains agreed objectives based on measurable parameters and the appraiser is impartial, the scheme can be effective for identifying the development needs of the staff member. The appraisal system loses its credibility when the agreed action points are not followed.

Any learning scheme should be well publicized and available to all staff.

3. Learning for a company-wide change programme

Change management and the need for change are covered in Chapter 15. Learning is an essential component of a company-wide change programme, whether it is TQM or a change of structure to empowered teams. Staff require learning opportunities in work process and analysis skills as well as so-called 'soft skills' such as inter-relating with team members. Managers need to learn how to make the transition from an out-of-date autocratic management role to that of coach and mentor. The learning for all employees and managers must extend beyond skills and include learning about the need for 'cultural' change. It is essential to generate trust between all members by following the same learning process.

4. Learning resources

The investment made by an organization in continuous learning includes money, time, key personnel and facilities.

A learning organization will allow the time required for both on-the-job and off-the-job learning for each employee. The total time will be variable depending on the change programmes of a particular company.

Example

Bell Canada allocate fifteen days per year for training for each person, and budget accordingly (Ruth Wright, 1995).

Consideration should be given to a budget for learning programmes, and the measurable cost of training and education should be expressed as a percentage of annual sales. Basu and Wright (1998) say 'The amount allowed should be no less than 0.5 per cent of sales and in some companies it is reported to be 2.0 per cent of sales'.

The use of a third party for specialist learning is usually successful. Each manager, supervisor and team leader should have responsibilities for the training of their own personnel. In addition, a senior manager should have the responsibility of co-ordinating the continuous learning programmes of an organization. (For smaller organizations this responsibility might be coupled with other responsibilities.)

Ideally an organization will have dedicated learning facilities including a learning centre, equipped with personal computers, appropriate training videos, presentation facilities and a library of relevant management books, periodicals and internal reports as a source of self-education and information.

5. Learning performance

The effectiveness of the education and training programmes of a company is usually assessed in terms of input as it is not easy to measure their output. The input measures are often expressed as:

- Number of learning hours per employee.
- Learning expenditures as percentage of annual sales (as discussed above up to 2.0 per cent of sales).
- Number of courses and seminars conducted.

Staff turnover is an indirect output measure of learning performance. A well-structured management development programme, and a reputation as an organization which provides good learning opportunities, will attract high-calibre candidates to an organization. A learning programme must be integrated with career development. If the management approach to human resources is well defined and considered, then most staff will repay their learning with longer service to the company. When a company loses people soon after they have been trained, then it may have got its training right but everything else is wrong.

Another assessment of learning performance involves the accreditation of learning programme against national standards. One such scheme is 'Investor in

People' in the UK. The scheme comprises four principles of employee development standards set by the Department of Education and Employment:

1. A commitment from the top to develop all employees.
2. Regular reviews of learning and development needs.
3. Actions to train and develop individuals throughout their employment.
4. Evaluation of achievement in learning and development.

The assessment indicators stem directly from the standard. If a company measures up to the National Standard as assessed by Training and Enterprise Councils (TECs), then it receives an accreditation certificate of 'Investor in People'.

The drive to continuously acquire new knowledge and transfer it into skilled people to achieve its business objective is the fundamental spirit of a learning organization. A learning organization is a leading organization.

Chapter summary

In this chapter we began by saying that people are an important resource, and like all resources the operations manager must manage people so as to get the most out of them. We showed that if people can be motivated, then they will be an extremely valuable resource; but it was stressed that management cannot motivate – people are self-motivated. All management can do is provide the correct environment for self-motivation. Such an environment includes getting the physical aspects of location, layout and process 'right', and having known standards and known levels of individual authority. The importance of money was discussed and it was suggested that provided that the money paid is sufficient and equitable, people can be self-motivated if the culture of the organization is positive. A positive culture is where the members of the organization, from the most senior person to the most junior person, believe in what the organization is doing, there is open communication, and every day each person strives to do the best for the organization. The importance of a mission statement was discussed, especially where a change in culture is required. Finally the need for annual appraisals aimed at the development of people, and the need for continuous learning, was stressed.

Case Study *John Smith meets McDonald's*

The case study used to illustrate the importance of setting standards, enthusing people, and the provision of learning programmes is McDonald's. The setting is initially Hong Kong but then moves to London.

Question

Consider the various references in the case to worldwide consistency for products and services. Discuss how McDonald's sets and controls standards for products and services and how their people management practices support these.

Hong Kong, July last year

John realized that the tram was going in the wrong direction, it was heading to Causeway Bay whereas he wanted to go towards Happy Valley. He pushed his way to the front and jumped off at the next stop, somewhere in the Wan Chai District. Although it was only 9 am he reckoned that the temperature must be in the high 30s and goodness knows what the humidity factor was. His shirt was already wringing wet with perspiration. John felt the need to sit down and to get his bearings, and looked round for somewhere out of the sun and out of the way of pedestrians. He then realized that he was standing outside a McDonald's.

Although he had seen several McDonald's in London – there was one at Charing Cross which he passed twice a day – he had never been inside one. But seeing one now in Hong Kong, a familiar name standing out against all the confusing signs in Chinese characters, was very comforting. John didn't hesitate, went straight inside and sat down at the nearest table. He looked around and was pleasantly surprised with what he saw and experienced. First, the place was very clean; there were two staff members clearing and cleaning tables and continuously sweeping the floor. Second, the seating was comfortable. And third, the menu with prices including special 'menus' was clearly displayed. As an accountant it was second nature for him to convert the prices from Hong Kong dollars to pounds sterling, and he was impressed with how reasonable the prices were.

John, accustomed to the time it took to be served in fish and chip shops back in England, had planned to make an order and go to the washroom and have a wash while the food was being prepared. From watching other customers he realized that this wasn't going to be practical as it seemed that the food was arriving freshly prepared to coincide with the arrival of customers. John watched in fascination for 15 minutes and at no stage did a customer have to wait for more than two minutes, and there were never more than two people in each of the eight or so queues at any time.

Finally John went to the washroom and had a wash before making an order. He was impressed with the cleanliness of what was obviously a frequently used facility. Later he was equally impressed with the very good quality of his 'Big Mac' and French Fries.

Singapore three days later

Three days later in Singapore, not far from the Raffles hotel, John noticed a McDonald's. He turned to Mr Lee and said 'Have you ever been to McDonald's? I went to one in Hong Kong, a most impressive place, you should see how they make those hamburgers. Come on, lets have lunch in McDonald's, my treat'.

Once inside John eagerly looked around and was pleased to see that this McDonald's was every bit as good as the one he had visited in Hong Kong. Cleanliness, friendly service and excellent value-for-money food, it was all there. He had wondered if Hong Kong was a 'one off' experience. Mr Lee didn't like to embarrass his young English colleague by telling him that he frequently had a meal at McDonald's, not this particular one but the one in the lower end of Orchid Road.

Six months later

The Head Office of John's company announced a restructuring and offered a voluntary redundancy package. John went home that evening to his apartment in South West London (Battersea) and over supper said to his partner, 'Susan, I think I'll take the redundancy offer and set up a McDonald's here in Battersea. Look at all the flats and apartments around here, there has to be a good opportunity. I am surprised that someone hasn't opened one already.'

Susan smiled and said, 'You are certainly

keen on McDonald's. Since you visited Asia, I think you must have taken me to every one in London, and I must agree each is as good as the other. It really is amazing how they get such a consistent quality and high level of service. Go on, have a look into it, but I'll stay with my job and don't expect me to fill in during the late night shift if you are short of staff!'

One week later

John has in front of him a pile of research material that he has gathered concerning McDonald's, including a booklet from the Head Office of McDonald's Restaurants Limited in London. He is explaining to Susan how McDonald's is able to get the same consistency of service and product quality around the world. 'At McDonald's nothing happens by accident. The recipe for the hamburger, the standards for the ingredients, the procedure for preparation, the service levels, the length of customer queues, the shape and size of the scoop for the French fries, and even what the serving staff say to customers has been pre-planned in Chicago, (USA). Every recipe and every task has been carefully analyzed, tested and designed. Every employee is expected to perform their tasks according to the job description and manual of procedures, and every hamburger and milkshake from Estonia to Edinburgh, from Hong Kong to Honolulu, from Peking to Paris has to reach the same world class standard.'

Susan replies that this sounds rather like old-fashioned 'Taylorism', 'with management doing the thinking and workers doing what they are told'. She adds, 'It is hard to understand how it could be that in all the McDonald's you have visited, from Wan Chai to Wimbledon, staff were enjoying what they were doing and even seemed to mean it when they told you to have a nice day. I wouldn't have thought it would be easy to instil such a cheerful culture when everything seems to be so pre-planned with little scope for individuality.'

John's reply is: 'My research shows that at McDonald's crews are taught not just to follow the standards, which are important, but they are shown why they are important. In the United Kingdom alone there are 800 restaurants and two million customers. These customers trust McDonald's to provide them with food of a high standard, quick service and value for money. They know before they walk into the restaurant exactly what the menu will be and what they will get. McDonald's crew members understand the need to provide this consistency, and they understand that the standard set is for worldwide consistency. McDonald's staff therefore not only follow the rules but are aware of the corporate values of quality, service and teamwork. They don't just follow the book, they have a strong motivation to reach and maintain individual high standards. Crew members are encouraged to work their way through a development programme into management. Unlike traditional 'Taylorism' the culture at McDonald's is very much customer led.'

Susan wonders 'How does such a large organization control suppliers, and more importantly the consistency of materials?' John answers 'McDonald's has three pillars supporting its business structure. One is the suppliers, the second is the owner/operator franchisees, and the third is McDonald's Systems. McDonald's Systems provides starting up instructions, operations procedures, specifications for food and other supplies, and performance measurements. Each country or state has its own division of McDonald's Systems, and it is Systems that negotiate and primarily communicate with suppliers. Suppliers often attend conferences with owner/operators, but owner/operators in the main deal through Systems regional warehouses when ordering supplies. Systems are also responsible for keeping owner/operators up-to-date with information as well as keeping suppliers up-to-date. For example, Systems have specialists in each field. The potato specialists inform suppliers and owner/operators on developments in potatoes and the preparation of French fries.' John

▶

adds that Susan might be interested to know that McDonald's and McDonald's Systems do not have formal contracts with suppliers, although many suppliers in various parts of the world supply only McDonald's. Business is done often on the shake of the hand. And, in addition to co-ordinating and informing suppliers, Systems maintains quality standards worldwide. This includes frequent visits, some not announced, to restaurants to check on quality standards and cleanliness.

Susan says 'But all this constant checking and supervision still reminds me of the bureaucratic approach of Taylor and surely this must lead to a sterile do-as-you-are told culture.'

John agrees that McDonald's does have tough standards and strong corporate values which members are encouraged to buy into, but adds that the culture is such that crew members are doubly motivated to do well. As an example he cites the annual McDonald Olympics where crews from around the world compete to make the best hamburger and so on, and winners are rewarded with Olympic-style gold medals. Thus members operate to the set procedures and standards, but members are personally highly motivated to maintain and reach the very highest standards.

John refers to page 24 of the booklet he had received from McDonald's Restaurants Ltd (London) and says 'Training is an important aspect of McDonald's commitment to their staff and to the organization's central focus of customer satisfaction. In England the company has recently upgraded its training programme for three core customer care posts – a customer care manager, assistant and children's party manager for each restaurant. This training teaches the difference between meeting basic customer expectations and delivering outstanding service. Staff who demonstrate "people skills", that is, people who are genuinely interested in people, are selected for these dining area positions where they are in close contact with customers. McDonald's expect their people to be motivated and customer focused.'

Thoughtfully John concludes 'I think the difference is that with "Taylorism" the process is designed around the technical competence of the organization with efficient use of resources as the prime focus. Whereas with McDonald's the culture is very much customer focused – this is the essential difference.'

Written by J. Nevan Wright © Henley Management College 1999

IV Part Four

This Part considers the six key operational issues of:

- demand and forecasting;
- capacity management;
- scheduling of activities;
- materials management and the extended supply chain;
- e-business and B2B alliances;
- project management.

The objective of capacity management is to have sufficient capacity to meet the organization's needs as determined in the business policy. The business policy determines what level of service will be provided to the customer. The business policy might well be full utilization of resources and to accept that, on some occasions, customers will queue and some customers may be lost to the system; thus customers' needs may not always totally coincide with the business policy. Part of the responsibility of the operations manager will be to determine:

- What resources are needed overall?
- What can be achieved with existing resources (feasibility)?
- The allocation of resources on a day-to-day basis in the most efficient way possible to achieve the policy of the organization.

Knowing what the capacity is – feasibility – is one side of the equation; the other side is knowing what is required – demand. Forecasting demand is therefore an important element of capacity management. **Chapter 8** begins this Part with an introduction to methods of forecasting demand and examines capacity management – a critical area for the operations manager.

Equally critical is the planning and timing of activities (scheduling) which is considered in **Chapter 9**. Likewise, what is feasible and what is desirable influences how activities are scheduled. Scheduling feasibility is mainly limited by the system structure, and influenced by what is desired by business policy and operational objectives.

Much of what is identified in the strategy of scheduling also applies to materials management (**Chapter 10**) and to the understanding and control of the extended supply chain (**Chapter 11**). The supply chain approach discussed in Chapter 11 encompasses the flow of processing of inputs through the system to the delivery of service to the customer. The flow of information and e-business is shown to be a crucial issue in modern day supply-chain management. **Chapter 12** considers a project management approach to planning and scheduling of activities, and considers project management for change.

8 Capacity management

Objectives

This chapter considers:

- Establishing demand and forecasting techniques.

- Types of forecasts.

- Capacity management and capacity management strategies.

- Practical day-to-day capacity management techniques.

Establishing demand and forecasting techniques

Events as important as numbers

Forecasting is used by various functions, for example the marketing function forecasts sales (the annual marketing plan), accountants forecast expenses (the budget) and the meteorological department forecasts the weather. Funny how none of them ever get it quite right!

The reason why it is so difficult for forecasts to be totally accurate is that although expected trends can be factored into the calculations, the basic information used is drawn from what has happened in the past. In considering the past, numbers alone are not sufficient, as the numbers will merely be a reflection of a variety of circumstances that influenced or determined the outcome. Establishing circumstances, or events that shaped past demand, will not always be easy as there can be no guarantee that all the circumstances of the past will be remembered or that they will occur in exactly the same way again in the future. The danger for statisticians and researchers is to concentrate on the numbers and to ignore the circumstances.

For some types of demand forecasting, seasonal trends and so on might well be sufficient to provide a reasonably accurate forecast. In other cases, and this is especially relevant to service industries, demand will often depend on a myriad of circumstances and events.

Capacity forecasts

Capacity decisions use forecasts at several different levels. Long-range capacity planning requires forecasts to be made several years ahead; this would include forecasts of capacity requirements for facilities. Short- to medium-term forecasts usually span two to three years, and are typically used to determine personnel and training needs, renting of premises and equipment, and details of service and products. In the immediate short term, forecasts are needed to plan, order and allocate resources on a monthly, weekly and daily basis. The shorter the time frame, the more accurate the forecast has to be.

Types of forecasts

There are three ways of looking at forecasts: the qualitative approach, the mathematical or time series approach, and the causal approach. In reality all three are interlinked and should be taken into account when determining a forecasted demand figure.

Qualitative forecasting

Qualitative forecasting uses judgement, past experience and existing past and present data. Due to the implicit nature of qualitative forecasting, two seemingly equally knowledgeable people given the same information are likely to arrive at different results. Because much forecasting is based on the past we must accept that to predict the future will require a certain amount of judgement of what the circumstances will be, and which circumstances from the past are relevant to the present. If forecasting on past results and based on current conditions was easy, the book-makers would soon be out of business!

Example

Past statistics show that our local football team has always won on its home ground. This does not prove that it will win next time they play at home.

Last spring our sales were twice that of the winter period. Further examination of the figures might show that this has been the trend for the last three years, i.e. spring sales double that of winter sales. However, the circumstances existing each spring might well have affected the results. For example, in the spring of the first year we launched a new service or product which had a short-lived success. In the second year our main competitor went out of business towards the end of the winter and our sales increased by default. In the third year, due to tough new competition, we were forced to cut prices and to advertise heavily to get the sales. The figures on their own could be misleading if we were not aware of all the other relevant factors. Knowing which of the factors to include and which to discount in forecasting the future requires knowledge of what happened and judgement as to what is relevant.

The best-known methods of qualitative forecast are:

- Expert opinion.
- Market surveys.
- Life cycle analysis.
- Time series forecasting.

Expert opinion

Delphi method

The Delphi method is considered by many to be the most successful of the qualitative methods. It is time-consuming and costly, and best used by large organizations. (The Delphi method was developed by the Rand Corporation and is named after the ancient Greek oracle.) The method uses a set of questions to a group of managers or 'experts' who, working without collusion, give their individual opinions. The opinions are then tabulated by a co-ordinator, and if individual results differ significantly, the results are fed back (names are not revealed) to the panel with a further set of questions. The process is repeated until consensus is reached. Questions and feedback generally continue for four rounds with the questions becoming more specific with each round. The benefit of the method is that a group opinion can be achieved without the team meeting together. The weakness of a face-to-face group meeting is that members might be swayed (group dynamics and team-think) by a dominant member, or perhaps an 'expert' member may be embarrassed to back down from a publicly stated opinion. The Delphi method has also been unkindly described as 'pooled ignorance' as the tendency is for the feedback questions to force a convergence towards the group centre.

Salesforce and 'jury of executives'

Two other 'expert' methods are:

- to invite the salesforce to give their opinions;
- the 'jury of executives' approach.

The problem with salesforce opinions is that they are likely to be influenced by recent events (memory and sometimes experience is short) and, as would be expected from salespeople, their forecasts tend to be optimistic (nobody hires negative salespeople – do they?).

The 'jury of executives' approach involves the averaging of independent estimates from a panel of company experts and sometimes from people from outside the organization. The danger of any panel approach is that a dominant person, or one who is best able to present their ideas, is likely to sway the other members of the panel.

The advantage of all the expert-opinion approaches is the use of experience and judgement of several experts and the obtaining of various points of view.

Market surveys

Surveys can be carried out by phone, personal interview and by mail. Market surveys use two approaches: a structured approach and an unstructured approach.

With the structured approach the survey uses a formal list of questions; the unstructured approach lets the interviewer probe and perhaps guide the respondent.

The framing of questions is an art. The key is to establish from the outset exactly what information is wanted, and then to design questions which will give the information required. Questions which are not relevant to the issue are a waste of time and money. Other problems are that sometimes people are unable to answer survey questions because they have never thought about what they do and why; or they may be unwilling to answer questions that they consider personal. Others might feel obliged to give an answer rather than appear uninformed even when they don't know or don't understand the question; or they might even try and help the interviewer by giving what they think are the required answers. Kotler (1997: 120) gives the following advice when creating questionnaires: 'Carefully choose the questions and their form, wording and sequence. A common error is including questions that cannot, would not, or need not be answered and omitting questions that should be answered. Questions that are merely interesting should be dropped because they exhaust the respondent's patience.'

Additionally the form of question asked can influence the response, and Kotler goes on to distinguish between open-ended and closed questions. Open-ended questions allow respondents to answer in their own words, whereas closed questions ask respondents to select an answer from a given list of answers. An easy form of market survey includes group interviewing or focus groups. With the focus group approach six to ten people are invited from a market target group to a meeting. They are sometimes paid a small fee, the conditions are relaxed with refreshments and so on, and after the interviewer has set the scene it is hoped that group dynamics will bring out actual feelings and thoughts. At the same time the interviewer attempts to keep the discussion focused on the subject of the research. The concern with this approach is that too much can be read into the opinions of a small and non-random sample. To some extent this can be overcome by holding several focus group meetings on the same subject and then pooling the results.

Market surveys are generally not used for forecasting demand for capacity management; they are perhaps more appropriate to determine the shape or style of a new service, or to find out why an existing service is not performing as well as expected.

Life cycle analysis

The classic life cycle S curve is shown in Figure 8.1. It is generally accepted that products and services have a time-based life cycle. The launch stage has few sales, the growth stage shows a rapid increase in customers and at the maturity stage the demand will be relatively stable. For most types of services life cycles are readily predictable and the rate of growth/decline will not be dramatic. For services such as medical, educational, legal, commuter transport and so on, it is a moot point whether a life cycle exists; and if it does the extended length of the cycle and in particular the decline phase will be sufficiently obvious for demand forecasts to be adjusted. However, for retailers of some fast-moving consumer goods or fashion items, growth can be explosive and decline equally rapid. Other fast-moving consumables such as toothpaste, soap or baked beans only reach the decline stage if there is a dramatic change in technology, such as canned peas being replaced by frozen peas; but even then, once the decline has settled, there is still a demand (easily forecast) for canned peas. Experienced managers who have been involved with the introduction of new products can, often with a high degree of accuracy, forecast how long a fashion item will stay in each stage of the life cycle. If an organization is in a market with a defined life cycle then knowing where a product is on a life cycle will enable decisions to be made, such as stockpiling items in anticipation of a high demand in the growth stage.

Time series forecasting

Time series forecasting uses mathematical analysis of past demand trends to forecast future demand. The accuracy of a forecast will not be known until after the event. However, a particular method of forecasting can always be tested for past accuracy. Accuracy is usually monitored by the deviation of the actual result from the forecast result. Calculation of standard deviation, total absolute deviation and deviation spread is explained later in this section.

Short-term forecasting involves taking historical data of demand patterns from a few past periods and projecting these patterns into the future. The simplest method is to take the last period's actual demand and use it for the next period's forecast, as shown in Table 8.1.

The method gives a quick response to a trend; if the trend is upwards then the forecast will be upwards but lagging behind. If, however, there are marked seasonal fluctuations then this method would, following a buoyant autumn, forecast high winter sales, when in fact past history shows that winter sales will always be

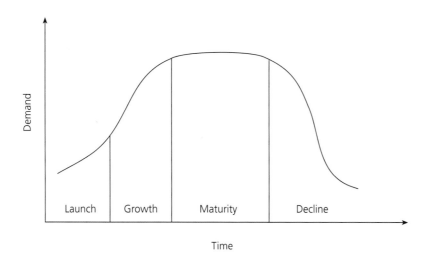

Figure 8.1

A product/service life cycle

Period	Actual	Forecast	Deviation	Table 8.1
Spring	20	–	–	
Summer	22	20	–2	
Autumn	23	22	–1	
Winter	18	23	+5	

Forecast from last period's actual

lower than autumn sales. In the above example, based on autumn sales actual results, the forecast for winter sales is 23 although past history shows that winter sales are always about 25 per cent below autumn sales.

Forecasting by past average

This method is to average the past results. The accuracy of the method is tested by the deviation from the actual (see Table 8.2).

Total Absolute Deviation (TAD) is the sum of all the deviations, ignoring plus or minus signs. Mean Absolute Deviation is the average of the deviations. In this example although there are twelve forecasts, there are only eleven deviations. 25/11 = 2.3 which is the Mean Absolute Deviation (MAD).

Periods 8 and 12 show large deviations from forecast to actual. If capacity had been arranged to meet the forecast demand of 21 then there would have been a shortfall for Period 8 of 16 per cent (4/25 × 100 = 16 per cent) and for Period 12 a shortfall of 15 per cent (4/26 × 100 = 15 per cent). Clearly in this case past average is not sufficiently reliable with this pattern of demand.

This method 'dampens' rapid responses when there are fluctuations, but it is slow to respond when there is a definite trend, either up or down. In the example, after Period 8 the trend is up but the forecast remains steady.

Forecasting by moving average

This method provides a reasonable response to trends, and also dampens fluctuations (see Table 8.3).

Calculations for the forecasts in this example were made by taking the previous three periods and dividing by three, e.g. the forecast for Period 10 is the sum of the

Table 8.2				
Forecasting by past average	Period	Actual demand	Forecast (average of all past actual)	Deviation (forecast to actual)
	1	20	nil	–
	2	18	20	+2
	3	22	19	–3
	4	23	20	–3
	5	21	21	0
	6	19	21	+2
	7	24	21	–3
	8	25	21	–4
	9	22	22	0
	10	23	22	–1
	11	25	22	–3
	12	26	22	–4
	13		22	

Total Absolute Deviation 25 (pluses or minuses are ignored)
Mean Absolute Deviation 2.3

Period	Actual	Forecast	Deviation	
				Table 8.3
1	20	–	–	
2	18	–	–	Forecasting by
3	22	–	–	moving average
4	23	20	–3	
5	21	21	0	
6	19	22	+3	
7	24	21	–3	
8	25	21	–4	
9	22	23	+1	
10	23	24	+1	
11	25	23	–2	
12	26	23	–3	
13		25		

Total Absolute Deviation 20
Mean Absolute Deviation 2.2

three previous periods divided by three, $24 + 25 + 22 = 71$, $71/3 = 23.7$, which rounds up to 24.

The number of periods used for averaging is a matter of judgement. If there are definite cycles the number of periods in the cycle can be used to determine the number of periods used for averaging. In our example the last two periods in each group of four have the higher demands (in the first four periods, 3 and 4 are the highest; in the next group of four, 7 and 8 are the highest; and likewise so are 11 and 12 in the next group of four), thus a four-period average might prove to be more accurate. We will test this theory in Table 8.4.

The discerning reader will have noted that we have used the same 'actuals' for each of the last three methods of forecasting. If we compare the MADs we will see that the last method proved to be the more accurate for this set of figures.

However, for a true comparison, as there are only eight forecasts in the last method we should only compare MADs calculated on the last eight forecasts for each method.

Method 1: Past average will now show a MAD of $17/8 = 2.1$

Method 2: Three-period moving average, MAD $17/8 = 2.1$

Method 3: Four-period moving average, MAD $11/8 = 1.4$

This shows that, for this example, the four-period moving average has given the most accurate forecasts.

Seasonal adjustments

Where there are distinct seasonal trends then the forecast can be further refined by adjusting for seasonality.

Table 8.4	Period	Actual	Forecast (four-period average)	Deviation (forecast to actual)
Four-period moving average	1	20	–	–
	2	18	–	–
	3	22	–	–
	4	23	–	–
	5	21	21	0
	6	19	21	+2
	7	24	21	–3
	8	25	22	–3
	9	22	22	+0
	10	23	23	+0
	11	25	24	–1
	12	26	24	–2
	13		24	

Total Absolute Deviation 11
Mean Absolute Deviation 1.4

Table 8.5		Actual	Average for year	Seasonal factor (percentage of average)
Seasonal factors	**Year 2002**			
	Qtr One	20		96.4 (20 is 96.4% of 20.75)
	Qtr Two	18		86.75
	Qtr Three	22		106.0
	Qtr Four	23		110.85
		83	83/4 = 20.75	400
	Year 2003			
	Qtr One	21		94.3
	Qtr Two	19		85.4
	Qtr Three	24		107.9
	Qtr Four	25		112.4
		89	89/4 = 22.25	400
	Year 2004			
	Qtr One	22		91.7
	Qtr Two	23		95.8
	Qtr Three	25		104.2
	Qtr Four	26		108.3
		96	96/4 = 24	400

Let us assume that Period 1 is the first quarter of a year and Period 2 the second quarter and so on. We can then recalculate our forecasts as in Table 8.5. The next step is to average the seasonal factor for each season:

Year	2002		2003		2004				
Qtr One	96.40	+	94.3	+	91.7	=	282.40/3	=	94.1
Qtr Two	86.75	+	85.4	+	95.8	=	267.95/3	=	89.3
Qtr Three	106.00	+	107.9	+	104.2	=	318.10/3	=	106.0
Qtr Four	110.85	+	112.4	+	108.3	=	331.55/3	=	110.5

By taking the four-period moving average for the last four actual results, which is 24 (96/4 = 24) and applying the seasonal factors, the next four quarters can be forecast as in Table 8.6. This gives us the same total (96) for Year 05 as for Year 04. As there is an obvious upwards trend, this is not logical. We therefore add a trend factor to our calculations.

Table 8.6

Forecast for 2005

Year 05	Forecast	
Quarter One	24 × 94.1%	23
Quarter Two	24 × 89.3%	21
Quarter Three	24 × 106%	25
Quarter Four	24 × 110.5%	27
		96

Trend factor

The trend factor is obtained by calculating a time lag factor. The formula for the trend factor is (Number of periods of moving average –1) / 2 +1. In our example:

(4 – 1)	=	3.0
3 / 2	=	1.5
1.5 + 1	=	2.5

Therefore our time lag factor will be 2.5.

We now return to our four-period moving averages, calculate the trend between successive moving averages and multiply each trend by the time lag factor (Table 8.7).

98.125/4 gives an adjusted average quarter of 24.5. Using the adjusted average plus the seasonal fluctuations we can forecast for Year 05 as shown in Table 8.8.

We now have a forecast for the next twelve months (four quarters) which is seasonally adjusted and which has allowed for growth based on the past trend. Naturally as each new 'actual' comes to hand we recalculate our moving forecast.

The main weakness of the moving average method is that equal weight is given to each of the historical figures used, and it is also necessary to have, or to build up, a history of information to test against and to forecast from.

Another disadvantage is the number of calculations involved, although with a computer spreadsheet once the formula is entered (and proved) this is not as onerous as it once would have been.

Actual (a)	Moving average (b)× 2.5	Successive trend × 2.5		Time lag factor (c)	Adjusted average (a + c)
20					
18					
22					
23					
21	20.75				
19	21.00	+0.25			
24	21.25	+0.25			
25	21.75	+0.50			
22	22.25	+0.50			
23	22.50	+0.25	2.5	0.625	23.125
25	23.50	+1.00	2.5	2.500	26.000
26	23.75	+0.25	2.5	0.625	24.375
–	24.00	+0.25	2.5	0.625	24.625
					98.125

Table 8.7

Adjusted average

Table 8.8

Adjusted forecast 2005

Quarter One	98.125/4	=	24.5	×	94.1%	=	23
Quarter Two			24.5	×	89.3%	=	22
Quarter Three			24.5	×	106.0%	=	26
Quarter Four			24.5	×	110.5%	=	27
							98

A method known as exponential smoothing (see Table 8.9) overcomes some of these problems without losing any of the accuracy.

Exponential smoothing

Exponential smoothing requires only the previous forecast figure and the latest actual figure. It allows the forecast to respond to fluctuations but at the same time it maintains a level of stability.

We begin by calculating a smoothing constant. The formula for the smoothing constant is:

$$\frac{2}{N + 1}$$

N is the number of periods we wish to smooth. For example, if six was the number of periods the smoothing constant will be:

$$\frac{2}{6+1} = \frac{2}{7} = 0.28$$

For our example (see Table 8.9), we will use an exponential smoothing constant based on four periods:

$$\frac{2}{4+1} = \frac{2}{5} = 0.4 \text{ exponential smoothing factor}$$

The actual demand for the last period is multiplied by the factor, and the forecast for the last period is multiplied by the sum of 1 – the factor. In our case using a factor of 0.4 the actual for the last period is multiplied by 0.4 and the last forecast is multiplied by 0.6 (that is 1 – 0.4 = 0.6). Forecast calculations for each period use the previous period's actual and exponential smoothed figure.

Starting with Period 5: (For Period 6)	Actual 21 and forecast 21. As there is a Nil Deviation no smoothing is required, and thus for Period 6 the forecast will be 21.
For Period 7:	The actual was 19 and the forecast was 21. Using exponential smoothing for Period 7 the forecast is: 0.4 (19) + 0.6 (21) = 7.6 + 12.6 = 20.0
For Period 8:	0.4 (24) + 0.6 (20) = 9.6 + 12.0 = 21.6
For Period 9:	0.4 (25) + 0.6 (22) = 10.0 + 13.2 = 23.2
Period 10:	0.4 (22) + 0.6 (23) = 8.8 + 13.8 = 22.6
Period 11:	as no deviation to actual for Period 10, forecast is 23
Period 12:	0.4 (25) + 0.6 (23) = 10.0 + 13.8 = 23.8
Period 13:	0.4 (26) + 0.6 (24) = 10.4 + 14.4 = 24.8

This example is given to demonstrate the mechanics of exponential smoothing. The next steps are to add a trend factor and a seasonal factor to update the exponentially smoothed average. In a four-seasonal forecast, the factor for Period 5 when the actual is known will be upgraded to provide a new seasonal factor for Period 9 and so on; it is in effect a closed loop based on the past. The problem is in deciding values for the smoothing constants. Such decisions are often arbitrary, based on past experience, and tested against past information. Computer programs exist which will do this systematically and are found in cash-flow forecasting programs and in inventory control programs.

Finding trends

When looking at a column of figures it is difficult to visualize if there is an increasing or decreasing trend. A simple method of determining if there is a trend is to calculate a mean and then to calculate the variation from the mean for each period (see Table 8.10).

In our example the first four periods total 20 + 18 + 22 + 23 = 83, and

$$\frac{83}{4} = \text{a mean of 21.}$$

Table 8.9	Period	Actual	Forecast (four-period average)	Deviation (forecast to actual)	Exponential smoothed average	Deviation
Exponential smoothed average	1	20	–	–		
	2	18	–	–		
	3	22	–	–		
	4	23	–	–		
	5	21	21	–		
	6	19	21	+2	21	+2
	7	24	21	–3	20	–4
	8	25	22	–3	22	–3
	9	22	22	–	23	+1
	10	23	23	–	23	–
	11	25	24	–1	23	–2
	12	26	24	–2	24	–2
	13		24	–	25	–
	Total Absolute Deviation			11		14
	Mean Absolute Deviation			1.4		2

Table 8.10	Period	Actual	Cumulative difference from mean							
Trends	1	20	–1	(20 – 21)	= –1					
	2	18	–4	(18 – 21)	= –3	+	–1	=	–4	
	3	22	–3	(22 – 21)	= +1	+	–4	=	–3	
	4	23	–1	(23 – 21)	= +2	+	–3	=	–1	
	5	21	–1	(21 – 21)	= (0)	+	–1	=	–1	
	6	19	–3	(19 – 21)	= –2	+	–1	=	–3	
	7	24	0	(24 – 21)	= +3	+	–3	=	0	
	8	25	+4	(25 – 21)	= +4	+	(0)	=	+4	
	9	22	+5	(22 – 21)	= +1	+	+4	=	5	
	10	23	+7	(23 – 21)	= +2	+	+5	=	7	
	11	25	+11	(25 – 21)	= +4	+	+7	=	11	
	12	26	+15	(26 – 21)	= +5	+	+11	=	16	
	13									

We can now clearly see that from Period 8 onwards there is a marked upwards trend.

Causal

In forecasting it is easy to get caught up with the method of calculating and to overlook the purpose. The purpose is to get the best possible forecast of what might happen in the future. Therefore forecasts (calculated on past events) must be carefully considered against all the known facts of what is happening or is likely to happen. The state of the economy and key indicators such as interest rates, inflation rates, currency exchange rates, employment rates, and factors such as the entrance of new competitors, new technology and materials, fashion changes and planned marketing drives will all have causal effects on future results, irrespective of carefully calculated results based on the past. Likewise, past results should be examined to determine how they were affected (caused) by similar events. Knowing the causes for changes in demand is important.

Commonsense

The commonsense approach with forecasted figures is to test them by asking 'Are these figures sensible, what happened before and what is likely to happen in the future?' Once the future demand forecast has been agreed then the operations manager must determine the future capacity of the organization, and anticipate what changes might be needed to meet the level of forecasted demand.

Capacity management

Capacity management is a key planning responsibility of operations managers. As defined by Wild (2002) 'Capacity management is concerned with the matching of the capacity of the operating system and the demand placed on that system'.

Capacity management involves the study of anticipated demand patterns for the medium- to long-term, and the organizing of resources to meet this demand. The organizing of resources includes acquiring resources, training people and the development of strategies for meeting changes in demand.

Capacity planning and management

Figure 8.2 shows the relationship between the various stages in capacity planning and capacity management.

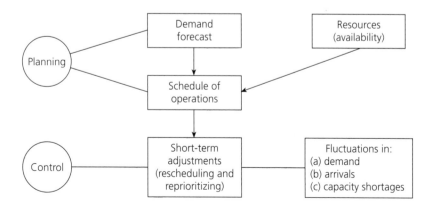

Figure 8.2

Capacity management

Measuring capacity

An organization has capacity if it has some of each of the resources required to carry out its function. For example, a bus service has capacity to transport a passenger if it has a bus with some empty seats, a driver, fuel, etc., but it must have some of each of the necessary resources (bus, seats, driver, fuel). In measuring capacity we concentrate on the key resource. The key resource is the most crucial resource for the provision of a service, and it may be determined by factors such as being the most costly, the most used, or the most in demand. Table 8.11 shows resources which are likely to be considered key resources.

Table 8.11	Service	Key resource
Measurement of capacity	School	Number of classrooms = limits number of students
	Hospital	Number of beds = limits number of admitted patients
	Professional practice:	
·	Dental, medical, legal, accounting, etc.	Number of professionals, dentists, lawyers, etc. and hours available
	Hairdresser	Number of chairs
	Restaurant	Number of tables
	Theatre/sports:	
	Arena	Number of seats
	Petrol station	Number of pumps
	Telesales	Number of phones
	Passenger service:	
	Airline/bus/train	Number of seats
	Retail shop	Shelf space
	Ice cream vendor	Capacity of refrigerator
	Accommodation:	
	Motel/hotel	Number of beds

Can service be stored?

In many service industries if capacity is not used when available, then that capacity is lost to the system. For example, aircraft seats cannot be stored; once an aircraft takes off with only half the seats occupied, although major costs have been incurred in providing the capacity, the empty seats have been lost to the system. The same applies for the theatre and sports events, professional consultants, hairdressers, restaurants, taxis, hotels and so on; service cannot be stored – without a customer the service capacity has been lost. In retail services the situation may be different; goods not sold today could well be sold tomorrow, the sale is not necessarily lost to the system (a customer might buy groceries only once a week and if the customer doesn't buy on their normal shopping day, then they will buy the next day, thus the supermarket's sales have not suffered for the week).

Controlling capacity

There are two basic approaches to controlling capacity: one is to manipulate capacity, the other is to manipulate demand. Most organizations will seek to match capacity and demand by a combination of both approaches.

Manipulating capacity

With the first approach, capacity is planned ahead to meet the expected demand, and if or when demand changes capacity is juggled to meet the new demand. If there is insufficient capacity, customers must either wait for service or customers will not wait and thus be lost to the system. If there is too much capacity, then resources will be under-utilized (the aircraft flies with empty seats). For many service organizations under-utilization might be considered more profitable than the loss of customers.

Manipulating demand

With the second approach capacity is fixed and demand is manipulated to match the available capacity. Common methods of manipulating demand are advertising, promotions, cheaper fares/rates in the off season, cheaper meals for early diners, happy hours (half-price drinks) in bars and so on. Where demand exceeds capacity prices can be raised, or customers might be allowed or even encouraged to go elsewhere.

Uncertainty of demand

If demand is known in advance and is stable, the operations manager's job is to plan and make the best use of resources to meet the demand. Minor fluctuations cause only minor problems. Where demand cannot be accurately predicted then, although the aim has not changed, operations management problems can become extremely complex. Uncertainty of demand has three dimensions:

1. The number of customers and their arrival times (a steady, even flow is obviously easier to cope with than peaks and troughs).

2. The length of time each customer will need (if the service is of exactly the same duration each time, or can be planned, such as half-hour appointments in the dentist's chair, planning is easier than when it is not known how long each service encounter will require).

3. The amount of resources and the scheduling (timing) of resources.

Capacity management strategies

Faced with uncertain and fluctuating demand there are two basic strategies which can be used:

- Efficient use of resources and the variation or adjustment of capacity.
- Eliminating/reducing the need to adjust capacity (Wild, 1995).

Strategy 1: adjustment or variation of capacity

Generally, system capacity can be changed to some extent. Staff can work over-time, unskilled people can be employed in busy periods to free up skilled staff, staff can be re-allocated from their normal duties to help in the front office and so on.

Table 8.12 summarizes ways of adjusting capacity.

Example

In busy periods a small supermarket will open up extra check-out counters, and office staff including the manager will help with processing customers. In quiet periods counters are closed, some check-out staff are re-assigned to stocking shelves and the office staff go back to their normal duties.

Table 8.12	Resources	Capacity additions	Capacity reductions
Strategy 1 – capacity management	People	Add permanent staff	Reduce staff
		Train staff (multi-skilled)	Re-assign staff
		Strong culture (willing staff)	Retrieve subcontracted work
		Add temporary staff	Retrain staff
		Work overtime	Work short weeks
		Re-assign duties	
		Delay (batch) paperwork	
		Subcontract	
	Space	Rent or purchase	Sub-lease or sell
		Reorganize layout	
	Machines/equipment	New machines/systems	Dispose of
	Information systems	Buy, hire or rent	Cancel contract
		Subcontract	
	Materials/goods deliveries	Add substitutes	Aim for just-in-time
		Increase suppliers	

Strategy 2: reduce the need to adjust

If the policy is never to keep the customer waiting, then it follows that there must be a surplus of capacity for most of the time. The aim will be to avoid adjusting capacity by having available surplus capacity.

It is more likely, however, that it will not always be possible to have sufficient capacity to meet every demand. Thus if the policy is not to adjust capacity then it has to be accepted that from time to time customers will have to queue, or customers will be lost to the system. In some service situations it might be possible to hold stocks of resources, such as in a retail situation, a restaurant, or a fast-food shop and the customer is buffered from waiting by being supplied from stock.

Example

A fast-food store will anticipate when customers are due and have a stock of made-up hamburgers. To maintain quality of food the store policy is that hamburgers will be only held for four minutes before being discarded. Thus the aim is to prevent customers waiting by having a buffer of stock and the store accepts that some stock might be wasted. The holding of output stocks, even where it is possible, will not in itself prevent queues if there are insufficient staff to serve the customer.

Strategy 2, avoiding adjustment of capacity has several sub-strategies which for convenience we will label 2a, 2b, 2bi and 2bii. Also see Wild (2002).

2a: Surplus capacity maintained at all times.

2b: Sufficient capacity held for most situations, but

2bi: It is accepted that customers might have to queue and that it is likely some business will be lost.

2bii: Output stocks are held to absorb (buffer) demand fluctuations. This is not always possible, for example a hairdresser cannot stock outputs.

Structure and capacity

In Chapter 1 we identified seven system structures. To a large extent the system structure will determine the capacity strategy that can be adopted.

In Figure 8.3 Strategy 1 applies; that is, the system can be adjusted to increase efficiency. This structure requires surplus capacity and does not allow for customer queues. Strategy 2a would also be applicable, and to a limited extent 2bi, that is loss of customers, but *no* customer queues.

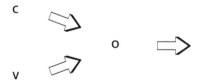

Figure 8.3

Surplus capacity, nil customer queue

In Figure 8.4 again Strategy 1 can apply. This structure also enables Strategy 2bi and 2bii (loss of trade and customer queues are both feasible).

Figure 8.5 shows the two structures where output stocks can be used to balance capacity, i.e. Strategy 2bii is applicable.

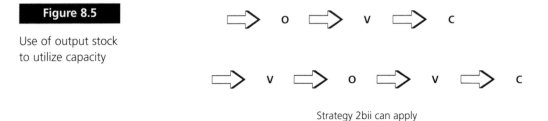

Strategy 2bii can apply

Practical capacity management techniques

As we have already seen, service systems cannot serve customers until the customer arrives. Therefore when demand falls short of capacity the result is idle capacity. Day-to-day management of capacity concerns attempting to alter demand and capacity levels so that they are in balance while still responding to random customer demands.

Planned and random demand

In the supply of most services, demand can be separated into two separate perspectives: planned and random demand. It is useful in day-to-day management of capacity to know the pattern and proportion of demand which can be reasonably predicted and therefore planned for, and the proportion which is random. Once this pattern is known it is likely that planned demand can be used to fill the troughs as much as possible and thus smooth the overall demand for a given period.

Due to the fluctuating nature of demand many service organizations could sell more capacity than they are able to accommodate in peak times and have a large amount of excess capacity in off-peak demand times. We are all aware of how the tourist industry promotes off-season specials (air fares, hotel rates, package deals and so on) and increases fares in the 'high' season to try and smooth demand. Other examples are variable phone-call rates, early-bird specials in restaurants and so on. Additional measures include offering complementary services to make waiting more palatable, such as a lounge bar for customers waiting for a restaurant table; and at airports, coffee bars, bookshops and souvenir shopping are provided for customers.

Where possible, capacity can be managed by encouraging customers to book in advance or to make reservations. The appointment book for doctors, dentists and hairdressers is in effect a queue of customers. Ideally the dentist would hope to be fully employed with no spare capacity and with patients arriving at pre-arranged times. The problem is that not all dental work takes exactly the same amount of time, and where half an hour might normally be adequate for an extraction, a complicated dental problem will take longer. Thus the service itself is variable in the time required. This variability of service time applies to most services.

Capacity management in service industries also includes doing as much of the work as possible in advance of the customer arriving. For example, the hotel will have rooms prepared before the customer arrives, the chef in the restaurant will have salads made up in advance and other food partly prepared before patrons arrive. Identification of core work which can be done in advance will speed up the actual service when the customer arrives. Another method of overcoming demand fluctuations is to increase customer participation.

Example

Auditors have peak periods at annual balance times. A method of overcoming the pressure is to provide customers with checklists and proformas of information required, so that when audit staff arrive the customer has much of the required information at hand and set out in a manner that makes checking straightforward. Another method is to carry out interim audits in advance, so that only a sample audit is required at balance time.

To overcome heavy demand periods, once the pattern has been established, if work cannot be delayed (paperwork held and completed after hours) or otherwise smoothed, then a bank of pre-trained temporary or part-time staff can be used (the demand anticipated and temporary staff trained in advance). In addition, in really busy periods, as discussed earlier (the supermarket example) back-office staff can be switched to front-office duties and so on.

Addition of people to increase capacity – learning curve

The addition of extra people, no matter how good the induction training, will not necessarily provide a fixed level of capacity. As discussed in Chapter 7, service industries rely heavily on people and a strong corporate culture will help overcome some short-term increases in demand. Additionally, the longer that people have been with an organization, the greater their ability to respond to sudden changes.

The 'learning curve' effect is shown in Figure 8.6. Thus experienced staff and a strong corporate culture will increase the capacity of a given number of human resources.

Queuing theory

Due to the random nature of customer arrivals (even when there is an arrival pattern) and due to the variability in time taken to satisfy each customer, no matter

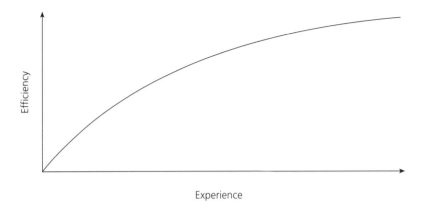

Figure 8.6

The learning curve

how good the planning of resources, queues will build up, disappear when there is a lull, and then reappear.

Your turn!

Some questions which you could consider for your department are:

How long should a customer wait, what is 'reasonable', and how long on average will customers be prepared to wait?

How much idle time is acceptable for service staff?

What is the cost of having unused capacity?

What is the cost of not being able to provide a service?

Variability of arrivals

It is often not possible, unless an appointment book or reservation system is used, to control the actual moment of arrival of a customer. The number of arrivals and the length of time between subsequent arrivals is not constant. By recording the number of arrivals a histogram can be used to show a frequency distribution, as in the example in Figure 8.7.

When the number of potential customers is large the probability of the next arrival does not depend on how many customers are already in the system. On the other hand, when the number of customers is finite and also small the probability of the next arrival will depend on how many customers have already arrived (supposing there are known to be five customers then the probability of the next arrival will depend on how many have already been served).

The assumption in most queuing systems is that arrivals occur singly, and therefore the concern is with the probability of a customer arriving or no customer arriving at any point in time or period of time.

Service units

The service mechanism for customers is probably the most controllable part of a queuing system. The simplest form is a single facility through which all customers

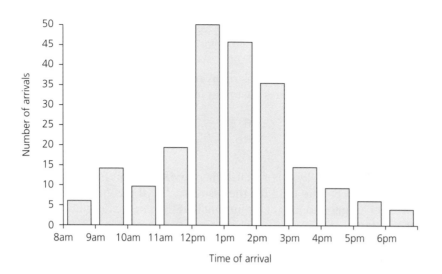

Figure 8.7

Example of a
frequency
distribution graph

must enter if they are to be served; more complicated systems will have several
serving units which may not all be the same. Multiple serving units can be
arranged in parallel, so that a customer might enter any of the units. A single
queue may form and a customer will go to the first unit that becomes available, or
alternatively a queue may form for each unit.

Queue discipline

Customers might form orderly queues where newcomers go to the back of the
queue and wait their turn (first in, first out), or the system might be that the last
one to arrive is served first (last in, first out); for example, when processing inward
mail, the last letter received goes to the top of the pile and is processed first. Other
methods might be to have a priority system for serving customers or to have no
system at all with customers being selected or selecting themselves for service at
random. Discipline or lack of discipline is not likely to affect the speed at which the
service unit operates, but will affect the waiting time for customers.

Service times

Some customers might take longer to serve than others, or all customers might
need exactly the same amount of time to process. Nonetheless, as in the case of
measuring the variability of arrivals, so too can the variability of service times be
measured and averaged. It might be observed that as the queue lengthens, the
average throughput increases, with the serving staff allowing themselves less time
per customer. If customers are being rushed through the system they might
believe that the level of service is below standard, or if they are kept waiting they
might become dissatisfied and leave the queue.

Queuing formulae

A measure for a simple queue is customer intensity, where:

$$\text{Customer intensity} = \frac{\text{Mean (average) rate of service}}{\text{Mean rate of arrival}}$$

For example, if the service time is on average six minutes and the inter-arrival time is on average eight minutes customer intensity will be:

$$\frac{6}{8} = 0.75$$

Thus 0.75 is the probability (p) of a customer having to wait for service. When p is below 1 there will be idle time for the resource, but if p is more than 1 then the queue will get longer and longer (assuming that the service does not speed up but remains constant).

For example, if a client for a consultancy arrives at the beginning of the hour and another client arrives every eight minutes thereafter and the average service time is six minutes, then at the end of 60 minutes, although the consultant could have serviced ten customers, only seven have arrived with one due in four minutes and only seven will have gone through the system. Therefore over a period of ten hours the consultant will have seen 75 people, but would have been able to have seen 100.

If, however, the arrival time was every six minutes starting at the beginning of the hour and each interaction took eight minutes the customer intensity would be 8/6 = 1.33. Thus at the end of the first hour seven people would have been served, one would be half-way through a consultation, one would have four minutes to wait, and the remaining one would have 12 minutes to wait. But if at the end of the hour a new client walks in the door, that client is going to have to wait 20 minutes. At the end of ten hours, the consultant will have seen 75 customers, and there will be a further 25 people waiting in the queue (that is, the last customer to arrive will have a wait of three hours and 12 minutes!).

The question can be addressed from a customer service perspective, i.e. how long do customers have to wait for service – or how long will they wait before they are lost to the system? Or, from a resource use perspective, how long are we prepared to have idle capacity in the system?

Your turn!

From Chapter 1 identify which system structure applies when the customer intensity is less than one, and which system structure applies when the customer intensity is more than one.

Chapter summary

Capacity management is a key responsibility for the operations manager.
Capacity management has two aspects: demand and capability.

Demand

In service industries demand is likely to be uncertain and to fluctuate. In this chapter several forecasting techniques were introduced. It was stressed that any forecast must be tested against past experience and the causes established (the commonsense approach).

Having established a forecasted demand the next uncertainty is the arrival times of customers and the duration of each service occurrence.

Capability

Establishing the capability of existing resources and knowing how resources can be manipulated and managed to adjust the level of capacity (up or down) is a key role of the operations manager. The major resource in service industries is usually people, thus training and motivation of people are important.

Strategies

Strategies for capacity management were identified and discussed. It was noted that to an extent systems structures limit the strategy that can be adopted.

In addition measures of capacity were considered and practical day-to-day capacity techniques were suggested, including an introduction to queuing theory.

Case Study *The Great New Zealand Carpet Bag Company*

The case study that is used to illustrate many of the issues addressed in this chapter is the Carpet Bag Company.

Question

Brenda Johns, the consultant, following her investigation of the situation, enters the office and states that the immediate objective must be to restore confidence with the bank and to improve the cash flow situation. She advises that her preliminary short-term recommendations are:

- Reduce head office staff by 50 per cent.
- Use the retail shops to attempt to dispose of surplus stock (at sale prices).
- Sell or close the retail shops after six months.

- Re-negotiate terms with the major department stores. The factory to manufacture only to firm orders.
- The factory to move to just-in-time procurement.
- Supply chain management to be the responsibility of Mr Chong.
- Mr Simpson to be responsible for Marketing and Administration.

If all of these recommendations are adopted, what will be the implications for the capacity management of the factory?

A Kiwi success story?

Patrick was standing in Bart's office on the 12th floor of the prestigious Plaza Tower Centre. He had his back to Bart and was looking out of the

▶

large 'picture' windows at a flotilla of yachts with rainbow-coloured sails passing under the Auckland harbour bridge. It was another beautiful clear day – totally out of keeping with the way he was feeling. He turned to Bart and said: 'We have come a long way in five years, don't let us fall out now. Bring in this consultant of yours and let us see what we can salvage out of this mess.'

The beginning

Five years ago Patrick Chong, a newcomer to New Zealand, had joined in partnership with his next door neighbour Bart Simpson. Bart had been the manager of a small branch of the Bank of New Zealand but had recently taken voluntary redundancy. Bart had $200 000 which he wanted to invest and was looking for a business opportunity. Patrick had been a manager of a factory making handbags in Beijing and, although he had little capital, he was also looking for a business opportunity. Bart had no manufacturing experience, but believed that he would be a good salesperson. Bart had for a long time had an interesting idea of using off-cuts of carpet to make hand luggage. He had explained his idea to Patrick when chatting together over the back fence. They decided to pool their strengths and to manufacture and sell hand luggage made out of carpet. Thus the Great New Zealand Carpet Bag Company was born.

After some investigation and preliminary planning they had leased a large disused warehouse at a very cheap rental in Huntly. Huntly is 100 kilometres south of Auckland and is on the bank of the Waikato River. Huntly was originally a coal mining town, but mining ceased some years ago and today it is a very pleasant clean rural town. It is also the home town of the Maori Queen. The local borough council was keen to attract new industry to Huntly to offset high unemployment and to arrest the tendency for young people to move north to the metropolis of Auckland. The advantages of locating in Huntly for Bart and Patrick were cheap rent and energy costs, location on the main trunk railway line and plenty of labour. For Patrick the extra advantage would be cheap housing and a good small town lifestyle for Ting Ting, his wife and their children. Bart decided to stay in Auckland where his children were already established in schools and of course Peggy his wife was not keen to move from her golf and bridge clubs.

From the start it was agreed that the partnership would be equal in all ways, but for each man to have clearly defined responsibilities. Patrick was to arrange all the resources required for the factory, including purchase of plant and equipment, and recruitment and training of labour. He was also responsible for liaison with the local authorities. Bart was to be responsible for marketing and selling and for negotiations with suppliers of materials from contacts he had made in his banking days. He was also responsible for accounting and tax returns, etc. To begin with they started with a staff of six people: four machinists and one cutter in the factory with Patrick, and one administration assistant working with Bart from an 'office' in his home.

The first twelve months

In the first twelve months the Great New Zealand Carpet Bag Company grew at a rate that completely bemused both men. They were both working twelve hour days and both were thoroughly enjoying the challenges and excitement.

Once the first dozen or so bags had been made Bart took samples to several large department stores in Auckland and across the Tasman sea to Melbourne and Sydney. The store 'buyers' were most enthusiastic at the novelty value of carpet as a material, and impressed with the obvious high quality of the bags and the price. (Bart had purposely set the price at 10 per cent below the wholesale price of other comparable bags.) Large orders were received in the first month of operations and Patrick had to gear the factory up accordingly. The partnership had to go into debt to finance the purchase of materials and pay wages until the first remittances were received from the buyers. On the strength of the forward orders Bart had no trouble in convincing his old bank to provide the funds required.

Some of the early problems were:

- Suppliers were not always reliable.
- Some machinery proved to be lightweight and had to be replaced. The factory could not keep up with demand.
- Bart in his enthusiasm promised early deliveries without consulting Patrick.
- Bart committed the partnership to large expensive offices in downtown Auckland without consulting Patrick.
- Patrick leased new machinery through a finance company without advising Bart. (Bart could have arranged a far better lease deal with the bank.)

Despite all these problems, most of them brought on by the need to react quickly to get things done, at the end of the first twelve months the partnership was working remarkably well and both men and their families were still good friends.

Due to the unreliability of suppliers the factory developed a practice of stockpiling raw materials. Patrick also aimed to build up a stockpile of finished goods (in fact it was three years before he achieved this). Patrick and Bart both agreed that quality could not be compromised and Patrick trained workers to accept responsibility for the quality of their work. Patrick was, however, continually frustrated with the erratic delivery of materials from local suppliers. He kept suggesting that they import materials, even though this would mean longer lead times and even bigger stockpiles. Bart, however, refused to do this. He steadfastly retained the responsibility of negotiating suppliers and prices. Bart believed in loyalty to his supplier friends.

The suppliers claimed to Bart that they did their best but:

- Orders received from the factory were frequently by word of mouth.

- Orders were always 'panic' orders.
- Often the factory did not clearly state what they wanted (specifically colour, quantity and delivery dates).
- When they tried to ring the factory to clarify what was required Patrick would become excitable and was often hard to understand and further misunderstanding would occur.

Bart maintained his original policy of keeping the price below the competition. However he was a little concerned to note that The Great New Zealand Carpet Bags were actually being retailed at a price higher than the competition, this was especially so in the Australian stores.

The rise and fall of the Carpet Bag

The initial demand and success of the carpet bags exceeded all the expectations of the partners. By the end of the first three years the operation had expanded to the extent that the factory employed 120 people. New equipment had been leased, including state of the art laser cutters. The factory was still housed in the original warehouse, but extra space had been leased for storage. Patrick was still working long hours and was still battling with the suppliers. The 'good' news was that at last the factory had caught up with demand and was now able to supply orders from stock. Patrick was so busy that he hadn't visited 'head' office for over twelve months, but once a month Bart dropped in to see him. The accounting and administration was still done in Auckland where the office staff now totalled 80 people. Patrick wondered if all these people were really necessary, but Bart assured him that they were and hinted at exciting new developments for year four.

The 80 office staff included the Marketing Manager, Jude Nye, the Sales Manager, Tracey Simpson (Bart's daughter), the Accountant, Charlie Chong (Patrick's eldest son), the Human Resource Manager, Hinemoa Henare, the Information Technology Manager, Zinzan Fitzpatrick, and the Purchasing Manager,

Freddie Starr. The office staff were young, friendly and enthusiastic, and liked to entertain clients and the major suppliers. Towards the end of year three Bart was only dropping into the office for a few minutes each day. On Fridays Bart and Peggy would join the 'head' office managers for drinks and dinner at one of the more fashionable cafés. The Great New Zealand Carpet Bag Company always paid the bill.

Despite the extravagances the business showed a healthy profit for year three. During the year the bank had been happy to increase the loan. Although the interest rate was higher than Bart would have liked, he had no real option but to accept the bank's terms.

In year four the demand for the carpet bags levelled off and towards the end of the year there was a noticeable drop in orders. During this year The Great New Zealand Carpet Bag Company opened six of its own retail shops in the main cities of New Zealand and Australia. It transpired that this was the 'big thing' which Bart had hinted at to Patrick. The retail stores were not as successful as hoped but they did manage to break even for the last month of the year. Also during year four the factory, at Patrick's initiative and to use up spare capacity, began manufacturing 'conventional' luggage (not using carpet). Again the emphasis was on high quality and in keeping the price below the competitors, and the new line was reasonably successful. By the end of year four there were still 120 people working at the factory, but unlike previous years no overtime was being worked. The finished goods store had an estimated six weeks of stock on hand. The office (due to the need to manage and market the retail stores) had grown to 95 people, and the number employed in the retail stores totalled 25. The profit for year four was less than in year three.

For the first six months of year five, the retail stores continued to stagger along; some months a small profit, others a small loss. Also during this period the demand for carpet bags almost dried up, but this was to some extent offset by the steadily growing demand for the 'conventional' luggage. Patrick was beginning to get worried. He now had a large stock of carpet bags, and had ceased making them; he also had at least one month's supply of 'conventional' luggage. The factory obviously now had an over capacity in people but he was reluctant to lay anyone off. Instead, he had reassigned some workers to painting the factory, and had begun a process of closing parts of the line for overhaul and maintenance, although in his heart he knew that the work being done was not strictly necessary.

Then in the seventh month Patrick was amazed to find a container outside the factory full of carpet bags returned from a department store chain in Australia. On contacting Bart he was shocked to learn that all 'sales' to the Australian stores were on a sale or return basis. Bart explained that the deal he had made (when the business was just beginning) was that stores only paid when they had sold the goods and that they had the option to return the goods if they hadn't sold after three months. He believed he had done a good deal because the stores had agreed to pay the return freight. Over the years he had seen no need to change the arrangement.

In the first year of sales there had been no problem with this arrangement as demand was outstripping supply and cheques were being received at regular intervals from the stores. No one had foreseen that the carpet bag was a novelty item and that the meteoric growth would be followed by an equally meteoric decline.

In months eight, nine and ten of year five, further smaller consignments of carpets bags were returned. However, the demand for the 'conventional' luggage was still slowly but steadily increasing and Patrick was still building to stock. Apart from the large number of carpet bags on hand and a small supply of raw materials for carpet bags, he now had two months' stock of finished 'conventional' luggage with about one month's supply of raw materials. Spare staff were being employed to landscape the grounds in which the factory and store were set. Factory numbers due to natural attrition were down to 108.

The crunch

It is now the last month of year five. Bart has just told Patrick that the bank is pressing for the repayment of the loan. Patrick is shocked to find that the amount owed is $2 000 000. Bart says the bank is prepared to agree to an arrangement of repayment over two years providing $500 000 is paid within seven days. He suggests that they both mortgage their homes to do this. He is confident that they can trade out of the situation and he has hired a consultant to look at the company and to advise them on what they can do to turn the organization around. Patrick turns away from

the view of the bridge, the yachts and the sparkling Auckland harbour and says 'We have come a long way in five years, don't let us fall out now. Bring in this consultant of yours and let us see what we can salvage out of this mess'.

Two months later

The consultant has made an appointment to present her main recommendations to Patrick and Bart. The day after that meeting Patrick and Bart are to meet again. On that occasion it will be Patrick's intention to discuss the impact of the consultant's recommendation on the management of the factory.

Written by J. Nevan Wright © 2001 Henley Management College.

9 Scheduling and time management

Objectives

This chapter considers:

- Scheduling issues and techniques.

- Time management.

Introduction

In this chapter we identify the various types of scheduling problems which may be encountered in different operations and we consider techniques for their solution. The management of time and the timing of activities are of concern to all managers and this is also discussed.

Scheduling

Scheduling is the art of:

- listing activities;
- deciding the order of completing activities;
- arranging the necessary resources, including inventory, to complete each activity;
- timing the activities.

Scheduling, like capacity management (Chapter 8), is a key issue for the operations manager. As with capacity management the task is to minimize the cost of having resources of people, equipment, goods and materials available and at the same time to meet stages of production and to achieve customer's delivery dates. The major elements of scheduling are:

- what;
- when; and
- how much

resource is required to fulfil planned activities. Theoretically it is possible to have just sufficient resources available, and just at the right time, to meet demand.

Service industries

Demand forecasts, as shown in Chapter 8, are generally not exact, and in a service situation arrival of customers can seldom be exactly known, nor can it be determined how long each service activity will take. Thus, for a service operation it is not possible to know precisely what resources will be required at any one time. The strategy has to be either to always have surplus capacity of key resource available (generally staff) so that customers do not have to wait for service, or to allow customers to queue and to keep the key resource fully employed. In a service operation it might be possible to buffer demand by having a queue of customers. The queue might be disguised in the form of making advance appointments, i.e. customers book ahead and resources can be scheduled to be available when required. In a service industry it is not possible to stock outputs (e.g. the hairdresser cannot cut hair in advance of demand, and once an aircraft takes off with empty seats that opportunity to carry passengers is lost).

Customers pre-booked

For some service systems customers have been conditioned to book in advance (restaurants, doctors, transport, etc.) and the service provider makes the booking to coincide with availability of capacity. In these cases the system controls the time of service delivery, and the scheduling of the necessary amounts of resources can be fairly exact. Efficiency is dependent on arrival of the customer at the pre-arranged time; if the customer is late service will be delayed, or if not delayed (the train leaves on time) the customer will miss out. In either case, resource utilization will be inefficient. Nonetheless, if customers keep to the prearranged booked times, and the time allowed for each service interaction is not overrun, a degree of accuracy and efficiency in the scheduling of resources will be possible. However, experience tells us that our local doctor will begin the day with a schedule of patients with set appointment times, but if your appointment is later in the day the doctor will generally be behind schedule (examinations took longer than expected, some patients arrived late and so on). In some areas of service, to overcome non-arrival of pre-booked customers, service operators will deliberately over-book.

Example

In the international air travel service, based on past experience of the non-arrival of passengers, an airline may frequently accept bookings for, say, 440 passengers although the scheduled aircraft only has 400 seats. When, as often happens, more than 400 customers arrive on time, then the front-line staff have the problem of placating customers who cannot be seated, or offering inducements for passengers to take a later flight. In this example the airline has placed the efficiency of the operation as its first objective, and scheduling of resources can be fairly precise.

Manufacturing industries

In a manufacturing operation it is possible to obtain forward orders and delivery dates and therefore schedule activities and resources to meet demand. In addition, even without forward orders a factory can make to stock, thus scheduling of resources in manufacturing can have a reasonable degree of exactitude.

Examples

Consider the printing of Christmas cards; if a factory did nothing else the strategy could be to make the same number of Christmas every day of the year and to stockpile for the expected high demand in December. In this example, on the first day of production after Christmas the factory would begin printing for the next Christmas.

Another example is where an ice-cream manufacturer in the southern hemisphere supplies a local chain of supermarkets for six months of the year, and then when the season changes exports to a chain of supermarkets in the northern hemisphere for the next six months.

In both these examples the strategy adopted is *level production*, i.e. the same amount made every week throughout the year. In the case of the Christmas cards, output is stocked to meet future demand; in the ice-cream example output can only be stocked for a short period, but the manufacturer has found an alternative market.

Lean or just-in-time

One 'textbook' approach in manufacturing is known as lean production. The aim with 'lean' also known as 'just-in-time' is to only make to order and deliver direct to the customer when the item is completed. An example would be one-off house building. The builder will only begin construction when a contract to build has been agreed. Activities will be scheduled and materials will be ordered to arrive only when needed (the pre-mixed concrete will be delivered and poured on the day required, the electrician will arrive and wire the house when scheduled and so on). When completed the new owner will take delivery.

Example   *Toyota's 72-hour car*

In the United States or Japan when purchasing a new car the buyer can visit a showroom and inspect a sample of cars. The buyer will then, with the help of a salesperson, sit down and enter his/her requirements into a computer terminal. For example, from a menu he/she will select the engine size, the number of doors, the type of sound system, the colour, the type of upholstery and so on. In doing so the buyer is making an order for a car to be assembled to his/her specifications (from a flexible range of options) to be delivered within 72 hours. Unknown to the buyer, he/she is not only making an entry to the master production schedule for the car assembly plant, but also directly placing an order to the various suppliers of the approximately 12 000 components which go into the assembly of a Toyota. Each supplier will then deliver the required components to the factory at the time required to go straight to the applicable station on the assembly line. Within 72 hours the car as specified by the customer will be delivered and paid for. Payment will be made before Toyota has paid the wages or the suppliers! With this model Toyota holds no stocks of input materials and has no stock of finished cars.

Your turn!

Ring any car dealer, other than for a Japanese brand, and ask how long it will take for a car meeting your various requirements to be delivered. Unless you pick a stock vehicle, and the colour you want is in stock, you are likely to be told that you will have to wait about 72 days!

Other lean examples

Dell Computers works in a similar fashion to Toyota. Computer components are acquired and assembled to meet specific orders by customers. A further example is Fisher and Paykel in New Zealand. Fisher and Paykel manufacture white ware (household washing machines, refrigerators, stoves, dish washers, etc.). When a customer visits a white ware retail shop they will see examples of Fisher and Paykel's products on display together with promotional material. The customer will select an item, and the salesperson will arrange delivery within three days for a time suitable to the customer. The customer could well assume that the retailer has a stock of finished goods in a warehouse, but in fact the unit the customer will receive has not yet been made, i.e. Fisher and Paykel manufacture to customer order.

Obviously the lean, or just-in-time system as per the examples of the small builder, Toyota, Dell Computers and Fisher and Paykel requires exact scheduling of activities and resources, very good communication with suppliers and the co-operation (input) of customers. Planning/scheduling has to be exact and staff and processes have to be flexible.

S.M.E.D.

Manufacturers using the lean approach require a flexible workforce and flexible machines. The workforce has to be able to adjust to each item on the line being different to the previous one, i.e. in white ware manufacturing on the line at any one time there might be a mixture of refrigerators, washing machines, stoves, etc. The approach used is known as S.M.E.D – *single minute exchange of dies*. In other words, set-up times of machines are measured in units of single minutes, and generally while a machine is running it is being reconfigured to meet the next requirement. The opposite to S.M.E.D. is the manufacture of large batches, i.e. in white ware manufacturing, for one week refrigerators of one size only would be made and stockpiled. This could mean that if a customer wanted a particular model they might have to wait a month for the next batch to go into production.

Just-in-time and service industries

For service industries a just-in-time system is not possible. If the customer is not to be kept waiting, then resources always have to be available. Or, if resources are to be kept fully employed (no idle capacity) then there has to be a 'stock' (queue) of customers waiting in line for service.

System structures

System structures for service and manufacturing operations are shown at Figure 9.1.

Example

No matter how experienced the general practitioner, the time required for a routine treatment will vary from patient to patient. If the doctor is determined that no customer is ever to be kept waiting in the anteroom then the doctor might schedule perhaps only one patient per hour. This might mean that for a good deal of the time the doctor would be idle. The dilemma faced by the doctor – either the doctor waits for customers or the customer waits for the doctor – is compounded for many other types of service operations. The doctor can at least make appointments in advance and therefore know with some degree of accuracy the time of arrival of customers, whereas for many service operators arrival times will be random.

Scheduling for forecasted demand

For most service systems the arrival of customers cannot be precisely determined and scheduling relies on the accuracy of forecasted demand. In such cases, if it is the policy not to keep customers waiting, then surplus capacity will need to be held. As seen in the section on queuing in Chapter 8, the problems are the random nature of arrival of customers and the variability of the amount of time required for each service activity.

This generally means that a third approach to scheduling has to be adopted – to try and have sufficient capacity most of the time, but to accept that queues will sometimes form and that there could well be some loss of business. The two basic strategies of capacity management discussed in Chapter 8, of either avoiding adjustment of capacity, or providing for efficient adjustment of capacity, equally apply to scheduling decisions. An example of this third approach, as shown in Figure 1.6 is a dentist, where for most of the time patients book in advance but some time is set aside for emergency treatment. On occasions during the time set aside for emergency treatment (the patient has chronic toothache and is not pre-

SERVICE OPERATIONS

Figure 9.1

(a) Customers are 'stockpiled' and drawn as required from a queue. It is possible to schedule exactly the right amount of resources at precisely the right time to meet the demand. Example: airline travel.

System structures and scheduling

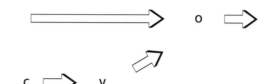

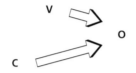

(b) The objective here is that the customer(s) will be served when they arrive. As demand and/or service time cannot be precisely forecast, surplus capacity is held.

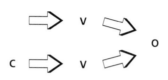

(c) In this system it is accepted that sometimes there is spare capacity, and sometimes queues of customers will form. Examples are the dentist and the service function of a restaurant.

MANUFACTURING OR RETAIL OPERATIONS

(d) The customer draws from a stock of finished goods. This system allows for the same amount of production each week i.e. 'level' production.

(e) Here input stock is held, orders are made to meet customers due date. In a retail operation this shows finished goods held, and the operation is the sale to the customer.

(f) Goods are produced and stocked. The customer is supplied from finished stock.

(g) The lean or just-in-time system, where materials are scheduled to be received direct into production just when needed, and finished goods are delivered direct to the customer.

pared to wait for two weeks!) it could be that there are no patients. In this case the dentist is idle, and at the same time the appointment book contains customers waiting to be seen.

For manufacturing, although the ideal might appear to be the just-in-time system, it is more likely that in practice some reserve stock of input material and finished goods will be held. In a mass production operation, such as car assembly, it is not likely that there will always be a perfect match of demand to capacity, and thus to balance the line some standard units will be made to stock. For example, if one day's demand only requires 800 units, when the capacity including the people is for 1000, it is not likely that the line will be slowed down for one day, or that 20 per cent of the people will be sent home; rather it is likely that 200 'standard' items will be made to stock. If, however, the demand permanently dropped to 800, then the capacity would be adjusted. If, on the other hand, demand is for 1200 for one day (when capacity is 800), then unless demand continues at this high level, the 72-hour target will not suffer unduly.

Scheduling: feasibility versus desirable

The broad approach to scheduling activities is influenced by business policy and, as shown in Figure 9.1, by system structure. Operations scheduling is thus limited by what is feasible given the resources (capacity) available and the limitations of the system structure, coupled with what is desirable in terms of customer satisfaction.

In considering scheduling it is necessary to understand two perspectives: those of the customer and those of the organization. The operations manager must know what these perspectives are; that is, what the customer expects, and what the organization is prepared and able to provide. These areas of conflict are likely to centre on timing or speed of delivery of service, cost of service, flexibility and responsiveness.

Timing of service

Customers may not expect to queue for service or wait for products, and if the organization's policy is to avoid queues then there will not be a conflict. If, however, the operations manager does not have sufficient resources available, or fails to schedule sufficient resources, then there will be a conflict. If the organization's policy is to accept that sometimes a delay in delivery will occur, but the customer has been led to believe or has assumed prompt service, or that the item will be on hand for immediate delivery, then when the customer has to wait for delivery he/she will be less than satisfied.

Where queues are accepted as almost the norm, such as at the supermarket checkout or at the Post Office, then customers will be aware that they might have to queue. In these cases, provided the queue is seen to be moving and service is equitable (no queue-jumping), then customers will be reasonably satisfied. If a new competitor arrives in our market and offers the same specified service but with no queues, then if we are not careful our queue will disappear for the wrong reason – we will lose our customers! The operations manager's job is to manage the scheduling of resources to prevent or at least minimize queues.

Scheduling techniques

Gantt chart, also a control mechanism

The Gantt chart or bar chart is the simplest method to schedule activities. The Gantt chart was first developed towards the end of the nineteenth century by Henry Gantt, a colleague of Frederick Taylor. In essence it is a bar graph with time shown on the horizontal axis and activities on the vertical. A variation is shown in the example in Figure 9.2, where it can be seen that some activities overlap; for example, applications can be sorted and screened/checked as they arrive, although the position is still being advertised.

As activities are completed they are colour coded; thus not only is the Gantt chart a scheduling aid but it is also a means of control to show which activities have been completed, which still have to be completed, and if the time frame is being kept to.

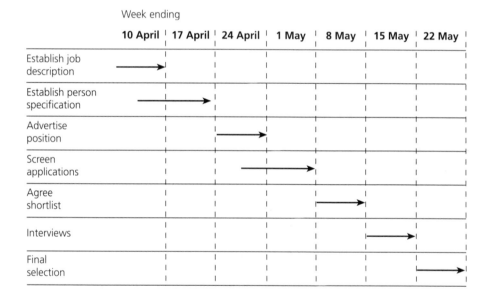

Figure 9.2

Schedule for recruitment of new staff member

Sales reps	Monday	Tuesday	Wednesday	Thursday	Friday
John	Holiday	Paris	London (exhibition)	Reading	Oxford
Jill	Bristol	Cardiff	Swansea	London (exhibition)	Hamburg
Harry	London (set up exhibition)	London (exhibition ————————————————➤	London	London	London final day)
Hannah	Edinburgh	Glasgow	Ayr/Carlisle	Sunderland	Scarborough

Table 9.1

Example of load chart

Load charts

Load charts are another variation of the Gantt chart. Instead of listing activities the Load chart shows departments or individual people on the vertical axis, and the operations manager can then see which resources are available for scheduling. If all resources are fully utilized then further work might be declined or steps taken to temporarily increase capacity as discussed in Chapter 8. Table 9.1 gives an example of a Load chart.

A similar approach is used when timetables (such as a school timetable) are being constructed.

Forward scheduling and reverse scheduling

Forward scheduling begins as soon as the demand is known. Service is performed to customer order and delivery is made as soon as possible. Orders are usually accepted on a first come, first served basis even if the scheduler knows that customers are going to have to wait. Often customer queues form. Examples are hospitals and restaurants.

Example

Customers arrive (not pre-booked) at a restaurant and if possible are taken to a table where they wait for service. If no table is available they are shown to the bar and will be called when a table is ready.

Reverse scheduling, also known as backward scheduling, begins with the due date. By working back from the due date activities and resources are scheduled one at a time so as to arrive at a start time. With reverse scheduling it might be found that the organization does not have all the necessary resources and thus the operations manager has the task of hiring equipment, arranging subcontractors, temporary labour, etc. to meet the requirements.

Assignment method

The assignment method of scheduling resources uses a linear programme model and follows the transportation models demonstrated in Chapter 6. The objective

Example

The due date for a wedding will be the day the bride and groom have booked the church. Working back from this date the other arrangements include hiring of a marquee, erection of the marquee, hiring of caterers, making of the bride's and bridesmaids' dresses with various intermediate fittings, booking hairdressers and photographers, the two mothers arranging their outfits, the timing of the hen and stag parties, the booking of entertainment, the hiring of cars and so on. On top of all this the poor bride and groom have to find time to occasionally see each other.

is to minimize the total costs or the time required. Examples include assigning salespeople to areas and people to tasks or projects. With the assignment method a limitation is that only one activity or person can be allocated to one area or activity at a time.

Example

A business has three staff members: Andreas, Jacob and Stefan, and there are three tasks to be completed. Each employee has different skills, and each employee has a different hourly wage rate. The estimated cost for completing each job per employee is as follows:

	Task A	Task B	Task C
Andreas	£33	£42	£18
Jacob	24	30	33
Stefan	27	36	21

Stage 1

Begin by subtracting the smallest number in each row from each number in that row. The table will now be:

	Task A	Task B	Task C
Andreas	15	24	0
Jacob	0	6	9
Stefan	6	15	0

Now subtract the smallest number remaining in each column from every number in that column.

	Task A	Task B	Task C
Andreas	15	18	0
Jacob	— 0 ——— 0 ——— 9 —		
Stefan	6	9	0

The next step is to draw a straight line passing through each zero. In our example there will be two straight lines as shown above, along the Jacob row and down the Task C column. If there are fewer straight lines than there are numbers of rows a further stage is needed to find the optimum solution. In our example, as there are only two straight lines and there are three columns, we will move to the next stage.

Stage 2

In this stage we take the smallest uncovered number, in our case Stefan and Task A:

	Task A	Task B	Task C
Andreas	15	18	0
Jacob	— 0 ——— 0 ——— 9 —		
Stefan	[6]	9	0

Subtract the smallest uncovered number from every other uncovered number, which in our case is Andreas Task A (15) and Task B (18), and Stefan Tasks A (6) and B (9), and *add* it to the number where the two lines intersect.

Stage 3

We now have:

	Task A	Task B	Task C
Andreas	—9———	12———	0—
Jacob	—0———	0———	15—
Stefan	—0———	3———	0—

In Stage 3 we draw sufficient straight lines to cover all the zeros. If, as our example shows, the number of lines is equal to the number of columns, we have arrived at an optimum solution. In this case we will assign Task C to Andreas, Task B to Jacob and Task A to Stefan. Note as Andreas has only one zero he must get Task C, which leaves Stefan with only Task A. The optimum cost is:

Task A	Stefan	27
Task B	Jacob	30
Task C	Andreas	18 = 75

This was a simple example with only six possibilities ($3 \times 2 \times 1$), which no doubt some of our

▶

readers could have solved in their heads without going through all the three stages. If there had been four staff members and four tasks the possibilities total 24 ($4 \times 3 \times 2 \times 1$), and if there were nine staff and nine tasks the possibilities are 362 880 ($9 \times 8 \times 7 \times 6 \times 5 \times 4 \times 3 \times 2 \times 1$), i.e. not quite so easy to solve in your head!

Dummy tasks

Earlier it was said that the assignment model requires only one task for each person, or an equal number of columns and rows. How then do we cope if there were an uneven number of rows and columns (three tasks and four workers)? This is overcome by creating a dummy task with a row which only has zeros in it. When the assignment is complete the employee who is assigned the dummy task is in effect unassigned as there is no task to be done.

The transportation model and its uses

The basic transportation approach allows for the allocation of people to tasks and projects, people to sales territories, contracts to bidders. The aim is to minimize costs and/or time, or to maximize profits or effectiveness. In our example another approach would have been to consider opportunity costs by subtracting every number in the first table from the largest single number (rather than the smallest number), thus converting our maximization exercise into a minimization result.

Scheduling strategy

Scheduling can be either internally oriented or externally oriented. Internal scheduling is possible when there is a buffer between the customer and the operation. In service industries the buffer is when the strategy is to have a customer queue. This means that the service provider schedules meetings with customers at a time to meet the service provider's programme. For example, the dentist, or other provider of services, schedules customers to arrive at a certain time (and can therefore take Wednesday afternoon off to play golf).

External scheduling in service industries is when the customer determines the time of the meeting and the service provider has to arrange his or her schedule to meet the needs of the customer. In manufacturing the buffer will be when the strategy is to supply the customer from a stock of outputs. Figure 9.3 summarizes scheduling strategies, and shows the importance of the flow of information, and of due dates from the customer.

Priority rules

Priority might be given to the first comer, i.e. the first person or job that arrives is the first to be processed (first come, first served). Or it could be that priority is given to the job which has the earliest due date. However, in certain circumstances it might be better to do the shortest or easiest jobs first, e.g. a clerk gets rid of six routine jobs in the first hour irrespective of when they are due, and then leaves the rest of the day free to work on a major report.

WHAT (task), WHEN (sequence), HOW MANY (number), HOW OFTEN (repetition)
CONSTRAINED by DEMAND and POLICY (objectives)

Figure 9.3

Scheduling
strategies

1. Externally orientated scheduling

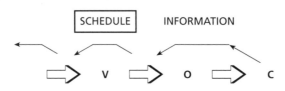

N.B. Importance of 'Due dates'

2. Internally orientated scheduling

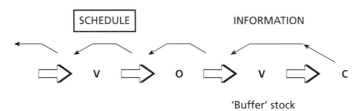

'Buffer' stock

Your turn!

Is your operation internally or externally orientated? How are jobs prioritized in your operation?

Bottlenecks

Bottlenecks are where the whole process is held up because one particular task takes longer than the subsequent task. For example, invoices are held up for mailing out due to the checking clerk being away sick, or mortgage approvals are held up due to the need for approval from the district office. Bottlenecks can be overcome by adding resources, by re-routing work, by method study at pressure points, or by rearrangement of layouts as discussed in Chapter 6. Eli Goldratt developed OPT – optimized production technology – for the minimization of bottlenecks in production. With OPT organizations determine where the bottlenecks are and where non-bottlenecks are and resources are re-arranged to minimize bottlenecks. The key is that an hour lost in a bottleneck will delay the whole process by a minimum of an hour and could well create further bottlenecks in subsequent stages of the process, thus the overall time lost could well exceed the initial loss of one hour. With non-bottlenecks, an hour saved will only be an illusion, as no benefit will accrue to the overall process.

Your turn!

Do bottlenecks occur in your workplace? If so what actions are taken, or could be taken to ease the bottleneck?

Theory of constraints – TOC

The theory of constraints is to improve overall performance of the operation by identifying and understanding what the constraints are. There are three basic types of constraint;

● Critical internal resource;

● demand;

● policy constraint.

Critical resource, i.e. the operation could be constrained by the number of staff in a critical process, thus there is a bottleneck, e.g. mortgage approvals held up due to a lack of legal staff, or in manufacturing the production line can turn out 20 items per hour but the paint shop can only process 15 per hour.

Demand constraint, the operation might have a higher capacity than market demand. If a manufacturing operation the policy might be to continue with level production in anticipation that demand will increase, but in service industries, as discussed earlier, it is not possible to stock outputs.

Policy constraint. The policy might be to limit the operation, i.e. no overtime, or five-day work weeks.

Network analysis

Network analysis is a key tool of project managers and there are many computer programs available. Project management is described in some detail in Chapter 12.

The approach for network analysis is:

● list all the activities needed to complete the project;

● allow sufficient time for each activity;

● monitor progress against the plan.

In the simple example given below the project is to shift an office to a new location.

Example

Activity		Duration	Preceding activity
Sign new lease	A–B	One day	None
Agree layout plan	B–C	Five	A–B
Pack for move	B–D	Three	A–B
Re-decorate	C–D	Seven	B–C, B–D
Wire for computers	C–E	Three	B–C
Move and install	D–F	Two	B–D, C–D, C–E
Staff move in	F–G	One	D–F

Until the lease is signed little else can be done. We assume that the new office is in the right location, the rent is acceptable, and the floor space is adequate (see Chapter 6). Thus signing the lease is the first step. Before we move in we have to decide where each department will be and where each person will be located. This has to be done before we wire for phones and computers. The time needed for wiring and installation of computers and for the redecoration will determine the date of the relocation of the staff to the new offices. Once the shift date has been established then packers and removal people can be arranged and staff briefed.

The network will be drawn to show the sequence of events, and it will be seen that some activities can occur simultaneously. For example, packing can begin while wiring and redecorating are taking place. But the actual move cannot take place until the wiring, redecoration and packing have been completed. The final step in this simplified example is for the staff to move in. If everything has gone to schedule, within sixteen days from the beginning of the project staff will be on site and operational.

Figure 9.4a shows the order (precedence) in which activities must occur. The convention for drawing a network is to have the arrows moving from left to right with no backtracking. Dummy activities allow the sequence of events to be maintained. In our example E–D is a dummy activity. Redecorating and wiring can occur at the same time, and both have to be completed before D–F can start. Redecorating has been shown as C–D, and to avoid confusion wiring has been shown as C–E with a 'dummy' activity E–F to maintain the sequence.

Time frames and critical paths

By adding the time required for each activity it is then possible to calculate the time required to complete the project. This is shown in Figure 9.4b. If we follow along the Path A–B, B–D, D–F, F–G we can calculate that this sequence of activities and the path A–B, B–C, C–D, D–F, F–G will take sixteen days, and the third path of A–B, B–C, C–E, E–D, D–F, F–G will take twelve days. Thus the longest path is sixteen days, and shows that the project will take sixteen days to complete.

If any activity on the longest path exceeds the

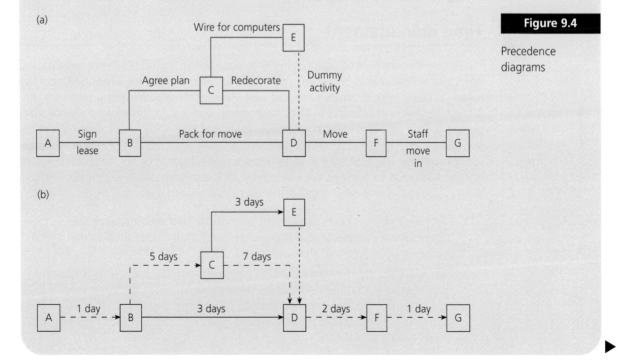

(a)

Wire for computers — E

Agree plan — C — Redecorate — Dummy activity

A — Sign lease — B — Pack for move — D — Move — F — Staff move in — G

(b)

3 days — E

5 days — C — 7 days

A — 1 day — B — 3 days — D — 2 days — F — 1 day — G

Figure 9.4

Precedence diagrams

allotted time then the entire project will take that much longer. For example, if redecorating takes nine days (instead of the allowed seven) the entire project will now take eighteen days. Thus it is critical that each activity on the longest path does not exceed the allotted time. Hence the term 'critical' path. To make the critical path obvious on the diagram it will be colour-coded.

An activity that is not on the critical path can be late finishing, provided that the extra time taken does not exceed the *slack* or *float* existing for that path. For example activity B–D where three days have been allotted could actually take twelve days without affecting the total time for the project. Thus activity B–D has a *float* of nine days. Likewise activity C–E has a float of four days. If the total amount of slack or float is used for an activity then that activity will become critical to the project

Our example is very simple and only gives the rudiments of the network approach. Many computer packages exist for critical path analysis and planning. Built into the software will be the ability to have a minimum of three estimates of time for each activity, e.g. the expected (most likely) time, the most pessimistic and the most optimistic times. The software will also show the earliest start time, the latest start time, and the most probable start time, and will calculate various critical paths. Printouts, on an exception basis, can be provided to show when and where activities fall behind schedule, thus allowing the manager to take corrective action. Corrective action might include adding extra resource, delaying one activity and transferring resources to another activity, etc. Adding resource will mean more cost, and a trade-off might have to be made along the continuum of accepting a delay to the project as a whole and the cost of adding extra resource to complete on time.

Time management

We began this chapter by identifying that scheduling includes timing (when) and how much resource is required. For customer satisfaction we identified the key issues as being specification, time and cost. Again, when considering resource utilization, time was also found to be an important element. In this section we consider personal time management. It will be appreciated that what you can do for yourself can be applied to staff when delegating tasks. As with all operation management problems the first step is to know what the objectives are, and the steps or activities needed to achieve the objectives. It is also important to prioritize objectives and steps. A five-step approach to personal time management is as follows:

1. List the problems/tasks facing you. Sort those that will advance the organization's interests and those that don't really add value to the business. Discard those that don't add value.
2. Prioritize; that is, determine which objectives are the most important and the order in which they should be done. This includes deciding which cannot be delayed, and which are not important. Sometimes it is possible to get rid of several small tasks in a short space of time, but don't get bogged down with a trivial task.

3. Having decided the order of objectives, then in the same manner list the tasks required for each objective and assign priorities to them.

4. Make a schedule of jobs to be done, and in brackets allot time to each.

5. Tick off items as they are completed (this is the best bit!).

This approach can be done at the beginning of each week, and then checked and reset each morning, but don't waste all morning reworking your schedule!

Most managers achieve 80 per cent of their important results in only 20 per cent of their time. In other words, 80 per cent of their time is spent on unimportant or time-wasting tasks. It is easy to go home feeling tired but frustrated because in reality you have achieved very little of value. Some writers suggest setting a regular amount of time aside each day for talking to staff, for checking the voice-mail, making phone calls, checking incoming e-mails and sending e-mails. If you are working across time zones a message sent at 10 am in the UK will arrive at 10 pm in New Zealand, thus messages don't have to be answered immediately.

By the same token you should try and make it a rule that all voice-mails, e-mails and faxes are replied to on the day received, if only just to acknowledge receipt. Technology is wonderful, but don't be deluded into thinking that just because you have sent a message it has arrived. Somewhere in the IT link a server can be down, and although you have not received a 'message returned' advice this does not mean that your message has gone all the way down the so-called superhighway. If you don't get a reply in a reasonable amount of time don't be shy in sending a message asking for confirmation.

Meetings don't have to be a waste of time

The greatest time-waster of the 1990s has proved to be meetings. A poorly-run meeting can run on for hours, waste everyone's time and achieve nothing. Minutes of meetings should only cover actions to be taken by members. At the next meeting the first task should be to check if actions have been completed, and then to discuss what else has to be done, what should be done, and to agree a fresh list

Chapter summary

In this chapter we have considered the key task of scheduling work. We showed that scheduling includes arranging resources and setting time frames so as to achieve objectives as efficiently as possible.

- Techniques and methods of scheduling were considered.
- The importance of stock management and basic approaches were explained.
- Finally, we discussed the importance of managing our own time.

We conclude this chapter with the thought that time is a precious commodity, and whether you are doing time, marking time or spending time, believe us: time is running out. Your only hope is to do it now – procrastination is the thief of time.

of actions. Unless any action follows from a meeting, why have it? One suggestion for running a meeting is to have no chairs; if everyone has to stand for the duration of the meeting it is surprising how quickly the meeting finishes. If this is too revolutionary, at least try not serving coffee; a meeting is not a social occasion – if it is a social occasion it should be billed as such, and we should not expect to achieve any worthwhile business.

Case Study *Microcell*

The case which applies to this chapter is Microcell.

Questions

Part A

Draw a schedule of activities, showing precedence and timescale needed to supply a batch of 100 000 PR10 cells to the regional warehouse. Make sure the plan includes allowances for scrap. How many cans need to be ordered from the supplier and what is the maximum time from order to delivery of the batch of 100 000 cells into the warehouse?

Part B

How can local management reduce manufacturing costs and reduce order time? Identify how you would go about the investigation and what additional information you would require?

Micocell

Microcell (GmbH) is a business unit within Permacell Inc. (USA). It is controlled as a cost centre (£45 million) in order to manufacture a range of small lithium oxide and silver oxide primary (not rechargeable) button cells for watch, calculator and photographic equipment applications. Microcell employs 250 people in a facility built 25 years ago. Many of the proprietary processes are between 10 and 25 years old – 80 per cent of process workers have more than 10 years experience in the plant, but a

similar percentage of senior managers have less than 3 years experience in the company.

The marketing activity at Permacell is a centralized function and is essentially Microcell's internal customer. Marketing owns and controls the supply chain into fast moving consumer goods outlets and into the technical photographic outlets, which take 80 per cent of Microcell's output.

Microcell's product range consists of twenty different cell types and 12 different batteries – a battery is a collection of cells joined together to satisfy different voltage, current and life characteristics for battery-powered equipment. Product volumes range from 100 000 per month to 2.5 million cells per month and are subject to monthly call off against an annualized forecast from marketing.

Cell manufacture is a complicated operation involving small component micro assembly on old automated machinery and batch chemical processing which involves mixing and preparing chemicals to provide the active ingredients in the cells. It is the chemical reaction between these active ingredients which provides the electrical energy in primary cells. The use of chemicals with their inherent variability of physical and chemical properties, together with inconsistent manufacturing processes on old equipment, results in the need to store completed cells for between 8–20 days. Storage allows defects in materials and in manufacturing processes to become evident and testing prior to packing screens out these defects.

Table 9.2 below details the manufacturing activities, production rates, scrap rates and order lead times required to manufacture the PR10 cell.

Senior management is concerned about the manufacturing costs at Microcell and also about the lead-time from Marketing's order to receipt of the product into the supply chain. Manufacturing data needs to be analyzed in order to answer searching questions at the next regional directors' meeting.

Activity no.	Activity	Preceding activity	Production rate per day	Order lead time – days	Scrap rate %	Table 9.2
1	Procure cans	–		20	0	Manufacturing activity at Microcell
2	Manufacture cathodes	1	5000		10	
3	Manufacture anodes		50 000		5	
4	Procure tops	–		15		
5	Manufacture separator		50 000		10	
6	Electrolyte, stock	–		1	0	
7	Assemble and clean	2,3,4,5,6	5000		15	
8	Age	7	10 days, fixed		0	
9	Test	8	20 000		10	
10	Pack	9	20 000	1	0	

Prepared by P. Race © Henley College 2002.

10 Materials management

Objectives

The objectives of the chapter are to understand:

- The importance of materials management.

- Techniques and models for management and control of materials.

For readers employed in service industries this chapter might not at first appear to be relevant. However, we urge you to read on. This is a short chapter, and often approaches used to manage one area of an organization can, with a little imagination, be adapted for use elsewhere. Such an example is provided in this chapter.

Note, this chapter discusses materials management and Chapter 11 covers supply chain management. Supply chain management considers relationships with suppliers and customers and includes the logistics of purchasing and distribution as well as the flow of materials through the process. In this chapter, the focus is on the minimization of the cost of holding materials, and issues considered are:

- when to order materials;
- how much to order;
- how much to hold; and
- how to manage and control stocks of materials.

Some texts use the term inventory management; for our purposes inventory management is synonymous with materials management.

For some service operations, stock control and materials management is not a major issue, e.g. for a lawyer, a travel agent, or a university. For other operations materials are a key issue. On the one hand, the concern will be with not running out of material – as any retailer or restaurant knows, a stock out generally results in a lost sale, and in manufacturing operations input materials are obviously essential. On the other hand, surplus stocks of materials lead to all sorts of problems resulting in losses due to risk costs, storage costs and finance costs.

Risk costs include:

- fashion/taste changes (style, colour, texture);
- past 'use-by date' for foods;

- deterioration;
- obsolescence due to new technology or to model changes which make 'old' models out of date;
- damage;
- pilfering.

  Storage costs include:

- Premises, rent of space, racking, special storage such as refrigeration or secure storage of dangerous goods;
- handling costs (specialized equipment, wages etc.).

  Finance costs include:

- interest on money invested in stocks of materials (either the organization has had to borrow money to pay for the stock held, or the money 'invested' in the stock could have been used elsewhere in the organization);
- insurance.

Most of the above requires no explanation; it is readily apparent that old stock, whether it is old technology or simply no longer fashionable, is hard to sell, and in some cases scrap value will not even cover the original cost.

Finance costs

For obvious reasons, accountants do not like high amounts of stock, and they have a means of measure for stock efficiency known as stock turn (what is a 'good' stock turn will vary from industry to industry). The calculation of stock turn is quite straightforward. The formula is

$$\frac{\text{Annual cost of goods sold divided by}}{\text{Value of stock on hand at balance date}}$$

Example

For a retail operation the cost of the goods sold in a year was £6 000 000, and at balance date £2 000 000 is on hand, the stock turn therefore is 3 (6/2 = 3). (*Note*: to simplify the calculation remove all the noughts.) This means that the stock on hand turns three times a year. Expressed in months this shows at balance date that the retailer is holding four months of stock based on past sales (12 months divided by 3 = 4 months).

To calculate how many days of stock are on hand divide the cost of sales by 365 (the usual number of days in a year); i.e. £6 000 000/365 = 16 438.36; as the amount of stock on hand is £2 000 000 then £2 000 000/16 438.36 = 121 days or four months.

If it is assumed that the retailer is paying for goods within a month of them being received into store, it follows that the retailer is carrying

▶

the cost of holding the stock for three months or 91 days. If this is a cash business (that is the retailer does not sell on credit – goods are paid for when the sale is made), and assuming an interest rate of 12.5 per cent p.a., the retailer will be either paying the bank if the account is overdrawn or foregoing a return on investment of close to £62 500. (£2 000 000 × 12.5 per cent p.a. = £250 000 and 250 000/365 × 91 = £62 329).

On top of the interest cost, or interest foregone, there will be the cost of insurance and the cost of storage space. The true cost, taking all factors into account, will be between 15 per cent and 40 per cent p.a.

Traditional materials management

Pull system

With a pull system a warehouse is viewed as independent of the supply chain, and materials are replenished with order sizes based on a predetermined stock level for each warehouse. The materials stock management system usually operates with a re-order level and a re-order quantity. As Figure 10.1 shows, when the stock drops to a certain level, a re-order is triggered for a predetermined amount. This system takes into account past usage and the lead time needed for a re-order to be satisfied. The aim is to have as small an amount of material on hand as possible at any one time and likewise the re-order quantity will be as small as possible.

Economic Order Quantity – EOQ

The EOQ system is a push system that works where there is an advantage in buying bulk quantities rather than making several small orders. An example for an importer would be to compare the cost of making several small air-freighted orders compared to one large sea-freight container load. The re-order system is

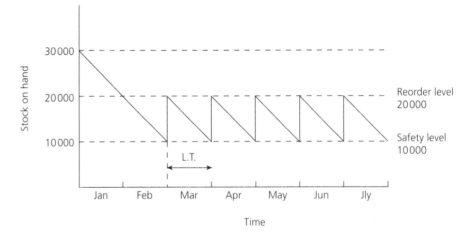

Figure 10.1

Example of a pull system

L.T. = Lead time for delivery ONE MONTH

Example

Annual usage 120 000 per annum (10 000 per month on average).

Lead time one month. (Lead time is the average time taken for a supplier to deliver once an order has been placed).

Stock on hand at the beginning of January = 30 000 items.

Safety stock level = the policy is to have one month reserve stock as a safety measure (in this example = 10 000 items).

If the aim is to hold a minimum of stock at any one time the question is how much to order and when.

generally a computer system which calculates re-order amounts using a formula known as EOQ – Economic Order Quantity. The EOQ assumes that:

- Demand is constant and known.
- Deliveries are complete, on time and to specification.
- There is no stock slippage (loss, theft, damage etc). This means that what the computer shows as being in stock will actually be there.

The formula and an example is shown at Table 10.1.

$$Q = \sqrt{\frac{2\,DO}{PH}}$$

Table 10.1

EOQ model

Where:
Q = Reorder quantity
D = Demand (units of material) per year
O = Cost of each order
P = Price per unit
H = Holding costs

Example
Demand is 3000 units per year
Cost of each order is £50
Price of each item is £12
Holding cost is 10 per cent p.a.

$$Q = \sqrt{\frac{2 \times 3000 \times 50}{12 \times 0.10}}$$

$$Q = 500$$

Cost of ordering

Cost of ordering might not seem to be a big cost (order form, an envelope and a stamp). However consider the savings made when the British Stock Exchange implemented an electronic share transfer system in the mid-nineties. Prior to this share transfer cost £30 per transaction; once share transfers were online or 'paperless' the cost was reduced to £0.30p per transfer. Many organizations have made savings of a similar magnitude by adopting an online purchasing system. For example, in the supermarket, barcoding at the check-out can trigger an automatic online re-order when stock of a particular item drops to a preset level. This will save on staff numbers which would in a manual system be required to physically count stock, calculate forecasted usage and raise order forms, etc.

Cost of holding

The cost of holding stock includes risk costs, storage costs and finance costs, as listed earlier in this chapter.

Centralized purchasing

Many organizations have a centralized purchasing department. The perceived benefits are:

- Larger order quantities leading to negotiation for better prices.
- Preferential treatment from suppliers when materials are in short supply.
- Large purchasing departments with specialized staff. For example, one staff member or group of staff can concentrate (specialize) on one particular product or group of products. For example, a supermarket chain will have a centralized specialist fruit department which will not only place orders but visit orchards, and advise on growing methods, pesticides to use, etc.
- Standardization of product and quality control of product.
- Lower transportation costs.

With online computer communication branches of a large organization can place orders direct to the centralized purchasing department or warehouse as in the supermarket barcoding example given above.

EOQ and lean production

It might be thought that the lean or just-in-time approach to purchasing is not compatible with an EOQ system. The answer is that generally EOQ is not applicable for ordering most components in a lean manufacturing as individual components are ordered and delivered just as required (see the Toyota and Fisher and Paykel examples given in Chapter 9, pp. 178–9). However, some items will be consumed in such quantities that buying one item at a time would not be sensible, i.e. the purchase of one nut and bolt when several hundreds are used daily.

Supply chain

With a total supply, or value, chain approach as introduced in Chapter 4 (Figure 4.1), and explained more fully in Chapter 11, supplier, manufacturer, distributor, retailer and customer are considered as one system. The aim is to be more responsive to customer needs, to reduce stock holding and to develop a close relationship with suppliers – in short with every stage of the supply chain. The value chain approach is to determine where value is being added with the intention of reducing cost in the supply chain. With a well-managed supply chain, the right quantity of product is always delivered on time and is always exactly as specified. In the past little loyalty was shown to suppliers, and the purchasing department, usually a separate function from operations management, would see their role as being to screw the best price possible out of suppliers and to 'shop around' for 'best' deals. Unfortunately 'best' was often seen as being synonymous with cheapest. Consequently the supplier was never certain as to their future relationship with the buyer, and there was little loyalty shown by either purchaser or supplier. As explained in Chapter 4, with the supply chain approach the supplier becomes part of the team and is judged on loyalty, ability to perform on time and to specification, with cost a secondary issue. Cost, of course, is still important, but it is no longer the key issue.

Balance date/stocktakes, or 'Where did the stock go?'

Organizations with large amounts of stock holdings will always be concerned about how accurate the stock records are. The only true way of knowing what is really on hand is to physically count it. The problem at balance date is that when the auditors count the stock and compare it to stock records generally there will be a discrepancy. Stock discrepancies only occur for a limited number of reasons:

1. The stock was never received (short deliveries or over-invoiced).
2. The stock was sold but the sale was not recorded.
3. Stock has been stolen.
4. Stock has been damaged or disposed of but disposal has not been recorded.
5. Stock has been miscoded on receipt or when sold (e.g. 200 hoses booked in, but actually 200 hose-clips received).
6. The stock was sold before it was booked in.
7. Stock has been 'borrowed' (in the sales representative's van for display demonstration purposes).

The rules we recommend (developed from bitter personal experience) to overcome these sorts of problems are:

1. Stock orders to be entered into the system.
2. Stock must be booked into the system when received. The system should be able to verify that goods received match those ordered (see Step 1).
3. Stock not to be sold before it is booked in.
4. Sales must be entered through the system.

5. Payment to be triggered by the system, not by suppliers' invoices. Let the suppliers do the reconciling; you will only be paying for what you ordered and for what you have received.

6. Carry out rolling stock-takes on a portion of the inventory on a weekly, fortnightly or monthly basis. This should overcome the drama of an annual stock-take, and should also reduce your audit account.

The above system relies on a standard computerized system.

With an integrated supply chain approach a heavy reliance is placed on the information technology system. Thus if goods are barcoded as they pass over the sensor at point of sale, the customer's statement is updated, a delivery docket and invoice raised, stock records of the retailer are updated, sales figures and margins calculated and recorded, and a re-order is triggered. If suppliers are tied into the system then the supplier will also be automatically notified of a replacement re-order. Figure 10.2 depicts an integrated inventory system.

Figure 10.2

Integrated point-of-sale system

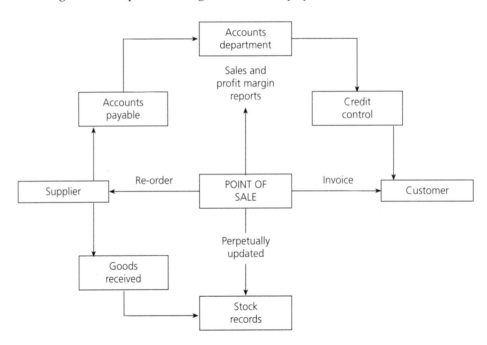

Variation on a theme

An advertising agency had great difficulty in reconciling invoices and statements received from radio, TV and print media. Their answer had been to increase the number of accounting clerks, but still they got behind and not only were they losing commission but they were in danger of losing their accreditation.

Our solution was to recommend that when the agency raised an 'order' on the media the agency's computer system would automatically record a payment advice calculated at the media's rate of charge. Subsequently, when the due date arrived the computer system would tally the advertisements ordered with the rates and automatically print a cheque that would be attached to a summary of payments. Invoices and statements from the various media companies then became irrelevant. The philosophy was to only pay for what was ordered, and to rely on the media to fulfil orders. Generally it was found that the media ran advertisements on the TV and radio more often than had been ordered and seldom was the agency short-changed.

The result was that within four months of the new system being put into place the accounts staff were reduced from fourteen people to three, and office space was able to be sub-let. Additionally, accounts were being paid on time and the relationships with the media had never been better. The only concern was that of the auditors who had difficulty in ignoring the media's statements, invoices and credit notes. Eventually we were able to convince them that the agency was paying for what was ordered and nothing else was relevant.

ABC analysis

ABC analysis is an adaptation of Pareto analysis (see Chapter 4). With Pareto analysis the assumption is that 20 per cent of the items held will account for 80 per cent of the value of materials on hand. With the ABC approach inventory will be categorized as high value, medium value and low value. The high value 'A' items will require the greatest control, the 'B' items will require less control, and the low value 'C' items (nuts and bolts) will require significantly less control. A breakdown of ABC items might look something like that shown in Table 10.2.

With ABC analysis rather than having an annual or periodic stock-take, stock taking can be on a cycle basis. With cycle counting a series of 'mini' stock-takes are made during the year. For example, all A class items might be counted weekly, and some B items might also be scheduled to be counted on a weekly basis.

	A Class Items	B Items	C Items
Number held	10%	30%	60%
Value	55%	40%	5%

Table 10.2

ABC analysis of materials held

Chapter summary

This chapter has considered the management of holding stocks of materials. For readers employed in some service operations this chapter might not appear to be relevant. Nonetheless, many service industries are reliant on materials to function and the cost of holding materials will be of concern. If we think laterally often an approach used in one aspect of management can be adapted for use elsewhere. An example of this is given with the integrated point of sale system and a media booking system for an advertising agency.

Case Study *Wiggo Kongstad*

See also Cyclone Furniture case study in Chapter 6, pp. 124–8.

Question

Advise Mr Kronholm how to change Wiggo's inventory policy, taking account of the impact this will have on customer service and resource utilization. Remember, Wiggo wants to retain its reputation as a customer-oriented supplier in a competitive and cost-conscious market. Use appropriate inventory management models to clarify the analysis of the data and say what additional information you require to improve your analysis.

The company

Wiggo Kongstad was founded in 1941. It is based in Esbjerg, Denmark and is now engaged solely in the supply of Personal Protection Equipment such as working gloves, clothing, footwear, eye and ear protectors, etc. Such goods are sourced in Denmark and also imported from elsewhere in Europe and from the Far East (including China), for sale to 'end-users' primarily in the food and metal industries in Denmark, with some exports to other parts of Scandinavia.

The company occupies a warehouse, a small workshop and office/administration facilities in an industrial area of the town.

Annual turnover last year was DKr 57 million. The current year forecast is DKr 58 million. Competition is high. Pressures on prices are high, and profitability has tended to be low.

The purchasing department

The purchasing department consists of three people, but also two others have responsibility for particular product groups (because of their particular knowledge):

Ms Else Kristiansen – Purchaser
Mr Peter Christensen – Purchaser
Ms Tina Begemann – Assistant Purchaser
Mr Jens Erik Peterson (Stock Manager)
Mr Ole Pederson (Sales Manager)

Group	Item numbers	Turnover (DKr)	Rate of turnover	
				Table 10.3
1. A	53	2 765 000	3.9	Number of/types of items and stock turnovers (last year) by product group
2. B	24	644 000	5.9	
3. C	16	209 000	7.4	
4. D	25	581 000	2.5	
5. E	27	898 000	20.9	
6. F	221	18 816 000	4.2	
7. G	840	9 432 000	3.3	
8. H	418	4 104 000	6.8	
Total	1624	37 449 000	4.1	

Note: Listed turnovers are items sold from stock. Additionally there is a turnover based on direct deliveries from producers to end users at app. DKr 20 000 000.

The role of the department is to ensure that the right goods are in stock at the right time, having been purchased at the right price.

The five people in purchasing share responsibility for the groups of products. Each product group comprises several types of items. The details of the number of items and turnover for groups are given in Table 10.3.

Inventories

Last year total turnover (at sales value) was approximately DKr 37m per annum (Table 10.3) but in addition approximately DKr 20m per annum of items were sold to customers as direct deliveries from suppliers. The stock turnover rate, then 4.1, is a measure of the utilization of that stock.

$$\text{Turnover} = \frac{\text{Sales}}{\text{Average stock}}$$

Stock levels are now considered to be too high – currently having a total sales value of DKr 9.1m. The cost of maintaining this level of stock is substantial (loss, breakage, holding costs, insurance, etc.) Additionally, often items required for customers are not available whilst other items not often required are held in large quantities and occupy valuable space.

In order to improve this situation Mr Kronholm has decided that the overall stock level should be reduced to DKr 6m, i.e. a level reduction of 30 per cent and an increase in stock turnover from 4.1 (at present) to 6.2. He expects that this will be achieved by eliminating (i.e. not stocking at all) items from the lower stock turnover categories – provided that no large or important customers are supplied with such items.

Stock turnover

The rate of turnover for each product group is shown in Table 10.4. It shows some major differences – which surprised Mr Kronholm, so he asked for the data in Table 10.5, which shows the items in each product group categorized by stock turnover rate. It shows, for example, that 588 of the total of 1624 different items stocked have a stock turnover rate of 2 or less and that 56 per cent of items types have a stock turnover rate of 4 or less. Table 10.6 examines the 588 items in the 0–2 turnover category. These items represent a total stock of DKr 3.79m, i.e. 42 per cent of the total and 10 per cent of the annual sales turnover value.

Product	Rate of turnover	Annual turnover DKr	Stock level DKr	Number of items
1. A	3.9	2 765 000	708 974	53
2. B	5.9	644 000	109 152	24
3. C	7.4	209 000	28 242	16
4. D	2.5	581 000	232 400	25
5. E	20.9	898 000	42 967	27
6. F	4.2	18 816 000	4 480 000	221
7. G	3.3	9 432 000	2 858 181	840
8. H	6.8	4 104 000	603 529	418
Total	4.1	37 449 000	9 064 445	1624

Table 10.4

The rate of turnover for each product group

Rate of turnover	0–2	2–4	4–6	6–8	8–10	10+	Items total
1. A	19	14	10	4	0	6	53
2. B	5	4	3	4	3	5	24
3. C	3	2	1	4	1	5	16
4. D	4	5	10	4	1	1	25
5. E	6	0	1	3	2	15	27
6. F	86	41	35	14	13	32	221
7. G	349	169	89	50	39	144	840
8. H	116	91	55	48	31	77	418
Items total	588	326	204	131	90	285	1624

Table 10.5

Turnover rate data

Rate of turnover below two	Number of items	Annual turnover DKr	Annual profit DKr	Profit ratio %	Stock level DKr
1. A	19	685 000	308 000	45	133 000
2. B	5	20 000	8000	41	23 000
3. C	3	23 000	7000	32	4000
4. D	4	120 000	33 000	28	53 000
5. E	6	8000	2000	30	2000
6. F	86	1 746 000	421 000	24	2 501 000
7. G	349	1 610 000	355 000	22	977 000
8. H	116	219 000	58 000	27	102 000
Total	588	4 431 000	1 192 000	27	3 795 000

Table 10.6

Data on items with stock turnover 0–2

Source: Ole Kronholm and Ray Wild, 1996

11 Supply chain management

Ross Milne

Objectives

Issues covered in this chapter are:

- The key elements of a supply chain and the growth in interest in supply chain management.

- The dynamic nature of the supply chain and the factors that drive inefficiency in supply-chain relationships.

- The roles of the various players in the supply chain and how these players add value.

- Strategies that can be used to improve supply chain performance.

- Metrics for evaluating supply chain performance.

Introduction

As described in the opening chapter, customer service is the mission – the reason for existence – of service organizations. Today we see a major change taking place in how organizations define, build and manage operations management systems. More and more, practicing operations managers are being required to co-ordinate activities outside the boundaries of their organization. They are doing this because it is the only way they can provide the types of value that their customers now want. If the operations manager is 'to make the mission happen' then he or she must work with what is now called 'the integrated supply chain'.

> The boundaries between companies will blur as they view themselves as part of an ecosystem, supply chain, or value chain.
>
> *Hasso Platner, co-founder and Vice Chairman, SAP*

What is a supply chain?

If you asked people involved in business to define the term supply chain you would get many different answers. Each definition would reflect the nature of the business and the inputs and outputs that it produced. For some, supply chain is related to purchasing and procurement; to others it is warehousing, distribution and transportation. For others it would be sources of capital and labour.

In a typical supply chain, raw materials are procured and items are produced at one or more factories, shipped to warehouses for intermediate storage and then shipped to retailers or customers.

Melnyk and Swink (2002) give the following holistic definition of the supply chain as:

> The entire network of organizations involved in (1) converting raw materials and information into products and services, (2) consuming the products and services, and (3) disposing of the products and services.

They further state that 'this definition treats the supply chain as a product cradle-to-grave concept, including all value-added activities required to plan, source, make and deliver products and services that meet customer needs.'

What is supply chain management?

As a result of the heightened expectations of customers, operations managers have been forced to focus their attention on managing the value-adding system that the supply chain represents. Thus we have seen the emergence and growth of supply chain management as a dominant force for operational success. But what exactly is supply chain management? Simchi-Levi et al. (2003) define it as follows:

> Supply chain management is a set of approaches utilized to efficiently integrate suppliers, manufacturers, warehouses and stores, so that merchandize is produced and distributed at the right quantities, to the right locations, and at the right time, in order to minimize system wide costs while satisfying service level requirements.

What does this definition suggest? It suggests that supply chain management must consider every organization and facility involved in making the product and the costs involved in doing so. It also implies that the objective is to be cost-effective across the whole supply chain, which requires a system wide approach to optimization. It also involves both strategic and operational level issues.

What about logistics management? Is there a difference between 'logistics' and 'supply chain' management? The Council of Logistics Management defines logistics management as:

> The process of planning, implementing and controlling the efficient, cost effective flow and storage of raw materials, in-process inventory, finished goods, and related information from point of origin to point of consumption for the purpose of conforming to customer requirements.

If we consider this definition we see it is very similar to the first and we can conclude that for our purposes the terms logistics and supply chain management are synonymous.

Structure of the supply chain

The supply chain in its broadest form consists of all the parties involved in the planning, sourcing, making, delivery, consumption and disposal of a product. This process begins with the extraction of resources from the Earth and ends with the return, reclamation or disposal of any associated residuals (waste). The supply chain brings together and integrates the activities of all the parties involved.

A supply chain can consist of many different partners each making a contribution. From a single operations perspective there are upstream suppliers, downstream suppliers, technology/resource suppliers, aftermarket suppliers and customers. Upstream suppliers typically provide raw materials, components and services, e.g. warehousing. Downstream suppliers typically provide enhancements to the operations' finished goods; for example, assembly, packaging and other 'value-adding' activities. Technology/resource suppliers provide equipment, labour, process design and other resources needed to enable and improve production processes. Aftermarket suppliers provide product service and support, such as maintenance, repair, disposal or recycling.

Actual supply chains usually involve many stages of sourcing, making and delivery, and these are not always sequential. If there are several stages in the upstream supply chain then each stage is referred to as a tier. The tier number (first, second, third, . . .) refers to how closely the supplier works with the organization. A first-tier supplier provides components and services directly to the operation. A second-tier supplier provides components and services to the first-tier supplier and so on. Each of these tiers could involve multiple suppliers.

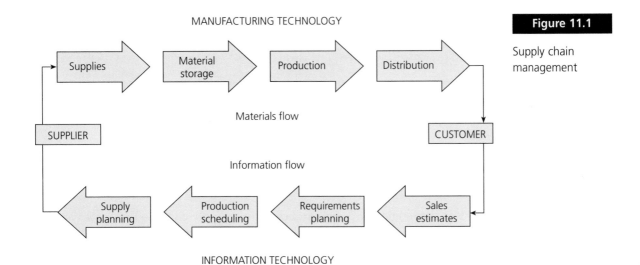

Figure 11.1

Supply chain management

There are also multiple levels making up the downstream portion of the supply chain. These levels are commonly referred to as echelons. A single echelon may consist of partners in locations all over the world. Further, the downstream may in fact involve different channels of distribution.

As one soon realizes, the entire supply chain for even a simple product can be quite complex. For most products there are literally hundreds of organizations involved in the harvesting, manufacturing, assembly, distribution and sales processes. To complicate things further suppliers may produce other products and have connections with suppliers and customers in other markets. Thus it is distinctly possible that all firms in an industry are ultimately connected to one another through various links in the supply chain.

Example

Consider the check-out operator at the super-market. As the goods are scanned at the point of sale what is happening? The barcode is read. What happens to the data? The data can be used to automatically re-order from the warehouse, the stock records are updated, the stores profit margin per line item is calculated. The barcode also allows the sales history of the product to be recorded and if the customer has a loyalty card then the sales data can be used to build up the customers purchasing profile. Not bad for just swiping the product over the scanner!

Your turn!

Take for instance that daily slice of toast. How many layers are there in the supply chain that provided you with that toast? Bread is made from, among other ingredients, flour. Flour is milled from wheat. Wheat is grown from seed and harvested. The bread from the baker is delivered to the retailer or may be baked fresh at the bread shop. The bread is toasted in the toaster. Butter is spread on the toast and it is eaten. What happens after the toast is eaten? Who supplied the electricity for the toaster? As an exercise try to identify as many layers involved in this supply chain and also what it is they supply. To undertake the exercise it is best to choose a position in the supply chain, either the flour mill or the baker. Identify the tiers and echelons from this position.

An additional exercise is to identify value-adding processes as opposed to cost-adding processes that occur in this supply chain.

What makes supply chain management difficult? We have a very complex logistics network to deal with. The following two observations about supply chains also add clarity to the situation supply chain managers have to face.

1. It is challenging to design and operate a supply chain so that total system-wide costs are minimized and system-wide service levels are maintained. Indeed it is frequently difficult to operate a single facility so that costs are minimized and service level is maintained. The difficulty increases

exponentially when an entire system is being considered. The process of finding the best system-wide strategy is known as global optimization.

2. Uncertainty is inherent in every supply chain; customer demand can never be forecast exactly, travel times will never be certain and machines and vehicles will break down. Supply chains need to be designed to eliminate as much uncertainty as possible and to deal effectively with the uncertainty that remains.

A interesting story

Did you know it takes a typical box of cereal more than three months to get from the factory to a supermarket. Why? Some reasons for this could be the time it spends in storage, in transport or even just waiting around to be packaged. Can you think of any other reasons why it might take this time?

Global optimization

What makes finding the best system-wide, or globally optimal integrated solution so difficult? Simchi-Levi *et al.* (2003) suggest the following factors make this a challenge:

1. The supply chain is a complex network of facilities dispersed, in many cases, throughout the world.
2. Different facilities in the supply chain frequently have different, conflicting objectives. Suppliers would like customers to commit to purchasing large volumes with flexible delivery dates. Customers would like to purchase in small volumes with fixed delivery dates.
3. The supply chain is a dynamic system that evolves over time. Not only do customer demand and supplier capabilities change over time, but the relationships also evolve.
4. Systems variations over time are also an important consideration. Time varying demand and cost variability make it difficult to determine the most effective supply chain strategy.

Managing uncertainty

Global optimization is made even more difficult because supply chains must operate in uncertain environments. A variety of factors contribute to this uncertainty:

1. Matching supply and demand is a challenge.
2. Inventory and back-order levels fluctuate considerably across the supply chain even when consumer demand for specific products does not vary greatly. In fact, as we will see later, distributor orders to the factory often fluctuate far more than the underlying retailer demand.
3. Forecasting doesn't solve the problem. It is impossible to predict demand for a specific item no matter what advanced forecasting technique is used.

4. Demand is not the only source of uncertainty. Lead times, manufacturing yields, transportation times, component availability and natural disasters can all have a significant impact.

Why supply chain management?

The emergence and growth of supply chain management as a key factor in business profitability has been driven by certain forces now present in the marketplace. The following are a few reasons for this fundamental shift:

1. *Demands for the flexibility of partnership.* In today's marketplace consumers have a degree of choice and greater ability to make comparisons. As a result, their expectations are rising and their needs constantly changing. Value in this environment is a moving target. Organizations must be flexible to be able to adapt to these changes. It is very difficult for a single organization to possess all the capabilities required to keep up. Organizations now look for suppliers who can provide the skills and capabilities needed as they require them. A firm can easily form partnerships with appropriate skilled suppliers that last as long as the need exists. As demand changes so to can the partnership arrangements.

2. *Advances in technology.* The merging of information and communications technologies has supported the growth in supply chain partnerships. These technologies have enabled extensive connectivity. Today's computer networks, open systems standards and the Internet enable people working in different areas of the supply chain to maintain constant contact. Since information transactions have become so easy, there is less of a need to restrict operations to within traditional organizational boundaries.

   These new capabilities offer the ability for supply chain partners to share information in real time. This enables the partnering firms to hold lower inventories and incur fewer transactions costs. These lower costs can in turn be passed on to the customer in the form of lower prices and better value. Or alternatively retained as increased profits.

3. *Collaborative networks.* Companies have now recognized that great improvements in value can be attained by co-ordinating the efforts of partners along the supply chain. When firms focus only on their internal operations they are making decisions in isolation and as a result this can lead to the overall performance of the supply chain deteriorating. As we will see later, firms who work together and share their plans and other information are actually able to improve the overall supply chain performance to their mutual benefit.

4. *Recognition of core competencies.* Recently there has been a shift away from focusing on markets and products towards considering what the organization's capabilities are. A focus on core competencies allows a firm to concentrate on those few skills and areas of knowledge that make the organization distinct and competitive. These competencies provide the firm with its competitive advantage. Recognizing what processes they are best at allows the firm to concentrate on these processes. This had led to

firms rationalizing what they do and has the effect of producing supply chains where each of the partnering organizations focuses on what they do best.

Example

Getting it wrong

Problems can arise when communication breaks down between marketing groups and supply chain managers.

In the mid-1990s Swedish car maker Volvo found itself with too many green cars in the middle of the year. The marketing wheels spun into motion to move more green cars off collective car yard floors.

The marketing worked fine, the problem was the supply chain planning group hadn't been notified of the promotion on the green cars and thought customers were finally buying green cars. As sales increased, production stepped up to match demand. The end result: Volvo was still left with a huge inventory of green cars at the end of the year.

Source: Hau Lee Stanford University

Supply chain dynamics

The dynamic nature of the supply chain is evident both in the changing nature of the supply chain structure and in the day-to-day activities of the players. In a typical supply chain, each participant can create disturbances, either independently or in response to actions taken elsewhere within the supply chain. These disturbances frequently create a chain reaction. This latter phenomenon is often referred to as playing 'the Beer Game'. This term 'the Beer Game' has its origins in a role-playing simulation of a simple production and distribution system developed at MIT in the 1960s. It has been used in countless courses throughout the world. A computer-based simulation game has been developed to allow participants to explore the issues associated with supply chain dynamics. Simchi-Levi *et al.* (2003) describe the beer game, the computerized beer game and the learning achieved from playing it. Essentially, the game is a simplified beer supply chain consisting of a single retailer, a single wholesaler that supplies the retailer, a single distributor that supplies the wholesaler and a single factory with unlimited raw materials that supplies the distributor. Each component in the supply chain has unlimited storage capacity and there is a fixed supply lead time and order delay time between each component.

In the beer game each player manages one of the supply chain components. Each week the retailer observes external demand, fills that demand if possible, records back-orders to be filled and places an order with the wholesaler. Each of the other components also observes the demand, fills the demand if possible, records the back-order situation and places an order or, in the case of the factory, schedules production. As a result of a change in external demand the whole supply chain has to react to this change. Order processing and filling delays are built into the simulation, which causes the delay in the system. As a result, the players tend to over order, especially when in a backlog situation. The system appears to experience widely oscillating demand that is amplified as we move further up the supply chain. Thus inventory and back-order levels usually vary dramatically from week to week during the game. At the end, players instinctively blame the other players for causing the situation. What they don't accept is that the system itself was capable of reacting in a way that they did not expect.

The game is also described in great detail in Senge (1990). There is no real beer in the beer game and it does not promote drinking, though it does lead to some interesting behaviour amongst participants. What is interesting about the beer game is that it has been played so many times yet the patterns of behaviour generated in the game are remarkably similar. What the beer game does so well is introduce the participants to the phenomenon now referred to as the 'bullwhip effect' – an effect that is observed in all forms of supply chain in practice.

The bullwhip effect

As Melnyk and Swink (2002) describe, the 'bullwhip effect' occurs when a small disturbance generated by a customer produces successively larger disturbances at each upstream stage in the supply chain. Bullwhip effects are of great concern because they incite excessive expediting (moving certain orders ahead of others), increased levels of inventory, uneven levels of capacity utilization (where plants go from being idle to working overtime) and, ultimately, increased costs.

Example

In examining the demand for Pampers disposable nappies, executives at Proctor & Gamble noticed an interesting phenomenon. As expected, retail sales of the product were fairly uniform; there is no particular day or month in which demand is significantly higher or lower than any other. However, the executives noticed that distributors' orders placed to the factory fluctuated much more than retail sales. In addition P&G's orders to its suppliers fluctuated even more. Here was a real life example of the bullwhip effect!

Source: Simchi-Levi *et al.* (2003)

Why does this effect occur? In the absence of information, suppliers are likely to over-react to changes in order sizes, whether upward or downward. The amplification of variations through the stages of the supply chain results in this effect.

The main factors contributing to the increase in variability in the supply chain are as follows:

1. *Demand forecasting*. Traditional inventory management techniques, practiced at each level in the supply chain, lead to the bullwhip effect. Forecasting is typically used to estimate average demand and demand variability. These are used to determine the reorder point and safety stock levels. The more variable the demand the higher the safety stock level and hence this can lead to changing the order quantities increasing variability.

2. *Lead time.* Increase in variability is magnified with increases in lead time. With longer lead times a small change in the estimate of demand variability implies a significant change in safety stock and thus reorder quantities, leading to an increase in variability.

3. *Batch ordering.* If the retailer uses batch ordering then the wholesaler will observe a large order followed by several periods of no orders, followed by another large order. Thus the wholesaler sees a distorted and highly variable pattern of orders. Requirements to ship full truck loads can also lead to the same order pattern. Similarly, end of season sales quotas or incentives can result in unusually large orders being placed on a periodic basis.

4. *Price fluctuation.* If prices fluctuate, retailers often attempt to stock up when prices are lower. This is accentuated by the prevailing practice in many industries of offering promotions and discounts at certain times of the year.

5. *Inflated orders.* During shortages or periods of allocations retailers will inflate their orders to ensure that they will receive supply proportional to the amount ordered. When the period of shortage is over they will resort back to standard orders – further distorting demand estimates.

These factors all contribute to increase the variability of orders placed within the supply chain. One of the first steps that can be taken to reduce the bullwhip effect is to ensure all stages in the supply chain have access to the customer demand information. By centralizing the customer demand information and sharing it with all stages the bullwhip effect can be reduced, but it will not be eliminated.

Simchi-Levi *et al.* (2003) suggest the following methods for coping with the bull-whip effect:

1. *Reducing uncertainty* by centralizing demand information, that is, by providing each stage of the supply chain with complete information on actual customer demand.

2. *Reducing variability.* The bullwhip effect can be diminished by reducing the variability inherent in the customer demand process. This can be achieved by using an 'everyday low pricing' strategy, offering a product at a single consistent price. By eliminating price promotions, a retailer can eliminate many of the dramatic shifts in demand that accompany such promotions.

3. *Lead-time reduction.* Lead time reduction reduces the amount of 'safety stock' estimated to be carried.

4. *Strategic partnerships.* Engaging in any of a number of strategic partnership initiatives can eliminate the bullwhip effect. These initiatives are outlined below.

Supply chain integration

Information enables the supply chain to be integrated. Within any supply chain there are many systems. Managing any one of these systems is a complex task involving a series of trade-offs: principally, the need to balance the two objectives of customer satisfaction and resource utilization. To manage the whole supply chain requires even more complex trade-offs. The complete supply chain needs to be considered as a whole and decisions concerning the whole need to be made. In many supply chains there is no common owner to co-ordinate the whole process. Without co-ordination each facility in the supply chain will do what is best for that facility; the result is local optimization. Each component of the supply chain optimizes its own operation without due respect to the impact of its policy on other components in the supply chain. What is desirable is global optimization which implies that we identify what is best for the whole system. To achieve this involves addressing two issues:

1. Who will optimize?
2. How will the savings obtained through the co-ordinated strategy be split between the different supply chain facilities?

These issues can be addressed in various ways.

Strategic alliances

In order to achieve an integrated supply chain the various players need to work together. The three most important types of supply chain-related strategic alliances are third party logistics (3PL), retailer–supplier partnerships (RSP) and distributor integration (DI).

Third party logistics (3PL)

The use of a third party to take over some or all of a company's logistics responsibilities is becoming more prevalent. 3PL is simply the use of an outside company to perform all or part of the firm's materials management and product distribution function. 3PL relationships are typically more complex than traditional logistics supplier relationships. Modern 3PL arrangements involve long-term commitments and often multiple functions or process management. As organizations focus on their core competencies they are looking for other specialist organizations to partner with.

Retailer–supplier partnerships

As customer satisfaction becomes more imperative and margins get tighter it makes sense to create co-operative efforts between suppliers and retailers in order to leverage the knowledge of both parties. The types of retailer–supplier partnerships can be viewed on a continuum. At one end is information sharing. At the other is a consignment scheme of vendor-managed inventory (VMI), where the vendor completely manages and owns the inventory until the retailer sells it.

In a simple quick response strategy, suppliers receive point of sale (POS) data from retailers and use this information to synchronize their production and inventory activities with actual sales at the retailers. In this strategy the retailer still prepares individual orders, but the POS data is used by the supplier to improve delivery performance and hence reduce supply variability.

Example

Delivering the goods

National Semiconductor, a manufacturer of computer chips, began looking at ways to improve supply chain efficiency in the early 1990s in an effort to improve its profitability. It discovered that it delivered 95 per cent of its products within 45 days from the time the order was placed. The remaining 5 per cent required as much as 90 days. Since customers could not be sure which 5 per cent was going to be late, they were required to hold 90 days of stock of everything. The system was overloaded with inventory.

By looking at the total costs of their system, National realized they needed to simplify the supply process. They proceeded to cut 45 per cent of their product line. To get the remaining products to their customers more effectively they simplified – going from 20 000 routes on 12 airlines involving 10 warehouses, to one central facility in Singapore. To speed up the delivery process they hired Federal Express to handle all the sorting, shipping and storage at the Singapore distribution centre. This has resulted in major operating improvements. National can move products from factory to customer in four days or less. Distribution costs are down from 2.6 per cent to 1.9 per cent of revenues.

Source: Henkoff (1994)

Your turn!

The National Semiconductor example offset inventory costs reductions with increased freight costs. In doing this they significantly reduced delivery time. What impact would this have had on inventory held by their customers? How would this have affected their financial accounts?

In a continuous replenishment strategy, sometimes called rapid replenishment, vendors receive POS data and use this data to prepare shipments at previously agreed-upon intervals to maintain specific levels of inventory.

In a vendor-managed inventory system, the supplier decides on the appropriate inventory levels of each product and the appropriate policies to maintain these levels. The goal of many VMI programmes is to eliminate the need for the retailer to oversee specific orders for replenishment. The ultimate aim is for the supplier to manage the inventory and only receive payment for it once it has been sold by the retailer – in essence the retailer is providing an outlet for the supplier.

Distributor Integration (DI)

Modern information technology has enabled this strategy in which distributors are integrated so that expertise and inventory located at one distributor is available to the others. DI can be used to address both inventory-related and service-related issues. In terms of inventory, DI can be used to create a large pool of inventory across the entire distributor network, thus lowering total inventory costs while raising customer service levels. Similarly, DI can be used to meet the customers' specific needs by directing those requests to the distributors best suited to address them.

The Internet and the supply chain

The influence of the Internet on the economy in general and business practice in particular has been tremendous. The direct business model employed by industry giants such as Dell Computers and amazon.com enables customers to order products over the Internet and thus allows these companies to sell their products without relying on third-party distributors apart from those providing the physical delivery service.

Similarly, the Internet and the emerging e-business models have produced expectations that many supply chain problems will be resolved merely by using these new technology and business models. Whilst it has promised so much, in reality the expectations have not been achieved. In many cases the downfall of some of the highest profile Internet businesses has been attributed to their logistics strategies.

Whilst the success of the business to customer concept has not yet eventuated, the use of the Internet for business to business integration has more likelihood of success. Integration of the supply chain players is made possible with the use of the Internet and the associated technologies.

Reviewing the impact of the new technologies on the supply chain provides an interesting development. The Internet and evolving supply chain strategies has seen a shift in transportation and order fulfilment strategies away from case and bulk shipments to single item and smaller-size shipments, and from shipping to a small number of stores to serving highly geographically-dispersed customers. This shift has seen the importance of partnerships with parcel and less than full load industries. It has also increased the importance and complexity of reverse logistics, that of handling the significant numbers of product returns. Thus, one of the big winners in the new developments is the parcel industry. Indeed, one of the important advantages of the parcel industry is the existence of an excellent information infrastructure that enables real-time tracking. Players in this industry who work to modify their own system in order to integrate it with their customers' supply chains are likely to be successful.

As businesses come to understand the role of the Internet we will see new models of business evolving. As yet, what those models will be is unclear, but one thing is for certain: the Internet will have an impact on how supply chains of the future will be managed.

Customer relationship management

The recent growth in availability of customer relationship management (CRM) systems has led to access to data that can be used to improve overall supply chain performance. The objective of CRM is to develop a customer-centred organization that ensures every opportunity is used to delight customers, foster customer loyalty and build long-term relationships that are mutually beneficial. The ultimate goal is to ensure that each individual customer's current and future wants and needs can be satisfied. This involves the capture of individual customer transaction details and developing a picture from this historical data of what customer needs and purchasing habits are.

CRM's relevance to overall supply chain management lies in the need to integrate such systems with the management of the supply side. The information gathered by the CRM systems can be used to improve the overall performance of the complete supply chain. As the need for supply chain transparency increases, businesses are looking for ways to improve the efficiency of supply. This has led to the development of the concept of total demand chain management

Demand chain management

The concept of demand chain management (DCM) can best be examined using the following relationship:

$$DCM = SCM + CRM$$

That is, demand chain management is about ensuring that the current and future needs of the customer are satisfied in the most efficient and effective way possible. This leads to co-ordinated product and supply chain design initiatives.

The Supply Chain Council

The Supply Chain Council is an independent not-for-profit organization that was established in 1996. It is dedicated to the development, promotion and support of cross-industry standards for supply chain management. Its role is to provide member companies with access to industry standards that allow for benchmarking against average and best-in-class. To learn more about the Supply Chain Council visit www.supply-chain.org

Also associated with this is the Supply Chain Operations Reference model (SCOR). This model is a set of metrics for measuring supply chain performance. A company can use the SCOR framework to evaluate its current performance and then compare this to industry benchmarks, enabling it to identify opportunities for improvement.

Measuring supply chain performance

The Supply Chain Council has proposed a metrics system that focuses on four areas: (1) customer satisfaction/quality, (2) time, (3) cost, and (4) assets. A range of measures are described for each category. Both predictive and outcome measures are suggested.

Three sample measures are as follows:

1. *Supply Chain Response Time* (SCRT) is a measure of the time it takes to react a major shift in market demand. It is the measure of how long it takes for the organization to recognize the demand shift, internalize that fact, re-evaluate demand and to adjust production by 20 per cent.

2. *Cash-to-Cash (C-to-C) cycle time* (CT) is the number of days between paying for inputs (raw material) and getting paid for the product. It is calculated as:

   CtCCT = inventory days of supply + days of sales outstanding – average payment period for material.

   Best in class have less than 30 days' cycle time, while medium performers can be up to 100 days.

3. *Perfect Order Fulfilment* is a measure of meeting customer expectations. This is similar to the concept of DIFOTIS, that of Delivering In Full, On Time, In Spec. That is, a perfect order meets the following standard:

   - All items on order are delivered in the quantities requested.
   - Delivered to the customers' required delivery date.
   - All documentation supporting the order is complete and accurate.
   - Delivered in perfect condition, no damage and to the customer's required specification.

   To have a perfect order all four of the above must be satisfied. Perfect order fulfilment is calculated as the ratio of the number of perfect orders to the total number of orders. Using this measure has proved revealing for many organizations. For many firms at first evaluation this measure can be as low as 27 per cent. And this measure is directly related to customer satisfaction.

Chapter summary

In this chapter we have discussed the concepts of supply chain management. The developments in the field of supply chain management have identified that the future success of business will depend on working in partnership with the players that operate within that business' respective supply chain. Developments in technology have enabled the sharing of POS information with suppliers. This has contributed to better management of customer demand. Businesses now know the importance of supply chain management in providing opportunities for improved organizational performance.

Case Study *Fresh Foods*

Questions

1. What are the customer service and resource utilization objectives at Evesham? Show the relative importance of selected criteria and identify their conflicts.

2. Identify the system structures for (i) Evesham, (ii) a retailer RDC. How do these structures support the operation's objectives? Comment on the robustness of these structures.

3. Identify the main capacity and scheduling problems that may be experienced at the Evesham depot. What strategies are used to deal with them?

4. Suggest, with appropriate reasoning, four key performance indicators for the Operations Manager at the Evesham depot.

(*Note*: To enable simplification and confidentiality data in this case study has been modified).

Christian Salvesen is a major European logistics business specializing in the strategic management of outsourced supply chains. The company employs 16 000 people and operates at 200 sites in eight countries.

A key task of the supply chain is to define its mission statement, such as: 'To meet customer service requirements consistently and reliably through a mutually cost effective supply chain'. This usually takes some time to achieve, not because it is either complex or controversial but because the supply chain can mean different things to different people. Furthermore, although the objectives are unanimous, the way in which each organization achieves them through their respective supply chains is different.

'It is these two elements – customer service and resource efficiency – that drive any supply chain', says Ian Baldwin, Logistics Director.

Let us examine Salvesen's experience in implementing these principles in the area of the supply of fresh foods through Evesham chilled depot. Here is a product group whose availability is measured in hours. Meticulous planning and co-ordination is required to customer demand in rigid 'delivery windows' and plans have to cope with the most unpredictable element of a supply chain – Mother Nature.

Evesham is a chilled depot of approximately 20 000 sq. ft. situated in the Vale of Evesham in Worcestershire, which is one of the major produce growing areas in the UK. It has a staffing level of 94 and nearly half are qualified reefer vehicle drivers. It is a stockless depot for cross-docking operation under temperature controlled conditions. The main function of the depot is to act as a consolidator of suppliers' produce and chill products received from various parts of the country for subsequent onward despatch to the majority of the UK and Irish Regional Distribution Centres.

Operating on a 24/7 basis Evesham is a critical link in the fresh food temperature controlled supply chain, and allows the speediest possible route from field to plate, thus preserving both product quality and maximum shelf life. The depot has an operating revenue budget of £7.6m.

The depot is obviously subject to seasonality due to the nature of its core volume product, but continues to develop its year-round chill business. The majority of its profits, however, are derived during the summer months of the produce season. The average throughput is 7600 pallets per week, but the volume peaks in August accounting for 21 per cent of the annual throughput.

Regular daily collections are made from suppliers/packers during the day and return to the depot during the afternoon/evening. Product is off-loaded into a cross dock/straight through chilled warehouse facility, where it is sorted for onward delivery destination and despatched anytime from 16.00 hours onward through until 01.30 that night.

Orders from the major retailers would have been received into Evesham between the hours of 11.00 and 17.00 that day. A typical example of the complexity of the physical operation would be for suppliers such as Flamingo/Wealmore which are based in the northwest of London.

10.00	Vehicle leaves Evesham to collect clean empty trays from Corby for delivery to Flamingo.
16.00	Arrives at Flamingo, off-loads trays and reloads half the vehicle with product for that day's retail orders.
17.00	Arrives at Wealmore to collect balance of load for that day's retail orders.
20.30	Arrives back at Evesham to off-load product into chill warehouse where it is sorted into delivery destinations for Ireland and Scotland.

Tesco	Dublin/Belfast/Livingstone
Safeway	Bellshill
Asda	Grangemouth
Somerfield	Pitreavie

(Irish product would leave asap).

▶

23.00   Vehicle leaves for Salvesen depot at Ormskirk in Lancashire.

01.30   Arrives at Ormsmirk where further product is put on (Ormskirk is a produce growing area) and the trailer is then taken on to Scotland by an Ormskirk driver, with the Evesham driver returning with another trailer (may be loaded) to Evesham.

07.30   Arrives at first of Scottish delivery points.

On completion of deliveries the vehicle would go into the Salvesen Operation at Camerons Wood (Livingstone, Scotland) to confirm all activities onto the Salvesen 'Track and Trace' Sharp system (confirms visibility of delivery to customer). The vehicle may then reload with produce or soft fruits collected earlier by Camerons Wood from the Scottish growers, and return it via the Ormskirk changeover link into Evesham for consolidation and onward delivery to the retail RDCs (Re-distribution Centres).

The transport fleet at Evesham comprises 34 owned tractors supported by 53 temperature controlled trailers, including 40 hired trailers. In addition to 10 tractor/trailers based at Ormskirk the operation has the flexibility to 'buy in' extra resource from other depots in the Salvesen temperature controlled network. The hired tractors are made up of both long-term rental contracts and short-term casual hire to meet the variable demand and seasonality in a changing market.

Currently Salvesen covers the following retailer RDC profile for fresh foods.

Tesco	11
Safeway	8
Somerfield	7
Asda	8
CWS	2
Marks & Spencer	3

The service level agreements with retailers include that delivery should be made within the limit of the delivery window. Any significant variation of delivery time is subject to penalty. There is no buffer stock, as such a short shelf-life of such a perishable product group does not allow for it. There are also other challenges, such as forecasting the effect of weather or promotions. The supply chain cannot afford any shortage of refrigerated trucks of appropriate capacity when needed. 'Even when we achieve 100 per cent availability on all products it may count for nothing if the absenteeism of drivers is out of control.'

Written by Ron Basu, 2002, with permission from Salvesen. For more information see www.salvesen.com/business/central/

12 Project management

Objectives

In this chapter we consider:

- The definition and purpose of project management.

- The project management knowledge areas or functions/specialist topics to assist with the management of projects.

- The project process by establishing an understanding of the project life cycle.

Introduction

We gave the definition of a service operating system in Chapter 1 as 'the transformation of inputs (people and other resources) to service outputs' and this definition is also appropriate for projects; that is, a project can also be seen as an operating system with the same key differences. Firstly, let's consider a definition of a project: 'a project is a *temporary* endeavour undertaken to create a *unique* product or service. It is those key differences – *temporary* and *unique* – that provide management with the key differences between projects and ongoing operations. Temporary means that every project has a definite beginning and a definite end. Unique means that the product or service is different in some distinguishing way from all similar products or services' (Project Management Institute, 2002). Examples of projects that can be encountered in service operations are:

- Editing a book series.
- Launching a new service product such as a new credit card.
- Developing an information system such as a customer relationship management (CRM) system.
- Implementing a revised customer service complaints procedure.
- Managing a change in culture from say a bureaucratic to an entrepreneurial culture.
- Performing an audit of a process as part of a quality programme.

> **Your turn!**
>
> Can you think of some examples of temporary endeavours to create unique services?

Modern management thinking views the management of change as a project. For example, The Office of Government and Commerce (OGC) in the UK provides a project management methodology called PRojects IN Controlled Environments, better known as 'PRINCE 2' and suggests a project 'in broadest terms is a managed collection of activities to bring about a desired *change* and PRINCE 2 provides a framework whereby a bridge between a current state of affairs and a planned future state may be constructed.' Therefore, a project gives the project manager a central role in steering an organization through a change process – and hopefully to improved performance! You can read more about managing change in Chapter 15.

Projects might be set up to manage tangible outcomes such as moving location, launching a new product or editing a book. Alternatively, they can be less tangible outcomes such as creating a quality culture. No matter what the scope of the project, it is important that the ongoing day-to-day operations of the organization are not compromised. Treating change as a project is a sound approach to managing change without compromising the day-to-day operation.

What are the basics of project management?

Projects are temporary and unique endeavours and show the following characteristics. Projects:

- Are influenced by goal driven activities of multiple stakeholders.
- Need resources across functions and from outside the organization.
- Require temporary involvement from people who often have other conflicting roles in the organization.
- Are managed through a series of phases or stages called the project life cycle. Those stages are project definition, project planning, implementing/ controlling the project and finishing the project.
- Often involve risks beyond those of an ongoing operation.

This chapter is structured around our project management framework shown in Figure 12.1.

We take a 'questioning'- the vertical axis – and 'process' approach – the horizontal axis of Figure 12.1 – to managing projects, where the project management knowledge areas such as *defining scope* are applied across the *project life cycle stages* – definition, planning, execution and closure of the project. The attention of project management is to plan and control each knowledge area against each stage of the project life cycle so, for example, managing scope involves scope planning and scope control in roughly equal amounts. However, managing objectives of quality, cost and time are predominantly controlling functions with a heavy focus during the execution phase of the project life cycle.

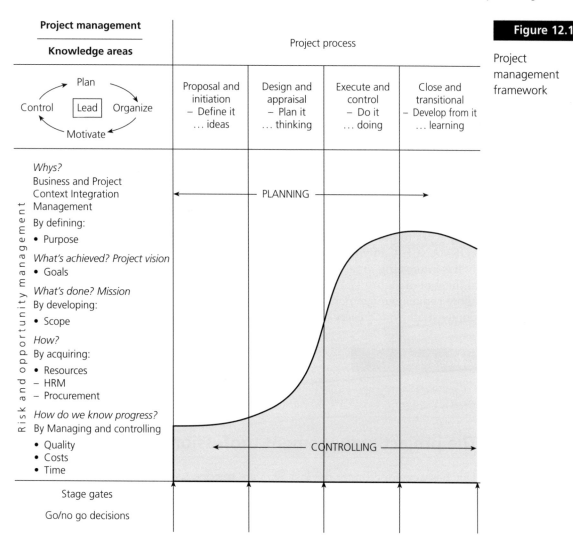

Figure 12.1

Project
management
framework

Let's consider the questions *why, what* and *how* to address the knowledge areas of project management:

WHY is the project being initiated?

It is necessary to understand the business context, the project environment (see frameworks and models in Chapter 3) and the need for integration with other activities and other projects. This will lead to an understanding of business NEEDS which will help define PURPOSE for the project.

PURPOSE can be influenced by: a problem to be solved, an opportunity to be exploited, a benefit to be gained or an inefficiency to be eliminated. (Turner, 1999: 107).

WHAT has to be achieved by the project? Communicate the vision.

This should be clearly presented as GOALS for the project and expressed as quantitative measures.

WHAT has to be done during the project?

This is managed by identifying the SCOPE of the project developed by breaking down the project into 'packages' of product and work, known as the Product and Work Breakdown Structure (see later).

HOW the scope is to be achieved?

This is addressed by identifying the ORGANIZATION, the RESOURCES and the CONTRACTORS needed to carry out the work of the project in order to achieve the QUALITY, COSTS and TIME objectives set out by the goals which will indicate when the project is completed.

Point of interest

When managing small projects it can be useful to abbreviate this questioning framework to the 4P's: management of PURPOSE, PROCESS, PEOPLE and PER-FORMANCE. Can you see the links?

It is interesting to see the boundaries between the stages of the project life cycle at the foot of Figure 12.1 as decision gates or go/no-go points in the project. These allow senior management to review and control projects against emergent corporate strategy and carry out a project audit.

Your turn!

Can you identify any projects that were halted following a stage gate review?

The project management profession

This has developed over the last 50 years to cope with the challenges and issues demanded by projects mentioned above and is dominated by the Project Management Institute (PMI), based in the USA and the various national associations such as the Association of Project Managers (APM), based in the UK (see references for web links). Project management is described as 'the application of knowledge, skills, tools and techniques to project activities in order to meet stakeholder's needs and expectations from a project.' (PMI: 6). The following knowledge areas have been identified to help manage projects through the life cycle stages (PMI: 7)

Project management knowledge areas

Let's consider the following areas where the project manager needs to acquire knowledge and understanding to better manage projects.

Project context

Projects and project management operate in environments broader than the project itself; therefore it is necessary to carry out a strategic analysis to identify influences and needs early in the project. The framework presented in Chapter 3,

Figure 3.1, where the project and its deliverables would occupy the centre of the diagram, provides useful issues which could impact upon the project and its outcomes, such as political, economic, social, technological, legal, environmental and competitor behaviour.

At the same time, it is necessary to address the question, 'Should the project go ahead?' Various tools can be used to help make this decision, such as an assessment of strengths and weaknesses of the proposal, resource capabilities and availabilities, funds, anticipated returns through discounted cash flow analysis, relationship to other project activity and risks.

Stakeholder analysis is also essential at this early stage to ensure effective management of all parties involved. Tools such as stakeholder force field maps, with power/influence and interests highlighted, as in Figure 12.2, can help identify 'friends and foes' and highlight communication strategies for effective management.

Example

Figure 12.2 represents the various stakeholder positions in the C-Direct case study, presented at the end of this chapter.

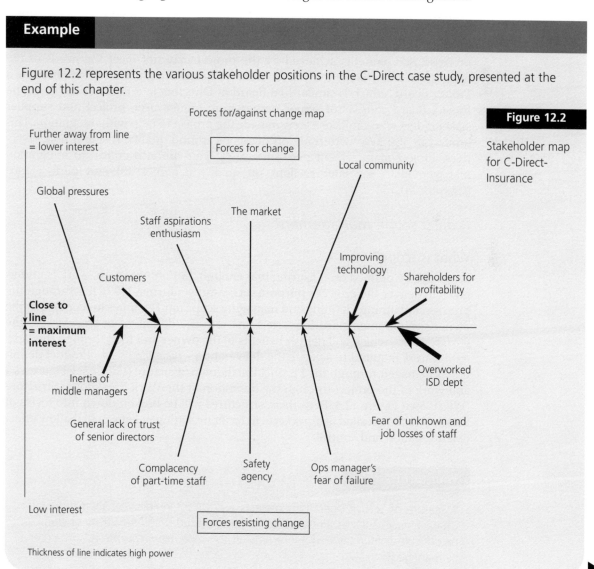

Figure 12.2

Stakeholder map for C-Direct-Insurance

▶

In short we need to identify:

- Who are the stakeholders?
- What are their interests?
- How can they influence the project?
- What are their strengths and weaknesses?

- What are their views?
- What is their anticipated behaviour?
- How can we gain their support?

By effective stakeholder management the likelihood of project success is greatly increased.

Integration management

Integration management is a crucial part of project management throughout the project life cycle. Consider for example the handover and transition stage of the project requires the deliverables of the project to be integrated with the future operations by effective management of the handover. Of course, unless there is effective integration at the front end of the project aligned to the owner's strategy processes, the benefits achieved by the project may not meet the needs of the owner and other stakeholders. In some projects, integration occurs through a Project Board, which is similar to a Board of Directors in a limited company. The Project Board consists of senior parties from owner, user, project and supplier stakeholders who can take a view outside the project to help with integration. This group can also help with trade-off decisions around quality, cost and time objectives. Project management performance systems are also critical to integration management – see later sections on quality (Chapter 13) and performance (Chapter 14).

Project scope management

What is scope?

Scope can be defined as: 'ensuring that enough, but only enough, work is undertaken to deliver the project's purpose successfully' (Turner, 1999). It is through the process of planning, defining and managing scope (and changes to scope), that the owner's requirements are converted first into the definition of *deliverables* – the *product scope* – which will deliver benefits to the owner and then through the *statement of work* required to achieve the deliverables – *the project scope*. Product definition is managed through the Product Breakdown Structure (PBS) – see Figure 12.3 and work of the project through the definition of the Work Breakdown Structure (WBS) – see Figure 12.4. Both these structures will be broken down into levels of detail sometimes called *work packages* to facilitate setting *milestones* that allow effective delegation and control.

Your turn!

A feature of service operations projects are the intangibility of their outcomes. Characteristics such as ambience of facilities, attitudes and sensitivity of staff can be difficult to quantify and hence difficult to scope. How can these 'soft' criteria be managed?

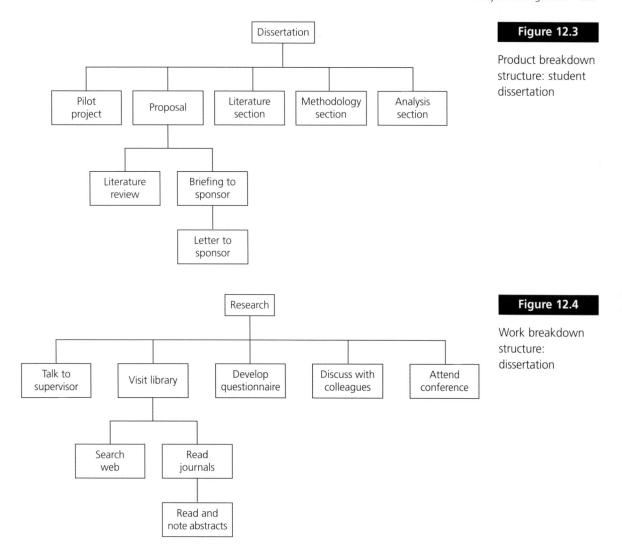

Figure 12.3

Product breakdown structure: student dissertation

Figure 12.4

Work breakdown structure: dissertation

The benefits of a good PBS are that it:

- Focuses on deliverables;
- Helps define scope;
- Gives a stable planning framework;
- Offers better control of the scope of work;
- Provides a framework for the control of the deliverables or product.

The features of the WBS are:

- It is a hierarchical structure that identifies the total work that has to be carried out.
- It divides the project into logical areas of work and hence enables us to exercise control
- It gives us a common structure for controlling:

  - scope
  - costs
  - technical activity
  - programme timing
  - documentation
  - materials and resources.

By using the PBS and the WBS it is possible to identify key events in the project such as the submission of the literature survey in Figure 12.3 and call this a 'milestone' – an event you know has been achieved! Identifying milestone events allows high level plans to be drawn which offer:

- Vision for the project.
- A strategic plan for the project.
- Specific results throughout the project.
- Describes what to achieve – not how to do it.
- Consists of intermediate conditions or states.
- Obtains commitment and cooperation from internal and external resources.

Example

An example of a milestone plan is shown in the commissioning document project definition example at the end of the chapter.

Project time management

The management of the project schedule is one of the most important project management knowledge areas. It is often erroneously seen to be what project managers do – draw bar charts and keep them up to date! So, what should a good schedule do? It should:

- Provide dates and durations of project activities.
- Indicate accountability for these activities – so providing a major communications document.
- Indicate key points within the project, milestones, links to other projects, etc.
- Allow progress against plan to be mapped and communicated to parties.
- Provide a baseline from which to forecast the future.

How is the schedule developed?

- Identify and appraise the business goal/objective.

- Define the scope and develop the PBS and WBS.
- Define activities.
- Decide relationships and precedence – activities that must be finished before subsequent activities can start.
- Draft the network and linkages following precedence.
- Assign time to each activity.
- Carry out forward pass – earliest times.
- Do backward pass – latest times.
- Difference is float.
- No difference identifies the critical path.

We recommend that you link these points to the details of scheduling presented in Chapter 9.

There are two fundamental ways of drawing schedules; networks and bar charts. Both can be seen in Chapter 9.

Networks – allow complex relationships between activities to be drawn and allows *critical path*, that is the shortest path, through the network and *float* or spare time on activities to be calculated. Of course, there is zero float on critical path activities – that means no spare time!

Bar charts are easier to understand and provide excellent communication and control charts.

It is important that the project team owns the schedule – get them involved when developing it.

Example

The use of 'Sticky-Notes' and group processes to develop the schedule starting with the last deliverable and asking the question 'What must I have done before I can start the activity?' and work backwards towards the start. Group the activities in parallel, i.e. run at the same time unless there are dependencies or resource constraints that prevent this. Assess resource requirements to look for levels/numbers required and plan around conflicts with other projects.

Project cost management

Money management of a project has the following elements:

- Estimating the costs and benefits of doing the project.
- Gaining funds.
- Estimating costs through PBS and WBS.
- Planning the baseline budget including risk and contingency planning.
- Tracking expenditure.

- Forecasting future costs and cash flows.
- Reporting accounts for reasons of governance.

Entire books have been written on these topics. Here we will focus on the linkages between them through the Product Breakdown Structure, the Organization Breakdown Structure and the resources needed to execute the project – people, materials, equipment, facility and overheads. These relationships are shown in the 'cost control cube' where each small cube represents an element of cost, which builds into the overall, budgeted cost. This allows aggregation and disaggregation of costs and expenditures to facilitate planning, monitoring and control of costs. A diagram representing the cost control cube is shown in Figure 12.5 (Turner, 1999).

Project quality management

Project quality management must address both the management of the quality of the product/service (the deliverables) of the project and the quality of the project process configured to deliver that product/service – the work required to achieve the deliverables.

Figure 12.5

Cost control cube

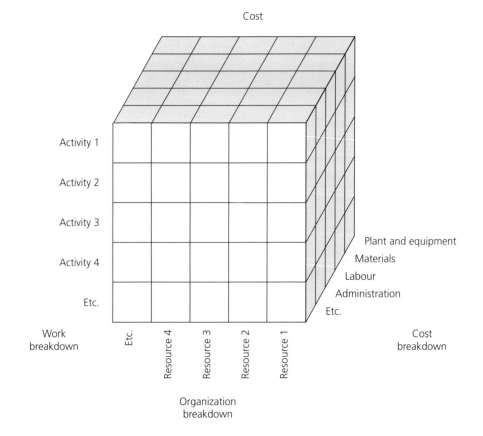

Example

For a book project, the details, accuracy and style of writing by the author contribute to product quality. The research, editing and desktop pub- lishing activity will contribute to the project process quality and especially effect the costs and timing of the project.

The elements of Project quality management which impact on product and project process are: quality planning, quality assurance, quality control and total quality management (see Figure 12.6).

Quality planning involves identifying appropriate quality standards of the products/services required by clients and determining how to satisfy them – defining 'fitness for purpose' as in Chapter 13.

Quality assurance involves exercising policies, procedures and processes to demonstrate that work has been done according to the quality plan.

Quality control is the monitoring and control of the results of project work to determine if they comply with the quality plans and standards and if they do not, take corrective action. If actions occur quickly this should help eliminate unsatisfactory performance – 'conformance to specification' (see also Chapter 13).

Total quality management encompasses all of the above elements and drives a quality culture throughout the project life cycle process as identified in this chapter. A quality culture involves individuals taking personal responsibility for quality planning and control and driving actions proactively through their ownership of problems and search for continuous improvements – not easy to achieve in fragmented project work!

Remember, quality, cost and time objectives will be subjected to trade-offs as discussed throughout this book. It can be useful to represent this trade-off in the objectives triangle, see Figure 12.7.

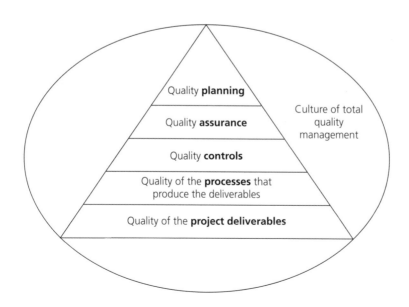

Figure 12.6

Quality management framework

Figure 12.7

Balancing objectives

Quality

● Indicates a focus on quality   ■ Indicates a focus on time   ✚ Indicates a focus on cost

Cost   Time

This objectives triangle is sometimes called the 'holy triangle of the project manager' and to bring the project to completion by achieving the quality, cost and time objectives was the mantra for those project managers with a narrow internal focus, who missed or indeed didn't have the responsibility for meeting multiple stakeholders needs and wants that were not always the same as those of the sponsor.

Project risk management

Risk has been defined as 'the chance of exposure to the adverse consequences of future events' (PRINCE 2) and can impact all stages of the project. It is essential to manage risk throughout the project by following a risk analysis and management process.

Risk identification, through discussing and highlighting risk issues at regular project meetings and maintaining a risk register.

Risk quantification, can be assessed by analyzing the impact elements of risk using the following formula:

Impact of risk = Likelihood of risk × Consequences of risk

An example of the use of this equation is lightning strikes (weather not industrial relations). There is small likelihood of lightning striking low buildings and the consequences of property damage are manageable if it does. With tall buildings, however, there is a higher likelihood of a lightning strike and of course consequences of loss of life are higher. So, lightning protection is commonly installed on tall buildings. Using a scale of 1 (low) and 5 (high), it is possible to draw up a simple risk register to illustrate comparative risks:

Table 12.1

Risk quantification

Type of building	Likelihood	Consequence	Risk
Low height	Low (1)	Medium (2)	Low (2)
High building	Medium (3)	High (5)	High (15)

Risk response development. This process includes management actions ranked as:

- avoidance, where the risk is life or death;
- deflection, where another party is better able to manage the risk;
- contingency planning, where the risk is less serious and if it happens, alternative plans can be executed.

Risk monitoring and control. Adopt a management control process that will record the plan, monitoring progress against that plan, recognizing any variances and taking positive steps to overcome them. Maintaining a risk register and reviewing this as part of regular project meetings sometimes facilitates these processes. See also Chapter 5, control cycles.

Managing opportunities. It is important to remember that whilst addressing risks, project management should also be vigilant for opportunities, which could improve project processes and deliverables. These can be identified, quantified and controlled using similar processes as risk management and can cover criteria such as technical, commercial and behavioural issues that could improve project performance.

Project human resource (people) management and project organization

As we saw in Chapter 7, people are the critical part of any operation. This is equally so in projects. Let's look again at some motivation theories developed earlier that provide pointers for project managers when executing projects.

Maslow's hierarchy of personal needs should be recognized and addressed by the project manager:

- Sustenance – satisfy basic Health and Safety needs – need for food, water and air.
- Security – need for shelter, security, safety.
- Belonging – need for friends and company, teams.
- Recognition – need for self-respect/esteem.
- Achievement – need for self-fulfilment from a job well done.

Turner (1999), has added the following factors – the 5P's, which help motivate teams when managing projects. A project must have:

- Purpose – a clear vision.
- Proactive culture – freedom to act.
- Progress opportunities – opportunity to learn.
- Professional recognition – respect for skills and experience.
- Profit sharing – to encourage an entrepreneurial culture.

The project manager needs to recognize these by effectively:

- Managing down – task, team and individuals.

- Managing out/across – peers, users and supporters.
- Managing up – sponsors, champions and consumers.

The project manager needs to assess availability of resources and choose the right people.

The project manager will need to be aware of *team roles* and try to select balanced teams with the following roles (remember individuals may take more than one role): co-ordinator, critic, ideas person, implementer, external contact, inspector, team builder.

It is important to recognize that teams move through a number of developmental stages before they can be classed as successful (Tuckman, 1965). The project manager should provide events and support to accelerate the team's recognition and management of these stages of team development:

- *Forming*, when team members work out what they are supposed to be doing and try to be a part of it.
- *Storming*, when members express strongly-held views which can lead to conflict and competition. Some push for power whilst others withdraw.
- *Norming*, when teams begin to organize themselves, listen more to each other and develop logical processes, agreeing criteria for future success.
- *Performing*, by now a sense of group loyalty has developed leading to an atmosphere of openness and mutual trust. The team now performs better than the sum of the individuals in the group.
- *Mourning*, when the task is finished, individuals leave the team and new members may join. Disintegration and integration must be managed and not left to chance. Teams eventually have to disband.

Organization structure

Organizations are often structured around what people do – their functions/ specialisms and who they report to – their boss/client. There are three main forms of organization: organization by function, by project/task or a hybrid of these two, the matrix organization. See Figures 12.8 and 12.9. Features of these are:

Functional organization. You carry out work as directed by your functional manager. Even if you work on a project, tasks will be allocated and controlled within your function. An example could be market research done by the marketing department for a particular project.

Project organization. You work within the project and the project manager manages you. You can be isolated from your function and your focus is on the task. An example could be a personnel specialist being transferred to a large change management project.

Matrix organization. The key feature of this 'half-way house' is having two bosses/ report lines. The authority for the details of the technical aspects resides with the functional manager, but the project aspects such as timing and costs reside with the project manager. Pleasing two bosses can be very challenging! People can work on a number of projects in a matrix organization. An example of a matrix organization could be a consultancy or an education establishment such as Henley Management College, where the lecturer reports to the faculty (functional) manager and to the materials development manager (project manager) for writing new books.

It is interesting to note that in Figure 12.8, in a functional matrix organization, the balance of power resides towards the function, and in a project matrix, the power resides towards the project. A balanced matrix can exist but it is rare and relies on excellent communications between all participants.

Organization breakdown chart

This is a way of linking resources, activities, timings and communication needs in a project (see Figure 12.10).

It is useful to allocate a coded communication protocol in the matrix, for example:

R = The person is *responsible* for doing the work on that activity at that time.

A = This person is *accountable* for the authorization of that activity and will approve outcome and pay the bill.

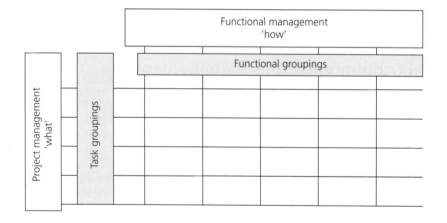

Figure 12.8

The 'what' and 'how' of matrix organizations

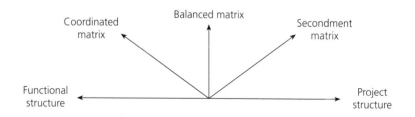

Figure 12.9

Types of matrix organizations

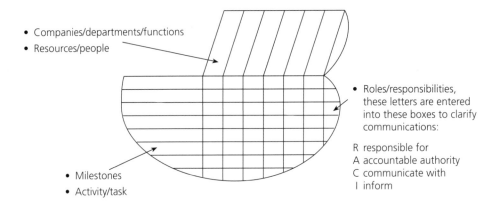

Figure 12.10

Responsibility chart

Resources identified and prioritized

- Companies/departments/functions
- Resources/people

- Roles/responsibilities, these letters are entered into these boxes to clarify communications:

R responsible for
A accountable authority
C communicate with
I inform

- Milestones
- Activity/task

C = *Communicate* with this person where communication means telling and listening – a two-way process.

I = *Informing* that person as a one-way process, telling or listening only.

The organizational breakdown chart provides an excellent communication document for the project and can be coupled to the bar chart for the project to provide single page reporting – very useful for communications and management controls.

Project communications management

It is often said that good management is all about effective communications. This is equally true for project management. Effective communications essentially revolves around key events such as launch parties, regular meetings and formal reports such as the project definition report.
Start-up/launch meeting:

- Create a shared vision – background, purpose, scope, objectives.
- Gain acceptance of the plans – bar charts, responsibility chart.
- Get the project team functioning – define your management approach.
- Repeat throughout the life cycle and to brief new team members.

Project definition report. This can be structured around the following headings and consolidates the outcome of the first stage of the project, the proposal and initiation stage:

- Background – business case for the project including financial justification.
- The project charter – including vision and mission statements covering purpose and goals of the project.

- Scope statement – including requirements specification, product and work breakdown structures for the project.

- Organization and resourcing requirements.

- Risks and assumptions.

- Budgets and time plans.

- Communications plan to various stakeholders.

  Regular *progress review meetings* to:

- Track progress to plan – time, cost, specification, risks.

- Formalize reports – forms, timing, circulation.

- Regulate meetings – attendees, agenda, chairmanship.

- Monitor suppliers.

- Resolve difficulties – problem-solving.

- Manage change – impact assessment, commercial considerations, communication, configuration management.

It may be useful at this point to highlight the section on 'model for change' in Chapter 15, which links the role of the project leader in the effective management of change.

Project procurement management

An important decision in project management is whether to carry out the activity using in-house resources or to subcontract to a contractor. Consider the factors that could impact upon this decision in Figure 12.11.

Partnering/collaborative working is often seen as a long-term strategy for procurement management today and the issues are presented more fully in Chapter 11 on supply chain management.

How do we manage the project process – the project life cycle?

As well as having understanding of the knowledge areas outlined above, we can see from Figure 12.1 that the use of the project life cycle can help us manage and control projects. Our approach in this book is to take a systems view of service operations. It is therefore possible to take a systems view of the stages or phases of the project life cycle and consider the inputs, the processes and outputs of each of the definition, planning, implementation and transition phases of a project. Unsurprisingly, the outputs from the definition phase will be an input to the planning phase and so on. It is also possible to use the stage boundaries as key points in the assessment of projects. Indeed, go/no go decisions for the management of projects can be integrated to these stage boundaries.

Table 12.2 The Project Process – project life cycle

Proposals and Initiation: Defining the project

Inputs	Process	Outputs
Business needs analysis – an understanding of the project environment, broadly covered by strategic analysis using PESTLE and SWOT analysis (Chapter 3) and specifically addressing questions such as:	Visioning – stakeholders meet to share their views about their vision of the end point of the project and to share their thoughts about what has to be done and what pathways have to be followed in order to achieve that vision.	Project definition report, with the following headings:
		Background – business case for the project including financial justification.
What business objectives will the successful completion of the project satisfy?	Scope definition – involves the definition of product/service scope and project work scope.	The project charter – including vision and mission statements covering purpose and goals of the project.
What are the outputs from the feasibility/pilot study, if one was undertaken?	Product scope is the features and functions of the product or service produced by the project, sometimes called the requirements specification.	Scope statement – including requirements specification, product and work breakdown structures for the project.
On what other projects is this one dependent and vice versa – programme and multi-project factors?	Project scope is the work that must be carried out to deliver the product or service.	Organization and resourcing requirements.
	Milestone planning. These are important events that allow for strategic planning of the project.	Risks and assumptions.
What are the priorities for resource management?		Budgets and time plans.
What are the uncertainties, risks and opportunities?	Stakeholder power, influence and interest analysis (see Figure 12.2).	Communications plan to various stakeholders.
Who are the stakeholders and what are their positions?	Resource planning:- scheduling/resource availability/capacity management.	
	Risk management: risk identification, quantification, response development, risk monitoring and control. This includes avoidance, deflection and contingency planning.	

Design and Appraisal: Planning the project

Inputs	Process	Outputs
The purpose of this stage is to break the project down into manageable work tasks or elements in order to allocate them to specific resources or agree contracts with suppliers. The project plan will also develop the quality, cost, time and risk plans for the project and cover the following elements:	Product and Work Breakdown structure templates, which can be based on headings/streams such as facility, equipment, people, systems, organization.	The project manual – this is a detailed report which explains how the owner's requirements are to be delivered. It covers the following areas:
	Deeper levels of breakdown or decomposition to allow planning at more detailed level for example 'the people workstream' could be broken down into recruitment, training, deployment, appraisal, rewards, in order to capture the work requirements at a detailed level.	Project charter – vision, goal and mission
The project definition report from the earlier stage.		Master project plan – budgets, schedules, quality specifications, risk register.
The scope statement.		Management plan – including organization charts and execution strategy.
Risk and opportunity analysis.	Organizational breakdown structures, which align work elements to the appropriate resource.	Performance specification for the project deliverable.
Resource limitations, skills and their availability.		Acceptance criteria.
Overlapping project requirements.	Schedule bar charts which detail sequence and duration of work elements.	Project constraints, risks and assumptions.
Historical information to aid estimation of costs and time – a knowledge management system.	Network charts.	
	Procurement schedule.	
	Budgets.	
	Quality plans.	
	Risk plans.	
	Validate and approve the plan.	

Table 12.2 *continued*

Execution and Control: Doing the project

Inputs	Process	Outputs
In this stage, work is carried out so expenditure is high. It is important to keep to budgeted plans and to maintain cash flow. This requires effective planning, control and management actions to address problems (see also Chapter 14).	Management control procedures – an understanding of the five functions of management: plan, organize, motivate, control and provide leadership.	Product and services that conform to plans: quality, cost, time, risk and budgets/cash flows.
	Change management process.	Forecasting completion.
A project manager who can communicate up, down and outside the project.	Project launch event – sharing the vision.	Rescue and recovery plans.
	Team building processes.	
The approved project plans for Product and Work Breakdown, quality, costs, time and risk.	Cross culture awareness.	
	Monitoring performance.	
Project execution plans detailing roles and responsibilities and contracting parties.	Problem solving – control and recovery.	
Experienced people.		
Resourcing criteria: assessment of needs versus abilities, training, negotiate involvement, confirm facilities are available when required.		

Close and Transition: Developing from the project

Inputs	Process	Outputs
The project charter – what were the goals?	Finishing the work: people don't remember the great start-up but they do remember an inefficient finish!	Satisfied client, users and other stakeholders:
Terms of reference; requirements specifications.		Project achieves stated purpose.
Various stakeholder needs.		Provides benefit to the owner.
Records of costs, schedule conformance.	Task force set-up to manage the checklist of outstanding items.	Satisfies the needs of other stakeholders.
Contract conditions.	Transferring the product/service to the client/user, preparation of manuals, training, maintenance agreements.	Output is to quality, cost and time objectives.
Waivers, deviation agreements.		Satisfies the project team and its supporters.
		Project 'as finished' documentation.
	Post-completion review.	Finalization report.
	Disbanding the team: planning the run-down, debriefing sessions, reward achievement and vice versa.	Lessons learnt fed into knowledge management process.
	Build relationships for the future.	Opportunities for future business identified.

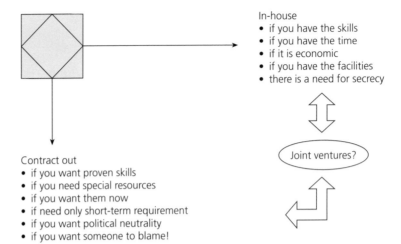

Figure 12.11

When to contract-
out chart

In-house
• if you have the skills
• if you have the time
• if it is economic
• if you have the facilities
• there is a need for secrecy

Joint ventures?

Contract out
• if you want proven skills
• if you need special resources
• if you want them now
• if need only short-term requirement
• if you want political neutrality
• if you want someone to blame!

Conclusion

Let's finish this chapter with three key observations and four recommendations of relevance to service operations management projects:

● Most employees of large organizations participate in projects.
● Most managers of large organizations play key roles in executing projects.
● Project management skills are an expected core competency for managers in service operations.

Our recommendations are:

● Choose the right projects:
   – Ones you believe in to sustain commitment and provide leadership
   – Ones that can succeed with clear vision, planning and control
   – Ones that develop you, your team and the business
● Choose the goals and end points in agreement with stakeholders.
● Choose the right team, motivate and energize them.
● Assess your own skills and motivation to make sure you're up to the job!

Chapter summary

This chapter has provided a digest of project management set against our model, Figure 12.1, which links together project management knowledge areas and tools, such as definition of scope, with the life cycle of a project. We have followed the PMI Body of Knowledge areas in order to develop our approach to managing projects:

● Project integration management.
● Project scope management.

- Project time management.
- Project cost management.
- Project quality management.
- Project risk management.
- Project human resource management.
- Project communications management.
- Project procurement management.

These areas were then linked across the following stages of the project life cycle, using a systems approach which identified Inputs/Processes/Outputs for each stage of the project to show which knowledge areas were best used at each stage:

- Proposals and initiation: defining the project.
- Design and appraisal: planning the project.
- Execution and control: doing the project.
- Close and transition: developing from the project.

Examples were used throughout the chapter to clarify concepts and illustrate application.

Appendix 1

An example of a project definition report:
Learning Resource Development Commissioning Document
Project Management, Part 2 MBA Module

Commissioned by:	Director of Programmes, IDT
Faculty Lead Tutor:	PR
Commisioned Author	MH
L&TS Project Manager:	LP
E-Learning Support:	EH
Resources Support:	JG
Course Designer:	MS
Completion dates:	March 2002

Proposed project outline

Purpose

To revise the Part 2 Project Management course material in order to provide contemporary coverage of the subject concepts in line with professional Bodies of Knowledge. To ensure delivery of new materials to production, within deadlines and to budget.

Goal

The goal is to develop new materials and resources, originating within Henley Management College, that will deliver subject content and learning support for those DL members undertaking the Project Management stream of the MBA Programme. Delivery is required in electronic format for DL and IBM programmes and with accompanying traditional print format for Overseas Associates students.
There are three aspects to address:

- The electronic delivery of the entire content of the module for the Henley-based DL students.
- The electronic delivery of the entire content and accessed via a Lotus LearningSpace (LLS) GroupWare environment.
- The continued support of the traditional DL student through combined use of technology and print in the delivery format.

The first of these three delivery modes is the priority.

Scope

1. Electronic DL pack (for Henley-based DL – Electronic Learning Programme)
The core material may consist of an electronic 'route map' providing students with an overview of the course objectives, resources available, the linkages between them and the intended learning outcomes. Resources to include:

- A core textbook (Gower Handbook of Project Management) on CD.
- Asynchronous e-learning environment (per intake) for interactivity between learners and tutor incorporating tasks and discussions over 4-5 month period.
- Synchronous activity?
- Further resources available through the College e-Library.
- Access to the general electronic assignment submission area through the website.

This forum will be facilitated by a subject specialist nominated by the Lead Tutor.

2. LLS Electronic DL pack (for key clients only)
The core material will be as for the electronic DL course, but provided in Lotus LearningSpace as the user interface/navigation. LLS will replace the web forum as the medium for:

- resources (electronic MediaCenter);
- discussion and questions with a subject specialist;
- reading list.

Access for electronic assignment submission will also be available through the website (assignments may also be submitted on paper).

3. Traditional DL pack
The core material will be as for 1 above with an additional printed guide or digest to the resources. There will be a web-enabled e-Learning support forum:

- updates on core material;
- discussion and questions with a subject specialist.

This forum will be facilitated by a subject specialist nominated by the Lead Tutor. (*Note*: this is not the same forum under 1 above).

There will be a website of further resources available through the Henley Management College e-Library. Access for electronic assignment submission will also be available through the website (assignments may also be submitted on paper).

Budget

- Faculty resources available to be agreed between Director of Graduate Business Studies, Faculty and the Dean and supported by the GBS Materials development budget.
- The same budget to support the trial process of the new learning resource.
- L&TS resources in support of presentation, e-Learning and other technologies, to be directed by the Manager Learning and Teaching Services.

2001 Budget allocation
Current MH contract covers material development (fictitious figures).

External authors   £5000

Testing   £1500 (to be carried into 2002 budget)

Signed: _____   Date: _____

Director Graduate Business Studies

_____   Date: _____

Academic Dean

_____   Date: _____

Lead Tutor

Manager Learning and Teaching Services

Development milestones for Project Management

Module will possibly comprise: Route map   CD-Rom containing textbook
Readings   Assignment guide

Total working days available		20	23 (4 × MH)	22 (4 × MH)	15 (4 × MH)	19	17	21	20	21	20
Item	Aug-01	Sep-01	Oct-01	Nov-01	Dec-01	Jan-02	Feb-02	Mar-02	Apr-02	May-02	Jun-02
Route map/Core resources	Faculty consultation and review Syllabus and AAC proposal drawn up (Fac)		Academic research and origination in Word (Fac)	AAC Approval sought 13 Nov 01(Fac) Course development (Fac)	Course route map, linking material to LTS through December (Fac)	Trial 4–21 Jan	Final revisions (Fac and LTS input). (NB if CD to be produced master to Lynic for reproduction 20 Feb 02)		Prepare companion printed matter for Overseas Associates students		
Assignment guide											
Readings			Readings identified (Fac/e-Librarian)	Reproduction rights (LTS)	Scanning, obtaining (LTS)						
Textbook			Identify (Fac)	Check availability, CD, web site (LTS)							
Copyrights				Identify and request permissions (LTS)							
ELMBA forum					Structure & design activities (Fac and e-Learning)						
WWW e-learning									Structure and design activities (Fac and e-Learning)		
LLS									Develop LLS databases for HMC08		
Complete course					Delivery to Intake 18–7 Mar						Delivery to Associates

Case Study *C-Direct Company Insurance*

Questions

1. Prepare the Project Definition Report for implementation of the policy change. This report should cover the purpose, scope, objectives and project organization for the project.

2. What are the risks for the project and how should they be managed? Comment particularly on the Operations/Project interface issues and recommend how these could be effectively managed.

The C-Direct-Insurance Company Background:
The C-Direct-Insurance Company (abbreviated as CD)

Call Centres have fast become one of the most important channels for organizations and their customers to interact. There are around 4000 call centres in the UK today, employing over 400 000 people. The direct-sell insurance industry is increasingly using call centres to access and service its market. The C-Direct-Insurance Company has its call centre in Newcastle, England. The company itself is just 6 years old and specializes in selling automobile insurance policies direct to customers.

The process

Advertising and promotion initiatives attract customers' interest and generate enquiries to the CD Call Centre. These lead to the provision of quotations for personal car insurance. In order to provide the quotation, CD operators need to collect the customer's personal and vehicle-related data (in total 17 items) and input them to the computer. The process is as follows.

Customers call the CD Call Centre (the focus of this case) by a freephone telephone number and submit the required information. This is entered directly into a computer terminal during the call, their questions are answered, and a quotation is provided within 1–2 minutes. Customers can pay by credit card and receive immediate insurance cover. Customers receive their personal insurance offer confirmed in writing by mail, about 2–3 days after initial contact.

Mr Small, the Operations Manager, is responsible for all operations in the Call Centre. The Call Centre employs 105 people in three shifts over a core day between the hours of 08:00 and 20:00. The resources for the Call Centre are: its *facilities*, e.g. buildings, the staff's workspace/workstations, the *equipment*, e.g. computers/systems, and the *people* that use them.

Car insurance is compulsory in the UK, so customers are price sensitive and tend to shop around to compare the company's offer with those of competitors. Only about 17 per cent of CD's offers are converted into policies.

The operations management strategies of scheduling, capacity and quality management were reactive rather than proactive; for example, poor forecasting of demand resulted in excess manpower being under-utilized. Staff were inflexible and showed little sympathy or understanding to frustrated and angry customers. The interfaces with support functions such as Marketing or Information Systems tended to be confrontational rather than supportive. Fortunately, in the early days, competition was not very tough and Mr Small had no special performance targets or formal control mechanisms – he was literally his own boss.

The policy change

After 5 years of high growth, over the last twelve months sales have only grown by 3 per cent and the company is beginning to struggle with diminishing profits. The main reasons for the slow-down have been identified: *new entrants*: Fifteen companies have entered the marketplace in the last 2 years, producing a wave of 'direct-insurance-start-ups'. These companies have targeted the same customer segment as CD, where the market has remained stagnant. *Customers* are more price sensitive and new entrants offer extremely low prices. Substitute products are unchanged – customers still require car insurance.

The new situation has forced management to review business policy options to provide a competitive advantage. Research has shown that for direct selling insurance products, the key market drivers are to:

- Offer a wider range of insurance products, so minimizing the need for customers to deal with many suppliers.

- Offer low price.

- Provide excellent service.

A recent internal report showed that the CD Call Centre still had potential to improve service levels and cost-efficiency. The decision was therefore taken to extend the product range and improve service by addressing:

Product flexibility. CD will respond to customer demand by launching a new product – 'household insurance' – and deliver it via the Call Centre, alongside car insurance. Household insurance is often requested by customers and they have been disappointed in the past not to source it from CD. Furthermore, the product margin for household insurance is high, thanks to low average claims. Since only a few competitors currently offer household insurance, management believe they can generate an above average profit margin in the first year after launch.

Responsiveness. In order to make the new product successful, it will also be necessary to fulfil customer expectations for 'time' response. Consequently, operations management will need to ensure quick access to the Call Centre and efficient treatment of customers for both products.

Quality. Improve customer service – at least to match competitors' standards. Internal analysis

has shown that the auto insurance 'lapse-rate' (customers not renewing their policies) – which is an indicator of customer satisfaction – is above the market average. To avoid this trap with the new product, significant improvement in service delivery of all CD's activities is needed (including settlement of claims, which is not part of the Call Centre's responsibilities).

Cost. Ensure price decrease of insurance premiums by reducing internal costs. All possibilities for further cost reduction must be exploited to permit a price-level lower than the top five price leaders.

By launching this policy change, senior management believe a successful implementation will lead to higher customer satisfaction and consequently to profitable growth.

Influences on the operation

The change in business policy will have an impact on Mr Small's current operations strategies. The policy change has been developed at corporate level but the benefits will have to be delivered by Mr Small, the Operations Manager, in the future. Therefore, Mr Small will need to address the changes to operating systems structures and operations management objectives. The determination of the trade-off between customer service and resource utilization will be a key factor for sustainable operation, especially in this competitive environment. The new business policy decision will affect Mr Small's current practice in two ways. First, he will have to interface with the project set-up to manage the launch of the new product and modifications to the delivery processes. Second, he will have to establish operations management strategies to allow the business to meet the objectives of the policy change.

The project phase

Workforce

The existing staff will be responsible for the new product, alongside the existing offering. Therefore an intensive training programme on

Information Technology (IT) enhancements and new product features will be required. To improve the overall quality and service provision, customer acquisition techniques and friendly handling of difficult customers will be covered during the training. Mr. Small will work with the training department to develop a training plan which will take at least four days per group to deliver (each group has about 10 employees). Therefore, he will have to schedule the training so that normal business will not be hampered by too few staff in the Call Centre. The new training approach will also have a long-term influence, because training updates for employees will be held at least once a year. One of the aims of the training is to reshape corporate culture so as to engender a commitment to high efficiency and excellent service. This will demand empowering the workforce to focus on customer service, together with better collaboration between staff, by using more teamwork to raise the overall efficiency levels of the operation. Mr. Small will also have to install a feedback process to evaluate the satisfaction level of the staff, to help identify continuous improvement areas. Better motivation will be achieved by introducing a new incentive system, using positive customer feedback as a measure for rewards.

Facilities and equipment

The current workspace/workstation for a Call Centre staff member is a small, open 'boxlike' area (less than one square metre), containing a terminal, keyboard and telephone. The boxes are very close together and do not have proper noise protection. Staff complain about the workstations, because with the background noise of five or more colleagues, concentration is difficult and the number of data input errors are high. Staff have little space to write notes, so, for example, noting down a telephone number to return a call to a customer is very difficult.

After looking at the staff's workspace, Small realizes they will have to modify the building in order to create more space and provide noise protection. He thinks that only by providing a

convenient and ergonomic workspace will he be able to ensure his staff's full commitment to performance improvements. A careful forecast of future demand will be necessary in order to install the right number of new workstations and avoid under/over utilization of resources.

Technology

A new terminal mask (template or standard screen) for the Call Centre needs to be developed by the Information Systems Department (ISD). This mask must contain all questions that need to be answered by the customer. To ensure service quality, ISD will have to create a flexible IT-system, which will enable the Call Centre staff to quickly switch from one screen to another, according to customer demand. The competitor benchmark for 'time to switch' screens is less than 3 seconds. Furthermore, high IT-reliability is vital, because breakdowns in the past have stopped all activities of the Call Centre (since they depend on online access to the mainframe) and customers cannot be served during that time. Mr Small wonders if an ISD/Call Centre staff taskforce should be set up to explore the main historical problems for poor reliability, define development areas and try to find the best possible solution?

Organization

Experience in the past has shown the first few months after a product launch to be critical. Therefore, a new role of a 'first-alert support person' needs to be established. The 'first-alert' person will help improve service by patrolling the Call Centre and helping the staff during busy times, in cases of difficult customer questions or with technical problems. Furthermore, they will have a coaching role for new employees and also support staff training. The Human Resource Department (HRD) will need to develop the job description, provide a career plan for that role, manage the necessary recruiting and training process and determine how this new position fits into the organization.

Written by Peter Race, 2003

V Part Five

In Part Three the overall approach to planning, implementation and control was covered. It was seen that for control to be effective, measurement in the form of standards and budgets was necessary. In Part Five the philosophy required to achieve a total quality management operation and the measurements that are needed is detailed.

- **Chapter 13** concentrates on the quality philosophy. It is acknowledged that there are many approaches to the subject of quality. It is argued that quality is not a separate discipline, such as accounting or marketing, but is an integral part of all management activities. It is shown that quality issues and the level of quality provided to customers, and the way in which the quality philosophy can be used to increase the efficient use of resources, is a matter of business policy.

- **Chapter 14** continues with the quality theme, the need to add value and to reduce non-value-adding activities. In this chapter it is shown that unless there are standards and measurement of performance, control will be less than perfect; and without measurement it will not be possible to know if performance is improving or not. The taking of measurements will take effort and therefore cost money; the taking of measurements alone does not add value to an organization. The bigger the organization, the more opportunities exist for well-meaning managers to seek returns, statistics and measurements, and not all of this effort will be justified. It is accepted that some non-value-adding measurements, such as required by government departments, have to be maintained. In this chapter, measurements that are important and measurements which should be taken are considered.

13 Quality performance

Objectives

This chapter considers the subject of quality. In particular the following issues are examined:

- Definitions of quality.

- Who determines levels of quality and service, and why?

- The cost of quality, including conformance and non-conformance costs.

- Levels of quality management.

- ISO 9000.

- Quality initiatives such as *kaizen*.

- Establishing quality controls.

- Quality beyond Six Sigma.

Introduction

There have been volumes of books and learned papers on the subject of quality. Some universities now offer quality as a separate subject or programme, the inference being that quality has become a discipline or subject in its own right, able to be studied in isolation from other disciplines. Our approach is different; we believe that in the management of operations, quality has always been important, and is inseparable from any management action. Quality cannot be put into a separate compartment, to be picked up and put down at the whim of a manager. In today's global economy quality has to be an integral part of all management actions if an organization is going to compete against world-class standards. This is especially true in service industries where customers rightly expect high-level service. This book recognizes this, and quality issues have been discussed in each chapter. Our underlying theme has been customer satisfaction and efficient use of resources. Both of these objectives require quality considerations. Customer satisfaction cannot be divorced from an understanding of what quality is, and likewise efficient use of resources requires a total quality management approach.

Having said that quality is an integral part of operations management, it is acknowledged that a separate section is required concerning the philosophy of culture, the costs of quality and some understanding of specific approaches to quality, such as ISO 9001:2000 and ISO 14001, Six Sigma and the new wave of quality beyond Six Sigma.

Example

Marty, after having quoted the wrong rate to a branch office after their third and urgent request, was heard to say in the cafeteria: 'Anything that can go wrong, will go wrong'.

Marty's manager loomed up, glared at Marty and said 'Especially if it involves people' and passed him an e-mail. The e-mail was from the branch and included comments made by their customer (now their ex-customer), which said many things and ended with the words 'and at the worst possible time'.

Definitions of quality

Applying inverse logic to the above, quality could be defined (as it often is) as 'The right thing, at the right place, at the right time'. Another popular definition is 'Get it right first time' and yet another is 'Fitness for purpose'. At first glance, it is difficult to fault any of these definitions, but the problem remains: 'What does "quality" really mean?'

Example

In 2001 Nevan and Joy visited England for six months. On arrival they bought an ageing car for £450. After travelling 11 000 miles over the length and breadth of the United Kingdom and over large parts of France, they sold the car for £300. Apart from three punctures, the car never once let them down. It always started first time, motored comfortably at some ten miles per hour above the speed limit, and all the bits and pieces such as the windscreen wipers, the indicators and lights worked. Applying the three definitions to this car we would find that 'The right thing, at the right place, at the right time' definition does not apply and likewise the second definition 'Get it right first time' also does not fit. However, 'Fitness for purpose' certainly appears to be appropriate. For Nevan and Joy, the requirement, or specification, was a reliable vehicle that would safely get them around Britain and France. For the six months they owned it, that car proved as reliable and as efficient as a vehicle that might have cost ten times as much. And yet, despite its proven record, it was still not worth any more than what they sold it for. Fitness for purpose? – Yes. Quality? – No. Not even the most optimistic second-hand car dealer could describe a rust-ridden, one hubcap-missing, £300 car as a quality vehicle.

Most people like to have a car that they can have some pride in. They are fussy about the model, the colour, the sound system, and they like to keep it clean. They are prepared to pay large amounts of money for the vehicle that best meets their rather ill-defined requirements. Reliability, performance and efficiency are taken for granted. Fitness for purpose is therefore only one aspect of quality. Quality can be divided into two parts – basic requirements and higher-level requirements.

As we saw in Chapter 2, customers have basic requirements of specification, cost and timing. The example used in Chapter 2 was the commuter bus service. First, unless the bus is travelling more or less to where we want to go (specification) we won't catch it. The second requirement is timing; if we start work at 9 am, we will be looking for a bus that gets us to work no later than 9 am and probably not too much earlier. The third consideration is cost. We would classify the route, the time and cost as basic requirements, and probably, depending on circumstances, rank them in that order. The alternatives, if the bus service did not fit our requirements, might be to use our car, share a car with a neighbour, walk some distance and catch a train, buy a bike, or not make the journey at all.

A bus service could meet all the above requirements and still not be a quality service. If the service was unreliable (sometimes late, sometimes early, sometimes did not keep to the route) then we would not consider it to be a reliable quality service. To be a quality service, the bus service needs to meet clients' basic requirements and be reliable (right thing, right place, right time). Supposing the bus did all these things, got you to work on time at a reasonable cost, and was always on time, but it was dirty, the driver was surly, the seats were hard and it leaked exhaust fumes. Then, although it met the criteria of right thing, right time, right place, there is no way you would describe that service as a quality service. Thus, apart from the basic needs, there are certain higher-order needs that must be met. In this case, we would look for polite service, a clean bus, reasonably comfortable seating and certainly no exhaust fumes. A truly high-quality bus might be spotlessly clean, have carpets on the floor and piped music as well as all the other attributes. But, no matter how comfortable the ride, how polite the service, how cheap the fare, unless the bus is going 'our way' we won't be interested in catching it. In other words, the specification must be reasonably satisfied.

Example

When Joy's car had a puncture, Tom, a young, friendly and helpful mechanic, fitted a new tyre. A week later, the new tyre was damaged when Nevan hit a concrete block on the motorway. When Nevan jacked the car up and tried to undo the wheel nuts he found that they were so tight he was unable to move them. The RAC came to the rescue and, by applying leverage, were able to solve the problem. The RAC man advised that over-tight wheel nuts were a common problem.

If young Tom had been instructed that the purpose of wheel nuts was to keep the wheel on and, to be effective they must be done up tight, Tom had got it right first time. Add the fact that he was pleasant and helpful, his manager probably thought that Tom was providing a quality service and indeed, for the space of a week, Joy and Nevan thought so too. It could be argued that Tom didn't get it right first time, because the nuts were too tight. But he didn't know that, nor did his manager and, for a time, nor did the customer.

The other definition, 'Get it right first time' is more of a slogan aimed at encouraging a sense of responsibility amongst lower-level staff to be accurate in their work (rather than relying on someone else to find an error). For anyone to be expected to do something right first time, they first have to know exactly what they are meant to be doing.

Thus the slogan 'Get it right first time' means that to get it right, we need to know what is right. In other words, a standard has to be set and the operator has to be informed as to what the standard is. Furthermore, there has to be some way in which the operator can check his or her work to ensure that the standard has been achieved.

Consider the case where Tom has now been informed of the correct tension to which to tighten the wheel nuts. Say the customer is in a hurry, but has been told to come back in an hour, and when the customer comes back, finds the job hasn't been started. Tom is at tea, the foreman calls him, and with bad grace the job is performed. Tom duly carries out the job to specification. But not only was Tom surly, he left grease on the steering wheel and also didn't replace the hubcap properly. Later, the hubcap comes off and is damaged. The customer would not regard this as quality service. In fact, the quality of the job was superior to the first scenario where subsequently it had proved impossible for the customer to remove the nuts.

'Fitness for purpose', 'Getting it right first time', or 'Right thing, right place, right time' may all fit the basic requirements. However, in the customer's eyes, these are the minimum requirements that the customer expects. Without satisfying the basics, you won't be able to give an acceptable level of service. To have your service or product described as a quality product, the customer will expect higher-level benefits, such as courtesy, attention to detail, pleasant surroundings and so on. These higher-level benefits are what gives an organization a competitive edge, and often the difference costs very little to achieve.

However, there is no point in an organization concentrating on friendly, clean service in the hope that this will make the difference if the service or product does not meet the basic specifications, costs too much or is not available when the customer wants it.

Example

The restaurant is in a good location, the decor is tasteful, the wine list is good and not too expensive, the menu is varied and interesting, the waiting staff are well-groomed and helpful, but the food is poorly cooked, almost uneatable. You don't go back and you will tell many people of your experience, and in turn these people will pass the bad news on, often with embellishments.

No-one knows how many potential customers are lost as the result of sub-quality products or inferior service. Such a figure cannot be quantified, it is unknown and unknowable.

Who determines quality?

When asked, 'Who determines quality?', most people will say, 'The customer'. But this is not the case.

In most cases, the level of quality that your organization will aim for is deter-mined by what your competition is offering. If you are a reasonable-sized player in your market, then you will be influencing the level of quality, and the competi-tion will be reacting to your initiatives. Even where you are seen to be leading the market in setting quality standards, the very reason that you will be doing so is because of your perceptions of what the competition is likely to do and your desire to stay in front. 'But,' you might ask, 'isn't what the competition does, and conse-quently what you do, a response to what the customer wants?' Up to a point the answer is yes, but only to a limited extent.

Example

When using an airline service most customers (unless they are travelling on the expense account, i.e. someone else is paying) want the cheapest airfare possible and to travel at a con-venient time. If the customer was deciding the level of service they would probably like free car parks at the airport, business class seats and service, and fares to be reduced by 50 per cent. This is, of course, not possible. No airline could afford to provide such extras. Each airline will provide prices and services similar to the competition.

Let us therefore accept that the customer's wishes are not always paramount. Thus the quality offered is determined in light of what the competition is offering and what the service provider can afford to give.

Cost to the supplier of a service is, and always will be, a limiting factor in the determination of the level of quality provided. Or, looking at it from another angle, any organization, no matter how inefficient it is, can, for a short period of time, provide a top-quality service or product if it ignores the cost of doing so. However, in the final analysis, unless that organization is making a profit, it will not survive. Thus, we are not likely to see free valet parking at the airport for economy-class passengers, nor will air fares drop to the extent that the airline does not, in the long term, make a profit. You will note that in our perception of how an airline passen-ger judges quality, we have not listed all the basic requirements, such as getting you, together with your luggage, to the right destination safely and on time. Such requirements are essential and are taken for granted by the customer. These will not form the basis by which the customer will judge quality. The customer's expec-tations will be greater than the mere satisfaction of the essentials. Quality will be judged by the price, plus intangibles such as friendly service, but most of all by the 'extras' provided. The extent of the extras that an organization provides will be limited by the cost which the organization is prepared or able to accept.

Social and political requirements

Other influences on the level of quality to be provided are political (for example, minimum levels of safety, hygiene, pollution and consumer protection can, and usually are, legislated for), and social opinion, including health and environmental concerns. Where social issues have not been legislated for, organizations like to be seen to have a social conscience. Frequently, in meeting the social needs, the provider will be just one step ahead of the legislators.

Technology

Another determinant of quality is technology. Technological advances, and how the competition uses the advances, will provide further opportunities or challenges to increase quality. But the greatest determinant on how much quality, or the level of quality an organization will give, is cost.

Efficient use of resources

In operations management, the classic conflict is between customer service and efficient utilization of resources. We saw in Chapter 1 that tangible resources and inputs to the service system are materials, machines, equipment, real estate and people, and intangible assets include knowledge and information. As seen in Chapters 8 and 9, if the policy at one extreme is for resources to be fully employed (i.e. there is no spare capacity) customers will be expected to wait or queue. At the other extreme, if the aim is to have no queues of customers, surplus (idle) capacity will be required. Generally, it can be assumed that from the customer's perspective queuing is not synonymous with quality.

In the context of the level of quality to be provided, the onus is on the organization supplying the service to determine a standard for the level of quality it aims, and can afford, to provide. The standard has to be clear and communicated to staff, ideally with an explanation of why service standards have been set at that level.

Determination of service level

As a provider of services, the question 'What market do we want to be in and why?' has to be periodically asked. The next question is 'What is the competition doing?' Logically the next question is 'What share of the market do we want and how can we hope to achieve this share?' The answers will be limited by what is feasible given the system structure and capacity of the organization. One of the main issues you will now find yourself looking at is quality; that is, quality as currently provided by the competition, and by your organization. Next you might go further and attempt to find out what the customers want. Having done this and discovered what the competitors are doing, and having attempted to gauge what the customers expect, you will be able to determine what level of quality is required and attempt to balance that against the level you can afford to provide.

Remember: 'Many organizations have gone bankrupt despite having loyal and satisfied customers' for 'given infinite resources any system, however badly managed, might provide adequate customer service . . . at least for a time' (Wild, 2002: 11).

Quality decision is not the customers'

The quality decision will be yours, not that of your customers nor of anyone else. Your decision will be based on what you can afford and what you are capable of doing. Of course, unless you provide the basic essentials expected by the customer, you will lose market share. On the other hand, if you want to gain a competitive edge and increase market share, you can readily do so by increasing your level of quality. The secret is finding out what you are capable of achieving. If cost is your greatest constraint (as it most certainly will be), then surely the solution must be in reducing costs. Thus the level of quality is determined by your own actions.

The importance of quality is that, to hold your place in the market, you must at least provide the same level of quality as the competition. To improve your position in the market, you need to demonstrate an increased and sustained level of improved quality above that of the competition. Quality, then, is the competitive edge that we are all looking for. The problem is of course that customers expect and, indeed, take for granted the basic requirements. They take for granted that food will be hygienically prepared, that a bus is roadworthy and that the driver is licensed. Quality in the eyes of the customers is the extras. Some extras cost little (courtesy, cleanliness), other extras cost money and cost will be the inhibiting factor as to how much quality can be afforded. But if the competition increases its extras, then, to hold your place in the market, it is essential that in some manner you step up your service just to keep your position.

Once extras have been provided by one player in the market and copied by the rest of the market, customers will take these extras for granted. What bank could afford not to provide automatic (hole-in-the-wall) banking? Which supermarket cannot afford to provide free car parking if a competitor opens up and provides plenty of free car parking?

Extras are provided to gain a competitive edge, but in service industries are generally easily copied by the competition. Often any increased market share gained by the introduction of an extra is short-lived, but once given it is difficult not to continue providing the increased service. (No marketing manager would be brave enough to try.)

How can organizations afford to provide extra services? The answer is found in increased efficiency and productivity. This has been achieved by a combination of:

- Taking advantage of advances in technology such as information technology, office systems and communications systems.
- The development of 'new' management techniques and philosophies to reduce cost and, at the same time, increase the speed and efficiency of service.
- Identification and elimination of costs or processes that don't add value, or the minimization of such costs where it was found they could not be totally eliminated.
- The adoption of philosophies such as total quality management, continuous improvement (*kaizen*), restructuring, empowerment and delayering of management (business process re-engineering) all of which require a change in organizational culture and a degree of carefully planned change management. Chapter 15 discusses change management in some detail.

The need to continually increase benefits and services to keep up with the market or to gain a competitive edge on the market, but without an increase in price to the customer, has led to the need to eliminate any cost that does not add value. The pressure to provide the customer with more for less will cost the service provider and will also set higher future expectations. *The level of quality provided must be a strategic decision based on what the competition is doing and what can be afforded, with a clear appreciation that once started there is no turning back.*

The cost of quality

Quality does not come cheaply. It is not free. To instill a quality culture into an organization will take time, require total commitment and will cost money. But the alternative is to lose your place in the market, and eventually your organization will be no more. The payback for the investment in quality is in the long term, and benefits of higher quality are the reduction of costs, higher profits, growth and survival.

Non-conformance costs

Non-conformance is when work or service is not performed to the standard set by the organization, and has to be corrected, done again or the customer has to be recompensed. The costs will include waste of wages for re-doing work, wasted time and perhaps waste of materials. Such costs should be captured and recorded. If we know how much extra expense we incur because of mistakes, then errors can be analyzed and procedures changed to make sure that such mistakes are not repeated.

Flow-on effects resulting from mistakes include stock-outs in warehouses and overtime worked as a result of errors. These costs may not be readily apparent but can be calculated after perhaps a lot of soul-searching and recriminations. However, the costs of lost opportunities and loss of enthusiasm by workers cannot be measured. For eventually, if errors and second-rate performance become the norm, morale will be such that there will be a general unwillingness to accept responsibility and an attitude of fatalism will pervade. The worst cost, however, cannot be measured, and that is the unknown cost of lost customers and lost opportunities. A really bad experience by a customer is likely to be repeated to at least ten other people, and the story will often grow in the telling.

So far we have discussed the usual costs of quality. Now let us explore the cost of quality from another perspective. Hopefully we agree that, if jobs are properly specified, if staff members understand what is required and are trained to do the job, and are prepared to accept responsibility, supervision should not be needed. Checking and correcting of their work will be the staff member's own responsibility. Ideally, jobs will be done right every time, and the customer will receive excellent service.

In operations management, the aim is to efficiently use resources to transform inputs into useful outputs. This is known as the transformation process. Anything done that doesn't add to the transformation is regarded as inefficient.

Example

Consider a simple process in an office where an invoice is received in the mail and is eventually paid. The lapsed time, or cycle time, between receipt and the raising of the cheque and mailing out might be three weeks. During that time, the actual amount of time spent on processing the invoice might be 30 minutes. Some of the actions taken might be: validity checked, that is, goods and services received; amount and price checked, discounts correct; then the cheque requisition is raised, the cheque is issued, and finally posted out. The balance of the time (three weeks less 30 minutes) the invoice will be waiting for processing. In the case of most invoices, some delay in payment might not matter, but in other cases discount will be lost or charges will be levied for late payment.

Your turn!

Make a list of costs of non-conformance to quality standards for your department.

Supposing you believe your organization is achieving 99.9 per cent quality; that is, 99.9 per cent of the time, you achieve exactly what you have set out to achieve. I would imagine that you would probably think you were doing pretty well. Thought of in this way, 99.9 per cent quality in the United Kingdom would mean:

- One hour of unsafe drinking water per month.
- Two unsafe landings at Heathrow airport per week.
- 12 000 lost items of mail per day.
- 300 incorrect surgical operations per week.
- 15 000 babies dropped by the doctor at birth each year.

For a typical management college, 99.9 per cent would mean 25 mislaid exam or assessment test papers a year. Because 99.9 per cent is simply not acceptable in some areas (such as how a college accounts for exam papers or how drinking water is controlled), the 'statistics' above refer only to what might be if standards were relaxed. This does not mean to say that any organization is 100 per cent efficient in all areas of its operations, but in crucial areas it has to be.

We are sure that you can think of examples of waste and expense which have been well publicized, such as the new road and flyover that was built for access to a refuse landfill. The only problem was that planning permission had not been obtained. Two years and £6 million later the road and tip were finally opened. Of course, government bodies can make large mistakes – they won't go out of business as a result. But what happens to a private company in a highly competitive world?

Conformance costs

How are such costs prevented? In some cases, a modicum of common sense might help. Generally, second-rate organizations – that is, those that have not embraced the philosophy of getting things right first time, or of giving all levels of staff responsibility for their actions – will resort to inspections, tests, close supervision and audits. These costs can be grouped under the heading of conformance. They are the costs of inspection and checking.

Example

How much is your audit account? If you know in advance what the auditors want it is possible that you could reduce your account by up to 50 per cent. This will require schedules to be properly pre-pared, support information to be ready, inventory count to be correct, debtors and the bank accounts reconciled; in short, the figures should add up and be in a convenient form for the auditors.

Your turn!

In your organization how many supervisors do you have? What is the cost of supervision? Would you need supervisors at all if every member of the company knew what they were meant to be doing, did it right first time, and were confident enough to take action or to seek advice if they thought things were not going the way they should be? If a staff member is bold enough to raise a concern but their fears are proved groundless, and the supervisor is sarcastic or disparaging, it will make the employee reluctant to speak up or make suggestions next time.

Example

We began this chapter with Marty's dilemma. Marty used the wrong manual when quoting an insurance rate; does this mean that Marty needs more supervision? Or does it mean that if Marty had been properly trained, the job was correctly specified, and if Marty knew the consequences of his actions, then perhaps no supervision at all would be necessary?

Supervision strategy

There are two possible strategies: the first is to increase supervision to prevent mistakes (increased ongoing cost); the second is to reduce the cost of supervision and to spend more time (one-off cost) on training. Which strategy do you think would be the most profitable in the long run?

Example

In one advertising agency, now out of business, the handling of invoices was so poor that accounts weren't paid when due, not because of lack of cash flow but because of inefficiency. Eventually the agency's telephones were dis- connected. Imagine an advertising agency, a business that depends on communication, without a telephone. What did that do for the customers' perception of the efficiency of the organization?

Levels of quality management

The four levels of quality management are:

1. Inspection.
2. Control.
3. Assurance.
4. Total quality.

Quality inspection and quality control

Quality inspection and control rely on supervision to make sure that no mistakes are made. The most basic approach to quality is inspection and correction of errors; the next stage, quality control, is to inspect, correct, investigate and find the causes of problems and to take actions to prevent errors re-occurring. Both methods rely on supervision and inspection.

Quality assurance

Quality assurance includes the setting of standards with documentation and also includes the documentation of the method of checking against the specified standards. Quality assurance generally also includes a third-party approval from a recognized authority, such as ISO. With quality assurance, inspection and con- trol are still the basic approach, but in addition one would also expect a comprehensive quality manual, recording of quality costs, perhaps use of statis- tical process control and the use of sampling techniques for random checking (see Chapter 14 for statistical control and sampling), and the overall auditing of quality systems.

Quality inspection and control and quality assurance are aimed at achieving an agreed consistent level of quality, first by testing and inspection, then by rigid con- formance to standards and procedures, and finally by efforts to eliminate causes of errors so that the defined accepted level will be achieved. *This is a cold and often sterile approach to quality.* It implies that once a sufficient level of quality has been achieved, then, apart from maintaining that level which in itself might be hard work, little more need be done. This does not mean that management is not taking into account what the customer wants or is ignoring what the competition is doing; it just means that the managers believe they know what is best and how this can be achieved. To this end, supervision and inspection become an important method of achieving the aim, with little input expected from staff members.

Total quality management

Total quality management (TQM) is on a different plane. Total quality management does, of course, include all the previous levels of setting standards and the means of measuring conformance to standards. In doing this, statistical process control (SPC) may be used, systems will be documented, and accurate and timely feedback of results will be given. With TQM, ISO accreditation might be sought, but an organization that truly has embraced TQM does not need the ISO stamp of approval.

Any organization aspiring to TQM will have a vision of quality which goes far beyond mere conformance to a standard. TQM requires a culture whereby every member of the organization believes that not a single day should go by without the organization in some way improving the quality of its goods and services. The vision of TQM must begin with the chief executive. If the chief executive has a passion for quality and continuous improvement, and if this passion can be transmitted down through the organization, then paradoxically, the ongoing driving force will be from the bottom up.

Figure 13.1 depicts a TQM culture, wherein management has the vision, which is communicated to and accepted by all levels of the organization. Once the quality culture has been ingrained in the organization the ongoing driving force is 'bottom up'.

Generally it is the lower-paid members of the organization who will be physically interfacing with the customers or providing the service, and it is the sum of the efforts that each individual puts into their part of the finished service that will determine the overall quality as experienced by the customer. Likewise, generally it is the lower-paid staff members, such as shop assistants, telephone operators and van drivers who are the contact point with the customer and the wider public. They too have a huge part to play in how the customer perceives an organization. It is on the lower level then that an organization must rely for the continuing daily level of quality. Quality, once the culture of quality has become ingrained,

Figure 13.1

Quality and the driving force

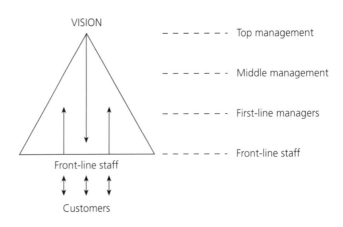

will be driven from bottom up rather than achieved by direction or control from the top. Management will naturally have to continue to be responsible for planning and for providing the resources to enable the workers to do the job. But unless the shop assistants, the telephone operators, the cleaning staff, the van driver and the junior account clerk are fully committed to quality, TQM will never happen.

TQM, however, goes beyond the staff of the organization; it goes outside the organization and involves suppliers, customers and the general public.

Japan and TQM

Total quality management has its origins in Japan. (The acronym used in Japan is TQC – total quality control. TQC is synonymous with TQM.) In the 1960s, Japan went through a quality revolution. Prior to this, 'Made in Japan' meant cheap or shoddy consumer goods.

The approach Japan used in the 1950s and 1960s to improve quality standards was to employ consultants from America, notably Dr W. Edwards Deming. Deming's philosophy was to establish the best current practices within an organization, establish the best practice as standard procedure and train the workers in the best way. In this manner, everyone would be using the same best way.

Deming's approach was to involve everyone in the organization and to win them over. He believed that quality was everyone's business. Deming said that to find the best way meant getting the facts, collecting data, setting standard procedures, measuring results and getting prompt and accurate feedback of results. He saw this as a continuous cycle: the continuous spinning of the quality wheel of plan, control, do and act. Deming argued that once a consistent standard or stable condition has been determined, control is achieved by reducing variability in the processes and that this can only occur if the results are promptly and accurately fed back so corrective action can be taken to eliminate variations to the standard (Deming, 1986).

Deming emphasized that people can only be won over if there is trust at all levels. This means that management are prepared to allow and encourage employees to take responsibility, and that employees are prepared to accept responsibility. Employee participation, through understanding processes and contributing through improvement suggestions, is a serious part of the Deming philosophy.

American and European approaches

In the United States and in Europe – perhaps because senior management, bankers and investors are concerned with the annual report, the bottom line and the share price, and perhaps because increasingly senior management calls upon consultants for immediate fixes – the tendency is to expect instant results. The time frame is short-term, and if results are not readily apparent, there will be a move to some other solution. The Japanese, however, know that success is rarely an overnight phenomenon. The implementation of TQM requires a total change in management thinking and a major change in culture, and will take years to internalize. Thus TQM has lost favour with some organizations because results are not instant. Where results are apparent in a short space of time, they may not always seem to be major. How, though, can you tell if there have been benefits and whether they are significant or not?

If after adopting TQM an organization is still in business and the results are slightly up on the previous year, is this something to be excited by? Maybe the shareholders won't see this as a triumph. But it may well be. If the organization had not begun its quality revolution, perhaps the results would have been much worse.

Sometimes, just a change in attitude and recognition of key problem areas can be sufficient to make a big difference. For example, when Jan Carlzon took over SAS, the airline was about to lose US$20 million. Within twelve months, by establishing where the moments of truth were between customers and front-line staff, he was able to turn a US$20 million loss into a US$40 million profit. Carlzon and moments of truth are discussed in more detail in Chapter 15. But this example is an exception: most benefits are incremental and goals are long term. The philosophy of TQM is to look for a continuous improvement, not major breakthroughs: any major breakthrough will be a bonus. No organization can ever say that TQM has been achieved – the quest for improvement is never-ending.

ISO 9001:2000

The International Standard Organization 9000:1994 series of 9001, 9002, 9003 have now been combined into one standard ISO 9001:2000. The predecessor to ISO 9001 was the British Standard BS 5750 (introduced in 1979 to set standard specifications for military suppliers). To gain certification, an organization has to meet rigorous standards and satisfy a third party, – the accreditation authority.

Total quality management means more than just the basics as outlined in ISO 9001:2000; indeed ISO 9000 could be seen as running contrary to the philosophy of TQM. As Allan J. Sayle (1991) pointed out:

> It is important to recognize the limitations of the ISO 9000 series. They are not and do not profess to be a panacea for the business's ills. Many companies have misguidedly expected that by adopting an ISO 9000 standard they will achieve success comparable to that of the over-publicized Japanese. One must not forget that the ISO 9000 standards did not exist when the Japanese quality performance improved so spectacularly: many Japanese firms did not need such written standards, and probably still don't.

What does ISO 9001:2000 achieve?

ISO 9001:2000 exists to give the customer confidence that the product or service being provided will meet certain specified standards of performance and that the product or service will always be consistent with those standards. It gives the customer confidence, so much so that some customers will insist that suppliers of services are ISO accredited. But what of the organization seeking ISO certification; are there any internal benefits?

First, by adopting ISO the methodology of the system will show an organization how to go about establishing and documenting a quality improvement system. To achieve accreditation, an organization has to prove that every step of the process is documented and that the specifications and check procedures shown in the documentation are always complied with. The recording and documenting of each step is a long and tedious job. Perhaps the most difficult stage is agreeing on what exactly the standard procedure is.

If an organization does not have a standard way of doing things, trying to document procedures will prove difficult and many interesting facts will emerge. The act of recording exactly what is happening and then determining what the one set method should be from now on will in itself be a useful exercise. Wasteful activities should be unearthed and, hopefully, overall a more efficient method will emerge and be adopted as standard procedure. Determining a standard does not imply that the most efficient method is being used. The standard adopted only means that there is now a standard method (not necessarily the most efficient), that the method is recorded, and that the recorded method will be used every time. The standard method not only includes the steps taken in the process but will list the checks and tests that will be carried out as part of the process. This will often require the design of new and increased check procedures and a method of recording that each check or test has been done.

From this it can be seen that the adoption of ISO, rather than streamlining an organization can actually serve to increase the need for audits and supervision. ISO, to this extent, can therefore be seen to be contrary to the philosophy of TQM. With TQM, staff members are encouraged to do their own checking and to be responsible for getting it right first time, and the need for supervision becomes almost superfluous. With ISO the standard method will likely be set by management edict and, once set in place, the bureaucracy of agreeing and recording improvements may stultify creative improvements.

ISO tends to be driven from the top down and relies on documentation, checks and tests to achieve a standard, somewhat bland level of quality assurance. TQM, on the other hand, once established, relies on bottom-up initiatives to keep the impetus of continual improvement. However, as the Deming method of TQM does advocate a stable system from which to advance improvements, the adoption of the ISO approach means that there will be a standard and stable system in place. To this extent, ISO will prove a useful base from which to launch TQM.

ISO 9001:2000 – 'the wedge'

As shown in Figure 13.2, ISO 9000 can be depicted as the wedge that prevents quality slipping backwards. The danger is that if staff believe that the standard is sacrosanct, and if they are not encouraged to make suggestions, ISO can also become the wedge that stops quality moving forward. In other words ISO, because

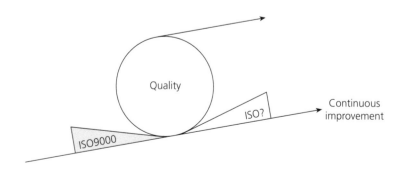

Figure 13.2

The wedge(s)

of the inhibiting nature of the paperwork and other hurdles needed to make a change, might actually act as a barrier to continuous improvement.

Notwithstanding the benefits of obtaining a standard stable system through ISO procedures, it must be queried why a true quality company should need ISO. If the customer or potential customer is not insisting on ISO accreditation, then the time and effort involved (and the effort expended will be a non-recoverable cost) make the value of ISO to an organization highly questionable.

Gaining ISO accreditation is a long and expensive business. Internally it requires much time and effort, and most organizations underestimate the time and effort involved. Generally, recording the systems alone will require the full-time efforts of at least one person for a period of time likely to be measured not in months but in years.

Example

One small print shop employing 20 people, and with one main customer, was sold on the idea of ISO accreditation by consultants. The management was advised that the process of obtaining accreditation would take nine months. The actual time taken was two years and three months. The main customer had not asked for accreditation, but the difficulties experienced by the print shop in getting accredited led the customer to query the efficiency of the organization and the account was almost lost. What of the expensive consultants? Well, they took their fee and rode off into the sunset.

Internal costs of obtaining accreditation are high – higher than most organizations are prepared to admit. Total internal costs will not be known unless everyone involved in setting up the systems records and costs the time spent, and this is seldom done. The external costs can be equally high. It is not mandatory to hire an external consultant, but there are advantages in doing so. Consultants are not cheap and quotes should be sought from at least three consultants. Briefing the consultants will force an organization to do some preparatory work, which, if properly approached, should help in clarifying the overall purpose and give some indication of the effort that will be involved. Once the consultant is employed, it will be the organization hiring the consultant that will do the work. Consultants point the way. They give guidelines and hold meetings, they will help with the planning; but don't expect them to get their hands dirty. They won't actually do any work – the organization seeking accreditation does the work!

Accreditation can only be obtained through an approved certifying body. The fee charged by the certifying body is relatively small. Fees depend on the size of the organization and the level of accreditation.

ISO 14000

ISO 14000 concerns environmental (green) issues. Again, if an organization has a social conscience and is environmentally aware, such as Canon in Chapter 3, why would it need ISO accreditation?

Throughout the ISO series, reference is made to documentation. To meet the ISO requirements, it is not necessary to have hard copies of quality plans, quality manuals and procedures. Indeed, when people have a computer terminal at hand, they are more likely to search the computer rather than leaf through large manuals. Also, with a computer system, it is easier to update the records with the latest procedures and to ensure that the user acknowledges receipt of change when using the system. In this way the system can be kept almost instantly updated.

The other important aspect of ISO is audits. Audits can be carried out internally and/or by external auditors. Audit requirements are more towards compliance checks after an activity has started or been completed. This type of check confirms that procedures are being kept to, or that an outcome complies with the standard. Where mistakes are found, they are retrospective. They will highlight where errors have occurred and thus indicate the need for corrective action for the future, but they don't stop the error happening in the first place. The most effective audit is the audit carried out before an activity occurs, with the aim being to prevent mistakes happening.

To be effective, the internal quality auditor should be trained in audit procedures and the purpose of auditing. Auditors should be there to help and guide, not to trap and catch. If the audit takes place before the event or process, it is preventative, and so much the better.

To summarize this discussion about ISO; with TQM the aim is continuous improvement, with the continuing impetus for quality improvement being driven from the bottom up. ISO will not achieve this. At best, ISO can be seen as a step on the way to TQM. At worst, it might actually inhibit TQM, as it relies on the setting of top-down standards and controls. A true TQM organization does not need ISO but, if ISO is insisted on by a customer, it can be made to fit into the overall TQM plan.

Quality initiatives

Kaizen

The Japanese have a word for continuous improvement: it is *kaizen*. The word is derived from a philosophy of gradual day-by-day betterment of life and spiritual enlightenment towards a long-term goal. *Kaizen* has been adopted by Japanese business to denote gradual unending improvement, but with a firm goal in mind. The philosophy is the doing of little things better to achieve a long-term objective. *Kaizen* is 'the single most important concept in Japanese management – the key to Japanese competitive success' (Masaaki, 1986).

Kaizen moves the organization's focus away from the bottom line, and the fitful stops and starts that come from major changes, towards a continuous improvement of service. Japanese firms have, for many years, taken quality for granted. *Kaizen* is now so deeply ingrained that people do not even realize that they are thinking *kaizen*. The philosophy is that not one day should go by without some kind of improvement being made somewhere in the company. The far-reaching nature of *kaizen* can now be seen in Japanese government and social programmes.

Zero defects

The core belief of TQM is that it is possible to get things right the first time: zero defects can happen. To make this happen, an organization has to know at every level exactly what the goals are and how to achieve them. There has to be a prompt and accurate method of feedback, there has to be a philosophy of continuous improvement, and everyone at every level should be looking daily for ways to make improvements.

Paradigm change

All this means trust. The managers have to stop being bosses and trust the staff; the staff must believe in the managers. This may require a major paradigm change for some people. The end goal is to gain a competitive edge by reducing costs and by improving the quality of the service. To determine the level of quality to aim for, it is first necessary to find out what the customer wants and to be very mindful of what the competition is doing.

The daily aim should be accepted as being *kaizen*; that is, some improvement somewhere in the business.

Quality circles

In the 1960s, Juran said 'The quality-circle movement is a tremendous one which no other country seems to be able to imitate. Through the development of this movement, Japan will be swept to world leadership in quality' (Juran, 1988). Certainly, Japan did make a rapid advance in quality standards from the 1960s onwards and quality circles were part of this advance. But quality circles were only one part of the Japanese quality revolution.

Quality circles have been tried in the United States and Europe – often with poor results. From first-hand experience of quality circles in Australasia and in the United Kingdom we believe that quality circles will work if the following rules are applied:

1. The circle should only consist of volunteers.
2. The members of the circle should all be from the one functional area.
3. The problem to be studied should be chosen by the team, and not imposed by management. Problems looked at by the circle may not always be directly related to quality or, initially, be seen as important by management.
4. Management must wholeheartedly support the circle, even where initially decisions and recommendations made by the circle are of an apparently trivial nature or could cost the company money (such as a recommendation for monogrammed overalls).
5. The members of the circle will need to be trained in problem-solving techniques and in how to present reports. The basic method study approach of asking Why, What, Where, When, Who, and How? (see Chapter 6) is a standard quality circle approach to problem solving.
6. The leader of the circle and the internal management of the circle should be decided by its members.

The overall tenor of these rules is trust and empowerment. Management of the organization has to be seen to be willing to trust the members of the circle to act responsibly and then must be active in supporting the circle. Although, initially, the circle may not appear to be addressing hard quality issues, as the confidence of the members increases very real benefits can be expected. Side benefits of quality circles, but nonetheless important, are the fostering of a supportive environment which encourages workers to become involved in increasing quality and productivity and the development of the problem-solving and reporting skills of lower-level staff.

In Japan, the quality circle traditionally meets in its own time rather than during normal working hours. Not only do circles concern themselves with quality improvement but they also become a social group engaged in sporting activities and outings. It is not expected, in a European country, that a quality circle would meet in the members' own time; few workers are that committed to an organization. However, there is no reason why, once the quality circle is up and running, management could not support and encourage social outings for a circle, perhaps in recognition of an achievement.

Quality project teams

A problem experienced in the United Kingdom with quality circles was the blurring of circles and quality project teams. The project team approach was top-down, that is, management selected a hard quality problem and designated staff from various sections to be members of the team. The top-down, conscription approach might appear to be more focused than the quality circle approach, but the fundamental benefits of a voluntary team approach are lost. With the pure, bottom-up quality circle approach, the members are volunteers and the circles consist of people who work well together and who want to contribute to the success of the organization.

Ishikawa (Fishbone technique) or cause and effect

The Ishikawa diagram, named after its inventor Kaoru Ishikawa (1979, 1985) or the cause-and-effect diagram, is designed for group work. It is a useful method of identifying causes and provides a good reference point for brainstorming (brainstorming is discussed below).

The usual approach is for the group to agree on a problem or effect. Then a diagram is drawn consisting of a 'backbone' and four (sometimes more) fishbones are shown to identify likely causes. Common starting points are people, equipment, method and material (see Figure 13.3a).

The following eight causes cover most situations:

1. Money (funding).
2. Method.
3. Machines (equipment).
4. Material.
5. Marketing.
6. Measurements.

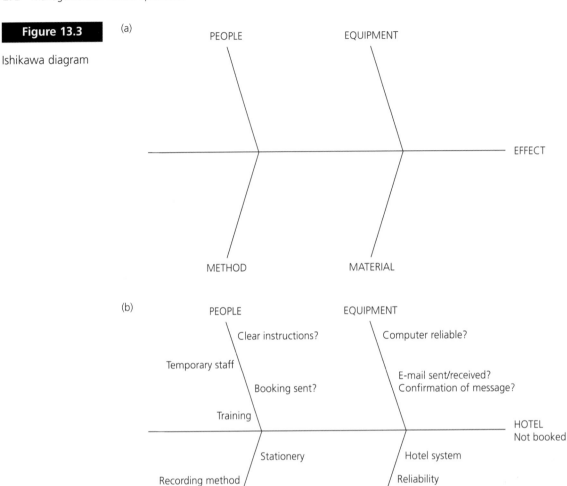

Figure 13.3

Ishikawa diagram

Example

Let us consider a situation where customers of a large international travel agency sometimes find that when arriving at their destination the hotel has no knowledge of their booking

In this case, to get started, the quality circle might begin with four basic possible causes: people, equipment, method and supplier (Figure 13.3b).

The circle will now have a clear picture of the possible problem areas and the linkages. The diagram will point the way for collection of data. In this example, training and standard procedures would appear to be worthwhile areas to follow up; a second likely cause might lie with the suppliers (hotel systems), and finally the e-mail system might need checking. In a more detailed problem, sub-causes may need further breakdown until the true cause of the effect is determined. As in the basic method study examine stage (see Chapter 6) the main question is: 'Why?'

7. Management and mystery (lack of communication, secret agendas, etc.).
8. Maxims (rules and regulations).

Brainstorming

Brainstorming is a method of identifying all the causes of a problem. It consists of a group of people being given a problem to consider with every person encouraged to make at least one suggestion.

Before the actual brainstorm process begins, it is important that the subject be defined and that the rules of the session are agreed. Members of the team will need at least five minutes of thinking time before the brainstorming proper begins.

Some rules for successful brainstorming are:

- One person to be responsible for recording suggestions on a whiteboard or large flipchart.
- Encourage everyone in the team to 'freewheel'. There should be no criticism of seemingly silly suggestions.
- Everyone in the team should come up with at least one suggestion, and other members of the team should not interrupt or make comments.
- Take suggestions by working around the room so that everyone has a turn.
- If someone is unable to contribute first time round, pass on to the next person.
- Typically, there will be a lot of suggestions in the first twenty minutes, then there will be a lull. Don't stop when this lull occurs but keep going, as usually there will then be another burst of ideas. Often the second burst provides the most creative ideas.
- Keep the initial ideas in front of the team until the end of the brainstorming session.
- When suggestions have dried up, the team should review the suggestions made and sort them into logical groups. Some suggestions will be found to be duplications and can be eliminated. One method of sorting the suggestions is to use a form of the cause-and-effect diagram.

Establishing quality controls

The classic approach to management control is for management to measure and correct the performance of subordinates to make sure that progress towards the organizational objectives is being made. Planning, it is said, creates standards of action, and controlling keeps the plans and actions in line. Control is therefore the function whereby every manager, from senior management to the supervisor, makes sure that what is being done is what is intended. However, because this system of control relies on feedback of results, control tends to be in the past tense rather than in the present. That is, the manager checks after the event to see that what has been done is what was intended. In this model the manager cannot control without having plans and goals. A manager will use the plan, consisting of goals and targets, to measure whether subordinates are operating in the desired way. The more detailed the plan, the more precise the control will be.

The control process can be at two levels. The traditional method is for the manager to attempt to control, top-down. The alternative method, the TQM approach, is to empower the worker, or a team of workers, so that control is exercised on the spot where the activity is being carried out.

For any activity, no matter how the control is exercised, whether it is through a top-down approach (where the aim is to control the activities of subordinates) or whether control is exercised directly by the staff, the same three control elements apply. The elements are: setting standards of performance; measuring performance against the standards; and correction of deviation from the standards.

Measurements and standards are covered in Chapter 14.

Six Sigma

The term Six Sigma means six standard deviations from the mean. In simple terms, with the normal 'bell'-shaped distribution curve one standard deviation (one sigma) will include 68.75 per cent of the total population; two standard deviations (two sigma) will include 95.45 per cent and six standard deviations (six sigma) will cover 99.99966 per cent of the total, or 3.4 errors per million opportunities (see Figure 13.4). Six Sigma team leaders receive special training in statistical measurement, and advance through the steps of Green Belt, Black Belt and Master Black Belt to Champion.

Six Sigma is, however, more than a statistical approach to measure variance, it incorporates all of the quality initiatives discussed above and includes the lean approach of just-in-time manufacturing (see Chapters 9 and 10). Six Sigma takes a whole systems approach to the improvement of quality and customer service with the aim of improving performance and profit, and in effect is TQM brought up to date by using a project management approach and the setting of a performance level that equates to 3.4 defects per million opportunities. The approach

Figure 13.4

Curve of normal distribution

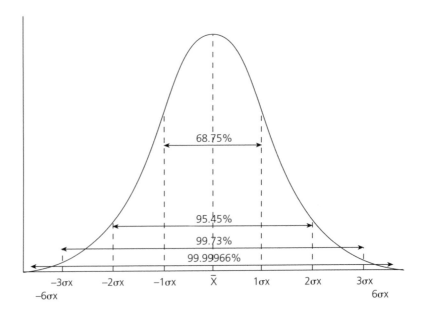

matured in the mid-1980s and was made famous by Motorola, General Electric and Allied Signal. It will be recognized that these are all large multinational companies.

The General Electric story (supplied by Ron Basu)

With over 4000 Black Belts and 10 000 Green Belts across its businesses, and Six Sigma savings of US$2 billion in 1999 alone, GE is a comprehensive Six Sigma organization. GE is the benchmark for Six Sigma programmes.

The company

General Electric has been at the top of the list of Fortune 500's most admired companies for the last five years, and without doubt their Six Sigma programme has played a key role in their continued success. In 2001 GE's turnover was over US$125.8 billion, they employed 310 000 people worldwide and their market value was US$401 billion. With earning growing at 10 per cent per annum GE also has the enviable record of pleasing Wall Street and financial analysts year after year. GE's products and business categories span a wide spectrum of automotive, construction, health care, retail, transport, utilities, telecommunications and finance.

Driver for Six Sigma

The CEO of GE, Jack Welch, is reported to have become attracted to the systematic and statistical method of Six Sigma in the mid-1990s. He was ultimately convinced of the power of Six Sigma after a presentation of Allied Signal's former CEO, Larry Bossidy, to a group of GE employees. Bossidy, a former Vice Chairman of GE had witnessed excellent returns from Allied Signals' experience with Six Sigma.

In 1995 GE retained the Six Sigma Academy, an organization started by two early pioneers of the process, both ex-Motorola, Michael Harry and Richard Schroeder. It was pointed out that the gap between Three Sigma and Six Sigma was costing GE between US$7–$10 billion annually in scrap, rework, transactional errors and lost productivity. With the full and energetic support of Jack Welch, senior management became fully committed to the Six Sigma programme. 'GE QUALITY 2000' became the GE mantra for the 1990s and beyond. Jack Welch declared that 'Six Sigma, GE Quality 2000 will be the biggest, the most personally rewarding and in the end the most profitable undertaking in our history!' While financial benefits and the share price were a driving force in Six Sigma deployment, GE identified four specific reasons for implementing Six Sigma:

1. Cost reduction.
2. Customer satisfaction improvement.
3. Wall Street recognition.
4. Corporate synergies.

Improvement programme

Although Motorola pioneered the Six Sigma programme in the 1980s to improve manufacturing quality and to eliminate waste in production, GE broke the mould of Motorola's original process by applying the Six Sigma standards to its service-oriented businesses – GE Capital Services and GE Medical systems. (*Note*: GE Capital Services accounts for nearly half of GE's total sales.)

The Six Sigma programme was launched in 1995 with 200 separate projects supported by a massive training effort. In the following two years a further 9000 projects were successfully undertaken and the reported savings were US$600 million. The training investment for the first five years of the programme was close to US$1 billion. GE also instituted a personnel recruitment plan to augment the cadre of dedicated full-time Six Sigma staff.

The GE programme revolved around the following few key concepts, all focused on the customer and internal processes:

1. Critical to quality; determination of and development of attributes most important to the *customer*.
2. Defect; identification of failure to meet *customer* wants.
3. Process capability; what the *process* can deliver.
4. Variation; what the *customer* sees and feels as against what the customer wants.
5. Stable operation; ensuring consistent and predicable *processes* to improve what the customer sees and feels.
6. Design for Six Sigma; designing to meet *customer* needs and *process* capability.

Model for roll out

There does not appear to be one universal model for roll out of Six Sigma amongst the companies that have implemented a Six Sigma programme. However, the Six Sigma Academy has advised that there is a general model which is effective and which has been adopted/developed by GE. This general model is shown in Table 13.1.

Key benefits achieved

The direct financial benefit achieved by GE was more than US$3 billion over a four-year period. This provides evidence of the very real benefits that are achiev-

Table 13.1 GE training model	Phase One	Business units select champions and Master Black belts. The Six Sigma Academy recommends one Champion per business group and one Master Black Belt for every 30 Black Belts.
	Phase Two	Champions and Master Black Belts undergo training. The overriding deployment plan is developed.
	Phase Three	Champions and Master Black Belts, with the assistance of Black Belts, begin identifying potential projects.
	Phase Four	Master Black Belts receive additional training, focusing on how to train other staff.
	Phase Five	Black Belts undergo training and the first projects are officially launched.
	Phase Six	Black Belts begin training Green Belts.

able from a Six Sigma programme. With Fit Sigma the next stage is to sustain and to grow the benefits.

At the second level of benefits, where the impact on savings is not direct, the achievements, average per year, include:

- 20% margin improvement;
- 12–18% capacity increase;
- 12% reduction in headcount;
- 10–30% capital expenditure reduction.

Some specific examples from business units are:

- GE Medical Systems: in the introductory year there were 200 successful projects.
- GE Capital: invested US$6 million over four years to train just 5 per cent of the workforce who worked full-time on quality projects, and 28 000 quality projects were successfully completed.
- GE Aircraft Engines: the time taken to overhaul engines was reduced by an average of 65 days.
- GE Plastics: in just one project, a European polycarbonate unit increased capacity by 30 per cent in eight months.

Market consultants and analysts have reacted favourably to GE's achievements with Six Sigma. Merill Lynch is quoted as saying 'Six Sigma balance sheet discipline plus service and global growth are helping fuel (GE's) 13% earning per share gains'.

On 8 May 2002, GE advised that they would deliver record earnings of more than US$16.5 billion, and was comfortably forecasting double-digit earnings growth for 2003.

Lessons learnt

At one level, to emulate GE may be considered as being beyond the reach of many companies. It is cash rich, and its business generates over 10 billion dollars per month (US$125.8 billion sales for 2001). It makes real things like turbines and refrigerators, and people buy their products with real money. However, on a closer examination there are some strong learning points from the GE Six Sigma programme that can benefit any company embarking on a quality programme. These learning points include:

1. *Leadership support.* There is absolutely no doubt from published data that the chief architect of success was Jack Welch. For any organization wanting to change a culture such as required for Six Sigma and Fit Sigma, strong unstinting leadership from the top is essential. Likewise, all senior management have to be engaged and believe in the philosophy.

2. *Definition of Six Sigma objectives.* The objective is to be world-class. World-class companies such as GE recognized that quality initiatives are synonymous with profit enhancement and share price. World-class means internal efficiency, best practice and a focus of customer satisfaction. The

lesson is that anything less than an ambition to be world-class simply won't do.

3. *Development of initial processes and tools.* At GE each problem was defined through measurement and analysis along a five-step DMAIC approach (DMAIC – Define, Measure, Analyze, Improve and Control), and the use of the seven quality 'tools' of: control charts, defect measurement, Pareto analysis, process mapping, root cause analysis, statistical process control and decision tree diagrams. The lesson is that a structured approach has to be followed for Six Sigma process management

4. *Alignment of Six Sigma with career paths.* At GE Black Belt status became essential for staff on the fast track for advancement. Black Belts were rewarded with share options (in most companies share options are reserved for senior management). The lesson from this is that recognition has to be given to motivate and retain valuable talent.

5. *Six Sigma and service industries.* The piloting of Six Sigma in GE Medical Systems and GE Capital Services incontrovertibly proved that Six Sigma is not just for manufacturing: the process is equally applicable to all operations including services. GE has opened the gate for service operations. In Western economies 80 per cent of gross domestic product is from the service sector.

Fit Sigma

Fit Sigma developed by Ron Basu is the new wave in the quality movement. Fit Sigma is based on Six Sigma. In *Quality Beyond Six Sigma* (Basu and Wright, 2003) it is shown how Six Sigma can be adapted to 'fit' any organization. The authors call this 'fitness for purpose' with the aim being to get an organization 'fit'. Having got 'fit' the important issue is how to keep 'fit'. *Quality Beyond Six Sigma* addresses all these issues and shows how small- and medium-sized enterprises can use the tools of Six Sigma and sustain the benefits gained in the longer term.

Chapter summary

This chapter has covered the question of quality. Our approach has been that quality is not a new or separate discipline, but pervades all management actions. Our philosophy is that quality is too important to be left to the managers: it is everybody's concern, not only those in the organization, but also customers and suppliers and any other stakeholder.

Quality has two main aspects: it can be measured from the customer's perspective – customer satisfaction; and it can be viewed from the perspective of efficient use of resources. These two seemingly separate objectives are in fact inseparable when quality is considered. An organization that wishes to compete in the global market must be efficient and provide a high level of customer satisfaction. No organization will be able to afford to provide world-class service unless its use of resources is efficient and non-value-adding activities have been minimized.

The level of quality an organization sets for itself is a policy decision, and to a large extent the decision is driven by what the competition is doing or is likely to do.

In this chapter we also discussed the various approaches to quality, including ISO 9000 and the total quality management approach. Specific techniques such as quality circles and cause-and-effect analysis were also introduced. The need for standards and control were reiterated, and the new wave in quality of Fit Sigma was introduced.

Case Study *Ridgeway Rubbish*

The Ridgeway Rubbish case illustrates the changes needed in the culture of an organization if it is to survive in a changing and threatening environment.

Questions

The operations manager now realizes that his department has to become more efficient and, due to the increased charge levied by the Council, that customers will not accept a drop in service.

1. Discuss, with reference to the 'Ridgeway Rubbish Dilemma' case, the distinction between customer service and quality, and consider what influences the standard of customer service and quality set by an organization.

2. Consider the implications for the operations manager should the Refuse Department become a profit centre, i.e. a separate trading concern owned by the Council. Assume that no immediate capital expenditure will be required (the Council will transfer all the assets currently used by the Department to the profit centre), but that in the longer term the Department is expected to be self-sufficient.

The Ridgeway Rubbish Dilemma

The direct customers for the Refuse Collection Department of the Ridgeway Town Council are considered to be householders. The service provided is a weekly collection of refuse. The Council has recently decided to add a surcharge to the rates (local government taxes) to partly offset the cost of refuse collection; until now there has not been a separate charge for refuse collection. The commercial (or business) district of the town also has refuse collected by the department, but commercial organizations are charged separately for this, and some organizations use alternative means of rubbish disposal. No competition yet exists for household refuse collection, but two private refuse collectors operate in a neighbouring town. The surcharge that will be charged by the Ridgeway Borough Council does not cover the full cost of the service and is much cheaper than neighbouring independent operators. Local body elections are due in eighteen months' time.

The operations manager (the manager of the Refuse Department) is worried that the charging of a fee by the Council suggests they are concerned with the cost of running the department. His other worry is that if householders are to pay for the service, they might become more critical and demand a higher service. In other words the Council have indicated that they are concerned with the cost of running the department, and customers are now likely to expect a higher level of service. The other worry for the operations manager is that the Council might consider out-sourcing (buying in) the service.

▶

To determine the requirements of the direct customers and the Council, and to see if there were any other stakeholders, the operations manager conducted a survey. The survey was designed to determine, firstly, what the customers and various stakeholders wanted; and secondly, their perceptions of what they are currently getting.

Results of the survey were as follows.

Requirements

1. *Householders* require a good service (ideally bins always properly emptied and left in a tidy manner with no rubbish scattered on the road). Householders also want a regular service (same day and roughly same time each week). Householders were not pleased when the surcharge for collection was made. They do not see a need for the Council to make a profit on refuse collection and the general opinion expressed was that being close to budgeted costs is sufficient.

2. *Council* requirements are for the Refuse Department to maintain a reasonable service (they are not concerned if the occasional bin is missed). They accept that it is desirable, but not vital, for collections to be on the same day every week for householders. For the commercial district collection is daily, but again the Council do not see that it is vital if a day is missed. Keeping to budget is regarded as essential.

3. *Commercial* ratepayers also see that keeping to budget is important. Many even suggested that the Refuse Department should actually run at a profit, and others suggested that the service should be outsourced. Commercial ratepayers provide 70 per cent of the Council's income and have a strong lobby group. They believe that they are subsidizing the householders.

4. *Other stakeholders*. The concern of the people who work in the department, and their immediate families, is with job security. They are confident that they can improve the efficiency of the service, and already they have made some useful suggestions such as providing customers with separate bins to enable recycling of glass and plastic materials. This suggestion is under active consideration.

Perceptions of existing service

All those surveyed agreed that the existing service is excellent. No bins are ever missed and the service is extremely regular and reliable. If the operations manager was only concerned with the level of service provided he would have been very pleased with the outcome of the survey. But as can be seen from the above survey's findings, some customers/stakeholders do not rate service as being the critical area of measurement. This suggests a rethink of the priorities of the department.

The operations manager now understands that the Council cannot afford to run the service at a loss. Prior to this analysis, the operations manager had not realized that the commercial customers had an interest in the service for householders, and he had certainly not considered that the commercial sector could actually threaten the overall future of the department.

The results of the survey indicate that if the department cannot keep to budget, the Council will put the price up or perhaps consider subcontracting to private providers. On the other hand, householders are very cost conscious and if the Council does contemplate a further price increase the householders might themselves lobby for private subcontractors. There is a chance that the whole refuse question could become a key issue in the election. Now that the operations manager realizes the importance for the department of not only keeping to budget but actually reducing costs, he is looking to see if some efficiencies are possible. Until now regular and high-level service rather than cost had been his main objective.

Written by J. Nevan Wright, 2002.

14 Measurement of performance

Objectives

In this chapter it is shown that measurement is needed:

- for control;

- to show that progress is being made.

The following key areas for measurement are considered:

- profitability;

- market performance;

- resource utilization;

- people performance.

Additionally, the following methods of measuring are considered:

- score cards;

- statistical process control;

- benchmarking.

Introduction

This chapter is concerned with the need for quantifiable measurements to:

- determine if progress/improvements are being made;
- effect control.

The importance of qualitative measurements, especially in relationship to customer service, is considered. Key measurements are identified and methods of interpreting measurements, including basic financial ratios, are discussed.

Some people might believe that measurement is the province of the accountants and not an important area of concern for operations managers. While it is accepted that figures are not everyone's strong point, unless standards are set which can be measured and results recorded, it will not be known if progress is being made or not. If all measurements are left to the accountants then control is abdicated to such an extent that they will drive major policy decisions. In Chapter 5 the financial imperative was discussed, along with hard (quantitative) and soft (qualitative) measurements of service. The need for measurement was further discussed in Chapter 13, our 'quality' chapter. In this chapter, the point is made that rather than the accountants pressing operations for returns and figures it should be the operations manager who is pressing the accountants to provide information.

This chapter therefore determines which measurements are operationally important and how the operations manager can use these figures to the overall advantage of the organization.

Measurement for control

The setting of standards is closely connected to planning and the setting of objectives. Standards have to be precise and communicated to and understood by all the members of the organization. Once the standards have been set feedback of actual performance and variations from standards are important. Feedback has to be made to senior management so that they can see if the overall objectives are being met, and to lower-level staff directly responsible for activities so that control can be exercised at the time, or close to the time, when activities are taking place. In this sense control refers to determining progress in achieving the plan and taking corrective action as deviations to the plan occur. Figure 14.1 expands on the control cycle shown in Chapter 5 (Figure 5.1) to show that feedback is required at two different levels. Detailed feedback is required at lower levels where the activity is occurring, and overall (global) information is required for senior management. At the operational level the day-to-day measurements that matter are those that set a standard benchmark and which provide feedback to let the person

Figure 14.1

Feedback in the
control cycle

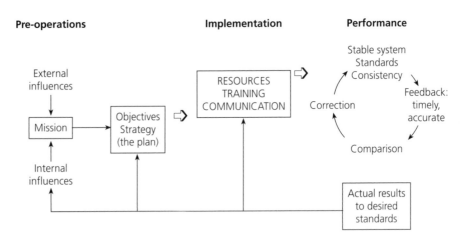

responsible for a particular task or activity know when something is slipping below (or too far above) the benchmark.

Measurement should not inhibit creativity

In some organizations, especially those relying on the skill, expertise and creativity of staff, standards are often poorly defined and variation from standards is a matter of perception rather than measurable. Too much measurement and too many standards are likely to stultify creativity; thus it is important to keep measurement restricted to the areas where it will do the most good. Care has to be taken not to impose detailed measurement on people who have been hired for their creative ability.

Key areas for measurement

The key areas for measurement in operations management are:

- Profitability, or (for non-profit organizations) not exceeding budget allocations.
- Market performance.
- Resource utilization.
- People performance.

Stable systems

Before any standards can be set, a stable system must exist; that is, each individual and the team must know what is currently being achieved and what can consistently be achieved. Once the existing standard is known, and the method of achieving this standard has been agreed, the basic standard (to measure against) can be set.

Profitability

We would all recognize that if any undertaking is to stay in business it has to make sufficient profit to:

- service its debts;
- make a return to the owners;
- invest in new resources for future growth.

For non-profit organizations efficiency has to be demonstrated and management has to be accountable for the funds and assets that have been provided.

Most people would see that recording and reporting profitability and/or being accountable for funds used is the responsibility of the accountants; however, every manager, in particular operations managers, must know how the figures are compiled and must be able to read standard accounting reports.

Accounting requirements

Much of the information gathered by accountants is not relevant to adding value to the service or the product. To be fair to the accountants, they must meet demands made from outside the organization, such as the Inland Revenue, the company's office, the stock exchange and other regulatory bodies. Obviously regulatory and statutory requirements have to be met. Likewise, people such as investors and bankers will also insist on financial reports that have been verified by external auditors. The collection of and the demands for any other information by accountants should be queried strenuously. For example, does internal charging between departments add anything to the value of the service or product? One question that should be asked is how does the time and effort required to collect and record a particular piece of information add to the value of the service being provided to the customer? In short, if this effort was not expended, what difference would it make to the customer?

Generally the customer won't care at all how costs are internally apportioned. The answer might be given that it is important to know what each section of the organization is costing, so that we can control those costs. But if the costs are inevitable, then knowing the electricity cost for one department does not really make any difference. If analyzed in this fashion, you might well be surprised how much information that is currently painstakingly gathered, reported and then queried with further information required is in fact of little, if any use whatsoever!

Example

One education institution records every piece of paper that is photocopied and charges the cost to the various sections in each faculty. At the end of the day the cost of photocopying does not change, but one clerk has been paid to track this useless piece of information. Occasionally an edict will come out that the overall cost of photocopying is too high and all staff (irrespective of which section) are urged to make all copying double-sided.

Example

An accounts clerk in an investment company calculated that the cost of each client newsletter mailed out, after all the transfer costs were calculated and a share of overheads were apportioned, was £88. Using this logic he believed that if the number of mail outs of newsletters was halved then the cost would also be halved, e.g. if 1000 newsletters cost £88 000 then 500 policies would only cost £44 000, and a saving of £44 000 would be made. The obvious truth is that the direct cost of each newsletter consists of the paper and printing, the envelope and the stamp. In short, each mail out had a direct cost of £2 to mail, and reducing the mail out by 500 would only save £1000 – if all the other transfer costs and overhead costs (including a share of his wages) were still there!

Most accounting departments could be cut by at least 50 per cent, and probably more, if they were restricted to recording what the operations managers wanted. The point is that while accountants keep themselves busy demanding useless information and challenging every other function for explanations and more detail, the other functions don't have the knowledge or time to challenge them.

Your turn!

How much does the accounting function cost your organization? If you don't know (and most likely you won't) ask the accountants for this information and then ask them how they plan to reduce their costs by 10 per cent. Explain to them that internal charges are not to be included in their calculations.

Traditionally accountants have seen themselves as the conduit through which quantitative information flows to management. Accountants work on historical data of what has happened and their reports cover arbitrarily set periods of time, with little allowance for the fact that business activities do not stop on the 30th of June or the 31st of December (or whatever other date has been designated as the time to take a snapshot of the financial position of the business). From a conventional point of view, and from the point of view of stakeholders such as shareholders and bank managers, there has to be a way of measuring the performance of an organization, and currently there is no better method than accounting reports. It follows, therefore, that for accountants to do their job of reporting to meet the conventional and regulatory requirements, information will be required from the operating arm of the business. This cannot be disputed. Therefore, if information is being provided, then it is useful to try and use that information to improve the efficiency of the organization.

Some information, such as that required for tax returns and annual returns, although it does not add value, has to be gathered. The question is: how can this expensive information be used to further the aims of the organization?

Basic financial measures

We will not delve into the sophisticated world of financial management involving the methods of financing, tax implications, currency hedging, etc. However, it is important that key financial concepts are understood, so that they are not used against what you are trying to achieve, i.e. the purchase of an important new piece of equipment.

Some key accounting terms are:

Sales or revenue
The total income of the business in money terms.

Net profit
The money made by the business after charging out all costs. This can be shown as before tax or after tax.

Equity

Equity or shareholders' funds equals the total of all the assets less all the liabilities. Thus equity is the net worth of an organization. The equation is:

$$\text{assets} - \text{liabilities} = \text{equity (ALE)}$$

Working capital

Working capital refers to the funds available, and is the difference between current assets (debtors, inventory, bank balances and cash) less current liabilities (creditors, short-term loans, overdrafts and the current portion of long-term loans). The equation for working capital is:

$$\text{Current assets} - \text{Current liabilities} = \text{Working capital}$$

It refers to the amount of money that would be still available if all short-term debts were paid and all short-term assets were turned into cash.

Increased working capital can only come from:

- Profits from operations.
- Sale of fixed assets.
- Long-term borrowing.
- Increase of shareholders' funds through the issue of shares.

A decrease in working capital can only be due to:

- Losses from operations.
- Purchase of fixed assets.
- Repayment of long-term loans.
- Distribution of profits (dividends).

The key indices relating to the financial objectives of a business are:

Trading margin	=	Net profit/Sales value × 100
Asset turn	=	Sales value/Capital employed
Return on investment (ROI)	=	Net profit/Capital employed × 100

Cash flow statements

Cash flow statements show where and how the working capital has increased or decreased.

Balance sheet (position statement) ratios

The balance sheet shows the financial position of an organization at a given date. It shows the assets, liabilities and equity (assets − liabilities = equity). The balance sheet is in effect a statement of financial position as at a given date. Many organizations now use the term 'position statement' rather than 'balance sheet'.

Example

Below is a simplified example of balance sheet figures. The numbers shown are to the nearest thousand to reduce the number of zeros for ease of reading and in making calculations.

Position statement as at 31 December 1999:

	£'000			£'000
Capital:				
Ordinary fully called	8000	Fixed assets		14 000
Unappropriated profits	2000	Current assets:		
Equity	10 000	Stock	4000	
Term debentures – 7%	6000	Debtors	1000	
Current liabilities	4000	Cash	1000	6000
Total funds employed	20 000	Total assets		20 000

Note: Assets – liabilities = equity.

Assets 20 000 minus debentures and current liabilities = equity 10 000.

1. Solvency ratios – these show the extent to which a company can meet its current commitments (i.e. pay accounts as they fall due and remain solvent).

    Current ratio = current assets   current liabilities
                = 6000   4000
                = 1.5 :   1
    This shows for every £1 owed there is £1.5 of current assets.

    The working capital is 6000 – 4000 = 2000.

    Liquid ratio = liquid assets   current liabilities
              = 2000   4000
              = 0.50 :   1

    For every £1 owed there is only 50p of 'quick' assets available to pay accounts as they fall due. Quick assets are cash and debtors. Stocks (of goods and materials) will take time to turn into cash.

2. Equity ratios – these show the extent to which the company is financed by shareholders:

    Equity/total capital (funds) employed = 10 000/20 000 = 0.5
    Debt 10 000 Equity 10 000   Debt: Equity = 1:1

    This shows that the shareholders' funds are 50 per cent of the total funds invested in the business. The balance of the funds has been provided by creditors and term debentures. If equity is less than 50 per cent the business is said to be highly geared, and in effect the creditors would have

▶

▶

a higher percentage of the funding of the organization than would the shareholders. With high gearing the future of the business depends on the continued support of the creditors and financiers.

3. Operating ratios – these show operating performance in terms of sales and capital employed:

The performance statement, or profit and loss statement, shows the operating results/performance for a given period.

Performance statement for twelve months ended 31 December 1999:

	£'000
Sales	12 000
Cost of goods sold	8000
Gross profit (margin)	4000
Operating expenses	2000
Interest	500
Net profit	1500

Return. (For these examples net profit is before tax. Some organizations use net profit after tax.)

Return on investment
= net profit/total funds employed
= (1500/20 000) × 100
= 7.5%

Return on investment (ROI), which is the same as return on assets (ROA), shows the earnings on the total funds employed. Return on investment is an indication of efficiency and can be used for benchmarking against other similar organizations. Return on investment is also used to assess the validity of further capital expenditure, such as an important piece of new equipment.

Return on shareholders' funds =
net profit/equity
= (1500/10 000) × 100
= 15%

In this example the business is returning 15 per cent on shareholders' funds. The actual dividend declared might well be less than this.

Return on sales
= (1500/12 000) × 100
= 12.5%

This is another measure of efficiency and can be used for comparing with other similar organizations.

Gross profit or margin %
= Gross profit as a percentage of sales
= (4000/12 000) × 100
= 33.33%

The key measure is return on investment (synonymous with return on assets). If the return is to be improved there are four areas which can be examined:

1. Increase the gross profit margin. This only applies to organizations that sell goods. The margin can be increased by:

   (a) increasing the price, or

   (b) reducing the cost of the goods. Reducing the cost of goods can be effected by buying materials more cheaply and/or by being more efficient in the manufacture of goods.

2. Reduce operating expenses. The aim is to be more efficient in the use of resources, i.e. less rent, wages, energy costs, delivery costs and so on. Operations managers should always be aware of costs getting too high and should be taking the initiative to control costs, otherwise it is likely (if costs are deemed to be too high) that senior management will make decisions for them. This leads to costs being cut that shouldn't be cut. For example, a 10 per cent across-the-board reduction of staff will lead to loss of morale, and the best (most marketable) staff are likely to be lost. If in our example expenses could be reduced by £120 000, profit would also increase by £120 000. Reduction of expenses of £120 000 has, in this example, the same effect on the profit as would an increase of sales of £360 000 (£360 000 additional sales at a margin of 33.33 per cent = £120 000). The same increase in profit could also be achieved by increasing the margin by 1 per cent from 33.33 per cent to 34.33 per cent. Sales of £12 000 000 at 34.33 per cent = £4,120 (an increase of £120,000).

3. Reduce fixed assets. This can be achieved by selling off assets, outsourcing (for example, selling off your delivery fleet and using contractors), relocating to cheaper premises and so on. Selling of assets and then outsourcing may not always be the best business decision in the long term, although in the short term return on assets will improve as will the ratios of working capital and equity.

4. Reduce working capital. A negative working capital has to be avoided, otherwise creditors cannot be paid when they fall due. But if working capital is high then debtors' collection might have to be improved, and the amount of stock held would need to be looked at. In our example debtors at balance date are £1 000 000 and sales for the year are £12 000 000, thus debtors equal one month of sales. If debtors had been £3 000 000 then this would show that debtors are taking three months to pay. Stock is £4 000 000 and the annual cost of sales (stock) is £8 000 000 which means at balance date we are holding six months of stock. This could well indicate that we are overstocked and stock holdings and inventory systems should be looked at.

Market performance

The first measure is the sales and the growth of sales, compared to market share. These measurements should be readily obtainable from the accounting department (sales, sales by service category or branch, and sales growth). The accounting department should also be able to furnish information on who are the biggest customers and whether these customers are increasing or decreasing their spending with the organization. If the accountants can't oblige one would expect that the marketing department would be passionately interested in this information, and would have it at their fingertips!

Chapter 4 discussed the requirements of the marketing department and Chapter 8 explained how important it is for marketing to provide accurate demand forecasts. Much of the information marketing requires will need measurement expressed in terms of delivery times, cycle times, length of queues and so on. These types of measurement should also be a 'must' for the operations manager.

Customer focus

Sorting out what is useful and what is not can be a problem. Usually what happens is that we rely on the accountants to tell us what they believe the key indicators to be. What an accountant sees as being important rarely has a customer focus. One method of determining which measurements are important in the market is to approach key customers and ask what they value; if speed of delivery is important to the customer then we should set a standard for speed of delivery and measure to see if we are achieving the objective.

Resource utilization

Using budgets to allocate resources

The master budget for an organization should be the means of allocating resources to various areas of the organization to best achieve the overall objectives of the organization. In Chapter 3 we discussed how business policy was set. Once the policy has been set then resources have to be allocated to make the policy happen. The budget can be the means of doing this.

The budget can be used to:

- communicate to all departments the overall objectives;
- determine what actions each department will have to take to achieve the objectives;
- enable each department to bid for the resources necessary to make it all happen.

Resources will never be unlimited, thus ideally resources will be allocated to the areas where they are most needed, or will do the most good. In this way any activity that does not directly advance the cause of the organization should receive few – if any – resources.

The budget should never be set on the basis of what was spent last year (plus 10 per cent), nor should bids for resources be made from a desire to increase one's importance by having a large department (office politics are counter-productive).

If the budget is to be a positive activity each department manager has to have a clear understanding of the goals and all should be working towards the best way of achieving those common goals. By working together each manager will gain a good understanding of the needs of other departments. The final budget will be the culmination of discussion and agreement between the whole management group and should be seen as a positive way of giving practical expression to the aims and policy of the business. Once set, it is important that the budget is kept to. For this to happen feedback of actual results has to be prompt and accurate. Ideally only summarized figures should be provided to operations managers as a matter of course; and, to prevent paralysis by analysis, only if there are variations to the budget should the operational manager call for detailed figures. As shown in the example in Chapter 5, panic measures to reduce expenses and time spent on writing reports to justify why expenses are above budget are not productive, do not add value and merely add to the overall costs.

Measure only that which really matters and from which real action can be taken.

Budgetary control: negative aspects

One of the dangers of budgetary control is that the system takes over and the accountants go to ridiculous lengths to budget.

Remember that accountants' time is expensive and don't forget the hidden costs of time and effort in meeting the accountants' requirements. *Any cost that does not add value to the service or the product is a wasted cost.*

If the budget is imposed without consultation and the operations manager is measured by his or her ability to keep to the budget, then budgetary control becomes a form of power play. The implication is that if the budget is not achieved, for example if there are not sufficient charge-out hours in a lawyer's office (revenue is not high enough), questions will be asked. Measurement for control purposes alone will not foster a climate of empowerment and is contrary to a culture where quality is the philosophy. Under such a method, many of the measurements will have nothing whatsoever to do with adding value to the product, but will be designed to control and to police.

Cost cutting

Cost cutting or cost-reduction exercises, if panic driven (or 'chairman's ten per cent reduction across the board'), will only give short-term results and will cause imbalances and disruptions in operations. Other concerns will be the negative effect on quality, innovation and customer service. The real business focus should be to survive and to retain the capability of competing in the future. Although strategy and innovation are important, the hard fact is that unless there is a positive operational cash flow the business cannot plan for the future. Therefore it is vital to have ongoing cost improvement even in a profitable company.

The approach must be cost effectiveness, not cost cutting.

Cost effectiveness

The key principles of a cost-effectiveness programme are:

- Understanding the strategic drivers of cost, i.e. volume/capacity, variety and variation and their impact in the marketplace and on competition.

- Evaluation of the effect of any saving measures on quality, safety and customer service.
- Identification of the leverage of cost structure and the setting of priorities for effort. As a rough guide the amount of effort allocated to manufacturing cost reduction should be proportional to the rest of the costs of the company.

Cost effectiveness is a continuous process for all organizations, but some businesses may require a quick and significant change in their cost structure. If so it may be expedient to form study or project teams to carry out *ad hoc* exercises, such as large-scale value analysis, restructuring or site rationalization (which might include office and factory closures).

People performance

Hard and soft measures

Measurement criteria can be 'hard' and 'soft'. Hard (quantifiable) criteria are those that can readily be measured. Measurements such as quantity, size, number of mistakes, scrap and wastage levels, number of customer complaints, warranty claims, days taken to collect money from debtors, cycle time of customers in a service system, cycle time of materials through production, value of inventory including the number of days inventory held, and delivery days, are hard criteria. If a system of recording is in place, hard criteria are easily gathered, easily checked and easily understood.

However, from the customer's point of view it is often the soft criteria that will determine whether the customer comes back or refers your service or product to others. Examples of soft criteria include aesthetics such as colour, taste, smell, ambiance and feel, as well as levels of finish (no rough edges, evenness of colour, flush fittings and so on). Other soft criteria include empathy, political sensitivity and genuineness of people (is the smile real? Do they mean what they are saying? Once the sale is completed will they still want to know me?). With a true quality culture the staff will all genuinely believe in the value of their product and service. The soft criteria will automatically be covered without the worker consciously thinking about what they are saying or doing.

Training for soft criteria

Some people will need training in new skills which may include grooming, acceptable language, basic manners and so on. However, a genuine desire to help, and faith in the product or service being offered, will overcome most social shortcomings. In any event, no manner of control from above can substitute for people who want to get things right and who want to improve quality, provided that they are empowered to do so.

Basic standards

The first and essential step is for basic standards of 'hard' criteria to be determined and agreed upon so that everyone knows the minimum level that is acceptable.

The criteria should be to only measure what is important, and only if it has a direct bearing on the quality of the product or service. In manufacturing, waste and scrap of materials, and down time due to plant or equipment failure are obvious measures and performance measurement might be by the number of items produced and shipped per day. In service industries it would seem harder to measure performance.

Example

Within a building society it is possible to measure what staff are doing. For example, how many customer contacts per clerk, how long on average each contact takes, the number of accounts per head of staff, the number of transactions processed per day, and of course the control of expenses within budget. It is not so simple to measure waste in a building society or in most other service industries. But how would the customer measure a building society's performance?

One large building society took a minimum of three weeks, but usually longer, to approve an application for a mortgage. All the staff agreed that the customers were not happy with the time taken, but management did not see the cycle time for the turn-around of a mortgage to be a key measurement. There were other in-house measures, all designed to control and police, but none at all designed with the customer in mind. What a difference it would make to that building society if all the policing measures were scrapped and the only measure taken was the turn-round of a mortgage application, especially if the target was set at 48 hours!

If the turn-around time achieved was 48 hours or less would it matter if Judy is ten minutes late to work on Monday, or if Doris takes Wednesday afternoon off to see her son's head teacher? And who cares if Charlie is occasionally back fifteen minutes late from lunch? The manager had a system whereby staff checked in and out on a time clock and the results were carefully tabulated and checked each week; just another example of non-value-adding work!

Need for score cards

All the big names in quality – Deming, Juran, Crosby, Feigenbaum and Oakland – agree that measurement is important in achieving quality. Without a score card it is not possible to see if improvement is being made. And further, if the organization is a group of 30 decentralized empowered teams, all striving to improve, it is highly unlikely that all will improve at the same rate. Therefore, by keeping a score card, it should be possible to easily see which ones are making outstanding progress, find out what they are doing and then pass the information on to the others. One of the greatest motivators for a team is to be the best and to be recognized as the best. This can only happen if there is a means of scoring and if the scoring is meaningful and result-oriented (customer focus, not cost saving).

Meaningful measurements

Meaningful measurements should be decided from three directions:

1. Top down.
2. Bottom up.
3. Customers: internal and external.

1. Top down

Management's responsibility is to provide leadership and to determine the strategy for the organization. Overall goals and targets are also management's responsibility. The key figure for profit-making organizations will be sales. Sales targets should be broken down into product groups and into customer groups using Pareto analysis. Pareto analysis will show who the top 20 per cent of customers are that make up 80 per cent of the sales value and will also show the top 20 per cent of products which make up 80 per cent of the sales value. The next stage of the analysis should then be to determine if the mix of products and clients has changed from the previous twelve months. For example, if twelve months ago a client was in the top 20 per cent of customers but this year has seldom used our services then we would need to know why. Staff will generally give us a quick and seemingly logical answer, but the true answer might not be what our staff believe. Glib explanations should not be accepted. The only real way to find out why is to ask the customer directly: 'What has happened? Are you not happy with our service? How can we improve?' Such questions must not be asked in a confrontational way, they have to be seen as a genuine desire to help and to improve the service. If your organization does not know who the top customers are, then these can easily be found from accounting records. Just sort through last year's statements.

For non-profit organizations, such as government-funded departments, or organizations including publicly funded hospitals and education institutes, the key measurement might be numbers of patients treated and student pass rates (not enrolment rates – but successful completions).

Non-conformance sales measures   Following on from the sales figures, we should also keep statistics of sales non-conformance costs; for example, how many orders are delivered late, or how many deliveries are wrong in quantity, quality, or even totally the wrong product? Likewise we could ask how long we took to get the invoice to the customer, and was the invoice correct? We should also monitor the number of days that the client takes to pay the invoice. You might say that these are not sales statistics – and that these figures would come from different departments. So what? These are the measurements by which your customer will judge you. The customer doesn't care which of your internal departments has got it wrong: as far as the customer is concerned, the XYZ company has fumbled again. And remember, it doesn't matter that 99 per cent of the time you get things right. It is when things go wrong that the customer judges you. When it suits them customers have long memories.

Non-conformance measures should be made to identify areas where extra effort is required so that problems do not recur, but never with the prime aim to catch out and punish.

Your turn!

Were you aware that according to research carried out by the Co-operative Bank (reported by the *Daily Mail*, 23 November 1998), office workers spend 45 hours every year stuck on hold, waiting for their phone call to be dealt with? Steve Jennings of the Bank's Business Direct team was quoted as saying that 'customers often get their first impressions of a business by the way telephone calls are handled'.

What is the policy in your organization over telephone answering?

As a customer, what are your views on voice-mail systems? (Consider positives and negatives and what else could be done.)

2. Bottom up

If an organization is serious about quality, it won't take long for the organization collectively to sit down and to agree what measurements are important. Once the overall targets and strategy for the organization have been communicated from top down, measurements that matter can be decided by individual depart-ments/teams. The setting of standards and the way in which conformance to the standards is measured will, therefore, be agreed from the bottom. These measure-ments will be smaller and will in some cases be self-directed and meaningful to the individual, but bordering on the trivial to the organization as a whole.

Key measurements are those that are important in setting meaningful stan-dards with the end view of satisfying the customer. It follows that measurements that matter are those where the impact of the outcome will be felt by the customer. These are the measurements which must be identified and which should be wide-ly circulated. Score cards should be kept and trend graphs should be highly visible in each department.

Other necessary measurements   There are of course other measurements that must be kept, mainly of a regulatory nature such as some accounting information and health and safety records. Such records should be kept to a bare minimum. Ways of using such information to improve the overall process should be invest-igated. If possible, those records, originally kept for another purpose, will now become part of the key measurement data.

3. Internal customers

The test for measurement is to ask if what is being measured adds to the quality of the product or service as seen from the customer's perspective. Further to the section on Internal Customers in Chapter 2 (pp. 22–4) this is where the concept of internal customers can be useful. At the individual level an internal customer can be considered as the next person in the process, or the person who passes work to you.

Pareto analysis

Using Pareto analysis (see note to Chapter 4), the aim is to identify areas upon which to focus effort so as to gain the maximum results.

Clerk 'A' passes a piece of work on to clerk 'B'. It is up to clerk 'A' to provide clerk 'B' with all the necessary information. Clerk 'B' does what he/she has to do and passes the work back to clerk 'A', either completed or asking for more information. Clerk 'B' will, perhaps sub-consciously, judge clerk 'A' for accuracy and legibility: likewise Clerk 'A' will be making similar judgements on the standard of work of Clerk 'B'. Both will be supplier and customer to each other. An improvement might be effected by clerk 'A' providing all the information needed first time and every time, and likewise by clerk 'B' advising clerk 'A' with a checklist of what is needed. A turn-around time might then be decided between the two clerks and a benchmark agreed. A simple example, certainly, and in most organizations setting such measurements will not be seen as a key measurement for the organization as a whole. But if an organization overall sets a target such as reducing turn-around time from three weeks to 48 hours as in our earlier example of mortgage approval in the building society, the target can only be achieved by the people who actually do the work getting involved and agreeing at their level what is reasonable, and how they personally can better process work between them.

Quality has to be practised and measured at every level within the organization. The point is that key measurements and benchmarks should be determined from the customer's perspective. Internally, the customer is the next person in the process and, for many people in an organization, they will be both customer and supplier, and the customer will be internal rather than external. Measurements that do not help the organization to turn out a better end product to the end customer are not key measurements and should be minimized. Key measurements should be highly visible for all to see.

Some areas of measurement that could point the way for Pareto analysis are:

- Frequency of effort.
- Amount of errors.
- Overtime generated by the need to correct errors.
- Number of customer complaints.

Statistical process control (SPC)

Statistical process control uses statistical sampling to determine if the outputs of a stage, or stages, of a process are conforming to a standard. With this technique, an upper and a lower limit are set. The sampling is to determine if the process is operating within these defined limits.

Sampling can also be used at the end of a process. This is known as acceptance sampling. In this method, a sample is drawn at random and tested for conformance or accuracy. Examples of acceptance sampling are: the checking of entries on a computer printout; the checking of final documents for accuracy; or an auditor's check such as testing a batch of invoices.

Two methods of statistical control can be used together: random checks during the process and random checks at the end of the process.

The procedure for statistical process control within a TQM environment is:

- Define the requirements, including upper and lower levels of acceptance.
- Set up a process which will achieve the requirements.
- Provide the staff member with a means of measurement for the process.
- Train the staff member to recognize deviations.
- Enable the staff member to take corrective action.

With TQM, once the person carrying out the task accepts the responsibility for the quality of the product, supervision and inspection can be phased out.

The basic statistical technique used is the calculation of the mean and the standard deviation. The upper control level is the mean plus three standard deviations, and the lower level is the mean less three standard deviations. Statistically, a normal probability distribution plus or minus three standard deviations (Three Sigma) will include 99.7 per cent of all of the cases. In effect, virtually all cases will fall within plus or minus three standard deviations of the mean; likewise 95 per cent of all cases will be between plus or minus two standard deviations (Two Sigma), and 68 per cent of the cases will be within plus or minus one standard deviation (One Sigma) of the mean. In practice it is not necessary to calculate standard deviations, and a range of upper and lower limits is used as a measure of variability in place of the standard deviation. Figure 14.2 shows how results of a sample can be plotted on a control chart to show variations from set limits.

The application of statistical process control requires two things: first, the process must be in a stable situation to be controlled; second, some knowledge of statistical techniques is necessary. It is strongly recommended that specialist

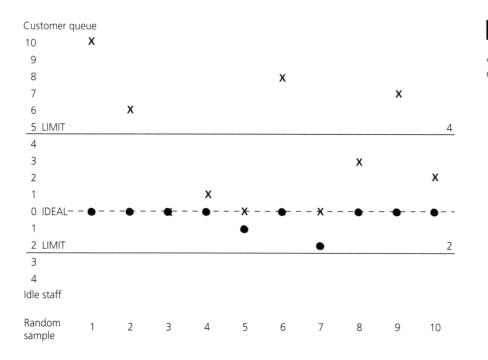

Figure 14.2

A service system control chart

Example

The policy in a service system is not to have more than two staff idle at any one time (the lower limit), and not to have queues of more than five customers (the upper limit), the ideal situation being no queues and no idle staff. The result of the random samples as plotted on the control chart shown in Figure 14.2 reveals that at least two of the four staff were always fully employed and only on two occasions was there some idle capacity, and that the idle capacity fell within the acceptable limit of up to two people idle. On the other hand, the target set for customer satisfaction has not been met. On four occasions more than four customers were queuing for service.

advice be sought when setting up a statistical control system. Once the control charts have been established then the maintenance of them becomes a fairly straightforward matter.

Those who wish to explore the subject of statistical quality control in depth are referred to *Operations Management* (Wild, 2002, Chapter 20).

Benchmarking

Benchmarking can be done in several ways. The purpose of benchmarking is to measure your organization against another organization. The other company may not necessarily be in your field.

The accountant's method of benchmarking is to compare published annual financial reports. It is fairly simple to obtain your competitors' audited accounts and compare them with yours by means of ratios and by looking at various key figures, such as stock turn, return on investment, cost of sales and so on. It doesn't matter if company 'x' has £50 million sales and companies 'y' and 'z' have £200 and £80 million sales respectively. If all three are in the same industry it could be expected that the percentage of costs to sales should be roughly the same.

Another example of benchmarking is given by British Airways who use the technique to spur action. They found that a Japanese airline could turn round a Boeing 747 in 40 minutes, but it was taking British engineers three hours to do the same task.

Unilever in England have entered into benchmarking agreements with other world-class manufacturers whereby the participants have agreed to exchange information about critical success factors. Some of the participants are American companies and some are European. The names of the organizations are not publicized and the participants enter into confidentiality agreements. In this type of benchmarking, the measure is not against competitors as such but against other manufacturers. The information given is used internally to highlight areas for improvement. Using this type of benchmarking in their distribution system, Xerox found that they had an additional layer of stockholding that could be eliminated.

Internally benchmarking can be achieved by comparing key measures of like departments, or even over the organization as a whole. Absenteeism could be a benchmark if it was considered that this was a problem area.

Benchmarking is a form of measurement and is useful for highlighting areas that can be improved. However, there is little benefit in knowing that another organization is more efficient than your own unless the method of improvement used by the other organization can be determined.

True quality companies are generally happy to share their experiences. Their philosophy is that the more efficient the competition, the more efficient they will be themselves.

In other cases it is found that the competition is not always happy to share information, and even when they do the circumstances in each organization will not be the same. Recognizing this, Basu and Wright in *Total Manufacturing Solutions* (1998) developed a new approach to benchmarking against world-class standards. Although aimed at manufacturers their methodology is easily adapted for service industries.

Chapter summary

In this chapter we have urged that operations managers need to take responsibility for deciding what should be measured and why. If there is no advantage to be gained from keeping a particular record then the gathering of that information should cease. No record gathering in itself adds value; all record gathering is an additional cost. It is accepted that accountants are required to gather and record some regulatory information for government agencies and for other stakeholders such as financiers, the stock exchange and so on. Where information has to be gathered then the operations manager should examine whether such information can be turned to an operational advantage. While there is some truth in the adage that 'if it can't be measured it can't be managed', on the other hand too much measurement will stultify, lead to extra expense and perhaps even inhibit creativity. Measurement should be used positively to advance the policy of the organization and not as a means of power play to rule and subjugate.

Case Study *Tex Rob (Israel)*

See also Case Study: Paua Bay in Chapter 5, pp. 86–93.

Questions

The case deals with the performance of product quality, reliability and serviceability. Here we will focus on two aspects – quality improvement and reliability management.

1. Discuss the TexRob approach to continuous improvement. What are the conditions that have to be met before improvement can take place?

2. What actions will the operations manager of TexRob need to take to ensure that his/her own technology and systems are consistently reliable?

Introduction

TexRob is a world leader in the field of Automated Machine Inspection (AMI). It

▶

designs and supplies Automated Machine Inspection equipment for the sophisticated printing industry – primarily for use in quality and process control.

The equipment – which combines advanced electronics, computing, optics, mechanics and mathematics – takes several years to develop. It is used for automated character recognition, automated plate alignment, automated colour adjustment and flaw (defect) detection. The printing industry is TexRob's main activity. Here its portfolio of products are market leaders. It is a highly competitive, growing, global industry.

TexRob, which is the result of a merger between two companies, has a turnover of US$135m (1995) and has subsidiaries in several parts of the world. It employs over 200 scientists and engineers.

Customer service

The mission of TexRob is

To provide innovative solutions that apply machine vision and related computer-based technologies to improve production processes.

As regards the customer service activity the aim of TexRob is to:

- Double the revenues within five years.
- Generate customer service revenues of at least 30 per cent of total revenue.

Customer service is a critical activity in this industry. Customers expect efficient service from the suppliers of their expensive and complex equipment. Downtime (i.e. time out of service) on such equipment is very expensive to them – often stopping their entire production process.

Customers of TexRob have two 'service options':

1. An annual service contract at a cost of 10 per cent of the system purchase price. This contract covers most of the parts of the system and response to service calls within 24 hours.

2. 'Time and Materials' provides response within 48 hours and charges each job for labour, materials, parts, etc.

Although TexRob would prefer customers to enter full annual service contracts, in general they have tended to sign full service contracts for less reliable systems and use 'Time and Materials' for more reliable systems.

Typically, TexRob has generated revenues from the service activity of less than 20 per cent of total revenue with low profitability. There is no external competition in the provision of service. To achieve the new objective TexRob changed its organization structure to recognise the need to elevate customer service in the company, in order better to be able to achieve the following:

1. To increase service charge revenues – by having more customers on service contracts by offering a more attractive service.

2. To increase the efficiency of the customer service operation, i.e. reduce costs whilst providing a better service.

TexRob recognize that in their type of business customers judge their quality on two aspects – product and service, and that their combined value and reputation is what matters to them and their customers.

The challenge for TexRob

The company now intends to:

- Shift its thinking and attitudes such that not only technological competition, but also service and quality are seen as parts of its 'competitive edge'.
- Improve the overall package of benefits provided to customers, i.e. product and service.
- Develop systems to support an incremental improvement in customer service quality and costs.
- Identify and create opportunities to expand or create markets through the

provision of market-leading customer service.

Specific action plans agreed for the Customer Service function include the following:

1. Develop improved procedures for measuring and monitoring product quality, reliability and serviceability.
2. Implement a Management Information System to support an improved customer service activity.
3. Improve documentation and training for customer service.

Product – quality, reliability and serviceability

The printing industry has low profitability and high capital equipment investment. A recent survey has shown that 25 per cent of manufacturers work three shifts, seven days a week, with another 35 per cent working with two shifts, six days. In such intensive usage of equipment the 'up-time' of the systems is the customers' first priority. In these circumstances, the quality of the products/systems focuses on two factors: 'Mean Time To Repair' and 'Mean Time Between Failure'.

Mean Time Between Failure (MTBF)
A high MTBF is the aim.

Preventative maintenance can be planned, i.e. maintenance should take place at shorter intervals than the MTBF and vulnerable items – likely to fail – should then be checked/replaced. In this way the need for repair, which will stop systems, is minimized and maintenance work can more easily be accommodated in system operation schedules.

Mean Time To Repair (MTTR)
The serviceability of the product is measured by MTTR. It is measured by the total time it takes to repair a broken system. The time countdown starts when the call for service is dispatched and stops when the system is up and running again.

From the equipment supplier's point of view the factors affecting MTTR are:

- The time required for the service engineers to access the system, e.g. the service engineer is not always available on site.
- The effectiveness of the 'remote diagnostic' causes; for example, the possibility of wrong actions being taken, such as the wrong spare part ordered.

(Systems are often equipped with remote diagnostic facilities. It enables the service engineer to access the system through a telephone line and a modem to run a diagnostic programme.)

Dealing with these issues is a matter for both equipment design and service department management in TexRob.

The Management Information System (MIS)

The main proposal of the MIS is to help the management in the decision-making process. In the case of customers' support management this means:

- Management of the inventory, in an efficient way, to reduce costs.
- Management of the customers' service calls and follow-up on the responses more effectively to improve the quality.

The 'modules' of the MIS are as follows:

- Open up Time System.
- Parts Management System.
- Problem Reporting and Tracking System.

Open up Time System
Basically this module is intended to manage the service calls, i.e.

- Managing the data flow and the history of the service calls – who is doing what, when and why?
- Calculate and control the involved costs – time, spare parts and expenses.
- Automatic 'escalation'.

▶

(The 'escalation' procedure requires the service engineer to notify his superiors whenever a failure of a system is not going to be fixed within 12 hours from arrival. The aim is to 'escalate' the problem – i.e. to draw attention to it and increase its priority. The MIS is planned to have such escalation as an automatic e-mail feature, and several other modules.)

Parts Management System

The principal feature of the PMS module is inventory management. Its main purpose is:

- To manage automatically the inventory levels held locally according to products and the geographical region where they are installed.
- Automatically order spare parts from local stock when appropriate.
- Transfer of parts between regions according to level of consumption and shelf time, thus more effectively managing worldwide inventory levels.

Problem Reporting and Tracking System

The main goal of this module is to computerize the manual procedure of 'bug' reports and improvement proposals. The procedure requires that the customer initiates a report about a problem (bug) in the system to the local TexRob office. The office sends the report via e-mail to R&D at HQ who follow up.

Training and documentation

The internal training of the service engineers is carried out by TexRob HQ. Training is provided for various reasons, such as:

- when new products are to be introduced;
- for newly recruited service engineers.

Under the new approach the requests and views of the customer service departments are reflected in the training provision. Amongst other things this results in the present practice of more frequent but shorter courses, more on-the-job training for new recruits, etc.

Managing high quality service

TexRob take the view that the best way to maintain a high quality service is through a continuous improvement programme. This is the customer service function's philosophy – when one programme of improvement is done the next one is ready to be carried out.

MTTR

Further improvements of the MTTR are planned. In future every new product will have a list of the sub-assembly parts with the required 'time to replace', none of which will exceed three hours.

For existing machines an engineering effort is being made to design and develop a fully functional 'Remote Diagnostic' for all the products. The immediate benefit will be the lower MTTR.

Life Time Costing

The selling price of an AMI system is based on the direct and indirect costs of manufacturing, plus a factor to cover costs of sales, R&D, overheads, etc. The service charge is determined as a percentage of the price, usually 10 per cent. The service cost to TexRob is affected by the reliability and serviceability of the system, or in other words by MTBF and MTTR.

The level of serviceability (MTTR) is achieved in engineering design and in manufacture. It is relatively easy to reach high serviceability and to calculate it. On the other hand, to calculate MTBF is difficult.

Records show that the calculated MTBF is achieved between the third and the fourth year of the system lifetime with significant deterioration after the eighth year.

Calculations show that the service profitability improves as the system matures, and falls significantly as MTBF deteriorates after year 8.

Case-based training

Further improvements in the training of service engineers is planned through the introduction of multi-media training. The objectives are:

- The new service engineers will be able to get some background information, prior to the course itself.
- To enable training 'in the field'.
- To provide training for customers for self-maintenance by the engineers.

Customers' satisfaction survey

The vice-president of customer service intends to use a survey every two years to measure the perceived quality of the service.

© David Furst, Ray Wild 1996

VI Part Six

This Part consists of **Chapter 15**, which considers change and change management. As stated in the Preface, the central theme of this book is that people make the difference in providing an efficient and 'quality' service. However, not all people in an organization have a passion for the mission of the organization, even when they know what it is and understand it. Some people come to work only for the money and do just sufficient to keep their jobs. They do not want to be empowered, they shun responsibility and consider management as being on a different plane. This attitude does not only apply to lower-level staff; there are plenty of examples of middle managers who are content to shuffle paper and wait for pay-day or retirement. In the twenty-first century, organizations with staff of this type will not survive for long.

This Part shows how to re-engineer an organization, first by getting the structure right, and second by achieving a cultural fit with the people of the organization so that everyone buys into the one vision and mission for the organization.

15 Change and change management

Objectives

The objective of this chapter is to excite and to stimulate. The subject for debate is that change is inevitable. Means of change, especially of corporate culture, are explored. As this is the final chapter, much of what has been discussed in preceding chapters is referred to.

Issues looked at are:

- Structure of organizations and re-engineering of structures.

- TQM, vision and cultural fit.

- Using the mission statement for change.

- Model for change.

- Project management for change.

- Training and communication.

Introduction

We live in a period of accelerating change. Great political events change our perception of the world. Fundamental changes in society restructure our lives. New technology means that the impossible becomes commonplace. Change is all around us and the capacity to manage change effectively is the crucial attribute of a successful manager in today's organizations (Carnall, 1993).

There is no doubt that people today are more travelled, better educated and consequently more discerning than ever before. Quality service, value for money and accountability are now taken for granted. Likewise, although innovation and technological advances are soon copied and any competitive advantage gained is only short-lived, failure to keep pace with changing technology could well prove to be a false economy.

Competitors are global, standards are world-class, and organizations that are not striving to meet world-class standards will soon be found out. The breaking down of national barriers (with the elimination of protective tariffs) and the opening up of worldwide competition is seen by some as a threat, and by others as a great opportunity.

What was adequate in the past when information and communication were slower is no longer adequate for today. To reap the benefits of the new technology, and the opportunities of the global market, organizations must have the appropriate structures and systems in place. Knowing what the appropriate structure should be requires a re-evaluation of: what the organization is trying to achieve (its core mission); what the customers want; what the regulators expect; and what the suppliers can provide.

The organization has to be structured around the whole extended process from supplier through to customer – ever mindful of technological changes and the competition – with the focus on adding value and the elimination of non-value-adding activities. In short the organization has to be re-engineered. In this chapter it is shown that re-engineering is not just redundancies and cost cutting. It is also shown that re-engineering requires major transformational change.

Needless to say the operations manager is at the cutting edge of competitive and technological change, and will be vitally concerned with both the process and the outcome of re-engineering.

For operations managers in service industries there are two basic types of change. One is the continuous and controlled change associated with the incremental philosophy of total quality management, and the other is major transformational change as brought about by the need to re-engineer to meet strong external forces.

Unless carefully managed, any change will lead to confusion. Elements of continuous improvement (incremental change) and the total quality management philosophy have been covered in Chapters 7 and 13. This chapter deals with the management of major transformational change and the overall change management process.

Communication revolution

Shareholders and other stakeholders can be excused for expecting that the rapid technological communication revolution of the last ten years would have by now resulted in increased performance, reduced costs and greater profits or surpluses. After all, communication of information is now meant to be instant, accurate and freely available. At the same time, with the well-publicized advances and promised benefits of technology, customers have come to expect, even to demand, improved service at less cost.

Management has been caught two ways: first, by the need to justify by results through heavy investment in technology; and second, by the expectations of the market for better service (including speed of delivery and up-to-date information).

Why then is it that so few organizations are seemingly no more profitable, and service is generally no better, than it was ten years ago? Figure 15.1 summarizes the operations manager's dilemma and indicates that the problem lies in organizational structures and communication blocks.

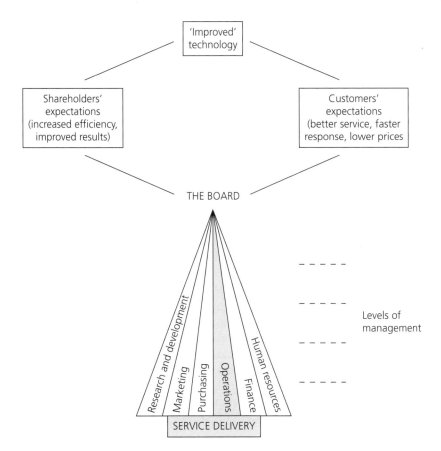

Figure 15.1

Service delivery

Unstructured reactions to change

Some organizations (perhaps many organizations) have taken an *ad hoc* approach to change with a series of knee-jerk reactions to major external threats and/or opportunities. With others there has been a reluctance to change and, as a compromise, matrix-type solutions have been superimposed on existing bureaucratic structures. In yet other cases, rushed major changes, in the guise of re-engineering, have been forced through without adequate planning and with very little appreciation of what the long-term effects might be. In most cases, whatever the approach to the changing environment, there has been a general lack of understanding of the magnitude of the changes that have occurred in the last ten years, and little appreciation of what is entailed in the management of change.

Change cannot be departmentalized

It has first to be appreciated that any change of a major nature cannot be limited to one department; for example, it is not possible to increase service by concentrating on efficiency in one backroom department in isolation from the rest of the organization. Effective change has to be organization-wide at all levels and the structure has to be such that it supports the intended changes.

Structure of organizations

Large organizations are still generally structured in the traditional hierarchical manner with defined functions: human resources, accounting, marketing, sales and operations, with each clearly separated into vertical departments. Typically each functional department is budget-driven, and each divisional manager guards his/her department from other departments and tries to get as large a share as possible of the budget irrespective of the legitimacy of other departments' requirements. This departmentalization can be compared to bunkers or silos where each department considers itself distinct and closed off from the other departments. In some cases departments become suspicious of the motives of other departments, power is jealously guarded and, in short, a bunker mentality emerges. Departments tend to become inward-looking, with the main concern being to meet the budget. Apart from the duplication of effort and wasted time in fighting other departments and in guarding borders and responsibilities, it is equally likely that customers seeking information will be passed from department to department with no-one wanting to accept responsibility.

Where the hierarchical structure of functional silos or bunkers is retained, the main problem is that improved communications technology has only served to speed up data collected within the silos; communication blocks between departments have not broken down. In short, the silos or bunkers now have more data, but information dissemination is no better than previously, and the power of each department has been most assiduously retained.

While organizations retain functional departments the benefits of improved communication and the real progress offered by becoming more open and more team-orientated will be squandered.

An organizational approach that attempts to break down communication blocks between departments is the matrix structure. With this approach people who work in one department are assigned responsibilities which are cross-functional. This approach attempts to superimpose a cross-functional team onto a rigid budget-driven departmental structure. The problems of the matrix approach are the divided loyalty of members of teams, arguments over priorities and of course the wrangling that arises from transfer of costs between departments and teams.

Figure 15.2

The budget-driven bureaucratic model

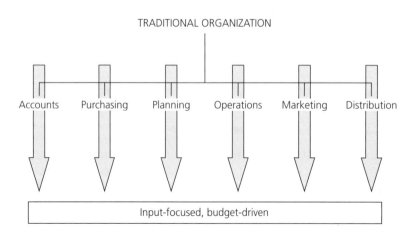

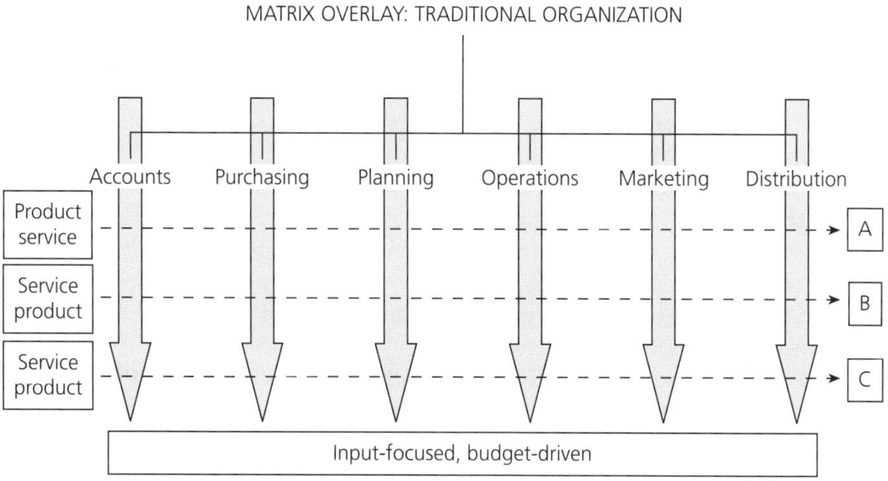

MATRIX OVERLAY: TRADITIONAL ORGANIZATION

Figure 15.3

The matrix structure

Accounts Purchasing Planning Operations Marketing Distribution

Product service — A

Service product — B

Service product — C

Input-focused, budget-driven

The budget-driven bureaucratic model is shown in Figure 15.2 and the matrix structure is shown in Figure 15.3.

Small organizations

The smaller the organization, the less opportunity there is to develop an organization consisting of separate functions. Very small organizations will of necessity be borderless with every member market-focused (rather than budget-driven), and each member will have a duty to satisfy a customer's query.

Example

A small business employing fewer than twenty people will not need a human resources department, a planning department or a marketing department. Certainly each person might have specialized tasks – one person might keep the accounts and pay the wages, another might be responsible for purchasing and so on – but all will be customer-focused. There will be little time for formal meetings with keeping of minutes, little time to write protective memos to justify actions taken and no time to maintain records and statistics which are never read or used. Each person will be too busy satisfying the customers' needs.

Re-engineering structures

'Re-engineering' means breaking down the silos and re-organizing around the process to gain real advantages from the investment in technology. This might sound dramatic, and indeed it is. Hammer and Champy (1993) describe their book *Re-engineering the Corporation* as a manifesto for business revolution. The term 're-engineering' emerged during the 1990s but many people are now confused as to what the term means. Many companies, especially in the USA, claim to be re-engineering but are, in reality, using the term to describe cost reduction and major restructuring. Major restructuring, involving the elimination of several layers of management and the creation of massive redundancies, is not re-engineering if the basic functional silos are still retained.

Re-engineering, properly applied, means that any activity that doesn't add value to the product, or any organizational or communication block that gets in the way of satisfying the customer, or anything that costs money without truly adding value, is eliminated. This means the whole organization has to be questioned and re-aligned. It means getting a blank piece of paper and starting from the beginning as if nothing existed.

It is not an exercise in trying to make fit what we already have. It is an exercise aimed at scrapping what exists and starting again. Re-engineering is not about incremental changes: re-engineering aims at quantum tenfold leaps in performance.

Example

IBM, without huge reductions in the workforce, claim to have saved £4.5 million a year by re-engineering, and Gateway Foodmarkets in the USA claim to have increased sales by 50 per cent and the margin on sales by 30 per cent.

Once re-engineering has taken place, then pressure has to be maintained to keep the new structure in place. Once stability has been achieved then a culture of continual (incremental) improvements has to be fostered.

People can change

The revolution should not start by scrapping all the middle managers and then subsequently hiring young graduates straight out of university. Many organizations are today regretting this approach. Loyalty and knowledge are hard to re-create. Some firms believe the only way to get a new culture is by getting rid of the existing staff (it is thought that they will be set in their ways) and hiring new people with open minds, the belief being that it is human nature to resist change or that it is simply not possible for people to change. The people who hold these sentiments naturally don't believe that it applies to them; they, of course, are the enlightened ones – they can change, it is everyone else who can't.

Your turn!

Are you personally capable of changing and of accepting new responsibilities?

Of course it is possible for people to change. People can adapt if they know the reason for change and can see a place for themselves in the new order of things. There is considerable evidence to show that a mature, experienced manager is more likely to cope with major change than younger managers who have not previously experienced change.

The only thing that happens if managers are fired without anything else changing (assuming that the managers who are dispensed with were actually doing something) is that, given time, the layers of management will return. Changing titles and changing people doesn't change anything; it is like re-arranging the deck chairs on the Titanic – an exercise in futility.

Example

In 2001 a service industry went through the agony of restructuring. Once there were 14 managers reporting to the Chief Executive; after restructuring took place the 14 were reduced to three, with some redundancies, some early retirements and some reductions in the ranks. The whole exercise caused uncertainty, a drop in morale and in overall effectiveness. Some good people, who had not been targeted for redundancy, resigned because they were suspicious of general management and felt it was better to jump before they were pushed. A massive investment was made in information technology.

Today there are 33 managers. True, only six report to the Chief Executive, but these six have all in turn appointed managers to report to them, thus creating a new layer of management that hadn't existed prior to the restructuring which took place only two years earlier! Although this organization believes it has re-engineered, and despite the heavy investment in technology and restructuring, income is only marginally up on the 2000 figures, costs have escalated and morale is still way down. Worse, market share is steadily declining.

Re-engineering: more than redundancies and restructuring

Re-engineering is more than restructuring and redundancies and it is more than the adoption of a horizontal, flatter structure with fewer levels of managers (this being, however, one likely and desirable outcome of restructuring). With re-engineering, the structure is designed to support the process. For instance, it might take on a circular form with several teams, each supporting a process, loosely connected and communicating electronically (see Figure 15.4). Obeng and Crainer (1994) suggest re-engineering produces a fist-full of dynamic processes more akin to a fist-full of writhing snakes as shown in Figure 15.5.

Focus of re-engineering

The essence of re-engineering is an appreciation that the focus is the satisfaction of the customer through increased quality and by the reduction of costs that don't add value. Work is organized around processes and outcomes and not around tasks.

Loosely connected
structure

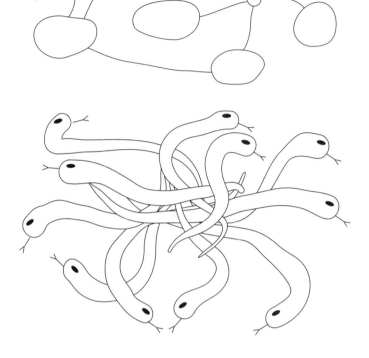

Dynamic process
structure

Re-engineering and structure

The old organizations were organized around functions and the flow of information. It was important for people at the top to have information about what was happening down the line. The bigger the organization, the further the information had to flow. Information was pushed up the line until it reached a person in the organization who had the authority to make a decision (see Figure 15.6).

Today, with cell (mobile) phones, faxes, electronic mail and its derivatives (Internet, Lotus Notes, AB Inform and so on) information is just a fingertip away. Information is instant, accurate, global and cheap. This gets rid of one structural shibboleth. As Obeng and Crainer (1994) say: 'The structure of the organization no longer needs to be the same as the information or reporting structure'.

Similarly, in most organizations, control is managed by setting departmental budgets and targets and by the allocation of resources to departments. Departments therefore are organized to fulfil a function and are usually groupings of specialists, such as accountants plus various levels of book-keepers in one group, marketing people in another group, and so on. The result is that each individual is set targets and then measured against these targets by their managers. Thus the aim is to keep to budget with the first priority being the function and not the overall process. (The process is only completed and the service supplied to the

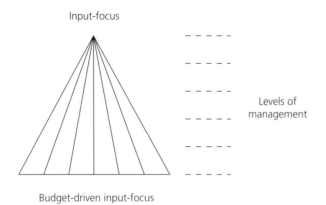

Figure 15.6

Budget-driven
input-focus

Input-focus

Levels of
management

Budget-driven input-focus

customer after several functions have had a direct or indirect input.) Likewise, the matrix structure, although designed to provide an output focus, is still very budget-driven (see Figure 15.7).

With re-engineering, one of the approaches is first to determine the key processes, second to recognize what has to be done and what resources and inputs are needed, and then to make those processes happen as efficiently as possible, always with the customer in mind. Attention will be paid to what really happens, and how the information networks exchange information and become meshed to make the process happen. In doing this, suppliers are regarded as part of the process. In this analysis the functional structure is ignored.

Adding value – quality of service and efficiency of operations – is seen as everybody's responsibility. Churchill once said that war is too important to be left to the generals. So too with adding value: everyone in the organization has to be involved and everyone, in the words of Tom Peters, must have a passion for excellence (Peters and Austin, 1986). But efficiency is more than an in-house concern; it is the concern of all involved in the extended supply chain. The supply chain begins with the suppliers of material and flows through the process to the customer (see Figure 15.8). Anything in the process where value is added to the product or service makes up the supply or value chain. Anything that doesn't directly add value to the product or service is outside the supply chain.

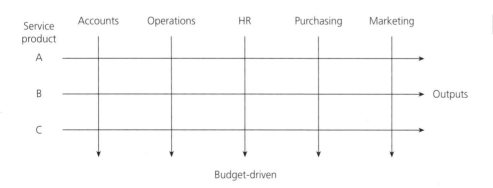

Figure 15.7

Matrix approach

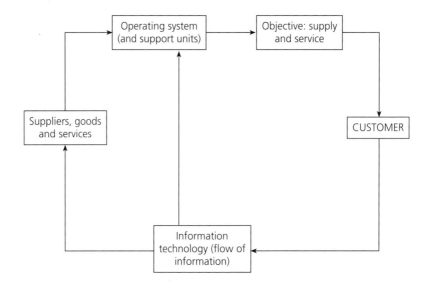

Figure 15.8

The supply chain approach

In the supply chain approach, not only are all members of the organization involved in quality and have the aim of making a daily improvement to the level of quality, but the suppliers are also expected to be imbued with the same enthusiasm. Likewise, if customers can be involved in advising and specifying what changes or improvements they would like, they too are a part of the supply chain and consequently are expected to be an integral part of the quality culture.

In this sense, the suppliers and the customers will, along with the in-house people involved in adding value to the product, be expected to incrementally force quality improvement on a daily ongoing basis. This is the basis of TQM: quality is everybody's business – not just the managers'.

Nothing is sacred

With re-engineering, nothing is sacred. This is the main drawback. Organizations that have been successful tend to look backwards for what is tried and true. The only problem is that conditions that apply today are not the same as those of even five years ago, let alone ten years ago.

Change is inevitable

We live in times of unprecedented change: organizations can no longer afford not to change. Those who ten years ago adopted TQM (see Chapter 13) have gone a long way towards re-engineering without the agony. For a start, they will have a culture that accepts change and is used to the self-empowered team approach. They will be in a good position to carefully assess how best to take advantage of technology with the aim of improving their product and reducing non-value-adding costs.

No organization can afford to be complacent. Change is here to stay.

The new structure

A chain of 40 retail stores, each employing up to 20 people, does not have a centralized purchasing department; each branch is authorized to phone, fax or e-mail their needs on a daily basis to designated suppliers. Goods are delivered directly to the branch and booked into the computer system by use of barcode wands. As each branch is electronically linked, stock transfer between branches is facilitated by the ease of access to information by any member of the group.

Head Office can monitor stock holdings at any time, but their prime responsibility is not to police stock holdings and stock turns, but to evaluate suppliers, look for new products and to negotiate global (discounted) prices.

Each branch and department of this organization works as a self-directed team, there is no large Head Office Human Resources Department (see Figure 15.9). The Human Resources Department consists of one manager and one clerk. They co-ordinate broad policies and issue one small, easy-to-read human resources manual. They also administer the payroll. Each branch manager, known as a team leader, acts as personnel manager and is responsible for recruit-ment, training of team members and for dismissals. Team leaders do not see themselves as supervisors but believe that their role is to chase Head Office to ensure that the branches have everything they need to perform efficiently. Team leaders and team members are encouraged to speak out if they think Head Office is not performing. The overall thrust is that front-line staff will suffer as little interference as possible; rules that exist are minimal.

An organization such as this requires a culture where lower-level staff take control and accept responsibility for their activities. It doesn't mean fewer people working twice as hard, but it does mean the elimination of several levels of management and it does get rid of the matrix of responsibility for human resources and other 'service' or staff departments as shown on the old-fashioned organization charts. With fewer levels of management, communication has become less confused and responsibilities (and areas of mistakes) have become much more obvious. Mistakes are publicized for all to learn from, and likewise improvements are not guarded but shared.

TQM culture

Achieving a TQM culture requires a vision of total quality from top management. Top management has to sell the vision and the rank and file has to buy into its vision. Once the rank and file is won over it will be the force driving the quality bandwagon. Once the culture of quality has been firmly entrenched within the organization it will permeate outwards to embrace suppliers and customers. When this happens management will no longer be attempting to dictate the level of quality and directing how the level might be achieved. Customers, suppliers and in-house, lower-level staff will be making daily incremental improvements and giving suggestions to management for larger, far-reaching improvements. As

Figure 15.9

Autonomous linked
teams

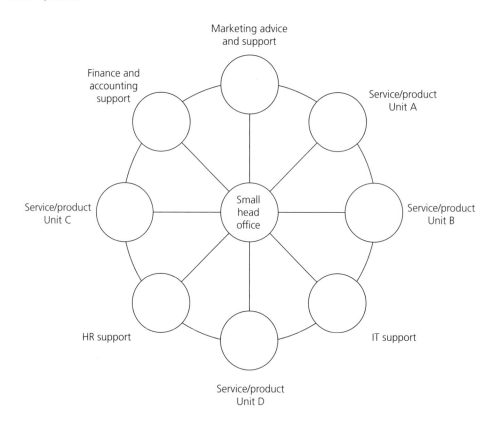

stated in Chapter 13, the drive will now be from the bottom up rather than
enforced from above, and with everyone sharing the same vision.

Vision and cultural fit

The word 'vision' suggests an almost mystical occurrence (Joan of Arc), or an ideal
(such as expressed by Martin Luther King: 'I have a dream'). The same connota-
tion is found when looking at vision in the organizational context. A leader with a
vision is a leader with a passion for an ideal. But unless the vision can happen, it
will be nothing more than a dream; see Wright (1996).

   To make a vision happen within an organization there has to be a cultural fit.
Corporate culture is the amalgam of existing beliefs, norms and values of the individuals who make up the organization ('the way we do things around here'). The
leader may be the one who articulates the vision and makes it legitimate but,
unless it mirrors the goals and aspirations of the members of the organization at
all levels, the vision won't happen.

   Culture and values are deep-seated and may not always be obvious to members. As well as the seemingly normal aversion to change by individuals, often
there is a vested interest for members of an organization to resist change. Often
middle management is more likely to resist change than are other members.
Machiavelli (1513) wrote 'It must be considered that there is nothing more difficult

to carry out, nor more doubtful to success, nor more dangerous to handle, than to initiate a new order of things.' Human nature hasn't really changed much since the sixteenth century!

Organizations are made up of many individuals, each with their own set of values. The culture of an organization is how people react or do things when confronted with the need to make a decision. As shown in Chapter 7, if the organization has a strong culture, each individual will instinctively know how things are done and what is expected. Conversely, if the corporate culture is weak, the individual may not react in the manner that management would hope.

Engineering a culture

To engineer or change a culture there has to be leadership from the top. Leading by example might seem to be a cliché but, unless the chief executive can clearly communicate and demonstrate by example a clear policy, how will the rest of the people know what is expected?

Mission statement and change

In Chapter 7 we noted that often a new chief executive will issue a new mission statement, ostensibly to signal a change in direction (although the real reason might only be to let everyone know that they have a new boss). Signalling a change in direction is a valid reason for the issue of a new mission statement and any effort to change an organization's culture is likely to require the articulation of a new mission. To be effective, as discussed in Chapter 7, it is important that the new mission is in tune with what the people of the organization believe. To achieve a mission that fits the culture it would seem sensible to get the involvement and interest of all the staff in the writing of the new mission. Thus, a change in culture could well begin with the determination and the 'buying in' of staff into a new mission.

Effecting a change in culture

To effect a change, there has to be leadership and a clear statement by the chief executive of exactly what is expected. Leadership does not have to be charismatic, but it has to be honest. Leadership does not rely on power and control. In Chapter 7 we stated that real leaders communicate face-to-face, not by memos.

Learning for change

If employees, organization-wide, are going to accept change, and themselves individually change, they will need to learn certain skills, such as:

- understanding work processes;
- solving problems;
- making decisions;
- working with others in a positive way.

All these types of skills can be taught. The main message that has to be taught is the need for cultural change and for people to trust each other; in particular, management has to win the trust of lower-level staff and learn how to change from an autocratic style of management to becoming coach and mentor. Lower-level staff, in turn, have to learn to trust management.

Hammer and Champy (1993) have defined five roles which they consider essential to make business process re-engineering happen. These are:

1. *The leader* – a senior executive who authorizes and motivates the overall effort.
2. *The process owner* – a manager with the responsibility for a specific process for re-engineering.
3. *The re-engineering team* – a group of individuals dedicated to the re-engineering of a particular process who diagnose the existing process and who oversee the re-design and the subsequent implementation.
4. *The re-engineering committee* – a policy body of senior managers who develop the organization's overall re-engineering strategy and who monitor its process.
5. *The re-engineering czar* – an individual responsible for developing re-engineering tools and techniques within the company and for achieving synergy across separate projects.

All of Hammer and Champy's roles are required to support the three constituents of the change process:

1. *Why* (vision and reason for the change).
2. *What* (aspects that have to be changed).
3. *How* (method of change including communication, training and the step-by-step implementation of the overall change programme).

Change is painful

Change will be painful and it will not happen overnight. Most writers and management consultants agree that to change a corporate culture will take at least three years. Change requires careful planning, harmonious collaboration and a willingness to listen and to accept criticism and suggestions.

The first step for a chief executive will be to win the Board over, then senior managers have to be convinced. Until there is wholehearted agreement and a determination at senior management level it won't be possible to sell the changes to the lower levels. At this stage, it is likely that some senior managers will opt for early retirement or will move on. Change and the 'giving up' of power will be too difficult for them to handle. As the change cascades down through the organization, it is likely that some middle managers and quite a few supervisors will also opt to leave. The problem is that for too long organizations have been built around those who give orders and those who take orders and it is hard for people to give up power and to trust the lower echelons to get things right.

Some, too, will find it difficult to give up the trappings of power. The company car, the car park, the private office are all treasured and outward evidence of power and success, not only within the organization but to friends and family. As the re-engineering process takes hold (together with the philosophy of total quality and value-adding), and is accepted at all levels, executive privileges will become less important.

A leader leads by example. A leader does not need a separate office; a true leader will want interaction and to be where the action is.

The action is on the front line

The action is not to pore over figures and budgets and draw up new mission statements; the action is on the front line. With a quality culture, there is no room for people or for expenses that do not add value to the process. It is best to let people go who don't want to or who can't change. This will be one of the hard decisions that will have to be taken.

'Structural teams provide the best means of distributing authority and accountability; thus they facilitate leadership that operates bottom up as well as top down' (Creech, 1994). Bill Creech believes that a decentralized team approach permits empowerment at all levels, especially on the front line, 'so that enthusiastic involvement and common purpose are realities, not slogans'. He adds that it doesn't matter how often the word 'empowerment' is used in the annual report; as long as centralized control is retained, leadership will not be able to operate from the bottom to the top.

Agreeing the need to change

The method for obtaining commitment and acceptance of change is, first, for senior management to agree on the need for change. Once the need is agreed, understood and accepted, the changes can be rolled down through the organization. This will involve strong leadership, discussion and agreement at all levels.

Schein (1988) points out that any change process involves not only learning and believing in something new, but unlearning something that is already present. Thus, no change will take place unless there is a motivation to change and the need for change is fully understood. All changes have to be negotiated, that is, agreed to, before a stable change can take place.

Loose cannons are dangerous

Empowerment is one thing but loose cannons are dangerous. As shown in Chapter 10 it is not for a staff member to decide a change in policy or to commit the organization to a course of action when they don't have the authority. The staff member must know what the policy is and his/her individual level of authority. Empowered staff are those who are encouraged to show initiative and to make suggestions for changes to policy; they don't unilaterally make spur-of-the-moment changes to policies.

In a stable system – where standards are known and consistency of performance is being achieved – staff should be empowered to make corrections at the lowest possible level. For this to happen people have to know what is expected, feedback of results has to be accurate and timely, and staff have to know what corrective actions they can take.

Example

A car salesperson will have authority to 'do deals' when selling cars, up to a certain level. The car salesperson does not have unlimited authority to make huge discounts or to give over-generous allowances on trade-ins. Part of the job satisfaction for top car salespeople is in negotiating and 'doing a good deal', thus a good experienced salesperson will be given more latitude to deal than will a less experienced person.

The actions of a car salesperson might well be isolated from the rest of the organization. In other cases, where a staff member is part of a larger process, then the dangers of unilateral decision-making will be obvious. Thus people cannot take it upon themselves to make a change that will impact on another staff member or on another department; such changes have to be approved at a higher level where the impact of changes throughout the system can be evaluated.

Example

Scandinavian Airlines (SAS) was a very efficient organization. They knew their business – transporting goods and people by air – and they did this with clinical efficiency. But when Jan Carlzon took over as President of SAS he found that the company was about to lose US$20 million. Within one year, he had turned the loss of US$20 million into a profit of US$54 million.

Carlzon determined that the airline had sufficient resources and well-trained staff and that 10 million passengers were carried each year. He then established that for each passenger there were five occasions when the passenger came into contact with front-line employees and that this contact lasted on average 15 seconds. He called these contact times 'moments of truth'. 'Last year 10 million customers came into contact with approximately five SAS employees, and this contact lasted an average of 15 seconds each time. Thus, "SAS" is "created" in the minds of the customers 50 million times a year, 15 seconds at a time. These 50 million "moments of truth" are the moments that ultimately determine whether SAS will succeed or fail as a company. They are moments when we must prove to our customers that SAS is their best alternative' (Carlzon, 1989).

Your turn!

When do 'moments of truth' occur in your organization? When does your customer come into direct contact with your organization?

For some organizations, the moment of truth might only be three times: once when the order is placed with the salesperson, once when delivery is taken and once when the invoice is received. In many service organizations there might only be one moment of truth: that is, the service will be provided and paid for at the same time. No matter how many moments of truth your customers have, there won't be many and they don't last long – as Carlzon discovered. And once the 'golden' moment has passed it cannot be recaptured.

A moment of truth is a moment when your staff have an opportunity to prove to the client that your organization is the best. Usually the person the customer will come into contact with will be one of the lower-paid members of an organization. It could be the telephone operator, it could be the cashier or the check-out person in the supermarket. Or it could be the driver of the van, which has your name emblazoned on it, who dangerously overtakes a potential customer. It is a good idea to have your name in large letters on the van, but not if the driver is an aggressive youth with seemingly suicidal/homicidal tendencies.

Establishing which staff are the contact points should not be hard to do. Training them in simple courtesy, good grooming and perhaps providing them with a smart uniform would be a good start. It would also be a sound investment to train these people in basic product knowledge, where to go for help and how to handle difficult customers. Such investment will be well rewarded. It should be stressed that the customer is not always right and that the staff member must therefore know what can be given or offered.

Continuous improvement should be to encourage – but as a team approach, not by one person 'doing their own thing'.

Specification

In considering Carlzon's moments of truth, it must be remembered that SAS was efficient in moving people and goods. Perhaps they weren't so good at distinguishing people from goods, but the basics were all there. Goods and people got to their destinations safely and on time. The corollary to this is that it is no good having polite and efficient front-line staff if the product or service is not up to the customer's specifications.

Once basics are being regularly and consistently achieved, moments of truth will help in selling the image that you want to your customers, but the basics must first be satisfied.

Example

Recently a dentist took over an existing practice. She asked advice on how to improve her service. Her own opinion was that the waiting room was shabby and needed upgrading. New carpet, a coat of paint, comfortable chairs, pot plants, current magazines and perhaps piped music; these were all improvements that she was considering. Without seeing the waiting room, my comment was 'But people don't want to be sitting in the waiting room at all. You should concentrate on keeping to your appointment timetable – this surely is more important that the comfort of the waiting room'.

In a dentist's surgery it is desirable to keep the moments of truth as short as possible!

Consider the restaurant where the owners have found the right location, spent a fortune on the decor, had the furniture ergonomically designed and a lighting expert determine the right level to eat by. The string quartet is obvious but not obtrusive and the serving staff are well groomed, courteous and helpful. Despite all of this, if the food is cold or overcooked the moment of truth will be very negative. The basics have to be right and the product or service provided must be what the customer wants.

Adding value

Does the customer care if the boss's office is well furnished? What benefit is it to the customer that the accounting section has pot plants and that the accountant has a new desk? The only concern to the customer is that the product or service is fit for their purpose, that is, it does what they want, is provided at the right time, the price is right and the staff they deal with are knowledgeable, helpful and pleasant. For the customer anything else is not important: they simply don't want to know. Within an organization, any money spent that does not add value to the service or product or which will not eventually add value (such as research and development) is a cost that should be queried and then queried again. Certainly you might be able to show that contented staff will give better service to the customer and therefore an up-market cafeteria is justified, but first it is essential to define the key points: where is value added? and where do moments of truth occur?

Nevan plays golf (*but not very well . . . Joy*). Sometimes he loses a golf ball (*often . . . Joy*). This means that, in a moment of stress (having just lost a ball and taken the required penalty stroke), he extracts from his bag a small box containing a new ball wrapped in tissue paper. Why do new golf balls come wrapped in a piece of tissue paper inside a small square box? From a customer's point of view, the paper and the box do not add value. A golf ball is not a delicate object, it is designed to be hit hard with a piece of steel. It does not need the protection of being wrapped in tissue, nor does it have to be cradled in a box. There is no useful purpose for either the tissue paper or for the box and they are both pieces of rubbish that Nevan is stuck with, just when he doesn't need any further stress. They certainly do not add value, but they most certainly have added to the supplier's cost. Only the customer can judge if a moment of truth is positive; only the customer knows what they want.

Learning for change

Having agreed that change has to be organization-wide, requires the development of a strong corporate culture and that people can change, what is required of managers? Managers will have to learn how to make the transition from being auto-cratic to becoming a mentor and coach. What of staff? Staff have to be given the opportunity to learn new skills and new technology. They also have to develop the skills of working with people and working as a team. These issues were discussed in Chapter 7.

Model for change

Many organizations start a change programme without going through the earlier stages of identifying the real requirements. Change programmes that are not care-fully planned and managed are doomed to failure, because not only is it likely that the improvement strategy will be wrong but also the necessary commitment and culture will not have been developed.

Making changes and improvements should be a continuous process, but to sus-tain continuous change is as difficult as initiating and implementing change. To keep the momentum going, it is necessary to evaluate if the change process has produced results and to keep developing ongoing improvement activities. The success of any project is underpinned by management commitment, organization and resources. Building a commitment for all the stakeholders, inside and outside the company, involves the understanding of why improvement is needed and the nature of improvement. It is a common phenomenon for various factions to appre-ciate why a change is required, but at the same time to believe that the need to change does not necessarily apply to them. As we have said in earlier chapters, the culture of the organization has to be such that everyone, from the cleaner to the chief executive, believes that they have a personal part to play in making changes. The prerequisite for change is the vision and the desire to change based on a cul-ture that will accept change.

It is vital that detailed discussion and agreement occurs throughout the com-pany as to what, how, when and where change should take place and whom should be involved.

The model for change given below is based on that developed by Basu and Wright (1998) and consists of four phases:

1. Start-up.
2. Self-analysis.
3. Making changes.
4. Feedback.

1. Start-up

The key task for senior management is to decide what improvement opportunity areas have the greatest impact for the business. However, a significant number of companies that initiate a change programme do so because they feel their survival is threatened. Our recommendation is that before any improvement is attempted, self-analysis takes place to identify the weaknesses and the gaps in performance. A self-analysis process does not start on its own. Any benchmarking programme requires full commitment, preparation and planning. The start-up phase contains three major steps:

- Recognition of need for change.
- Organization.
- Launch.

Recognition of need for change

It is vital that top management and the Board wholeheartedly recognize the need for a change programme. This recognition may be prompted by a reaction to current company performance, a threat from a new competitor or a strategic change (e.g. a merger or an internal report from any of the key stakeholders). The Board and management must believe that serious action has to be taken. Major, panic-driven changes can destroy a company. Poorly planned change is worse than no change. Change has to be planned, methodical and relentless.

At this stage it may be helpful to conduct a limited number of consultation workshops with key stakeholders to acquire agreement and understanding about the need to change. The outcome of this will be the full commitment of top management and the support of the stakeholders. The programme begins with the formation of a project team.

Project management for change

The organization phase involves a clear project brief, appointment of a project team and a project plan. The project brief must clearly state the purpose of the project and the deliverables expected from the project. There is no rigid model for the structure of the project team. Basu and Wright (1998) recommend a project structure as shown in Figure 15.10.

Figure 15.10

Project structure

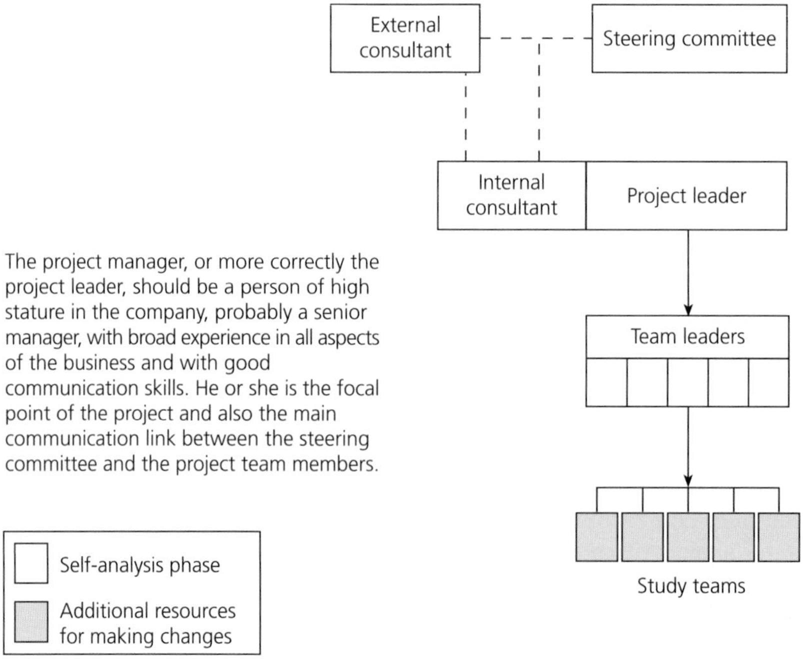
External consultant
Steering committee
Internal consultant
Project leader
The project manager, or more correctly the project leader, should be a person of high stature in the company, probably a senior manager, with broad experience in all aspects of the business and with good communication skills. He or she is the focal point of the project and also the main communication link between the steering committee and the project team members.
Team leaders
Study teams
Self-analysis phase
Additional resources for making changes

Steering committee

To ensure a high level of commitment and ownership to the project the steering committee should be drawn from members of the Board and include senior management. Their role is to provide support and resources, define the scope of the project consistent with corporate goals, set priorities and consider and approve the project team's recommendations.

Project leader

The project leader should be a senior manager, with broad experience in all aspects of the business and with good communication skills. He or she is the focal point of the project and also the main communication link between the steering committee and the project team members.

The role of the project leader can be likened to that of a consultant. However, if a line manager is given the task of project leadership as an additional responsibility to his or her normal job, then an experienced staff manager can be co-opted to support the leader. The project leader's role (similar to Hammer and Champy's czar – see above) is to:

- provide necessary awareness and training for the project team, especially regarding multi-functional issues;
- facilitate the work of various project groups and help them develop design changes;
- interface with other departments.

In addition to the careful selection of the project leader, two other factors are important in forming the team. First, the membership size should be kept within manageable limits. Second, the members should bring with them not only analytical skills but also in-depth knowledge of the total business covering marketing, finance, information technology and human resources. The minimum number of team members should be three, and the maximum number should be six. Any more than six can lead to difficulties in arranging meetings, communicating and keeping deadlines. The dynamics within a group of more than six people allows sub-groups to develop. The team should function as an action group rather than as a committee that deliberates and makes decisions. Their role is:

- to provide objective input in the areas of their expertise during the self-analysis phase;
- to lead activities during the making-changes phase.

For the project leader the responsibilities of the project include:

- education of all the members of the company;
- establishing study teams to recommend changes;
- regular reporting to the steering committee;
- regular reporting of progress company-wide to all the members of the company.

Obviously the project leaders cannot do all this work themselves, but they have to be the type of people who know how to make things happen and who can motivate people to help make things happen. To assist in various phases, study teams should be formed to work with the project leader.

We strongly recommend Eddie Obeng's book *All Change! The Project Leader's Secret Handbook* (1994) as essential reading for project leaders.

Study teams

In general, study teams should be formed after the self-analysis phase, but in selected areas. However, some members of study teams can assist in the original data-collection phase and also in the analysis phase. The members of the study team represent all levels of employees in the organization and are the key agents for making changes. Their role is to develop design changes and submit recommendations to the project leader.

External consultants

The use of an external consultant at various stages of the project might be useful to supplement your own resources. However, a consultant cannot know your company as well as your own staff do. It could be argued that a consultant not only brings his or her expertise and experience but will also act as a catalyst during the total implementation process. Likewise, in the initial stages, consultants can be effectively used in training the staff of organizations in both analytical tools and in assisting with culture change. In our opinion the best time to employ a consultant is probably after self-analysis has been completed and after the selection of a change strategy has been made.

Launch

It is critical that all stakeholders (managers, employees, unions, suppliers and key customers) who may be immediately impacted by the programme are clearly identified. Internal stakeholders must be consulted and kept fully informed at every stage of the programme. After the organization phase the next milestone is the formal launching of the programme. The nature of launching can be either low key or a big bang. It is recommended that before self-analysis a low-key, but not secretive, approach is more appropriate. Too much excitement and too high an expectation could be counter-productive if it leads to uncertainty. It will be only after self-analysis that an improvement strategy can be finalized. A high-profile launch would therefore be more appropriate once the change strategy has been approved by the steering committee.

The nature of the launch sets the tone for how future communication will take place. It is absolutely essential that senior management give strong and visible support.

2. Self-analysis

After the launch the project team will be involved with the self-analysis of the organization. This is basically do-it-yourself benchmarking. The steps are to establish key measures as discussed in Chapter 14 and analyze how well the organization is performing against these measures. Additionally, obtain reports on the best organizations known to you in your field and try to judge your performance against theirs. Identify the vision, mission and key values of your organization. How does actual performance compare to the stated vision and mission? Are resources, system structure and your people capable or sufficient to meet your service objectives? How is quality determined and measured? And so on. Once a questioning attitude such as this has been introduced it will be surprising how many weaknesses will be discovered. However, it is not only weaknesses that must be recognized; it is equally important to know your strengths. Remember, this is not a witch-hunt but an honest attempt to recognize the need for change and what has to be changed.

3. Making changes

In this phase the change process moves on to the action programme to make the changes happen. Having chosen the improvement strategy, the detailed work of implementing the changes will be influenced by the strategy. We have found it effective to name the total initiative, e.g. Project 2004, so that everyone in the organization can identify it as a 'single issue improvement culture' that transcends divisional boundaries.

4. Feedback

It is possible that after spending several weeks with the self-analysis phase employees outside the core project group may demonstrate scepticism. If this shows signs of occurring it may be necessary for top management to re-launch the initiative; for example, '2004 Stage Two'.

If this is done the project team will need reconfirmation. There is an obvious advantage in continuing with some of the same people involved in '2004 Stage One'. Their experience, new-found company-wide knowledge and their belief in the recommendations should not be undervalued.

The project leader will be responsible for writing implementation plans indicating key tasks, responsibilities, deliverables, resource requirements and target dates. It is recommended that the project plan includes a critical path, and that periodic reviews and reports by the project leader are made to the steering committee.

Process design

Process design relates to the actual transformation of an operation, procedure, organization or facilities from the current state to a desirable future state.

The steering committee should be kept informed of all changes and their progress. There is no advantage to be gained by being secretive. A world-class organization does not have secrets or hidden agendas.

Training and communication

Training and communication of people throughout the organization is essential. Key points are:

1. The objective is to share information and change processes among the stakeholders at all levels of the organization, for example:
   - Top management and the Board must understand enough about the improvement programmes to know how the changes will affect the business. They must know what is happening and show leadership so things will happen.
   - Project team education. The study team needs to have a detailed understanding of what is planned for their area and a good overall understanding of the big picture. They are the ones who will be responsible for working with and training people in process design changes in sections and units of the company.
   - Middle management and staff education. While everyone cannot be on project teams, everyone has a role to play in the improvement programme. Therefore everyone on the staff must be informed of how their work will be affected.
   - Employee training. No change process will work if the employees in the front office oppose it either directly or indirectly. Employee involvement and training are vital to the success of an implementation plan.
   - Communication to trade unions. It is critical that the representatives of unions and other staff representative bodies are kept informed at critical stages of the implementation of how the change process will affect their members.

2. The communication among the stakeholders should be full and open. A change programme cannot be built upon any false pretence. Success depends on trust. Secret agendas don't remain secret for long. Leaked information is always more damaging than official information. Damage limitation can be costly and time-consuming.

3. Learning programmes should be properly structured.
   - There should be a learning manager with a focused role.
   - On-the-job learning should be accomplished through team leaders.
   - An external human resources consultant may be valuable in guiding the learning and to effect a culture change.

Installation

The installation phase involves the planning and physical actions necessary for putting the changes into place. Separate capital proposals may be required and these should be channelled through the steering committee. Other likely expenditure will include modification of premises and office layouts. It is important that proper authorization be obtained for any expenditure before it is incurred. The project has to lead by example and cannot be seen to be taking short cuts.

The installation stage consists of a large number of concurrent and parallel activities including selection of equipment, revising layout, improvement of process capability, commissioning, training and so on. It is useful to prepare a project schedule showing the critical path and all the necessary resources.

Some people understand a system conceptually but cannot accept it unless they can see it in action. Pilot projects can demonstrate results and validate the purpose of the change. It can be a great advantage to move along the learning curve by a trial at a group of branches rather than going organization-wide in one hit.

Feedback

The phase of feedback involves the continuous need to sustain what has been achieved and to identify further opportunities for improvement.

It is at least as difficult to sustain changes as it is to design and install them. Keeping the change process going by regular feedback is a different process from that of making changes. It usually calls for different approaches and sometimes the responsibility of this phase may shift to a different team. The feedback phase contains two inter-related milestones – evaluation and continuous development.

The progress of the changes should be monitored at regular intervals, usually by comparing the actual results with target performance levels.

All the staff of the organization have to understand the purpose of the project, believe in it and wholeheartedly support it. It goes without saying that the lead must come from the top of the organization. To get the full commitment of the whole organization might mean a major change in culture. Changing the culture is likely to be part of the improvement strategy.

Chapter summary

This chapter has covered the need for change, the process for re-engineering, the need for an organizational structure which will support re-engineering and the constituents of a successful change programme. We have found that in service industries the most important element for success in an organization is the people. People include management and staff at all levels. As has been stressed elsewhere in this book, if the overall culture is right then there is very little that an organization cannot achieve.

Case Study *Trinidad Highways*

The case study which is relevant to this and earlier chapters, especially Chapter 12, is Trinidad Highways.

Question

What advice would you offer the Highways Division on how best to prepare for the change to contract out all routine and periodic maintenance to private sector contractors?

Introduction

The Highways Division of the Ministry of Works and Transport is responsible for the development and maintenance of all highways, main and secondary roads and bridges in Trinidad and Tobago.

Under this division there are eight districts. In this study we deal with one district (Caroni) which has 31 monthly paid staff and 361 daily and weekly paid employees ('force account'). The monthly staff consist of a district engineer, technicians, supervisors and clerical personnel. The daily paid workers consist of road overseers, tradesmen (carpenters, painters, mechanics, masons), foremen and labourers (male and female). The district engineer is the senior manager responsible for the operations in the district and charged with the task 'To sustain a quality road transportation network that is good, safe, reliable and facilitates an easy flow of people, goods and services'.

The district is thus responsible for periodic and routine maintenance of all highways, main and secondary roads (a network ranging from the major highways to the local roads) and bridges under its regional control. It also provides advice estimating and consulting to the external clients, e.g. for county councils and municipal corporations.

Periodic and routine maintenance

Periodic maintenance (e.g. major patching and base repair, vehicles and equipment repair and maintenance, and bridges and culverts repair) is mainly done by force account (approximately 80 per cent) and the remainder contracted out externally to contractors.

All routine maintenance activities (e.g. pot hole patching, crack sealing, roadway edging, minor land-slip repair, grass and tree cutting, ditch clearing, culvert clearing, bridge maintenance and repair, etc.) have been undertaken utilizing force account (direct labour).

Periodic maintenance

In general there have been four aspects – maintenance planning, work schedule, work control and management, reports and performance evaluation:

1. *Maintenance planning*

Prior to actual maintenance work, the following is undertaken:

- prepare and finalize work programme including emergency work requests or citizen complaints;
- conduct field inspection;
- determine split of work between in-house workforce and sub-contracts;
- calculate the work programme based on design and cost estimates;
- smooth the work loading activities for force account labour;
- prepare resource requirements:
  - prepare list of personnel, equipment and material to accomplish work programme;
  - prepare subcontractor work programme and sub-contract documents.

2. *Work scheduling*

- determine specific work requirements;
- establish procedure to process emergency work requirements;

- gather citizen requests for work needs;
- conduct field inspection to identify location and quantities of specific work needs;
- prepare work calendar;
- establish work schedules for maintenance activities;
- mobilize supervisors and crew to accomplish work;
- perform maintenance work;
- supervise activities.

3. *Work control*

- conduct inspections of labour force;
- internal programme for training;
- ensure field adherence to maintenance standards;
- direct labour management;
- equipment and material management.

4. *Management reports and performance evaluation*

- the reports include tracking actual expenditures by maintenance activity to compare with actual expenditures against the work programme;
- assessment of resource allocation;
- adherence of work performance to pre-determined standards;
- contractor performance;
- financial analysis of work performed.

Routine maintenance

The road supervisor has been the first line manager for the district roads maintenance function. The district is sub-divided into three sub-districts each managed by a works supervisor who reports directly to the roads supervisor. The works supervisor implements roads maintenance via the use of gangs (made up of men and women) who have fixed work areas.

There have been five gangs to each sub-district. Each maintains approximately 75 km of road with one road overseer, one female labourer and eight male labourers.

The bridges maintenance function has been managed by a works supervisor who is responsible for the works in the entire district of approximately two hundred bridges and culverts. His resources generally comprise one truck, one jitney and one gang of 13 persons (skilled and unskilled). He reports directly to the district engineer.

Works that are contracted out would require the division engineer to prepare contract documents which include: bill of quantities, works specification, technical drawings, tender evaluations and award of contracts. In this case the work control would include mainly an effective quality assurance programme with the following elements:

- meeting with contractor to review quality assurance programme;
- establish procedures for random selection of field sections to measure adherence to the maintenance standards;
- meetings with contractors to review the random selection procedures;
- conduct inspections on the frequency established;
- document inspections and review results and ensure adherence to the standards.

A change of policy

The Government of Trinidad and Tobago decided in 1996 (a) to contract out *all* routine and periodic maintenance works to private sector contractors; and (b) to provide incentives for the participation of existing employees to form themselves into 'micro-enterprises' and small contractors to implement works on a competitive basis.

Some of the reasons for this new policy are:-

- Excessive use of labour (use of labour to material cost ratios have been as high as 85:15); the labour component has

▶

therefore been in excess of 80 per cent of the total recurrent budget.

- Lack of standards.
- Long response time to citizens' maintenance demands accompanied by increasing maintenance expenditure.
- Lack of proper accountability (contracting out offers the advantage of full accountability of maintenance costs and greater flexibility in managing increased maintenance demands resulting from an expanding road network as well as increasing traffic densities).
- Inappropriate allocation of transportation system related revenues.

In addition, the government wanted to create an environment to allow for private sector participation in road maintenance and allow its public sector managers to:

(a) be more creative in developing strategies to deliver high quality performance;

(b) encourage the development of an increased cadre of entrepreneurs;

(c) take advantage of the opportunity to procure services in a competitive environment;

(d) develop criteria for measuring performance;

(e) be more accountable; and

(f) be given the opportunity for greater transparency in the whole process of spending public funds.

Thus inter-related objectives of the proposal are to:

1. increase service;

2. improve condition of the main highway and secondary roads network;

3. accomplish maintenance on a planned basis as opposed to only in response to complaints;

4. use personnel and attendant short- and long-term personnel costs;

5. avoid capital investments in equipment;

6. increase production;

7. reduce overall costs and improved cost-effectiveness;

8. improve capabilities; and

9. reduce citizen complaints of poor roads and inefficient crews.

The district was thus required to develop transition and implementation plans for the new policy to be completed within three years. This was the responsibility of a programme director who would manage the change through the district engineers. The purpose of the plan was to document the requirements that resulted in the decision to contract out all of the maintenance activities and describe the actions necessary to implement the programme. Figure 15.11 shows what the plan should cover.

The transition plan included the following:

1. Critical success factor (associated with the nine plan objectives)
A continued governmental support of new policy. Dedicated funding.
Co-operation of the trade unions.
Positive stakeholder and worker response to programme.
The existence of a capable local contractor in the construction industry with sufficient capacity for contract maintenance works.
The ability to administrate and manage the new policy.

2. Change management strategy
Organization re-structuring of districts.
Financial planning.
Employee database updating.
Options for dealing with employees.
Severance packages development.
Assistance programme for employees.
Developing an effective public relations programme.

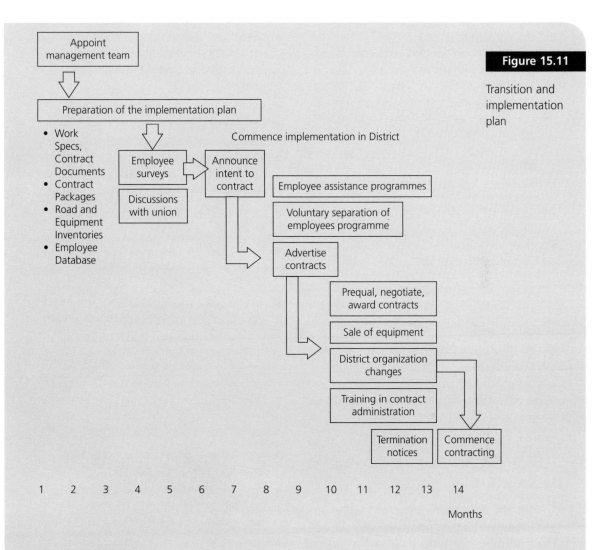

Figure 15.11

Transition and implementation plan

3. Maintenance plans

Inventory of physical features to be maintained.

Definition of appropriate work activities and measurement units.

Establishment of quality standards (service levels to maintain the inventoried items).

Updating performance standards which specify crew size, equipment, materials, correct work methods and production estimates.

Deciding what portions of the works are best performed by different types of contractors.

Calculation of performance budget using a combination of lump sum price and unit price estimates.

The creation of an annual work calendar to distribute the workload in the most effective manner.

4. Contract approach

This approach must decide on the most effective and efficient approach to contract works.

5. Treatment of resources

Development of strategy for disposal of equipment and facilities.

Inventory and valuation of equipment, materials and facilities.

Disposal plan.

6. Development of contracts

Work specification for all maintenance activities.

Modes of payment.

Contract packages.

General and special conditions of contracting.

Sample standard contracts.

7. Administration

Work plans.

Management information systems.

Pre-qualification, tendering and award procedures.

Contract administration procedures.

Training requirements for contract administration.

Involvement of other ministries.

The impact of the change

The new policy is likely to change the nature of the market as the demand for consulting, costing, advice and project managerial services can all be expected to increase. The contracting out of maintenance work is intended to be more competitive and there will be the ability to control cost. The competitiveness generated will also result in cost reduction and effectiveness. More private sector contractors with new technology will also enter the market.

With the implementation of the policy, it is expected that (a) the customers will have better roads and not have to wait for services relating to routine and periodic maintenance work, and (b) private contractors would be more responsive, provide increased productivity and efficiency. There will be cost reductions and the elimination of unproductive time and overtime costs associated with in-house works.

An efficient transition and implementation plan would therefore be required to adjust the capacity and productivity through contracting out works. Organizing to accomplish maintenance by contract involves significant advanced planning. The actions and decision which need to be accomplished include the following:

- developing the approach to be used to implement the contract maintenance programme to ensure the support needed;
- defining the organizational functions and activities required;
- assigning organizational responsibility and authority.
- determining levels of effect and required staffing;
- identifying and developing procedures, policies and methods;
- assembling the necessary data and information to support the contract maintenance effort.

Such planning will considerably improve the efficiency and effectiveness of the organization in the control maintenance area and help to ensure a successful programme.

Implementation of the policy will have an impact on inventory held by the district.

The elimination of materials and equipment requirements by the Ministry of Works and Transport would have the following benefits:

- no need to maintain large stores and large inventories of equipment;
- closing down the stores and facilities or entering into leasing/sale arrangements with contractors to use the facilities;
- elimination of losses in stocks due to thefts;
- elimination of (a) increased mark-up by suppliers on materials and spare parts, and (b) losses due to materials misordering and inefficient purchasing;
- reduction of staff and the removal of unproductive labour;
- freedom in the districts to rent/lease vehicles and equipment as and when required.

To accommodate contract maintenance the district engineers will have to develop an implementation plan for contracting road maintenance or to obtain work elsewhere in the private sector.

The implementation plan when completed will provide:-

1. A set of strategies for dealing with the staffing and assets used in road maintenance.

2. Contract documents and contract packages, procedures for the prequalification of contractors, tendering and award of contracts, contract administration procedures and work specifications.

3. Organizational requirements for administration of contracts and requirements for training in contract administration.

4. Implementation of a maintenance management information system, completion of road inventory and condition databases and development of work programme for the initial contracts.

5. A plan for the distribution of plant and equipment used in road maintenance;

6. Programmes to assist employees in establishing contracting enterprises or in seeking employment elsewhere, procedures for determining terminal benefits and a relocation programme.

The implementation plan will provide the district engineer with all the information and tools necessary to commence contracting maintenance. It is expected that there will be a transition period during which contracting will be introduced in a staged manner, and this will need to be decided in the implementation plan.

Delivering service quality

In order to ensure high, consistent quality of service provided in the district a number of co-ordinated actions will be required. Emphasis must be placed on management of quality systems and some of the specific requirements are anticipated below:

- maintenance operations are carefully planned and prioritized, based on rolling programmes;

- continuous attention to be paid to quality, productivity and performance standards;

- employee acceptance of new performance initiatives will be sought through effective performance evaluation systems;

- enhanced accountability to be targeted through measurement and comparisons;

- a well-planned public relations programme targeting key stakeholders will improve communications on achievements implemented;

- development and management of information systems which are essential to effectively and efficiently manage the district. To have access to appropriate information in the required form at the required time is imperative for effective decision-making;

- a balanced and sustained focus on road-user satisfaction will be essential;

- priorities for maintenance of roads and bridges will need to be established within budgetary constraints;

- there should be effective management horizontally and with the district organization;

- increased attention to environmental management;

- commitment and support of top management is critical;

- the district engineer should have the knowledge, commitment and skill to implement the new programme and be a pro-active manager.

These actions should be intended to result in:

1. greater value for money;

2. consistency and uniformity;

In finished works everything should benefit by clearly defining and establishing what is expected, how it will be verified and the consequences of non-compliance. The programme should also encourage contractors to do the work right the first time, which is usually the most efficient method. The structured system of tests and inspections should result in every contractor being dealt with in a fair and consistent way. This will enable comparisons of performance to be made on an equitable basis.

3. proper use of time

The programme should result in a system whereby the supervisory personnel can properly schedule their duties so as to achieve the proper sampling of contractors' work in an efficient and time-effective manner.

The aim must also be to achieve:

1. *Quality control.* The district engineer must monitor actual work quality continuously by comparing random samples of completed work with greater criteria defined in the performance standards. If sub-standard work is detected, the contractor must be required to correct it at his expense.

2. *Quality monitoring.* The district staff must check that the contractor's work is being undertaken to the standards as set in the specifications and according to the contract documents. These checks must be conducted on representative samples of the contractor's work in progress or on representative samples of the road network.

3. *Compliance review.* The overall effectiveness of contracting out road and bridge maintenance must be assessed. The district engineer must use the programme as an effective tool in the administration of contracts under his control. The results of the programme must be used to rate the performance of each contractor. The quality assurance programme itself must be assessed for its overall effectiveness and deficiencies, the system must be corrected and finally there has to be feedback on the maintenance standards themselves so that they can be improved and/or modified.

The role of the district engineer

The programme director and the district engineers believe that for the district engineers there will be a significant role change resulting from the new policy. The district engineer is responsible for the planning and scheduling of all maintenance activities and ensuring the undertaking of these activities mainly through force account, involving the implementation of procedures for instructions and directions in one form or another emanating from the top and proceeding down through line managers and supervision to the workers who actually carry out the work.

Under the existing system the responsibilities are as follows:

(i)   inspections to update the inventory of the condition of the roads;

(ii) planning work programmes to determine which roads and what activities will be undertaken and when;

(iii) budget preparation and allocation of funding for road maintenance activities;

(iv) quality assurance inspections;

(v)   allocation of assignments to work crews through the road supervisor and works supervisor;

(vi) assignment and re-assignment of personnel as the need arises;

(vii) administrative responsibility for the preparation of paysheets for employee wages, including responsibility for employee deductions, etc;

(viii) administrative responsibility for the recording of employee data, e.g. record of service;

(ix) resolving employee issues and being the arbitrator in labour disputes;

(x) taking disciplinary action when the need arises;

(xi) meeting with unions regarding labour matters.

The change from directly undertaking the operation to a situation where maintenance is contracted out will change the way in which the existing activities are accomplished. Under the new policy, items (i)–(iv) above will not be changed, but the role of the district engineer with respect to items (v)–(x) will become the responsibility of the various contractors. The district engineer will then have the following new responsibilities:

1. Management of change (transition).
2. Organization restructuring and job re-design and development of personnel towards:

   - development of supervisory skills;
   - team-building skills;
   - testing and quality control;
   - knowledge of engineering standards and codes of practice;
   - compiler literacy and systems;
   - performance-based evaluation systems.

3. Prequalification of contractors.
4. Tender evaluation and award of contracts.
5. Quality measurements and preparation of certificates for payments.

In the long term it would be possible for item (iv) (under existing responsibilities) as well as items 2–5 above to be contracted out. In such a scenario, the district engineer's role would essentially be one of planning and ensuring the performance of all the contracts in the system.

Short term, the contracting out of main-tenance works will impact significantly on the activities of the operations manager. Before the new policy is implemented, the district engi-neer will have to manage the transition plan with extreme skill. An effective system of com-munication and public relations must be in place. Employee and industrial relations will have to be carefully managed. In general, to achieve the objectives of the new policy the engineer would be concerned with the follow-ing in the short term:

(a) developing an effective transition plan for the gradual change over to the new system with minimum negative impact for employees;

(b) dedicating more time communicating with top management about the potential impact of the changes, especially his views for cushioning the negative effects of the policy;

(c) co-ordinating with the human resource development department to ensure that procedures for separation are complied with;

(d) updating the employee database.

A primary and fundamental task for dealing with the employees is the development and creation of a staff database which would include general human resource information as well as payroll information. The staff database will facilitate the separation exercise by:

- providing an accurate head count of employees;
- identifying the number of workers to be separated and their respective job classifications;
- allowing for the accurate qualifying of individual employee's separation packages based on the application of either a volutary separation formula or a retrenchment formula;
- identifying and quantifying any outstanding benefits and/or entitlements due to employees; for example, accumulated mobilized leave;

- allowing an estimation of a global cost for the separation of the work force.

It will also serve as a skills databank to employee group companies, micro-enterprises and existing companies in search of labour to carry out projects which become available. It will also be a mechanism available in the awarding of contracts for the verification of information supplied by contracting companies purporting to be owned by, comprised of or have employed former employees.

(e) implementing training programmes for supervisors;

(f) increasing the frequency of meetings with his subordinates to facilitate ownership of new strategies and empowerment;

(g) updating the road inventory.

Medium to long term the district engineer will be concerned with:

(i) contract administration, planning, budgeting and financial control;

(ii) ensuring that the district has adequate up-to-date equipment for testing, data collection and word processing projects, management, etc.

(iii) performance audits;

Iiv) liaising with top management to ensure compliance with policy, training and performance targets;

(v) facilitating team-building and performance evaluation;

(vi) continued development and evaluation of the computerized information systems for bridge and road maintenance. Pavement management systems and development of database related to contractor performance;

(vii) project management.

Written by Kendrick Burgess and Ray Wild 1996.

References

Association for Project Management (APM) (2003) *The Books of Knowledge*, Revision 4, www.apm.org.uk

Basu, R. and Wright, J. Nevan (1998) *Total Manufacturing Solutions*, Oxford: Butterworth-Heinemann.

Basu, R. and Wright, J. Nevan (2003) *Quality Beyond Six Sigma*, Oxford: Butterworth-Heinemann.

Bateman, T. S. and Zeithaml, C. P. (1993) *Management Function and Strategy*, Chicago, IL: Irwin.

Berry, L. L., Parasuraman, A. and Zeithaml, V. A. (1988) 'The service quality puzzle', *Business Horizons*, July–August: 35–43.

Carlzon, J. (1989) *Moments of Truth*, New York: Harper Row.

Carnall, C. (1993) *Managing Change*, London: Routledge.

Christopher, M. (1992) *Logistics and Supply Chain Management*, London: Pitman Publishing.

Creech, B. (1994) *The Five Pillars of TQM*, New York: Truman Talley Books/Dutton.

Deming, W. E. (1986) *Out of the Crisis*, Cambridge, MA: MIT Centre for Advanced Engineering.

Dulewicz, V., MacMillan, K. and Herbert, P. (1995) 'Appraising and developing the effectiveness of boards and their directors', *Journal of General Management*, 20(3) 1–19.

Hammer, M. and Champy, J. (1993) *Re-engineering the Corporation*, London: Nicholas Brealey Publishing.

Henkoff, R. (1994) 'Delivering the goods', *Fortune*, 28 November, 1994: 64 –78.

Herzberg, F. (1966) *Work and the Nature of Man*, Cleveland, OH: World Publishing.

Herzberg, F. (1968) 'One more time: how do you motivate employees?' *Harvard Business Review*, January–February, 53–62.

Ishikawa, K. (1979) *Guide to Quality Control*, Tokyo: Asian Productivity Organization.

Ishikawa. K. (1985) *What is Total Quality Control? The Japanese Way*, trans. D. J. Lu, Englewood Cliffs, NJ: Prentice Hall.

Juran, J. M. (1988) *Juran on Planning for Quality*, New York: Free Press.

Kotler, P. (1997) *Marketing Management*, Englewood Cliffs, NJ: Prentice Hall.

Lewis, B. R. (1994) 'Managing service quality', in B. G. Dale (ed.) *Managing Quality*, London: Prentice Hall.

Machiavelli, N. (1513; 1952) *The Prince*, trans. Luigi Ricci, revised by E. R. P. Vincent, New York: New American Library of World Literature.

Masaaki, I. (1986) *Kaizen: The Key to Japan's Competitive Success*, New Jersey: Random House.

Maslow, A. H. (1943) 'A theory of human motivation', *Psychological Review*, 50: 370–96.

Maylor, H. (2002), *Project Management*, 3rd edn., Harlow: FT/Prentice Hall.

Melnyk, S. A. and Swink, M. (2002) *Supply Chain Structure and Strategy*, New York: McGraw-Hill/Irwin.

Obeng, E. (1994) *All Change! The Project Leader's Secret Handbook*, London: Pitman.

Obeng, E. and Crainer, S. (1994) *Making Re-engineering Happen*, London: Pitman.

Parasuraman, A., Zeithaml, V. A. and Berry, L. L. (1985) 'A conceptual model of service quality and its implications for future research', *Journal of Marketing* 49 (Fall) 41–50.

Parasuraman, A., Zeithaml, V. A. and Berry, L. L. (1991) 'Understanding customer expectations of service', *Sloan Management Review*, 32(3): 39–48.

Peters, T. and Austin, N. (1986) *A Passion for Excellence*, London: Fortune.

Peters, T. and Waterman, J. R. Jnr (1982) *In Search of Excellence*, New York: Harper Row.

Porter, M. E. (1990*) The Competitive Advantage of Nations*, London: MacMillan.

PRINCE 2: An Outline (1999) CCTA, Norwick, England, ISBN 011330854X now Office of Government and Commerce, www.ogc.gov.uk/prince/

Project Management Institute (PMI) (2002) *A Guide to the Project Management Body of Knowledge, 2000*, www.pmi.org

Sayle, A. J. (1991) *Meeting ISO 9000 in a TQM World*, UK: AJSL.

Schein, E. H. (1988) *Organizational Psychology*, Englewood Cliffs, NJ: Prentice Hall.

Schein, E. H. (1991) *Organizational Culture: A Dynamic View*, San Francisco: Jossey Bass.

Schonberger, R. (1986) *World Class Manufacturing*, New York: Free Press.

Senge, P. (1990) *The Fifth Discipline: The Art and Practice of the Learning Organisation*, London: Century.

Simchi-Levi, D., Kaminsky, P. and Simchi-Levi, E. (2003) *Designing and Managing the Supply Chain*. 2nd edn, New York: McGraw-Hill/Irwin.

Skinner, B. F. (1971) *Contingencies of Re-inforcement*, Norwalk, CT: Appleton-Century-Crofts.

Smith, A. (1776; 1950) *An Enquiry into The Nature and Causes of the Wealth of Nations, Book One*, 6th edn, London: Methuen.

Taylor, F. W. (1987) 'The principles of scientific management', in Boone, L. E. and Bowen, D. D. *The Great Writings in Management and Organizational Behaviour*, New York: McGraw-Hill.

Tompkins, J. A. (1989) *Winning Manufacturing*, New York: Free Press.

Tuckman, B. W. (1965) in Torrington, D. and Hall, L. (1998), *Human Resource Management*, 4th edn, Hemel Hempstead: Prentice-Hall.

Turner, J. R. (1999), *The Handbook of Project-based Management*, 2nd edn., Maidenhead: McGraw-Hill.

UK Government Statistics (2003) www.statistics.gov.uk

US Bureau of the Census (2003) www.census.gov/

US Department of Labor Occupational Safety and Health Administration (2003) www.osha.gov/sltc/computer

Vroom, V. H. and Jago, A. G. (1988) *The New Leadership: Managing Participation in Organizations*, Englewood Cliffs, NJ: Prentice-Hall.

Vroom, V. H. and Yetton, P. W. (1973) *Leadership and Decision Making*, Pittsburg: University of Pittsburg.

Wild, R. (1995) *Production and Operations Management*, 5th edn, London: Cassell.

Wild, R. (2002) *Operations Management*, 6th edn, London: Continuum.

Wright, J. Nevan (1996) 'Creating a quality culture', *Journal of General Management*, 21(3): 19–29.

Wright, J. Nevan (2002) 'Mission and reality and why not?', *Journal of Change Management* 3(1): 30–44.

Wright, R. (1995) *Managing Labour Relations in a New Economy*. Montreal, Canada: The Conference Branch of Canada.

Zeithaml, V. A., Parasuraman, A. and Berry, L. L. (1990) *Delivering Quality Service: Balancing Customer Perceptions and Expectations*, New York: The Free Press.

Index